HARVARD ECONOMIC STUDIES

Volume CXVIII

The studies in this series are published by the Department of Economics of Harvard University. The Department does not assume responsibility for the views expressed.

Ragnar Nurkse

Equilibrium and Growth
in the World Economy

Economic Essays by

RAGNAR NURKSE

edited by
GOTTFRIED HABERLER
and
ROBERT M. STERN

with an introduction by Gottfried Haberler

HARVARD UNIVERSITY PRESS
Cambridge, Massachusetts

1962

Distributed in Great Britain by Oxford University Press, London

HB 33
.N8

Library of Congress Catalog Card Number: 61–11007
Printed in the United States of America

CONTENTS

Book Reviews

Bibliography

INTRODUCTION

by Gottfried Haberler

Ragnar Nurkse was born on October 5, 1907 in Kaeru (the name of the estate where his father was overseer) near the village of Viru in Estonia. His father, William Nurkse, was Estonian; his mother, Victoria Nurkse (née Clanman), who survives him, is of Swedish origin. His two younger sisters died many years ago. Ragnar went to the Domschool in Tallinn (formerly Reval), the capital of Estonia, and later to the University of Tartu. In the early 1930's his family emigrated to Canada. In 1928 Ragnar went to Edinburgh University and took a first-class degree in economics under the late Professor F. W. Ogilvie, who became his close friend and regarded him as his outstanding pupil.

In 1932 he was awarded a Carnegie Fellowship to study at the University of Vienna where I met him for the first time. During his two years' stay he became well acquainted with several members of the Austrian school, Hayek, Machlup, Mises, and Morgenstern. Here also started lifelong friendships with Martin Hill and Peggy Joseph (now Mrs. Hemming), Karl Bode, and Alfred Stonier, who were studying in the Austrian capital at the same time. Hugh Gaitskell also belonged to this group.

In Vienna, Nurkse wrote his first article on economics (in German), "Causes and Effects of Capital Movements," which is reprinted in the present collection, and his first book on the same subject (also in German), which appeared in 1935.

In June 1934 Nurkse joined the Financial Section and Economic Intelligence Service of the League of Nations. He was a prominent member of a remarkable team of economists who, under the inspiring leadership of Alexander Loveday, did outstanding work during the interwar period and continued to function during the war in Princeton, New Jersey. Other members of the group were the late Folke Hilgerdt, J. B. Condliffe, Martin Hill, Louis Rasminsky and Marcus Fleming; James Meade and others spent considerable periods working at the League in Geneva before the outbreak of the war.

After the war, Nurkse was offered a high position in the International Monetary Fund, but he decided to leave the international civil service and accepted a professorship in Columbia University in New York City, which he kept until his untimely death in May 1959. From the fall of 1945 to June 1958 (with the exception of the academic year 1954–55, which he spent abroad on sabbatical leave, mostly at Nuffield College, Oxford) he taught at Columbia, where he made a profound impression on a generation of economic students. International economists trained and inspired by him can be found literally around the globe and in all international economic agencies.

For the academic year 1958–59 Columbia University awarded Nurkse a Ford Research Professorship. He spent the year in Geneva pursuing his studies on economic development. Later, Princeton offered him a professorship and asked him to act as director of the International Finance Section. The choice was difficult because he was greatly devoted to his colleagues in Columbia; on the other hand, he disliked working in a large city, so he accepted the offer from Princeton. In the spring of 1959 he paid a visit to Sweden and in Stockholm delivered the *Wicksell Memorial Lectures,* which were a great success and are reprinted in this volume. He returned to Geneva very tired. On May 6 he travelled to Vevey at the other end of Lake Geneva and took a walk on Mont Pèlerin in the famous narcissus fields. There on a warm spring day he suddenly collapsed and died of a heart attack or stroke before he touched the ground.

Ragnar Nurkse was a man of great charm and culture and many achievements. He was very reserved, disliked and avoided large gatherings, but greatly enjoyed small parties and the company of friends. In 1946 he married Harriet Berger of Englewood, New Jersey. The marriage was most harmonious and very stimulating to his work. Two sons, Peter and Dennis, survive him.

Languages and philosophy were Nurkse's intellectual hobbies and music meant a great deal to him. In his early years, he studied music at the Conservatory of Music in Tallinn, and later continued under Professor Donald Tovey in Edinburgh; he was himself a fine pianist. In addition to his native Estonian and English, he spoke German, French and Swedish fluently and had a good knowledge of Russian and Italian. In his Geneva days, Mr. Loveday used to say that nobody in the League of Nations could be silent in so many languages as Ragnar Nurkse.

Nurkse's main interest was international economic problems; to them he devoted most of his life's effort. Characteristic of his entire work in economics is the strong theoretical foundation and "the delicate manner in which he used — but did not over-use — available statistics as well as his sense for finding balanced proportions between theory and historical facts in interpreting the trends of economic development," to quote from Professor E. Lundberg's moving introduction to the posthumously published Wicksell Lectures.

His first article (reprinted below in English translation) is a theoretical analysis of international capital movements. His models are interesting because they deal with certain aspects of capital movements which have been rarely treated in the extensive literature — namely, those which stem from the fact that different "stages in the structure of production" may be located in different countries. The analysis runs in terms of the "Austrian capital theory" ("lengthening in the period of production," etc.) which makes it difficult to relate his treatment to those in vogue nowadays. Richard Caves in his remarkable book, *Trade and Economic Structures*,[1] has briefly reviewed Nurkse's contribution to the theory of capital movements and refers to scattered places in the literature where these problems are hinted at. Nurkse's article was later incorporated into his book (in German) on the same topic which contains much empirical material.

The second article reprinted here is a fine piece of abstract-schematic analysis. It deals with the Austrian theory of the struc-

[1] Harvard University Press, Cambridge, Mass., 1960, 137–138.

ture of production in its relation to business-cycle theory. It was inspired by Hayek's famous book *Prices and Production,* but tries to build a bridge between the Böhm-Bawerk-Hayek "linear" and the Marxian "circular" or "departmental" representation of the structure of production.

These two articles are prewar and pre-Keynesian. Like most economists of his generation, Nurkse was quickly drawn into the stream of Keynesian thought. His most Keynesian essay is the next in the present collection, "Domestic and International Equilibrium," which appeared in 1947 in S. E. Harris' Keynes memorial volume, *The New Economics.*

During the twelve-year period 1935–1947 Nurkse did not publish anything under his own name because he was working for the League of Nations, where regulations prescribed anonymity. However, in the League of Nations anonymity was not as strictly enforced as it is at present in the United Nations, whose official publications never mention or give credit to the author if he is a member of the UN staff. Thus the volume, *International Currency Experience,* was ascribed in the preface by Mr. Loveday to Ragnar Nurkse (with the exception of chapter VI on "Exchange Stabilization Funds," which was written by William Adams Brown). This book is generally regarded as a classic in the field of international finance. The subsequent shorter treatment in *The Course and Control of Inflation,* of which Nurkse wrote the first analytical part, deserves the same reputation but is, in fact, not so well known as the earlier book.

Nurkse's work for the League of Nations was by no means confined to these two volumes. He was the "monetary specialist" in Mr. Loveday's section, largely responsible for the annual *Monetary Review.* While F. Hilgerdt was the principal trade expert, Nurkse occasionally wrote parts of the well-known annual *Review of World Trade.* Also parts of the later issues of the famous *World Economic Surveys* (after the departure of J. B. Condliffe and J. Meade, who wrote the *Surveys* until the outbreak of the war) were his work and, together with others, he was actively involved in the writing of the report of the Delegation on Economic Depressions, entitled *The Transition from War to Peace Economy,* published in 1943. Most of the League of

Nations publications were the result of real teamwork and Mr. Loveday usually took a hand in revising and putting in the finishing touches. It is therefore impossible to be more specific in the attribution of individual parts to different authors.[1]

Essays 3, 4, 5, and 8 deal with various problems of international monetary equilibrium. The reader's special attention should be drawn to Essay 7, which presents a comprehensive discussion of the theory of the balance of payments mechanism with special reference to the British postwar experience. Essay 6 is of a more theoretical-methodological nature.

Essays 7 and 9–11 deal with various problems of economic development which occupied Nurkse during the last years of his life. They thus supplement, elaborate, sometimes amend, and overlap his well-known book, *Problems of Capital Formation in Underdeveloped Countries.*

Nurkse's work on the problems of economic development and international trade has strongly influenced contemporary thinking on these matters, both in developed and underdeveloped countries. He was much in demand as a lecturer, and practically all of his writings in this area during the last years of his life grew out of lectures he delivered in Cairo, Istanbul, Rio de Janeiro, Singapore, Stockholm, not to mention his regular lecture courses in Columbia University.

He continuously strove to clarify, elaborate, improve, and modify his theories. This is especially true of the difficult and somewhat elusive notion of "balanced growth," which he had done so much to make popular in his development book. Essays 10 and 11 have much to say on that topic. The appendix to Essay 10, which had been published as a posthumous note in *The Oxford Economic Papers* (October 1959, here reprinted as it originally appeared with the explanatory remarks by John R. Hicks), should be of special interest. Unlike many others, Nurkse did not draw protectionist conclusions from his theory and did not say that "balanced growth" requires central planning.

He was somewhat pessimistic — too much so in my opinion — concerning the trade prospects of the underdeveloped countries,

[1] I am grateful to Messrs. A. Loveday, M. Hill and Louis Rasminsky for advice.

being much impressed by the alleged lag in exports of the poorer countries as compared with total world exports in recent years (1928–1959). But he does not fail to mention that such a lag can be found only in the *exports* of the poorer countries and that it is sizable only if oil-exporting countries are excluded; and that *imports* of the poorer countries, including or excluding the petroleum countries, have risen faster than world imports. (The overall aggregate hides, of course, great differences between individual underdeveloped countries and groups of them.) The gap between exports and imports reflects larger capital imports and grants.

This, obviously, is by no means an undesirable situation so long as it lasts, although one can be pessimistic about the possibility of maintaining the capital flow in the future. Again, unlike many others, Nurkse does not draw the conclusion that the poorer countries should cross bridges before they are reached; he does not recommend that they should restrict trade artificially on the ground that at some (uncertain) future date their export market will decline and their terms of trade deteriorate. In the Wicksell Lectures he expresses the view that this is an adjustment which can be left to the market. If and when the (factoral) terms really deteriorate, "factors of production will tend to move from export industries to home market industries." There is no sense in committing suicide in order to avoid death.

The Wicksell Lectures were Ragnar Nurkse's last words on trade and development. He had evidently spent much care on their preparation. But he was fully aware that he left many loose ends, and he was full of plans for further work. He intended to write a comprehensive volume on trade and development and had started to draft parts. His untimely death at the age of fifty-two has deprived us of any further help from his fertile mind and wise counsel; it was a grievous loss for economic science as a whole, to say nothing of his many friends. Let us hope, however, that the present collection will stimulate many others to follow the leads which he has given and to explore the lands which his researches have opened.

*   *

*

Mrs. Ragnar Nurkse has greatly helped in the preparation of this volume, and has selected the photograph of her late husband. Thanks are due to Mrs. Margarita Willfort for editorial assistance, proofreading, and preparation of the index, and to the Department of Economics of Columbia University for making a grant from the Seager Fund towards the incidental costs of preparing this volume.

ECONOMIC ESSAYS

Causes and Effects

of Capital Movements

(1933)

The theory of capital movements has not been treated systematically, so far, in the literature of economics. The reason
for this neglect may well be found largely in the fact that the
classical doctrine of international trade, the theory of comparative costs, rests on the fundamental assumption that while the
factors of production, labor and capital, are freely mobile inside
a given country, they are lacking external freedom of mobility.[1]
This basic premise of the international immobility of capital
seems to have prevented the possibility of a theoretical approach
to capital movements, at least from the standpoint of international trade theory.[2] It is significant that whenever the so-
called problem of transfers comes up in the orthodox theory of

Translation by Mrs. Ragnar Nurkse.

[1] The question of mobility does not arise, of course, with regard to the third
factor of production. Land is immovable.

[2] Capital theory has not been concerned with the question of capital movements, either.

international trade, the discussion is always[3] concerned with indemnity payments between governments and matters of this kind, never with spontaneous, economic money transfers, i.e., with capital movements in the strict sense.[4]

Secondly, the theory of capital movements undoubtedly suffers from the fact that the transfer problem, which arises in capital movements as well as in indemnity payments, has taken up far too much room at the center of the stage. No attempt has been made to look beyond it, either at the causes of capital movements or at their effects. The discussion has been limited to the immediate process of international transfers, in the belief that practical and theoretical problems could be seen here which actually have turned out to be largely spurious. After the war, the mechanism of transfer naturally attracted more attention than ever on account of the question of reparations. It was generally held that everything there was to observe on the subject of transfer of reparations must also apply automatically to the case of capital movements. This assumption was, to say the least, somewhat premature. Since the causes and effects of capital movements are utterly different from those of reparations and indemnity payments, differences are bound to arise as well with regard to the mechanism of transfers; only a few of these can be mentioned here later. (The general theory of transfers can be assumed to be understood and will not be discussed in this paper.) What it is that divides the causes of capital movements from those of indemnity payments and similar unilateral money trans-

---

[3] Even F. W. Taussig while giving numerous examples of transfer, confines himself to compulsory payments (America to Germany).

[4] We need not be detained here by historical research into the reasons why the classical economists made the assumption of the international immobility of the factors of production the cornerstone of their trade theory. We can agree with Bertil Ohlin, whose own words may be quoted from the article, "The Connection Between International Trade and International Labor and Capital Movements," *Zeitschrift für Nationalökonomie*, II (1930), 162: "That classical economists have shown so little concern with this important problem need not be attributed to the fact that international capital movements were less important 100 years ago than they are today. The root of the matter is more likely to be found in the structure of their theory of international trade as a labor theory of value. On the other hand, the study of international trade on the basis of the modern theory of the interdependence of prices (i.e., the reciprocal dependence between cost of factors of production and price of products) must obviously lead to an investigation of this problem."

fers is obvious, and needs no explanation. The main difference lies in the fact that the latter are not economically oriented. They move in an opposite direction from that indicated by profit expectation; otherwise the transfer would have taken place earlier, of its own accord. There will be no further reference to reparations and indemnity payments in this paper. We are exclusively concerned with the study of spontaneous, economic and productive capital movements.

II

The immediate cause of profit-oriented capital movements is an interest-rate differential. The main point is to find out how this interest-rate differential can come about. A useful though somewhat superficial view consists in assuming the interest rate to be the outcome of capital supply and demand. Consequently, a change in the interest rate can be induced either from the supply or from the demand side.

An interest-rate differential, hence a capital movement from A to B, can thus come into being in the following way: country A, for one reason or another, saves more than country B; in other words, the supply of capital rises. Or both interest-rate differential and capital movement in the same direction are caused by a fall in the savings rate in country B, which means a decline in the supply of capital. (The possibility of creating an interest-rate differential by increasing the capital supply in country A artificially through credit creation may be mentioned briefly as a factor on the supply side.) These variations in the savings rate have no problems to offer. Of greater interest are the variations that occur in the demand for capital and produce both interest-rate differentials and capital movements.

To begin with, suppose that a technical discovery or an improvement in methods of production takes place in country B, that B's products become cheaper on this account and that physical output expands. But the value of output will obviously rise only if the elasticity of demand in the relevant sector of the demand curve is greater than one. Industrial profits go up in B, the entrepreneurs strive to increase production, this in turn drives up the cost of the factors of production — including the interest rate — and the result is a capital movement towards B. The more labor-saving the discovery in B and the greater the elasticity of demand for B's product, the more extensive the ensuing capital influx. An opposite effect is conceivable: the improvement in technical methods of production may release capital in B and lead to an export of capital from B. But this is not very likely to happen. It can occur only if (a) the invention is a capital-saving one,[5] and (b) the elasticity of demand is lower than one. That the first requirement alone is not enough is shown by the fact that even if the discovery is only relatively capital-saving, a high elasticity of demand can lead to such substantial extensions in production that surplus capital will be necessary.

In the case we have just considered capital movements were brought about, in the last analysis, by a change in the technical requirements of production. In the case we shall take up next, the cause of capital movements is a shift in demand for various end-products as the result of a change in consumers' tastes.

For the sake of simplifying the demonstration, a gold standard will be assumed. Further, labor as a factor of production is assumed to have no external mobility. Lastly, we will suppose that the world consists of different "countries" in the following sense: each country manufactures several kinds of consumer goods, and the higher stages in production required for the manufacture of each of these consumer goods are to be found in the same country as the end-product. For the purpose of this example, international trade is assumed to consist of consumer goods alone, and no exchange of intermediate products or capital goods takes place among different countries.

A transformation in consumption habits, a widespread change in consumer preferences will be followed by a decline in demand for the products of country A, for instance, and a rise in demand for those of country B. In the former country export prices fall, in the latter they go up. Production in A becomes less profitable and is therefore reduced. Capital will be released, or at any rate no new savings capital will be available for investment. The reverse is the case in B: the producers of the consumer goods

[5] Capital-saving discoveries are relatively unlikely. See J. R. Hicks, *The Theory of Wages* (London, 1932), 125.

that the shift in demand has favored make more profits, and develop a wider demand for capital in order to extend production. The interest rate goes up.[6] The outcome is a capital movement towards B. A higher proportion of the flow of new savings finds its way into the country whose products are more intensely desired and have consequently risen in price.

It might seem that the rise in demand for B's export goods will not necessarily provoke a rise in their prices. If the industry favored by the shift in demand is subject to the law of increasing returns, that is, if it operates with diminishing costs, prices to all appearances can fall instead of rising. A case of falling costs of this kind becomes a little more involved under our present assumptions. Let us imagine that country B specializes, among other consumer goods, in the manufacture and export of pencils. Now let us have an increase all over the world in the demand for pencils. Country B shows an export surplus for the time, and gold flows into B. The influx of gold shifts the consumers' monetary-demand curve in B to the right. In the same way, a rise in the monetary cost and supply curves might be expected. The pencil industry's supply curve can display a negative slope: because of the gold influx (because of the greater quantity of money in B), the curve presently shifts upward all along the line so that the rise in demand makes the price of pencils go up instead of down. But this would not be a defensible argument. If an upward shift occurs in the pencil manufacturers' individual monetary-cost curves (on account of the gold influx and of their increased demand for means of production), a falling or negative supply curve cannot be valid for the pencil industry as a whole. In these circumstances it will have to have a positive slope, and there is little cause for surprise if the price of pencils goes up.[7] Nevertheless we reach the same result — rise in price as the result of a general rise in demand — even if the pencil industry

[6] More precisely, the demand curve for capital shifts to the right. Either a higher interest rate can be paid on the former capital supply, or a greater quantity of capital can be used at the former interest rate. If the capital-supply curve is a horizontal one, the interest rate need not rise at all in the present case, or will rise imperceptibly.

[7] Concerning the connection between cost and demand curves, see especially Jacob Viner, "Cost Curves and Supply Curves," *Zeitschrift für Nationalökonomie*, III (1931).

shows a falling supply curve in a sense presently to be explained. Supposing that we let the rise in demand for pencils take place in country B alone, it may proceed at the expense of some other product also manufactured in B for which demand will decline. Means of production in the latter industry will be released for expansion of the pencil industry. Because the means of production required for its expansion are placed at the disposal of the pencil industry while costs remain constant, external savings can be achieved that will not be overcompensated by a rise in the cost of the means of production and that produce a negative slope in the corresponding sector of the collective supply curve. Should the rise in demand for B's pencils occur outside country B and happen at the expense of a product not manufactured by B, but rather by country A, the international immobility of labor presumably prevents an adjustment of the real wage rate, which goes up in B. This counteracts the tendency towards external savings and falling costs in the pencil industry, and may convert the pencil industry's supply curve from a falling curve to a rising one. This seems to be a reason for assuming in the theory of foreign trade, at least in the case of international shifts in demand, that supply curves have in general a positive slope.[8]

The price increase of export goods in country B which induces a capital flow towards B will mean an improvement in net terms of trade for this country.[9] It is well know that discussions of the transfer problem have been mainly concerned with the question of whether capital movements in themselves create a change for the better or for the worse in the net terms of trade. The "orthodox" viewpoint has it that capital transfers bring about a deterioration in the net terms of trade for the paying country and an improvement for the receiving country. We have just seen that the causal connection between capital movements and the net terms of trade can take the opposite direction: an im-

[8] Professor Lionel Robbins has indicated the basis in general theory for the above remarks in a lecture on the theory of costs delivered at the Economic Society in Vienna in April 1933, in which he refers to the impossibility of postulating negatively inclined supply curves without shifts in demand. The latter release the means of production in one place for use where they are needed in another.

[9] Variations in the actual rate of exchange (Taussig's "net barter terms of trade") are measured by the relation between export and import prices.

provement in the terms of trade is the cause of capital imports. Because of this fact, certain difficulties appear in verifying these mutually conflicting transfer theories — a subject to which we will briefly return below.

The immediate effect of the rise in demand for B's product is to create an export surplus in that country, followed by an influx of gold with the function of closing the gap between exports and imports, and of providing the inhabitants of country B with a greater share in the "world product." The gold influx is succeeded by certain price movements that remove the discrepancy between exports and imports after a while. At the same time, the increase in demand for B's product calls for a capital movement towards B, and this provokes a second gold influx, with the function and effect of inducing a discrepancy between exports and imports in the other direction, of bringing about an import surplus. Capital flows into B in the shape of goods. It is evident both that the first kind of gold import will not be enough for this purpose, and that the two kinds are only to be distinguished one from the other by analysis; they are separable neither practically nor temporally.

Let us consider briefly what effects the increase in demand for its product and the subsequently induced capital imports will have on the general structure of production in the pencil-producing country. Since the land and labor supply remains unchanged in B and only the capital stock is enlarged, it means a transition to more roundabout methods of production in B, to a more capital-intensive structure, while in A, the country whose products have suffered a decline in demand, there follows likewise a shortening of the methods of production. If we observe the pencil industry in particular, we find that it is led by wage increases to replace labor with capital. More capital is used in relation to the other factors of production, the "average period of production" becomes longer, the "coefficients of production" have altered in favor of capital — whichever way one wants to put it. It will not be the same, of course, if the shift in demand takes place among consumers in a single country or if, regardless of whether it happens all over the world, the industries affected by the shift in demand, whether favorably or unfavorably, are

to be found in the same country. If within each "country" full
freedom of mobility is assumed for the factor of production labor,
the industry favored by the shift in demand develops "horizontally," with no change in the existing coefficients of production.
Conversely, the industry that has been prejudiced will shrink
"horizontally" and there is no incentive for a change in its
"average periods of production." [10] In the latter case, the increase
in consumer demand for pencils is met by an extension of production as a whole through intensified application of all the
factors of production in approximately the same ratio, with no
essential change in methods of production. In the former case,
on the other hand, consumer wants are satisfied, thanks mainly
to the increase in output afforded by more roundabout methods
of production.[11]

III

We have considered capital movements as being due to shifts
in demand and fluctuations in the price of end-products. Let us
now give up the assumption that international trade consists of
consumer goods alone. From a mainly "horizontal" analysis, we
move on to a "vertical" one.

In fact, the world's international trade is made up not only of
finished goods ready for consumption but also, and to a far
greater extent, of capital goods, "intermediate products," and

---

[10] The immobility of the third factor of production, land (inside a country
as well), can obviously not impair this result and is compensated for by the
mobility of the remaining factors of production, which tend to settle where
land is cheapest — taking into account all the advantages of situation,
quality, etc.

[11] What has been said under the assumption of the external immobility of
labor applies inside a country as well, in the case of "noncompeting groups."

Further, our assumption of a system under a gold standard is not quite as
unrealistic as it may seem at first. Any theoretical discussion which is based
on the gold standard is applicable to any country in a domestic sense, even
if no international gold standard exists. Ohlin, in *Handelns Teori* (Stockholm,
1924), 119, says, "A discussion on the basis of the gold standard — i.e., of a
rigid exchange system — is altogether valid not only for trade between different countries under a gold standard but, with insignificant modifications,
for trade between different regions in the same country as well."

We shall go on making use of both these assumptions. The third is about to
be discarded.

"goods of higher order." [12] Even if a country specializes in a certain consumer commodity, the principle of comparative costs determines that the goods of higher order required in the capital-intensive production of this commodity are not all manufactured in the same general neighborhood as the end-product. Needless to say, the principle of comparative costs applies to capital goods as well as consumer goods. From the standpoint of average length of the capital-intensive process of production, the geographical distribution of the various districts where each separate stage in production takes place is accidental and unimportant. [13]

Capital movements that originate in a shift in demand for goods of higher order will now be discussed. With this in mind, let us imagine a closed economy — the world, for instance — divided into three geographical sections of equal size. The first region, which we will call A, specializes in the highest stages of production, i.e., farthest from the consumer (primary production, mining, etc.). In the second region, B, we have a concentration of industries devoted to the "middle" stages of production, nearer

[12] If capital is viewed as an "aggregate of intermediate products" (with Böhm-Bawerk et al.), any kind of trade in capital goods would have to be considered as a capital movement even if it takes place for ready cash. But the transport of capital goods is not of theoretical interest in itself. When we speak of capital movements, it is evidently a matter of "capital supply." That exports of machinery in Britain were prohibited in the time of Ricardo, for instance, did not affect freedom of "capital" in any way in the sense of "capital supply." The concept and terminology of real capital and capital supply are lucidly interpreted in Fritz Machlup's *Börsenkredit, Industriekredit und Kapitalbildung* (Vienna, 1931), ch. 2.

[13] In practice, a strong correlation probably exists between the length of the roundabout processes of production in time (capital-intensity), and of those in space, the latter being detours in a literal sense, although the connection is meaningless from the standpoint of capital theory in which space is neglected. This correlation would not be hard to explain. As more and more steps in production are fitted into the process of production, it becomes less likely that a single specific region will be the most suitable place for production at all stages. The various stages of production will tend to be more and more widely scattered. On the other hand, it may be chiefly the opportunity for a longer roundabout method of production in space (an opportunity increased through improvements in the transport system and restricted by customs duties), which first allows the adoption of correspondingly longer methods of production in time. This parallel is suggested in certain passages of Eugen Böhm-Bawerk himself. See, for instance, his *Positive Theorie des Kapitales,* 3rd ed. (1909–1912), 131, 133.

consumption (machinery, semimanufactured products), while the third region, C, is connected with the final stages of production, those nearest to consumption. All consumer goods (the "real income" of our closed economy, A, B, C) are therefore exclusively produced in C. Out of this flow of consumer goods C retains one third, shall we say, to pay for its own initial means of production. Two thirds are handed over to region B, where C's intermediate products come from. B in turn keeps half the consumer goods it receives from C for itself, and exchanges the other half for the intermediate products farthest removed from consumption produced by A, which leaves A provided with one third of the total real income.

Now let us find out what happens when the supply of capital increases in C: when the savings rate goes up — or when inflationary credit creation takes place there. The resulting "capital surfeit" leads to lengthening of the stages of production that are found in C, the structure of production in C becomes more capitalistic, which means more intensive and continuous use of capital goods or intermediate products. In consequence, demand rises for the products of country B and this creates an improvement in B's net terms of trade. The increase in the price of products from the lowest levels of production in B extends the price margins between all the levels of production in B, which drives up the interest rate in B. Because the interest rate has gone up in B, part of the newly available capital supply in C, say one third, finds its way into B in the shape of C's consumer goods. This leads to an extension in the processes of production in B, hence to a rise in demand for country A's products. As formerly in B, the interest rate rises in A and calls for a capital import: the residual third of the newly created capital supply in C is fed into A. And again it happens by means of an increase in the import of consumer goods from C to A, which first enables A to extend its processes of production, since during the transition to more roundabout methods of production A's exports will fall and so fail to provide for the usual amount of consumer goods. But once the transition has been completed, thanks to the capital import from C, A will be in possession of a much larger "subsistence fund," a greater quantity of intermediate products on their way to be exchanged for C's consumer goods.

We have seen how price movements at different levels of production — and consequently variations in the "terms of trade" for the regions or countries concerned — furnish the mechanism by means of which an increased flow of savings capital becomes evenly distributed among all the levels of the vertical structure of production, through the medium of interregional capital movements. The mechanism operates in exactly the same way if the increase in the supply of capital in C is due to an extension of credit and not to a rise in the savings rate. But in this case, the increase in the capital supply leads to an extension of the roundabout methods of production which no longer corresponds to an increase in the net subsistence fund. "A time comes inevitably when the means of subsistence ready for consumption are used up before capital goods in the process of production have turned into consumer goods. . . . The price of consumer goods will (then) rise on the market, while the price of producers' goods will go down." [14] This change in price relations is the cause of a shrinkage in the process of production, a depression.

A further observation should be made in connection with the interrelations between price fluctuations and capital movements which we have been discussing, with the help of our model of the three regions. The question could be raised of why the increase in the capital supply in C does not lead to an immediate export of capital to A and B. It must promptly cause a fall in the interest rate in C, while in the other two regions the interest rate stays at its former level. Both interest-rate differential and capital movements are the direct result, with no need for the roundabout methods of demand and price increases as described above. However, the earlier demonstration is more in keeping with reality because of the fact that a number of "frictions" and sluggish periods have to be overcome before an interregional

[14] Ludwig Mises, *Theorie des Geldes und der Umlaufsmittel*, 2nd ed. (Munich and Leipzig, 1924), 371.

capital movement can take place. Capital mobility, whether in a single "region" or between several "regions," is never absolute. Among other adverse factors, the risk factor should be mentioned as perhaps the most significant. It may be compared to a threshold, which must be crossed before a capital movement can take place. The risk factor induces a certain amount of "idling": if the interest-rate differential stays within a certain range, no capital movement takes place. We have a complete analogy here with transportation costs in commodity movements. If a commodity has the same price in two districts, A and B, a decline in the price in A will not lead at once to an export to B. In spite of the price margin, there will be no commodity movement as long as the price margin is less than the cost of transportation from A to B.

Aside from risk, entrepreneurial savings may be mentioned as another serious obstacle to capital mobility. To go back to our model, when the increase in the savings rate in C is due to entrepreneurial savings alone, the outcome is as follows: the entrepreneurs save more and invest the proceeds in their own undertakings, without placing them on the capital market and without reducing their previous demands on the capital market. This spells a transition to more capital-intensive methods of production and means a greater need for goods of a higher order, which improves the net terms of trade in B as described, makes production more profitable, and drives up the interest rate. Now at last an interest-rate differential occurs, to draw some of the capital out of C's capital market into B.

The risk factor has a similar effect. At first, the increase in the capital supply in C will only make the interest rate in C go down. As long as this is not enough to overcome the risk threshold, new capital will be invested in C itself. Then the demand for B's export goods rises, their prices go up, country B makes more profits, its activity is stimulated, and this alone improves conditions for the influx of foreign credit. Now the interest rate goes up in B, which widens the interest-rate differential already produced by the decline in the interest rate in C. The risk period and other "elements of friction" are overcome and a capital movement from C to B is brought about.

The mechanism runs its course essentially according to the earlier model.

From this standpoint, it would be interesting to investigate the variations in price relations between raw materials and finished goods on the world market, and subsequent fluctuations of the net terms of trade of the countries involved, in connection with capital movements to primary producing countries. The practical difficulty is, of course, that in reality successive stages in production are not as neatly and distinctly organized, each in a separate region, as our former example would assume. So-called industrial countries export consumers' end-products as well as machinery and other equipment for production. Where so-called primary producing countries are concerned, products such as timber, rubber, nitrate, tin, etc., should no doubt be classified under higher stages in production than cotton, for instance, or wheat, coffee, etc. There has been no attempt so far to bring ordinary statistical distinctions between "primary products" and "finished goods" (besides finished consumer goods, the latter often include equally "finished tools and machinery"), or between raw foodstuffs and industrial raw materials on one hand, into somewhat closer harmony with the "vertical" model of the successive stages in production of capital theory. The obstacles to an empirical view are further increased by the fact that retail trade, the nearest step in production to the consumer, is necessarily dispersed. Therefore in a depression, when wholesale prices fall, the well-known phenomenon of the comparative rigidity of retail prices is unable to influence the "net terms of trade" of any particular region. On the whole, though, it can be said that so-called "primary producing countries" specialize on the average in higher stages in production than so-called "industrial countries" that turn out finished products.

An account of capital movements and the net terms of trade for the period 1921–31 appears in an excellent study of statistical material published by the League of Nations (*Balances of Payments, 1930*). "Of the years considered . . . [1921 to 1931], 1924, 1925 and 1928 were those during which price relations were most favourable to the countries exporting raw materials . . . and the same years also mark the apex of capital exports from the lending countries. In the years 1926 and 1930–31, on the other hand, the terms of trade of the countries exporting raw materials became unfavourable and the capital supply shrank." [15]

This brief report offers a good example of the main difficulties and dangers in verifying economic theory. The orthodox theory of transfers teaches that capital imports improve the net terms of trade and that capital exports have the opposite effect. The facts that have just been quoted seem to provide splendid empirical "proof" of this assertion. That the striking correlation between capital movements and variations in the terms of trade can be explained quite differently is evident from the analysis sketched above. From our point of view, the analogy between capital movements and variations in the terms of trade does not lie in the fact that the latter are caused by the former. The two are actually two closely related symptoms of a common cause, which is the extension of credit and the formation of capital savings in the lending countries.

These considerations are evidence for the practical impossibility of verifying transfer theory, the impossibility of establishing empirically whether a capital movement improves or deteriorates the terms of trade of a particular country. If we must speak of a causal connection in cases where capital movements inevitably go hand in hand with an improvement in the terms of trade and where the improvement is the cause of the capital import rather than the other way round, it becomes difficult to determine whether and, if so, in which direction the capital movement in itself exercises an autonomous influence on the terms of trade. When capital movements are caused by an improvement in the terms of trade, it seems hardly possible to find out what proportion of the improvement is caused, on the contrary, by the transfer of capital. And while it has been correctly maintained [16] that a capital transfer is as likely to induce a deterioration in the terms of trade for the receiving country, we fail to discover how far the terms of trade would otherwise improve if capital transfers had no such influence on trade conditions.

[15] Page 18.
[16] See Gottfried Haberler, "Transfer und Preisbewegung," *Zeitschrift für Nationalökonomie*, I (1930).

IV

A few of the effects of capital movements will now be briefly discussed from another point of view. The example of three regions in which the successive stages of production are located will no longer be required. For the moment, the possibility of creating inflationary credit will be excluded. The market rate of interest corresponds to the natural rate of interest, everywhere and at all times.

Let us assume that for some reason — various possible causes have already been reviewed — the interest rate in country B goes up in relation to the interest rate in country A. Capital flows from A to B. The interest rate in A rises to a certain extent. The demand for producer goods (intermediate products) declines in A, their prices go down.

At first the capital flow from A to B will consist of newly created capital savings.[17] But if the volume of new savings being channeled into B is inadequate to close the interest-rate differential between A and B, the capital flow will also be fed in part from the volume of "retained" savings in B. It is inconceivable that the amortization quotas (this shorter term is used to indicate retained savings) will have been impaired as a result of the capital export before all of the new savings have been transferred to B. For the fact that more roundabout methods of production imply diminishing profits, the gap resulting from the migration

---

[17] A clear distinction should be made here between the two sources of free capital supply. The first consists in actual, new savings that arise from a reduction in consumption spending. The other may be called, with Gustaf Åkerman, "retained" or "accumulated" savings, and consists in previously accumulated savings which the saver has refrained from consuming. It is represented by amortization quotas, renewal funds, and reinvestment of circulating capital. According to Dr. Åkerman, *Realkapital und Kapitalzins* (Stockholm, 1923), 51, "They could perhaps be described as savings that have been held on to. Meanwhile, as long as they are reinvested for the saver's benefit, sustained savings also belong to the supply of loanable funds which therefore includes actual savings in part, in part sustained savings. Even in a static society where real savings do not take place, there is a capital market with loanable funds and it will consist of 'accumulated,' 'disentangled savings' alone (*ausgereift*)." The difference can also be expressed as follows: economically speaking, the volume of new savings serves to extend the average periods of production, while "sustained" savings insure the maintenance of existing length of the production period.

of part of the amortization quotas will obviously be filled at once by the amount of new savings still remaining in A. This flow of savings still available to A will not be used instead for a lengthening of the roundabout methods of production in A.

If we assume that the interest-rate differential margin[18] is too large to be closed by the export of new savings from A, the amortization quotas themselves will migrate from A to B. The second of the main sources of free capital supply will be tapped. Let us examine the reactions in A. Amortization varies a good deal according to different capital goods. For circulating capital, e.g., the turnover rate, can amount to five a year (i.e., the whole of the capital supply that is tied up in circulating capital becomes available five times in the course of one year). For fixed capital goods, the turnover rate may amount to as little as one fifth a year if durability of the capital is five years. It is clear that the amount of "retained" savings that finds its way into B as a result of the interest-rate differential will be drawn mainly from such capital goods as can be more quickly used up or consumed. These capital goods are not replaced, and the fixed capital loses its complementary capital goods. Isolated capital goods are generally unprofitable, however. Different kinds of capital goods complement each other but as they have different amortization rates, each is the more dependent on the cooperation of "circulating" capital goods in proportion to its own durability and comparative lack of mobility, i.e., to the longer time required in order to release the capital supply. To the extent that sustained savings are involved and become diverted in the process, the mere fact of shifting the capital supply in a geographical sense will result in a certain depreciation (or virtual destruction) of fixed capital.[19]

[18] The circumstance referred to above, that within certain limits the interest-rate difference can be ineffective on account of risk and other factors, does not concern us here.

[19] Depreciation of capital will not be avoided if, in order to keep his durable capital goods active and to preserve their value, the owner is prepared to pay a higher price for use of the cooperating circulating capital. The yield of the corresponding durable capital goods will be reduced, which again causes depreciation. See also Machlup, "Theorie der Kapitalflucht," *Weltwirtschaftliches Archiv*, October 1932, 513.

This form of capital depreciation through capital movements could obviously be avoided if all capital goods had the same amortization rate. Secondly, there would be no loss of capital regardless of unequal amortization rates if the savings rate (the new savings) were adequate to close the interest-rate differential. Here we see the advantages of a progressive economy. In a stationary economy no net new savings occur; hence every one of the causes that call for capital movements will produce capital depreciation at the same time.[20]

There is another form of capital depreciation, not to be confused with the above. If an unforeseen shift in demand occurs, the producers for whose products demand has declined will not be given time or opportunity to wait until the capital that is tied up in their capital goods can be released, and transferred to the industry that has been favored by the shift in demand. Capital depreciation takes place at once, and would do so even if all capital goods had the same amortization rate.

We have not included the general theory of transfers in the range of these observations, if only because the bulk of transfer literature is already swollen to an almost disproportionate extent. At this point, we may be allowed to isolate one particular effect of the process of transfer in capital movements, and no more. To put it briefly, the usual view is that at the beginning of a capital movement, the rise in demand for foreign currency pushes the rate of exchange in A down to the export point of gold. Gold flows from A to B and this raises the general price level in B. Commodity imports go up in this country, exports go down, and capital is transferred from A to B in the form of an additional flow of goods. Of what kinds of goods this flow is composed is not, as a rule, specified: they may be capital goods at a distant stage in production just as well as luxury goods and other end-products for immediate consumption. In the latter case, means of production for the manufacture of capital goods will be released in the importing country. What kinds of goods will be imported and, on the other hand, which

---

[20] This does not mean that new savings, sufficient only to compensate for existing capital losses, are excluded from a "static" economy.

are the export goods that in whole or in part cease to be exported, is generally assumed to be unascertainable. All depends on the scale of comparative costs.[21]

This reasoning would apply if the transfer of purchasing power that accompanies a capital movement should provoke a general, uniform price rise in debtor country B, or at least if uneven price increases were to follow at random for a variety of goods. But capital imports encourage price increases for a particular class of goods, namely capital goods and intermediate products.[22] Capital movements alter the scale of comparative costs.[23] The capital import in B makes it probable that capital goods and intermediate products (producer goods, in short) will make up most of the additional flow of imports. It is also to be expected that the first goods that B ceases to export will be producer goods, even if a consumer commodity happened to come next in the scale of comparative costs before the capital transfer began.[24]

A more familiar approach yields the same result. The capital

[21] Wilhelm Röpke has expressed it in the following way: "Whether the additional imports attributable to foreign credit are composed mainly of capital goods or consumer goods . . . depends on whether it is more expedient for the extension and renewal of the apparatus of production that means of production should be drawn from foreign or from domestic industries. If means of production such as machinery of all kinds are not imported, and consumer goods are imported, it does not imply that instead of contributing to the extension of the apparatus of production in Germany foreign credit has become consumer credit in the economic sense." "Auslandskredite und Konjunktur," *Schriften des Vereins für Sozialpolitik,* CLXXIII, 25–26.

[22] If total monetary demand is divided among producer goods and consumer goods, the capital import will cause a shift in favor of the former. The price of consumer goods is not affected at first by the capital import. Price margins between the stages in production are reduced only by the rise in price of producer goods. In this connection, see F. A. Hayek, *Prices and Production* (London, 1931).

[23] Producer goods move down on the scale, consumer goods move up to take the place formerly occupied by producer goods. Of course, the nature of the scale may favor the importation of consumer goods and the exportation of producer goods to such an extent that a shift of this kind will not yet influence the composition of imports and exports in terms of goods. What we have is a tendency in the direction that has been indicated.

[24] The reason why the classical theory of foreign trade contains no reference to variations in the scale of comparative costs as a result of capital movements may be explained by the fact that it rests on the assumption of the international immobility of capital (as well as of the other factors of production).

import in B leads to a decline in the interest rate in B, which brings about certain changes in price relations. Because the various branches of production have average production periods of varying length, i.e., because the proportion of "capital" in relation to the other factors of production is unequal, consumer goods that require comparatively more capital decline in relative price while goods in the production of which less capital is needed go up in price. These shifts in relative prices of end-products undoubtedly cause a change in the scale of comparative costs. It can also be said, however, that intermediate products in general have a shorter production period behind them than is the case with end-products, and therefore less capital is needed in their manufacture. In this way, we come to the conclusion, also on the supply side,[25] that the new imports following a capital transfer are more likely to consist of producer goods than of end-products ready for consumption, because the scale of comparative costs has altered in favor of the former.

When the interest-rate differential that leads to a capital movement from A to B has not been prompted or followed by a rise in the savings rate,[26] the capital transfer has similar effects on the composition of the additional exports from A. The demand for producer goods declines in A, the price goes down and they are exported in greater quantity.

It is therefore by no means as unlikely as is often assumed in the discussion of transfer problems that the goods that are affected by the rise in monetary demand in the debtor country will be the same as the goods that are released by the decline in demand in the creditor country. This applies especially to intermediate goods in the highest stages in production: the higher the stage, the less specific the producer goods.

But if the rise in the interest rate in B leads to a rise in the savings rate in A and if the resulting additional savings are transferred to B, then the goods that are released in A, that decline in price and are exported, will be consumer goods. There is no change in the interest rate in A. Even so the scale of comparative

[25] A more detailed account of the circumstances cannot be attempted here.
[26] According to whether the interest margin occurs because of a decline in the interest rate in A or a rise in B.

costs will shift, and this time in favor of consumer goods. As against our earlier observations, the likelihood of a case of this kind occurring in practice is remote. It can generally be assumed that the supply of savings does not respond to a change in the interest rate as long as the change keeps within ordinary limits. The response may even take the opposite direction.

The study of transfer effects of this kind in capital movements reveals one of the characteristics by which capital movements differ from movements of other factors of production: labor, for instance. The capital movement alters the material conditions of transfer. The transfer does not happen simply as the result of an unspecified increase in the flow of goods in the direction of the capital movement. Normally, it has a tendency to proceed in the form of specific kinds of goods, specifically in such a way that the confusion between movements of the "abstract capital" (capital movements proper) and movements of "capital goods" may be less harmless than appears at first sight.

The connection between movements of capital and movements of capital goods disappears if the interest margin, the means by which the capital movement is released from A to B, is the outcome of a decline in the interest rate in A through an extension of credit. When a capital import is induced in this way, the demand for producer goods rises in B. The demand for the same kind of goods rises in A as well. The price of producer goods will therefore rise in both A and B, in which case the transfer of capital from A to B will not "release" any goods for additional export to B as was the case in "normal" capital movements. Increases in the price of producer goods in A and B tend to push each other up and the capital transfer in the shape of goods from A to B takes place according to the old scale of comparative costs. It is no longer possible to determine in advance what goods the import surplus in B will consist of.

The problem of the effects of "inflationary" capital movements can be examined no further in this paper. It is evident that the part which capital movements play as "business-cycle carriers" must furnish a chapter in business-cycle research with the task of explaining the spatial propagation of trade cycles and the synchronization of cyclical phases between various countries. A more complete theory of capital movements than has been available so far in the economic literature is an indispensable foundation for the study of the international, or more generally the interlocal, aspects of business cycles.

The Schematic Representation
of the Structure of Production

(1935)

Recent discussion on trade-cycle theory has served to emphasize the importance of a clear recognition of the fundamental characteristics of the productive system in general, largely by bringing into prominence the particular view of the structure of capitalistic production which underlies the "Austrian" approach to the theory of capital. It is the purpose of the present note to examine the adequacy of that picture as a representation of reality, and to contrast it with a different view of the productive process which, although it might claim to be the common-sense view, has perhaps been unduly neglected.

I

The first picture of the productive process which we will here consider is that which forms the basis of the Böhm-Bawerkian theory of capital. The fundamental point of Böhm-Bawerk's position lies in his conception of capital as the aggregate of

Review of Economic Studies, June 1935, by permission of the publisher.

intermediate products: capital goods merely represent the intermediate form which the "original" factors (i.e., labor and land) assume on their way to final "maturity" as consumable commodities or services. Since — it is argued — neither fixed nor circulating capital is capable of satisfying men's wants directly, these two types of producer goods are treated on the same footing and are both included under the significant designation of "intermediate products."

This view of the nature of capital leads naturally to the concept of the "period of production." The longer the period for which original factors are invested, the larger the total stock of intermediate products at any point of time. Indeed, a simple measure of the capital-intensity of the productive system, viz. the average period of production, is obtained by considering, for every unit of original factors, the period which elapses before its product matures in consumable form, and by dividing the sum of all these individual periods by the number of units of original factors.

The graphical expression of this view of the process of capitalistic production has become familiar in the form of the triangular constructions used by Professor Hayek in his *Prices and Production* and elsewhere. At the top of the triangle, original factors alone produce the first intermediate products, which thereafter, through successive applications of original factors in the lower stages of production, gradually increase in value as they move towards their goal of final transmutation into consumer goods at the base of the triangle. If the process be regarded as "synchronized," the area of the triangle represents the total stock of intermediate products, i.e., of capital, in existence at any moment. The height of the triangle shows the absolute period of production, while its base indicates the amount of original factors employed.

Böhm-Bawerk's graphical representation[1] takes the form of a system of concentric circles, in which all goods are grouped according to their distance in time from the consumer, and which — like Professor Hayek's triangular figure — is used to illustrate

---

[1] *Positive Theorie des Kapitales,* 3rd ed. (1909–1912), bk. II, sec. 4. See also *The Positive Theory of Capital* (New York, 1923), ch. V.

both the *structure* of production maintained by a given "time-distribution" of original factors, and as a picture of the synchronized productive *process*. Each circle of Böhm's *Ringschema* represents intermediate products; the innermost circle (the "highest stage") is constantly renewed completely by original factors without the aid of intermediate products, while the outermost circle passes each year into consumption. It is clear that the *Ringschema* is completely identical in meaning with the triangular type of representation, and that it — like the triangle — expresses what may be called a *linear* view of the productive process.

This picture of the productive system is intended by its authors to be an unbiased representation of the given elementary technological facts of capitalistic production and, as such, merely to form the basis for theoretical reasoning proper.[2] The question is whether that linear view — the view of "intermediate products" steadily moving down the *strictly one-way* road of the productive process towards their final goal of consumption — really takes account of the essential data of the technique of capitalistic production.

On the basis of this scheme, one obviously ought to be able to trace the period of production either backward (taking consumer goods in the *present* and noting the points of time in the *past* at which the original factors contributing to their production were applied) or forward (considering the *future* dates at which the products of the current services of the *present* stock of original factors mature in consumable form).[3] In its backward-looking aspect, the essence of the linear view is that present consumer goods, if their process of production be followed back in time, resolve themselves into original factors. The present stock of consumer goods is the result of labor[4] and intermediate products;

[2] See Böhm-Bawerk, 142: "Here it is not our task — as it is, for example, in the theory of interest — to find the right *explanation* for complicated phenomena, but merely to *describe* the facts correctly; facts, moreover, which are entirely familiar to everyone." (My translation.)

[3] I.e., the "completed" and the "anticipated" period, as distinguished by Mr. Martin Hill in his article, "The Period of Production and Industrial Fluctuations," *Economic Journal*, December 1933.

[4] Following Böhm-Bawerk and Hayek, we may for the sake of simplicity neglect land, the other "original" factor.

these intermediate products must again be resolved into labor and intermediate products, and so forth. In this process of splitting up of intermediate products we should, according to the linear view, at last arrive at the highest stage (at the top of the triangle) where the first intermediate products are produced by labor alone. It is clear, however, that in this way we can, in the end, actually arrive only at that point in the history of the human race where primitive man, with his bare hands, first fashioned a tool. True, the earliest labor units would have practically no influence on the *average* period. We are not, however, here concerned with a problem of measurement, but with the precise meaning of a concept; and it must be clear that the backward-looking aspect of the linear view leads to a production period of a historical order, which today even the followers of Böhm-Bawerk for the most part seem to dismiss as an absurdity.[5]

According to the forward-looking aspect we should, if the linear view were even in rough accord with the facts, expect to see the highest stage (the innermost circle of Böhm's *Ringschema*), a stage where labor and land, without the aid of capital, continuously produce the "first" intermediate products of the synchronized productive process. But the "beginning," in this sense, of the productive process — the top of the triangle — is, in fact, impossible to locate in the real world; and it is, indeed, difficult to imagine why labor in the highest stage should be refused the assistance of capital goods, without which its productivity would bear no comparison with that in the lower stages, where labor does cooperate with capital.

Clearly these and similar difficulties arise from an unsatisfactory treatment of fixed capital in the "Austrian" representation of the structure of production. For the picture fits circulating

---

[5] The uselessness of the "historical" production period as an index of capital-intensity may be illustrated by two examples. In the first place, the average period of production as conceived in this historical manner would quite possibly turn out to be shorter today than it was a hundred years ago, since in the meantime capital equipment has been so rapidly expanded as to shift the average, the "center of gravity," nearer to the present. Secondly, even if our present economy were henceforward to continue in a strictly stationary state, our "period of production" would constantly increase through the mere lapse of time, simply because we should move further away in time from that point in history where man and nature combined to produce the first tool.

capital excellently: here we can indeed in most cases point to a highest stage (in the sphere of what in everyday language is well named "primary" production), where no raw materials or semifinished goods are taken over for further treatment from an earlier stage. But when fixed capital is likewise conceived as intermediate products moving essentially in the same way to "become" consumable goods and services, the resulting *tableau économique* proves deficient mainly in two respects. First, the origin of fixed capital goods is left obscure in the triangular picture.[6] Second, the linear representation does not adequately show the place of the productive services of durable instruments[7] in the structure of production.

II

An unbiased view of the productive process of society demands recognition of the fact that fixed capital not only adds value to the circulating capital (i.e., the "goods in process") to which, in common with the "original" factors, it is applied, but that it *reproduces itself* (in the sense to be developed presently). For "production is in reality no such linear process from the original factors to the consumable commodity. The iron and machine industry, for example, produces for the lower stages (for the consumption industries) as well as for the preceding stages, e.g., for the mining industry. . . . The process of production takes no straight path; its course is, rather, a circular line which turns back into itself any number of times before reaching the final stage of consumption."[8]

[6] If it is implied that fixed capital goods (even if only in the highest stages) are continually reproduced by barehanded labor only, this picture of capitalistic production is of course manifestly untrue. Dr. G. Åkerman's work, *Realkapital und Kapitalzins* (Stockholm, 1923), a painstaking attempt to deal with fixed capital from the "Austrian" point of view, proceeds entirely on that unreal assumption.

[7] As distinct from durable goods yielding *consumer* services whose "output function" was analyzed by Professor F. A. Hayek in his article, "The Relationship between Investment and Output," *Economic Journal*, June 1934.

[8] Thus Professor Gottfried Haberler in his contribution to the Spiethoff-Festschrift (*Der Stand und die nächste Zukunft der Konjunkturforschung*, 1933), 98–99. The passage quoted was not, however, intended by its author as a criticism of the fundamental linear representation of the structure of production, but rather as an appeal for caution in its application to trade-cycle analysis.

In order to demonstrate the nature of the circular process of the self-reproduction of fixed capital, we may divide the total process of production into two "sections" or "departments." "Department I" may be taken to represent the industries producing instruments of production (such as machines, tools, buildings), while "Department II" produces only consumption goods. Each department consists of a number of stages of manufacture,[9] the final stage of each department yielding "finished goods," that is, finished capital goods in the case of I, and finished consumer goods in the case of II. In every stage in each department, fixed capital cooperates with labor and land in pushing forward the goods in process (the circulating capital) towards their finished state. Part of the finished output of Department I goes to replace the worn-out capital used in Department II. The remaining part of the output of instruments of production replaces the fixed capital used up in Department I itself — and this is precisely what is here meant by the self-reproduction of fixed capital. Department II supplies, on the one hand, consumption goods to the workers in Department I, who, of course, produce only non-consumable goods themselves, and, on the other, provides its own workers with their means of subsistence.

To illustrate these relationships graphically, we may construct a picture in which the small dotted rectangles represent current services of fixed capital, the crossed rectangles those of labor and

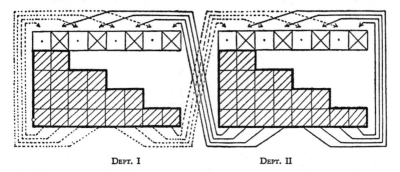

DEPT. I   DEPT. II

[9] Dept. I contains, for example, all the stages of production, starting from the mining of metal ores, which precede the making of tools and machines, while Dept. II may be characterized, for example, by the four stages of woolgrowing, spinning, weaving, and tailoring.

land, the two shaded areas (which, with continuous applications of fixed capital, labor and land, assume triangular shape) showing the volume of goods in process in each department. The arrows indicate how each department retains part of its output for its own "replacement" use, the remainder being supplied to the other department.[10]

Thus an exchange of fixed capital goods against consumable commodities takes place between the two departments. Our graphical illustration assumes the two departments to be of equal size, which will hardly be true in the case of a highly capitalized economy. Taking a numerical example, we may suppose Departments I and II to produce, in a given period of time, goods to an amount of 300 and 100 value units respectively. Of the 100 units of consumption goods, Department II retains, say, 25 to remunerate its own workers, giving up the remaining 75 to Department I. The latter uses, say, 225 units of its output of fixed capital goods for its own replacement needs, and hands over the remainder, 75 units, to the consumption department.

This exchange of instruments for an *equivalent* amount of consumption goods holds only under stationary conditions. When, through the appearance of a net flow of new saving, the economy

[10] In this connection, I venture to reproduce another, simpler figure to illustrate in particular the self-reproduction of capital: here the "ring" is equivalent in meaning to Dept. I, and the "spout" to Dept. II pouring forth its output of consumable goods. The output of Dept. I divides itself at the dotted line: part of it flows back into the ring (to maintain fixed capital

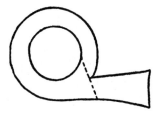

in Dept. I itself). This picture, though less informative than the departmental scheme in bringing out the internal exchange relationships of a capitalist economy, may nevertheless be useful in illustrating the circular process of capital reproduction as lying, in a sense, behind the purposive orientation of economic activity directed towards the creation of consumable income.

becomes "progressive," demand shifts from the products of Department II to those of I, in consequence of which a corresponding transfer of labor takes place to carry out an extension of Department I. That labor will continue to receive its means of subsistence from Department II, which means that the stream of consumption goods to Department I is increased. At the same time, the contraction of the output of consumption goods entails a decline in the replacement demand from Department II, and part of the output of fixed capital goods by Department I is thus set free to be used for the extension of that department itself. When stationary conditions are re-established, the proportion in which the "consumption" department divides its output between exchange for capital goods from the "investment department" on the one hand, and the remuneration of its own labor on the other, will have increased from 75:25 to, say, 80:20; its output in *absolute* terms will, of course, have risen in view of the employment of more fixed capital.[11]

Conversely, in a "regressive" economy, where capital is not maintained intact, the physical self-reproduction of capital instruments is correspondingly reduced: Department I will contract through a transfer of labor to the consumption department and a neglect of replacement in Department I in favor of a temporary extension of Department II. The stream of capital goods from I to II will be larger than the flow of consumption goods in the reverse direction.[12]

Let us, however, consider further the case of a "progressive" economy where, as the result of a shift of demand from consumption goods to productive instruments, the process of ex-

[11] I.e., owing to "the simple 'technological' fact that it is possible to increase the volume (time rate) of production after any interval by the use during that interval of part of existing productive resources — in large part the *same* resources previously and subsequently used for producing 'current consumption income' — to produce *instead* of current consumption income, instruments and agencies of various sorts, tangible and intangible, which when produced become 'productive' of *additional* current income." F. H. Knight, "Capital, Time, and the Interest Rate," *Economica*, 1934, 258.

[12] A more detailed discussion of the effects of saving and dissaving on the physical structure of production as conceived on the above ("departmental," "circular") lines is given by Erich Preiser, *Grundzüge der Konjunkturtheorie* (Tübingen, 1933), ch. 2.

change between the two departments is altered in such a way as to create an "active balance of trade" for Department II and a "passive" one for Department I. The shift of demand involved in the activity of saving will tend to raise the prices of the products of Department I and to depress the prices of the products of Department II, in other words, to shift the "terms of trade" in favor of Department I. This change in relative prices is, however, only a temporary phenomenon. The price fall of consumption goods forces entrepreneurs in Department II to restrict production, and thus to set free the productive resources required in the investment industries. When the output of Department II has contracted (and that of Department I expanded) in exact proportion to the shift of demand, when, that is to say, the full transfer of factors from the production of consumer goods to the production of instruments has taken place, the prices of consumption goods may be expected to return to their former level. Their temporary reduction only reflects a lag of the adjustment of output behind the shift of demand. Until the appropriate transfer of factors has been completed and the prices of consumer goods return to their original position, part of the saving will, in fact, go to waste, since the reduced prices of consumption goods enable the nonsavers to raise their real rate of consumption.

The only reason why the original price relationship between the two departments should not in the long run be restored, is the existence of immobile or "specific" factors of production in Department II, whose inability to adapt themselves to the new demand situation and to migrate to Department I naturally results in a permanent reduction in their prices and in those of their products. Complete specificity and immobility of factors as between the two departments will permanently lower the relative price level of consumer goods to such an extent that the *total* volume of new saving goes to waste, since the corresponding "investment," i.e., the change-over of production from consumer goods to producer instruments, proves impossible. On the other hand, a complete restoration of the original prices does not, of course, presuppose complete mobility of *all* productive resources, but may easily be brought about — in spite even of a possible predominance of immobility — as long as there is sufficient mobility on the margin.[13]

One may at first sight be tempted to take the ratio of the output of Department I to that of Department II as an index of the capital-intensity of production. This, however, would not be strictly legitimate owing to the possible distorting effect of general variations of the durability of instruments. It is easy to see that the output of Department I must, *ceteris paribus,* vary inversely to the length of life of fixed capital. If all instruments of production were of infinite durability, a Department I would not exist at all in a nonprogressive society.

In all except such purely imaginary cases, however, the self-reproduction of capital is an elementary "technological" fact of capitalistic production. (It is, indeed, so elementary that it can be conceived even on a primitive level of production where fixed capital in the ordinary sense may not be used at all. Take the example of seed corn: part of the crop is consumed, and part flows back into the "ring" to reproduce itself in the next harvest.) And in the picture of the structure of production which takes account of this fundamental datum — a picture which, it seems safe to assume, is commonly taken for granted in all non-"Austrian" economic discussion and which only requires to be clearly brought to the surface[14] — the period of production be-

[13] The considerations set out in the last two paragraphs above may be contrasted with Professor Hayek's elaborate reasoning in ch. 3 of his *Prices and Production* (London, 1931) concerning the movements of prices and profit margins in the different stages of his linear structure of production which result from changes in the relative expenditure on consumer goods and producer goods, these price margins being represented as determined by the rate of interest. Obviously his whole argument is not applicable to the price relationship between consumer goods (output of Dept. II) and producer instruments (output of Dept. I), which is governed by the completely extraneous factor of the mobility of resources (elasticity of supply), however relevant it may be when strictly confined to "goods in process," to the stages of production in the narrow sense of actual stages of manufacture.

[14] The main lines of the "departmental" representation of the structure of production were already clearly propounded by Karl Marx: see *Das Kapital,* part 3 (on "the reproduction and circulation of society's total capital") of vol. II, especially sec. 2 (on "the two departments of social production") of ch. 20 (pp. 370f of the German edition edited by Engels, 1893). Dr. F. Burchardt has drawn attention to this fact in his article, "Die Schemata des stationären Kreislaufs bei Böhm-Bawerk und Marx," *Weltwirtschaftliches*

comes meaningless. For, in the realistic circular view, the productive process has no "beginning" except (a) in a historical
sense, or (b) in relation only to goods in process, in which case
the beginning is found in "primary production."

III

We have seen that both the *Ringschema* and the triangle give
an extremely unreal picture of the structure of production. We
may now briefly consider the origin of the "linear" view and ask
how a picture so far removed from the technological facts which
it purports to represent came to be constructed. It must be remembered, of course, that the "linear" structure was not developed for its own sake, but as a basis for a theory of capital.
And there is undoubtedly a certain justification for the Böhm-
Bawerkian view of capital as "intermediate products." Capital
goods have no intrinsic utility of their own, they are incapable
of serving human wants directly. Men do not build up capital
equipment except with a view to an increased consumable product. But such reflections on the existence and fundamental purpose of capital in human society are, so to say, of a broad *sociological* order. They should not be allowed to distort our view
of the structure of capitalistic production, that is, of facts of a
technological order, as is the case when capital is conceived as
intermediate products in the actual productive process on the
basis of the "linear" view.

But even if this "sociological" aspect may be one of the factors
making the linear representation appear plausible, the actual
historical reasons and motives for its adoption are probably to

Archiv, XXXIV and XXXV, 1931-32, to which the present note is greatly
indebted. See also Alfred Kähler, *Die Theorie der Arbeitsfreisetzung durch die
Maschine* (Leipzig, 1933). It is curious to reflect how much better in some
respects the triangular picture of the productive process — with its emphasis
on labor as the "original factor of production" — would have suited Marx.
With the fundamental idea of labor as the "source of all wealth," the labor
theory of value ("modernized" by Marx) and the wage-fund doctrine
("modernized" by Böhm-Bawerk) both flow from a common stock of conceptions and misconceptions of classical economics. Mention must also be
made of J. B. Clark, whose *Distribution of Wealth* (New York and London,
1899), 269-275, contains a brief but lucid description of the "departmental"
organization of social production.

be sought elsewhere. Böhm-Bawerk's central point of departure in all his economic thought was, of course, the newly discovered doctrine of subjective value. And in that part of the doctrine which constitutes the theory of imputation (i.e., the determination of the separate values of complementary goods and thus also of productive factors) the phenomenon of interest presented a problem of first importance. For according to that theory the process of imputation can never stop at produced goods, but must always be carried through to the original productive factors, to which the product of a capital instrument must therefore be imputed as rent or wages. Interest actually existed, although — according to the only "correct" imputation procedure — it had no right to exist.

Böhm-Bawerk saw the solution of this problem in the element of Time. The introduction of the time factor enabled him to escape the rigid and ruthless consequences of "time-less" imputation theory and to fit the phenomenon of interest into the general framework of the theory of value. On the supply side, interest thus came to be explained in terms of the supposed premium on present goods and the underestimation of future wants, while the demand side was covered by the doctrine of increased productivity of more time-consuming (more "roundabout") methods of production; and the necessary "factual" substructure of that doctrine was found in the linear view of the productive process which established itself naturally in accord with the linear, irreversible nature of Time itself. Thus Böhm-Bawerk's structural view was not obtained by way of disinterested description of the elementary phenomena in question (although, once it had implanted itself in men's minds, it was firmly believed to be a simple and objective description of this kind), but was — in its very origin — so highly "predetermined" that, in consequence, it bears no confrontation with reality.[15]

Since Time constantly tended to degenerate into "historical" time, Böhm-Bawerk was led to confuse two entirely different things, namely the (historical) conditions of the original building

[15] I owe the above tentative reconstruction of the genesis of the linear representation of production largely to an article by P. Joseph and K. Bode, "Bemerkungen zur Kapital- und Zinstheorie," *Zeitschrift für Nationalökonomie*, June 1935.

up of capital equipment and the (present) conditions of the maintenance of an existing capital structure.[16] And his fundamental distinction between "original factors" and mere "intermediate products" is tenable on a historical view only: in the beginning was Nature and Man.[17] It is in this connection that the true relevance of the following passage from Bentham, quoted by Professor Hayek,[18] appears to me to lie: "In the order of history labor precedes capital: from land and labor everything proceeds. But in the actual order of things, there is always some capital already produced, which is united with land and labor in the production of new values." In the "actual order of things" capital is completely "on a par" with labor and land.[19]

Moreover, a "nonpredetermined" description of the role of capital goods in the "actual order of things" naturally suggests a sharp distinction between fixed and circulating capital, between (active) "instruments" and (passive) "materials," though there may be cases in practice where the distinction is not easy to draw.[20] The essential difference in the place and function of these two types of goods in the process of production, while it receives

[16] It is significant that his examples (e.g., of the fisherman) intended to illustrate the nature of capitalistic production nearly always relate to primitive times where Man and Nature first combine to produce an implement for further production. That is, he illustrates the process of production not on the clarifying assumption of stationary conditions (the fact that Böhm was not conversant with the all-important methodological distinction between statics and dynamics was already pointed out by Knut Wicksell in *Ueber Wert, Kapital und Rente,* Jena, 1893, 119 and also appeared from the famous controversy between Böhm and Schumpeter on the latter's "dynamic" interest theory), but in terms of the original building up of capital equipment, in terms of transition from one "degree of capitalism" to another.

[17] See the title of sec. 1, part I of the *Positive Theory:* "Man and Nature."

[18] "Investment and Output," 227.

[19] Dr. Hayek's admission that capital goods may become "original factors" through unforeseen changes (see "Investment and Output," 228–229) does not appear to meet the problem. Is it in the essence of capital goods that, by reason of unforeseen changes, they should be put to uses other than those originally intended? Surely the building up of capital equipment is independent of unforeseen changes: and in a stationary economy, where such changes are ruled out *ex hypothesi,* the dichotomy between original factors and mere "intermediate products" would still be of questionable validity.

[20] To cover such cases, Burchardt (see n. 14 above) forms a third group of producer goods — clearly of far less importance than the other two — viz. that of "auxiliary materials" (*Hilfsstoffe*), of which lubricating oil may be taken as an example.

its natural emphasis in the "departmental" system described in the preceding section, is, of course, completely veiled by the linear view. True, the latter does distinguish between "durable goods" and "goods in process"; but it is not the different durability of the two types of goods which, in our view, constitutes the essential difference, since individual "instruments" may well be of shorter durability than the span of life of goods in process.[21]

It may, of course, sometimes be profitable to invest new savings not in the form of fixed capital but in an addition to the quantity of goods in process existing at any moment, by lengthening the period of production in the literal, technological sense. In fact, however, the duration of production — the time which individual goods take to pass through the productive machine — is primarily determined by technical conditions relating chiefly to the kind and quantity of fixed capital employed.[22]

A simple and definite meaning could indeed be given to the triangular construction by restricting it to circulating capital and regarding all instruments (fixed capital) as "original" factors of production. On the basis of our "departmental" scheme it is possible, by putting together the two triangles for the "goods in process" of each department, to draw a single triangle, covering all goods in process, which would show the growth in value of raw materials through the process of manufacture and illustrate the average delay period between the application of all factors — including capital instruments — and the emergence of finished goods, capital and consumable alike. But since, as the "technological" period of production can have no significance as an index of capital-intensity, a triangle of this kind would be of no particular interest, and would, in any case, be entirely inadequate as a representation of the general structure of social production.

According to another possible view of the triangle, it should not be taken literally at its face value; it should be interpreted, as we interpret a map (where height, for example, is indicated by shad-

[21] See J. B. Clark, *Distribution of Wealth*, 148n.
[22] Thus all those who have misunderstood the Austrian production-period theory have probably been quite right in pointing out that an increase of capital generally shortens instead of lengthening the duration of the productive process (which, of course, was thought of in the narrow sense referring to goods in process).

ing or color), so that, for example, the imaginary time indices attached to the different points of the triangle "really" represent something else, that the top of the triangle is not to be taken too literally, etc. With the possible meanings and uses of the triangle other than the representation of the structure of production[23] we are not, however, concerned in this note, which merely deals, as it were, with the "technological," descriptive basis without which economic reasoning proper (on capital, interest, etc.) must needs proceed *in vacuo*.

Lastly, the triangle may simply be considered as an instrument precisely of such abstract reasoning *in vacuo*. "The Böhm-Bawerk theory, or at least a theory correctly worked out along the same line, may be quite 'correct' as an exercise in pure logic, i.e., with reference to the imaginary situations under discussion." [24] It is quite possible to imagine a world where the productive system of society works in the "linear" manner as shown by the triangular *tableau économique;* but it is not the world in which we live.

IV

An application of the "departmental" representation of the productive process to the theory of industrial fluctuations cannot be attempted here. The present note is primarily concerned with the "anatomy" of the productive system and not its "physiology" or even "pathology." The importance of a clear and accurate "anatomical" view of the general structure of capitalistic production — even if inevitably only a skeleton view — as an elementary requisite of trade-cycle analysis, will, indeed, probably be obvious.

---

[23] The triangle may thus be used, for example, to illustrate the scale of time anticipations, ranging from the immediate to the more distant future, of individual entrepreneurs. Nobody will object to the following statement of Professor Hayek ("Investment and Output," 221): "Surely it cannot be seriously argued that investments are made without some definite anticipation not only of the value of the services expected from them, but also of the time when they will mature. . . . The time when the product is expected to mature is as much a datum for the decision of the entrepreneur as its expected value." But a recognition of the very "real" periods and time anticipations in the minds of individual producers with regard to their own particular output (finished or unfinished, consumable or instrumental goods) can in no way justify the construction of a completely unreal picture of the structure of production of society as a whole.

[24] Knight, 262.

Yet it may not, in conclusion, be out of place to indicate, though only very briefly and inadequately, the relevance of the "departmental" scheme to the phenomena of the trade cycle.

We may take relative variations of demand for the products of the two departments of production to constitute the central fact of cyclical changes. A rise in the rate of saving means an increase in the demand for the products of Department I. Industries producing capital equipment will consequently be expanded by means of the increased funds available for investment: a transfer of factors, as already described above, takes place from Department II to Department I. The addition thus made to the productive capacity of Department I will, however, only prove permanent if the rate of saving — the demand for "machines" — remains at a sufficiently high level to employ the increased capacity of the machine-producing plant. Now the additional "machines" which go to increase the productive capacity of Department II [25] will, after a time, as they wear out, come to be replaced. Replacement demand for the output of Department I will thus gradually increase, and the rate of saving may to an equal extent fall off without causing a decline in the aggregate demand for productive equipment. Should the flow of new savings decline more suddenly, a sharp contraction of Department I will be inevitable.[26]

What holds for voluntary saving is equally true of forced saving.[27] In the case, however, of forced saving which is deliberately

[25] For the sake of simplicity, we neglect the fact that part of the output of the additional capacity of "machine" production will go to increase the capital equipment of Department I itself. The circular character of the structure of production makes it possible that new machine factories, power plants, ironworks, etc., are constructed to produce more machine factories, power plants, and ironworks. And this piling up of capital equipment in the investment industries (i.e., within Department I itself) is in fact a characteristic feature of the boom.

[26] This is merely a restatement in "departmental" terms of the argument put forward by Professor Hayek in his article "Capital and Industrial Fluctuations" (*Econometrica*, April 1934, 153–158, now reprinted in the 2nd ed. of *Prices and Production*), where it is based on the triangle and enshrined in the usual Austrian terminology, which yields us no additional knowledge. In contrast to the realistic "departmental" representation, his discussion in terms of higher and lower "stages," "uncompleted roundabout processes," etc. seems, in fact, unnecessarily inexact.

[27] A *prima facie* reason why the latter might appear to be more fluctuating, and therefore more likely to cause disturbance, exists only insofar as a constant

brought about through credit expansion, it is at least conceivable
that the process may be so controlled as to secure stable additions
to productive equipment by slowing down the rate of forced saving in the way described, though the difficulties of ascertaining
the concrete conditions of stability (the rate of increase of replacement demand, etc.) may in practice prove to be insuperable.
But there is, of course, no reason to expect that voluntary saving
— and, similarly, such additions to the demand for instruments
as may result from equally "voluntary" dishoarding — should
behave in the required manner. There is no guarantee that the
rate of saving will decline, when it chooses to do so, at the "right"
pace determined by the gradual rise of replacement demand,[28]
and in such circumstances it may be beneficial to introduce forced
saving in order to obviate the disturbances arising from variations
of voluntary saving, from the uncontrollable acts of individual
entrepreneurs and income-receivers. If we remember, further, that
such uncontrollable fluctuations of the demand for the output of
Department I frequently arise from technological inventions and
improvements, which — again — take place without regard to the
"conditions of stability," it must be clear that, in the absence of
"society's control over the forces of progress," "the technical obstacles to the maintenance of anything which can be called 'stability' must always be extremely formidable." [29] Economic progress renders the top-heavy structure of capitalistic production
peculiarly sensitive and vulnerable: Department I must, naturally,
be subject to sharp fluctuations if the accumulation of capital
equipment does not proceed at a steady rate. Generally speaking,

---

rate of forced saving means credit inflation at an increasing rate, so that the
forced saving would eventually come to an end with the total collapse of
the monetary medium. But, as Professor Hayek himself so convincingly shows,
a *constant* rate of saving is not necessary in order to secure a net and
permanent addition to capital equipment; the rate of forced saving may, as
with voluntary saving, be allowed to "tail off" gradually as replacement
demand increases.

[28] The gradualness of the rise of replacement demand — and the consequent
"vulnerability" of the structure of production — is clearly due to the durability
of fixed capital. If capital instruments had a very short duration of life, replacement demand would appear much sooner to "protect" the structure
against fluctuations of saving.

[29] D. H. Robertson, *Banking Policy and the Price-Level* (London, 1926),
23, and "Mr. Keynes' Theory of Money," *Economic Journal*, 1931, 410.

it seems that, with a few isolated exceptions, economists have paid too little attention in the past to the relation of economic progress to the business cycle. The general body of economic doctrine has centered round the analysis of economic equilibrium; and industrial fluctuations, not unnaturally, have come to be treated simply as oscillations about a basic (stationary) equilibrium position. The corresponding statistical procedure for investigating business cycles has usually consisted in "eliminating" the secular trend in order to "isolate" the wavelike cyclical movements around a horizontal straight line. The organic connections which may exist between the "trend" itself and the accompanying cyclical phenomena would seem to demand more adequate treatment.

The "setback" which occurs in Department I whenever investment demand falls off at the "wrong" rate will in all probability spread itself throughout the economic system, owing to the "monetary" reactions of the "deflationary spiral" type which it is likely to provoke. The original contraction of demand for the output of Department I may, owing to the circular nature of the self-reproduction of capital, lead to a cumulative shrinkage of replacement demand within Department I itself.[30] The fall of money incomes in Department I will mean a decline in the demand for the product of Department II, and that department will be led to reduce its replacement demand for "instruments." In short, the replacement demand of Department II being a derived demand, from which, in turn, the "internal" replacement demand within Department I is itself derived, the "vicious spiral" may perhaps most naturally be explained by an application of the principle of backward acceleration of derived demand (as expounded particularly in the writings of J. M. Clark) to the "circular" conception of the structure of production. A contraction of demand may thus tend to perpetuate and reinforce itself through the circular paths of the productive system.[31] Professor Hayek and his followers speak of the Secondary Deflation, meaning this cumulative contraction of purchasing power in the crisis, which they apparently

[30] The counterpart to this process is found in the "circular" expansion of Dept. I in the boom (see n. 25 above).

[31] Analogous considerations may hold for the cumulative process upwards in the ascending phase of the cycle. The typical revival of replacement demand at the end of the depression may suffice to call the upward spiral into action.

do not regard as inherently conditioned by the structure of production. It would seem, however, that the phenomena of the "spiral" or "cumulative process" type are closely bound up with the structural peculiarities of capitalistic production; the "spiral" may, perhaps, be fundamentally conditioned by the "circular" character of the productive structure.

It is for this reason, on the other hand, that an explanation of the trade cycle in purely monetary terms — an explanation which would apply equally to a community of, say, peasant proprietors exchanging consumable goods and services only, and to the system of capitalistic industry — can never be wholly satisfactory. The monetary processes are always conditioned by the technological characteristics of the structure of production. It is one of the great merits of the "Austrian" approach to trade-cycle theory that it directs attention to the sphere of capital production which forms, as it were, the background to the output of consumable goods and services; that it connects the monetary phenomena with a structural view of the general productive process. But the inherent unreality of the particular "linear" structure envisaged would seem to render it inadequate as a basis for the explanation of the trade cycle.

3

Domestic and
International Equilibrium
(1947)

INTRODUCTION

The impact of Keynesian Economics on the theory of international monetary relations has been powerful. Keynes himself, though he was well aware of the international policy implications of his doctrines, did very little to apply his *General Theory* to the analysis of international equilibrium. But he provided a theoretical framework which subsequent writers had no trouble in adapting to the special case of international relations. From this work of adaptation there emerged a whole system of international economics, set up in terms of the money income and expenditure analysis.

The income approach to international trade was not by any means entirely new. For over a century, writers on international trade had referred occasionally to shifts of purchasing power or changes in relative demand.[1] The Keynesian approach, however,

Copyright 1947 by the President and Fellows of Harvard College.
[1] See Jacob Viner, *Studies in the Theory of International Trade* (New York, 1937), ch. VI.

seemed to yield a more comprehensive and consistent account of
international monetary relations than had ever been given before.
It furnished at one and the same time an explanation of two related matters: (a) the adjustment process of the balance of payments and (b) the international transmission of fluctuations in
economic activity and employment. The result has been a fruitful
marriage of two subjects that previously led quite separate exist-
ences under the conventional names of international-trade theory
and business-cycle theory.

National frontiers as such are basically irrelevant to economic
analysis; it is only government policies that make them relevant.
And yet a political boundary line may be useful to the economist
because it forms, as it were, a zone of light through which economic processes pass and at which at least some of them can best
be observed. Customs, immigration and other officials, recording
the international movement of goods, people, and money, give us
information such as we do not possess for interregional movements within the same country. Accordingly, it is often in its
international aspects that any monetary or business-cycle theory
is apt to meet its stiffest test in regard to verification. There have
been theories that have not been successful in meeting this test
of international application. For example, the traditional price-
specie-flow doctrine, which represents the quantity theory of
money in its international aspect, was found by one of its last
distinguished proponents to be quite unrealistic.[2] Again, the
"neutral money" school, when one of its leading authors attempted to apply it to international shifts, led to rather strange
results.[3] By contrast, in the income-and-expenditure analysis of

[2] See F. W. Taussig, *International Trade* (New York, 1927): "The process
which our theory contemplates . . . can hardly be expected to take place
smoothly and quickly. Yet no signs of disturbance are to be observed such
as the theoretic analysis previses; and some recurring phenomena are of a
kind not contemplated by theory at all" (p. 239). Taussig found the facts
"baffling" and "puzzling" (pp. 242, 261), and his celebrated statement that
"things just happened so" was an honest admission of defeat.

[3] See F. A. Hayek, *Monetary Nationalism and International Stability* (London
and New York, 1937), 25-34. Hayek apparently maintained that, under
modern banking conditions, gold movements were bound to cause "monetary
disturbances" similar to those which, in *Prices and Production*, he had
described for the closed economy: deviations of the "market rate" from the
"natural rate" of interest, leading to elongations and contractions in the

the Keynesian type we have a theoretical apparatus which lends itself very simply and naturally to international monetary analysis, and which yields a realistic account of both the adjustment mechanism of the balance of payments and the propagation of economic fluctuations from country to country. The "adjustment problem" and the "propagation problem" appear in this analysis merely as two aspects of the same dynamic process of income change. The former relates primarily to the international monetary accounts, while the latter directs attention to fluctuations in domestic income and employment. It is the "propagation" aspect that is mainly significant for the international policy implications of Keynesian economics, though the "accounting" aspect also, as we shall see, imposes itself constantly on any consideration of national policy.

Before taking up the policy implications, we must briefly indicate the nature of the income approach to the mechanics of international equilibrium. A highly simplified account is all that can be attempted in the space available.

National Income and the Foreign Trade Multiplier

There is a two-way relationship between national income and foreign trade. On the one hand, changes in income generally entail changes in the same direction in the demand for imports. On the other, changes in the volume of exports tend to produce changes in domestic income.

If an expansion gets under way in one country, there will be an increase in imports into that country, which means an increase in exports for some other country. It is through this increase in exports that the expansion is transmitted to the other country. Let us see how this happens. The increase in exports will lead directly to an expansion of income and employment in the export

---

capital structure of production. That the adjustment of the international balance of payments should necessitate such convulsions is neither plausible a priori nor confirmed by the facts. Taussig (*International Trade*) found the adjustment to work more smoothly and directly than even the price-specie-flow theory had pictured it. So did many other writers, including notably C. Bresciani-Turroni (*Inductive Verification of the Theory of International Payments,* Cairo, 1932) and Harry D. White (*The French International Accounts, 1880–1913,* Cambridge, Mass., 1933).

industries. Some part of the additional income earned in the export industries may be spent immediately on imported goods, so that an equilibrating tendency toward greater imports to match the increase in exports comes into play at once. But this first increase in imports will usually be far from sufficient to restore an even balance. A part, and presumably the greater part, of the additional receipts of the export industries will be spent on home-produced goods. The increase in incomes spreads to domestic industries. At each step in the sequence of successive spending, a part of the increased money income will be diverted to swell the demand for imports.

To assume that each increment of income is entirely spent, either on imports or on homemade goods, is unrealistic; some part is likely to be saved. If there were no increased investment to absorb this saving, the rise in the total income flow would inevitably be arrested before the point at which imports become equal to the higher exports. In fact, however, the increased flow of spending on homemade goods is likely to have the "acceleration effect" of inducing a higher rate of capital expenditure, which will tend to offset the additional saving.[4]

In short, total money income in the country considered will tend to expand until the increased expenditure on imports equals the original increase in exports. In this way the increase in exports will have generated a multiple expansion in money income at home, and out of the increased income there will be an increased flow of expenditure on imports. The balance of payments comes back into equilibrium at higher levels of both national income and foreign trade.

In this successive-spending analysis, the proportion in which an increment of income is devoted to purchases of imported goods is evidently the central determinant of the process. This propor-

---

[4] Fritz Machlup in his excellent presentation of the multiplier analysis (*International Trade and the National Income Multiplier*, Philadelphia, 1943) excludes such induced investment by assumption. I find no need for this assumption here. The acceleration effect due to induced investment may be unpredictable; but so is the multiplier effect of the successive spending flow, since the marginal propensity to import is not likely to remain constant. In any discussion of general tendencies, both the acceleration and multiplier effects have their place.

tion is known as the "marginal propensity to import" or the "marginal import ratio." The higher it is, the more rapidly will imports increase after the initial rise in exports, but the smaller will be the expansion of national income associated with the restoration of external equilibrium. The smaller it is, the larger will be the ultimate increase in national income, but the longer will presumably be the time it takes for the balance between imports and exports to be restored. The increment in total income generated by the rise in exports, compared with the increment in exports itself, gives us the "export multiplier." This is simply the reciprocal of the marginal propensity to import, the reciprocal of the fraction of additional income spent on imports. If this fraction is one third, for example, the increment in total money income will be equal to three times the increment in exports.[5]

In the event of a decline in foreign demand for the country's exports, the multiplier mechanism operates in reverse. Equilibrium in the balance of payments will tend to be restored, this time at a lower level of trade, through a reduction in national income by an amount equal to the decrement in exports multiplied by the reciprocal of the marginal import ratio. Total money income will tend to fall to a level at which people's expenditure on imports will balance the diminished receipts from exports.

All these changes — upward in one case, downward in the other — which we have traced in national income, exports, and imports, are changes in terms of money value. To what extent they reflect changes in real volume will depend on the elasticity of supply. At less than full employment, supply is likely to be relatively elastic, so that movements in money value will signify real changes in the same direction. The particular supply conditions for exports and imports may show some elasticity even in a state of general full employment, so long as shifts are possible between production for the home market and for export. They may, on the other hand, be inelastic, if they depend heavily on

[5] This assumes that additional saving is offset by a larger volume of investment, induced in the way just indicated. If increased domestic investment does not provide the necessary offset to the additional saving, the income expansion will be arrested before imports have risen to the new level of exports, and there will remain an export surplus; which means, in effect, that the additional saving is offset by *foreign* investment.

certain specific factors of production. The extent to which money values reflect real changes need not be the same for exports, imports, and national income. For all three, however, some degree of correspondence between monetary and real changes is likely to exist below the level of general full employment.

The income approach to the study of foreign trade movements, as exemplified in the multiplier technique, is useful mainly in explaining fluctuations in the *volume* of trade. The classical doctrine of comparative costs in its various formulations was primarily concerned with the *composition* of a given volume of trade. In the international sphere, therefore, Keynesian economics has had the effect of shifting our center of attention in a manner analogous to the general shift which it promoted — from the traditional preoccupation with the optimum distribution of a given volume of employment to the analysis of the forces determining the volume of employment itself.

It is true that the multiplier analysis, though always mechanically applicable, is most appropriate, in the sense of most likely to yield significant results in real terms, when changes in total money income come about through changes in the volume of employment rather than through changes in money wage-rates and prices.[6] It is clear that, in the adjustment process, price changes work generally in the right direction for the restoration of equilibrium. But, insofar as they occur at all, they are essentially a by-product of the changes in the volume of employment and productive activity. These latter changes are therefore to be regarded as the primary equilibrating factors.[7]

The multiplier mechanism accounts at the same time for the adjustment of the balance of payments and for the transmission

---

[6] Machlup's book (*International Trade*, 19f) proceeds entirely on the assumption that prices remain unchanged. But even Keynes was not so Keynesian as to ignore the price effects of income and employment fluctuations. (See his admirable chapter 21 in *The General Theory of Employment, Interest, and Money,* New York, 1936.)

[7] "The problem may be synthesized by putting the question: Why should an inflow of gold raise industrial costs and so reduce exports? Surely only by setting up a keener competition for the means of production. . . . The mode of operation through an expansion of activity must therefore be considered the true theory and the phenomena which the classical view tends to stress a by-product." R. F. Harrod, *International Economics* (London, 1939 ed.), 140.

of income and employment fluctuations from country to country. An increase in a country's exports leads to an expansion in the volume of domestic income, expenditure, and employment, so that external equilibrium tends to be restored through an upward shift in the country's demand for imports. We have assumed that the increase in exports is induced by a boom in a foreign country. The expansion initiated in that country is transmitted through the multiplier process, which thus tends to produce a synchronization of economic fluctuations in different countries. It is only in the rather special case of an "autonomous" increase in exports (due, say, to devaluation of the home currency, a tariff reduction abroad, or a spontaneous shift of consumer's demand as between homemade and imported goods) that the favorable effect on income and employment at home will be accompanied by an unfavorable effect abroad.

Any expansion or contraction originating in the domestic economy tends to spread abroad through its effects on the demand for imports. A domestic investment boom will "spill over" to other countries since part of the increased money income "leaks out" for the purchase of additional imports. This leakage, while it checks the growth of income at home, is what transmits the expansion process outward. The size of the leakage is determined by the marginal propensity to import; if it is small, the boom at home can go on for a long while before it leads to an import surplus large enough to stimulate a parallel expansion abroad; if it is large, the boom will not go so far before it "spills over" to other countries.

The special "autonomous" factors tend to produce opposite changes in income and employment in different countries, and so cancel out for the world as a whole. It is in the sphere of domestic expenditure that *general* booms and depressions originate. The propagation mechanism we have described is a passive factor from the world point of view. It is neither expansionist nor contractionist in itself, but reflects the balance of forces at play in the domestic economies, and serves to pass on from country to country the expansionist or contractionist influences originating in one place or another.

The relative strength of the expansionist or contractionist im-

pulses which a country imparts to the outside world as a result
of domestic income fluctuations is determined by its marginal
propensity to import. But the relative amplitude of the fluctuations in its demand for imports may be wider or narrower than
that of the corresponding domestic fluctuations. If a given percentage change in national income produces the same percentage
change in imports, the "income elasticity of demand for imports"
is said to be equal to unity.[8] An elasticity greater or smaller than
unity means that expenditure on imports has a wider or closer
percentage range of variation than the national income. A country whose national income is relatively variable in itself, and
whose imports, in addition, have an income elasticity of demand
greater than unity, is particularly troublesome as a source of
cyclical change in the world economy. The United States in recent
times seems to have corresponded to this description.

The synchronization produced by the multiplier mechanism is
naturally imperfect, not only because different countries have
different marginal import ratios and income elasticities, but also
because the successive-spending process of the multiplier analysis
takes time. In consequence, fluctuations in one country will lag
behind those in the other. The "lags" in the propagation aspect
of the mechanism are associated, in the adjustment aspect, with
"gaps" in the balance of payments.[9] Transfers of gold, exchange
reserves or private short-term funds are needed to *fill* such gaps
temporarily; it is the change in domestic income flows that sooner
or later *closes* them. In the traditional doctrine, gold movements
played a central part as a causally significant factor. In the modern view, they act rather in a passive manner as stopgaps in the

---

[8] The "marginal propensity to import" and the "income elasticity of demand
for imports" are two distinct concepts, but there is a simple relation between
them. The former is defined as $\Delta M/\Delta Y$ while the latter is $(\Delta M/M)/(\Delta Y/Y)$,
which can also be written as $(\Delta M/\Delta Y)/(M/Y)$. ($Y$ stands, as usual, for
income and M for imports.) Thus the income elasticity of demand is equal
to the *marginal* divided by the *average* propensity to import. In the United
States, $\Delta M/\Delta Y$ is relatively small, but M/Y is still smaller, and the expression as a whole is therefore large. In England, on the other hand, imports
are much greater in relation to income, but they consist more largely of foodstuffs, for which the demand is relatively steady; so that $\Delta M/\Delta Y$, though
large, is not as large as M/Y and the whole expression is smaller than unity.

[9] See *Economic Stability in the Post-War World* (League of Nations, 1945),
103f and *International Currency Experience* (League of Nations, 1944), 100f.

balance of payments, covering discrepancies in foreign receipts and expenditures which, in time, bring about their own adjustment through changes in domestic money incomes.

This explanation of the adjustment process applies, of course, to a system of fixed exchange rates. What it shows is essentially the working of international monetary and cyclical relations in the old days of the automatic gold standard. The gold standard was a system for maintaining equilibrium of external payments among the member countries. It paid no regard to internal equilibrium in any of the member countries, or to the equilibrium of the system as a whole. It required that countries should not seek to control their national money income deliberately by domestic means; it presupposed a laissez-faire economy. These prerequisites to its smooth working came to be less and less adequately fulfilled as nations became conscious of a desire for economic stability, and as national policies were framed increasingly with a view to promoting employment and social security. The income approach to international economics would be of purely historical interest if its usefulness consisted merely in a better explanation of the international economy under Queen Victoria. It is useful, more generally, in that it shows what the automatic tendencies of monetary adjustment and cyclical synchronization would be in the absence of governmental or other interferences. Above all, it is useful in any analysis of the external effects of various national policies aimed at internal equilibrium. It is a necessary foundation on which to consider the international policy problems arising from national employment policies.

If internal equilibrium is defined as a level of national income such that there is neither general unemployment nor an inflationary tendency for prices to rise, while external equilibrium is essentially a balance of payments that maintains itself without the persistent need for monetary "stopgaps" on the one hand or, to anticipate, increased trade barriers on the other, then the central policy problem is concisely described as that of harmonizing the requirements of internal with those of external equilibrium.

Keynes gave a great deal of thought to the international policy implications of the search for internal equilibrium, but he did not explicitly set out the mechanics of external equilibrium himself.

The preceding sketch does not correspond in all particulars to Keynesian doctrine.[10] The multiplier analysis admits, as Machlup has shown, of almost endless variations and refinements in detail. Yet in its essence the application of the income approach to the case of international adjustment is simple and self-evident. It is perhaps for this reason that Keynes did not undertake it himself. In his celebrated controversy with Ohlin (*Economic Journal*, 1929), he had adopted an entirely "un-Keynesian" attitude, stressing the price effects in the transfer process and largely ignoring the income effects. But Keynes never had much difficulty in repudiating his previous views, and it would be hard to believe that the silence he maintained on the international aspects of the *General Theory* was due to a vested interest in his earlier position.

THE PURSUIT OF FULL EMPLOYMENT IN AN OPEN ECONOMY

Turning to the international policy implications of Keynesian economics, the first general principle is that responsibility for the maintenance of a high and stable level of employment in any given country lies primarily in the field of domestic policy. Nothing can absolve a country from the necessity of taking measures to put its own house in order through the maintenance of a sufficient volume of effective demand at home to keep its productive resources employed at the maximum level that can be continuously sustained without an inflationary rise of prices.

The next point to recognize is that a country in pursuit of this objective — in pursuit, in short, of "full employment" — should never be deterred by difficulties, actual or anticipated, in its balance of external payments. There exist specific methods of

[10] Thus, we have found no use for the "instantaneous" interpretation of the multiplier as Keynes expounds it in the *General Theory,* and have relied instead on the "serial" interpretation which expressly recognizes the time element in the successive spending process. Also, we have implicitly contradicted Keynes' statement that "the effects of loan expenditure (i.e., home investment) and of the foreign balance are in *pari materia."* (*The Means to Prosperity,* London, 1933, 36.) In our sketch, which follows Machlup's treatment in this respect, the foreign balance arising from an increase in exports leads to a flow of additional income which, so long as exports remain at the higher level, maintains itself even when the foreign balance has fallen back to zero through the induced expansion of imports. In the case of home investment, on the other hand, the net investment expenditure must go on continuously at a steady rate if income is to be maintained at the increased level.

influencing the balance of payments so that, regardless of the behavior of its neighbors, and without injuring its neighbors, a country can effectively seek to preserve external equilibrium while pursuing the full employment objective at home.

It is true that these methods can also be resorted to as instruments of a "beggar-my-neighbor" policy, aimed at improving domestic employment by creating external disequilibrium. This policy must for obvious reasons be barred. In fact, no country that knows how to keep up employment by constructive domestic measures will want to adopt it. From the point of view of a national economy, creating employment through an export surplus is just like "digging holes" at home.

The behavior of its neighbors need never deflect a country from the pursuit of full employment. The classical free trade doctrine showed that it was both beneficial and practicable for an individual country to abolish its trade barriers even in the face of a protectionist world. In the same way it is always to some extent possible for a single country to pursue a full employment policy unilaterally. The relative importance of foreign markets, the dependence on imported raw materials, and other similar conditions vary, of course, from country to country. Yet, to some extent, it is always possible for a single country to go ahead with a domestic expansion policy even in a world of depression and unemployment. The expansion will inevitably, under these conditions, produce an adverse balance of payments. So long as there are ample liquid reserves to meet the external deficit, there is no reason to worry about it. When liquid reserves have run out or are not available to start with, there is usually some change in the exchange rate that will preserve external equilibrium. Alternatively, there is the possibility of adopting import restrictions, not in order to reduce imports, but just enough to prevent them from increasing. This will prevent the expansion from "spilling over" abroad, but will not actually hurt the outside world. It is a defensive measure aimed at maintaining the equilibrium of foreign payments, and is to be sharply distinguished from the aggressive and unneighborly policy which operates through a disruption of external equilibrium.

The balance of payments is the test of whether a change in

exchange rates or import restrictions is a defensive or an aggressive measure. Nothing is simpler; yet this attitude of "relativity"
is repugnant to many laymen and economists alike. People often
tend to regard a policy measure as either good or bad in all circumstances. In reality, "it all depends." Devaluation or import
restrictions may be justifiable, as in the case of a unilaterally expanding country, when they are intended to close a deficit or
preserve equilibrium in the balance of payments. They are not
justifiable when their purpose is to create a surplus in the balance
of payments or to enlarge a surplus already existing. The distinction was evidently quite clear in Keynes' mind when, in speaking
of the Bretton Woods scheme and the United States Proposals for
the Expansion of World Trade, he said: "Both the currency and
the commercial proposals are devised to favour the maintenance
of equilibrium by expressly permitting various protective devices
when they are required to maintain equilibrium and by forbid-
ding them when they are not so required." [11] The balance-of-
payments test is no doubt subject to a great many qualifications
in practice; but it is fairly clear in principle.[12] Surpluses and deficits in the balance of payments reflect the external employment
effects of economic fluctuations and policies in different countries.
The balance-of-payments test may seem a superficial one, but it
corresponds in every case to the deeper needs of employment
policy. For instance, a country suffering a depression at home is
likely to develop automatically a surplus in its balance of payments. Devaluation or import restrictions in these circumstances
are the opposite of what is required for external equilibrium. Nor
are they required for internal equilibrium; for it is evident that
internal equilibrium, in the sense indicated earlier, can and
should be attained by domestic measures of expansion; and its

[11] Speech in the House of Lords, 18 December 1945, "The Anglo-American
Financial Arrangements," in *The New Economics,* ed. Seymour E. Harris
(New York, 1947), 393.

[12] The proper criterion is the balance of payments on account of all current
transactions and productive capital movements, excluding for obvious reasons
gold movements, short-term funds, and hot money flights. I have discussed
this more fully in *Conditions of International Monetary Equilibrium,* Essays
in International Finance, No. 4 (Princeton, 1945). Compare also *International
Currency Experience* (League of Nations, 1944), ch. IX, sec. 3 ("Exchange
Adjustments and Exchange Control").

attainment would tend incidentally to restore the equilibrium of external payments as well.

For purposes of employment policy, import restrictions are on a par with exchange devaluation. In their effects on foreign trade, however, the two types of measures are very different. Exchange policy is far preferable to commercial policy, though the latter, being much more effective in emergencies, may have its legitimate uses for temporary purposes. Exchange adjustments and import restrictions alike may serve the ends of a defensive or an aggressive policy. The universal rise of trade barriers in the pre-war decade was due to both these policies and finds its explanation not in the theory of international trade, but in the theory of employment. But to discard permanently the gains from international trade is foolish and, besides, quite unnecessary for internal equilibrium. The case for import restrictions as a defensive measure is sometimes extended far beyond its narrow legitimate scope. It is argued that the domestic policies aimed at full employment can be more easily carried out in a closed economy than in an economy maintaining trade relations with other countries. There are two possible grounds for this proposition. The first is the fear that foreign disturbances may interfere with domestic stability and full employment, and the aim is to lessen the danger of such disturbances by reducing economic intercourse with the outside world to a minimum. This anxiety is groundless. There exist effective methods of offsetting or averting the impact of foreign disturbances by appropriate variations in domestic expenditure combined with the use of external monetary reserves, or by measures designed to protect the equilibrium of external settlements. There is no need to sacrifice the benefits of international trade for the sake of maintaining a stable and satisfactory level of domestic activity.

The second argument for autarky amounts to saying that the employment problem is less serious in a poor community than in a rich one. There is some truth in this. The international division of labor is a laborsaving device. Destroying it, just like destroying machines, may increase the number of jobs in times of unemployment; but it will leave us permanently worse off. Balance-of-payments equilibrium which is obtained by curtailing the international division of labor cannot therefore be regarded as a true equilibrium position. Just as free trade by itself cannot ensure full employment, so the suppression of trade, though it might increase employment numerically, can never bring real prosperity. It is utterly senseless to create employment by reducing the level of economic efficiency. There are other ways of solving the employment problem.

The use of import restrictions may be inevitable when a deficit arises in the balance of payments which cannot be met from liquid reserves, and for which exchange adjustment would be too slow a remedy. Such a deficit may arise from a depression in one of a country's export markets. If the gap is closed by import restrictions, a surplus will develop in the balance of payments as soon as the foreign market recovers. The proper way then to eliminate the surplus is neither exchange appreciation, nor foreign lending, nor anything else except the removal of the import restrictions; it is the only way of restoring balance-of-payments equilibrium together with the pre-existing degree of international specialization.[13]

We have referred earlier to the case of a deficit arising in the balance of payments of a single country trying to raise its level of employment at a time of general depression. The problems of national employment policy may be considered a little more closely in the case of a country which is successfully maintaining both external and internal equilibrium at full employment, but which suddenly finds itself faced with a depression abroad. Here also, a deficit arises, but this time from a fall in exports rather than a rise in imports. The export industries will suffer a depression which, through the multiplier mechanism operating in reverse, will tend to spread to the whole domestic economy. The maintenance of internal equilibrium in these circumstances calls for offsetting the fall in foreign expenditure on the country's products by an increase in the volume of domestic expenditure.

---

[13] This does not concern import barriers which a country chooses to maintain more or less permanently, for social, military, or other reasons. Starting from his *Means to Prosperity* (p. 25), Keynes repeatedly contrasted these special or structural trade barriers, which we have to take for granted, with the restrictions arising from a general search for employment or from the general state of the balance of payments.

This offsetting policy, which is the opposite of what the gold standard rules would require, is subject to limitations;[14] but insofar as total employment depends on total outlay, the compensatory increase in domestic demand will tend to prevent a general depression in the given country. It does nothing, however, to correct the external disequilibrium. The gap in the balance of payments resulting from the fall in exports must be filled by drawing on the country's gold and foreign exchange reserves. How long the offsetting policy can be continued depends entirely on the size of these reserves. If they are ample, the depression abroad may right itself before they run out; it may be followed by an inflationary boom abroad, in which case the country's reserves of international liquidity will be replenished. If, however, the reserves become exhausted or unduly depleted before recovery abroad restores equilibrium in the balance of payments, then resort must be had to other measures: measures designed to correct the balance of payments.

When liquid reserves are inadequate to meet the external deficit, then and only then is the time to take measures to correct the balance of payments. Chief among these measures are exchange depreciation and import restrictions.[15] For the sake of completeness, deflation may also be mentioned here. If it were possible to carry out general wage cuts by government decree overnight, this might be an effective way of righting the foreign balance without adverse effects on domestic employment. The effect of wage reductions in a closed economy are somewhat doubtful, the Keynesian position being that they improve employment, if at all, mainly through their repercussions on the interest rate. In an open economy, by contrast, the efficacy of wage reductions — though not their desirability — is undisputed. Like exchange depreciation, wage reductions act as a beggar-my-neighbor policy of stimulating home employment when their effect is to create a surplus and not, as in the present case, to close a deficit in the balance of payments. In practice, however, it is

---

[14] See, e.g., *Economic Stability in the Post-War World*, 232, or *Conditions of International Monetary Equilibrium*, 11–14.

[15] This is not the place to discuss the various types of import restrictions. They include, of course, import quotas and exchange controls as well as tariffs.

generally only through unemployment that wage reductions can be brought about. Deflation is a possible means of correcting the balance of payments, but it is destructive of internal equilibrium and therefore out of the question.

We are left with (a) changes in exchange rates and (b) measures of commercial policy. Both operate on the balance of trade either by restricting imports or promoting exports or by a combination of the two. Besides correcting the foreign balance, however, they also contribute on their own account toward offsetting the fall in expenditure and employment which tends to result from the drop in exports abroad. Those measures which operate by restricting imports serve to direct the flow of expenditure from foreign goods to the home market; those which promote exports tend to increase or rather, in the present case, to restore employment and income in the export industries. The effect on aggregate employment and expenditure in the country considered is favorable. But this favorable effect could equally well be obtained by domestic expansion. It is clear, therefore, that these measures are strictly necessary only to correct the balance of payments and are to be judged only in this capacity.

Exchange adjustments or import restrictions should come into play only when the offsetting policy which we have described cannot be continued because of a shortage of liquid reserves. Once they do come into play, however, their effects on domestic employment and expenditure make it necessary, if inflation is to be avoided, to cancel some or all of the compensatory increase in expenditure which characterized the offsetting policy. This may seem an unnecessary theoretical refinement. In practice, the effects of the successive measures can never be observed or judged so closely. Yet even for policy-making there can be no harm in clarity as to the detailed implications of full employment policy in an open economy. The general principle remains: total outlay on the country's output should be kept at a level corresponding to the maximum volume of employment attainable without inflation. The complications introduced by the existence of foreign trade relate, as we have seen, to the need to compensate for changes in foreigners' outlay on the country's products by inverse changes in domestic outlay and, similarly, to offset the incidental effect on total outlay of measures taken primarily to right the balance of payments.

So far we have discussed the problems arising from a depression in the country's export markets abroad. The opposite case, an inflationary boom abroad, has the opposite effects and calls for the opposite policy measures for the maintenance of internal equilibrium. The rise in exports, and also the fall in the marginal propensity to import due to the rise in import prices, will have to be offset by a reduction in domestic expenditure. If gold and exchange reserves become excessive, an appreciation of the currency or a lowering of import barriers is the appropriate remedy. Here again the secondary adjustments required in domestic expenditure need not be overlooked. A tariff reduction tends to direct expenditure from homemade to imported goods; its effect is deflationary; and to compensate for this, an expansion will be required in domestic expenditure so as to keep total outlay on the country's output stable.

Such, in brief, are the rules of conduct which emerge from the Keynesian system to guide an individual country in search of internal equilibrium at full employment. In the preceding pages some readers may have missed a discussion of comparative cost structures, the play of relative prices, the forces of international competition, the shifts required between production for home needs and for export, the constant adaptation of a country's export industries to changing world markets, and other similar topics. All these are valid subjects of theoretical inquiry and practical concern; they are on a different level of discourse, but they retain their validity within the Keynesian system. The classical analysis concerns itself essentially with the optimum division of labor between countries. It is under conditions of full employment that this type of analysis comes most fully into its own. The Keynesian approach demonstrates that any single country can and should do something to realize these conditions within its borders, without hurting its neighbors and without throwing away the gains from international trade. Speaking for his own country, Keynes made this resolute statement: "whilst we intend to prevent inflation at home, we will not accept deflation at the dictates of influences from outside." [16] And he welcomed the postwar trade and currency schemes as an attempt to "combine the advantages of freedom of commerce with safeguards against the disastrous consequences of a laissez faire system which pays no direct regard to the preservation of equilibrium and merely relies on the working out of blind forces." [17]

International Coordination of Full Employment Policies

As we have seen, any single country has means at its disposal for warding off or neutralizing the impact of cyclical disturbances emanating from abroad. On the other hand, each country must agree to have its freedom of action limited by the obligation to consider the effects of its policies not only on the domestic situation but also on other countries. This implies in particular an obligation to refrain from the beggar-my-neighbor policy of creating a surplus in the balance of payments and so improving the employment situation at home at the expense of other countries. Even without deliberate policy, a surplus in the balance of payments tends to result automatically when there is a depression in domestic income and employment, and will, automatically, provide some relief from that depression. But just as other countries are entitled to take steps against this disequilibrium in international settlements, so the surplus country itself should help to eliminate it, if not by domestic expansion then at any rate by such measures as foreign lending or tariff reduction. It is true that the removal of the surplus by tariff reduction would tend to have unfavorable effects on domestic employment in the surplus country; but clearly there is nothing to prevent these effects from being offset by domestic expansion.

The outlawing of beggar-my-neighbor policies means that full employment must be pursued by domestic measures alone. The international paradox of countries scrambling for export markets and shutting off imports is merely a reflection of the domestic

---

[16] Speech in the House of Lords, 23 May 1944, "The International Monetary Fund," in *The New Economics,* ed. Seymour E. Harris (New York, 1947), 374.

[17] Speech in the House of Lords, 18 December 1945 (above, n. 11), 393.

paradox of unemployment and "poverty in the midst of plenty." A solution of the domestic problem gives a solution of the international problem as a by-product, or at any rate creates the conditions required for the solution of the international problem. This view is expressed very strongly in the *General Theory*.[18]

In his *Means to Prosperity*, Keynes had already stated the case for international coordination of domestic employment policies. Writing at the bottom of the depression in March 1933, he said: "We should attach great importance to the *simultaneity* of the movement towards increased expenditure. For the pressure on its foreign balance which each country fears as the result of increasing its own loan-expenditure, will cancel out if other countries are pursuing the same policy at the same time. . . . Combined international action is of the essence of policy." [19] The same idea appears, ten years later, in the *Proposals for an International Clearing Union,* of which Keynes is believed to have been the main author: "if active employment and ample purchasing power can be sustained in the main centers of world trade, the problem of surpluses and unwanted exports will largely disappear." [20]

The doctrine of international coordination of national policies for the maintenance of productive activity and employment has undoubtedly a strong appeal. If it can be realized, then it is possible that a high degree of exchange stability may be secured as a result of domestic stability in the various individual countries. Few nations, if any, will nowadays endure a severe deflation or inflation just for the sake of a stable exchange parity. It is only as a result, and not at the expense, of domestic economic stability that we may hope for some stability in international currency relations as well. Under the gold standard, exchange stability was, in effect, achieved through the synchronization of business fluctuations in the various countries. Under the new system, exchange stability would be achieved not through the synchronization of business fluctuations, but through the coordination of

[18] Pages 349 and 382.

[19] *The Means to Prosperity*, 24.

[20] *Proposals by British Experts for an International Clearing Union* (British Information Service, New York, 1943), 14; see "Proposals for an International Clearing Union," *The New Economics,* 334.

national policies to keep employment and production at the maximum level attainable without a general rise in prices.[21] We may even imagine a central international authority or council directing the coordination of national policies so as to make domestic equilibrium in the individual countries compatible with equilibrium in the international accounts.

But this idea of "combined international action," pleasing though it may be to the imagination, can be carried too far. Keynes, a master of *political* economy, seems to have viewed it with skepticism in his later years.[22] Any scheme aiming, however discreetly, at some super-national regimentation of domestic fiscal and monetary policies would be certain to encounter political and psychological obstacles in the world as we find it. Besides, it would be unnecessarily ambitious. Keynes was concerned to preserve some freedom of national action, hoping no doubt that nations would sooner or later adopt the correct internal policies spontaneously. We can hardly hope for more at the present stage. Even the gold standard system of the past was never based on any formal international convention, or possessed of any central executive machinery; it grew up freely and spontaneously through the recognition of a common primary objective (exchange stability) by a number of like-minded nations. In the same way, it is from a common recognition of the need to main-

[21] This maximum level may, of course, differ in the various countries, since the strength of labor unions, government controls, and other circumstances differ. In some countries, the minimum degree of unemployment attainable may be 3 or 4 per cent, while in others it may be 6 or 7 per cent.

[22] Here are a few quotations to illustrate his attitude: "There should be the least possible interference with internal national policies, and the plan should not wander from the international terrain." (*Proposals for an International Clearing Union,* Preface; see "Proposals for an International Clearing Union," *The New Economics,* 324.) "The error of the gold-standard lay in submitting national wage-policies to outside dictation. It is wiser to regard stability (or otherwise) of internal prices as a matter of internal policy and politics." (*Economic Journal,* 1943, 187.) "We must solve it (i.e., the problem of domestic stability) in our own domestic way, feeling that we are free men. The suggestion of external pressure will make the political and psychological problem of making good sense prevail more difficult." (*Economic Journal,* 1944, 430.) In his speech of 18 December 1945 in the House of Lords, Keynes recommended the monetary and commercial policy proposals in these words: "The plans do not wander from the international terrain, and they are consistent with widely different conceptions of domestic policy."

tain a high and stable level of employment that a new system of stable international currency relations may spontaneously develop. Meanwhile it is right and proper that any single country pursuing this objective at home, without attempting to "export unemployment," should have access, under appropriate conditions, to exchange-rate adjustments or other "protective devices" needed to ensure equilibrium in its balance of payments.

In the world as we find it, what matters is not so much the international coordination of national full-employment policies as the successful pursuit of such policies in one particular country, the United States. The effective realization, without inflationary disturbances, of stable and active employment conditions in the United States could do more than anything else to help other countries in their search for domestic as well as external equilibrium. As Joan Robinson puts it, "the problem which lies before the United States is what to do with her prodigious productive capacity — whether to use it for home consumption, to use it for the development of other countries, or to waste it in unemployment. No amount of ingenuity in devising currency schemes can influence the main issue." [23]

Apart from the variability of foreign investment, the external impact of economic fluctuations in the United States operates through the great variability of imports into the United States.[24] In contrast to British imports, where foodstuffs play the leading part, American imports consist very largely of industrial raw materials and are therefore closely geared to fluctuations in the volume of industrial production. Moreover, they consist very largely of the storable and standardized commodities in which price speculation, forward buying, and inventory fluctuations play such an important role. For this reason, as was shown by the experience of the years 1936–1938, the value of imports is apt to

[23] "The International Currency Proposals," *Economic Journal*, 1943, 169. (See Robinson, "The International Currency Proposals," *The New Economics*, 350–351.)

[24] United States imports before the war constituted, on the average, only about one tenth of total world imports. But their range of variation was such that from 1937 to 1938, for example, the reduction in United States imports alone accounted for about one third of the reduction in total world imports. (See League of Nations, *Review of World Trade*, 1938, 20–21.)

vary even more widely than the tempo of domestic industrial activity. Buffer stocks must be mentioned here as a possible remedy for this state of affairs. Keynes was a keen advocate of this method of offsetting cyclical fluctuations in the demand for and prices of primary products.[25] It has been common in the past to speak of buffer stocks as a means of protecting primary producing countries from the effects of business cycles originating in the industrial countries. Given the circumstances just indicated, it is clear that the buffer stock idea deserves to be discussed as a means, more particularly, of mitigating the impact of American business fluctuations on the rest of the world. As far as the outside world is concerned, stabilizing the United States' demand for imports by means of buffer stocks may to some extent be an acceptable substitute for stabilizing the course of domestic business activity in the United States.

KEYNES AND ECONOMIC NATIONALISM

Keynes has been widely regarded as the high priest of economic nationalism; but even the slightest insight into the international implications of Keynesian economics must lead to a rejection of this view. In the *General Theory*, it is only incidentally that Keynes adverts to the international aspects of his doctrine. The remarks on mercantilism which he included among the "Short Notes Suggested by the General Theory" may well have misled unwary readers into believing that Keynes was advocating a reversion to mercantilism. The belief is utterly erroneous, though it is not difficult to see how it might have arisen, especially since Keynes gave us no positive and systematic account of international relationships in his system. All he was concerned to point out was that the mercantilists were essentially right in affirming, and the classical writers unrealistic in denying, that an improvement in the trade balance was likely to have stimulating effects on domestic business conditions. The multiplier analysis of foreign trade makes this proposition a self-evident one today. Keynes was quite clear as to the "beggar-my-neighbor" character of the

[25] See his article, "The Policy of Government Storage of Foodstuffs and Raw Materials," *Economic Journal,* 1938.

mercantilist policies, and he was far from advocating them.[26] It was the rigid gold-standard system which, in his view, fostered a spirit of nationalism since, under conditions of laissez faire, the beggar-my-neighbor policies of mercantilism were the only means available to an individual country for the revival or maintenance of domestic employment.

The Keynesian position on international economic policy is perhaps best summarized by the following three quotations from the *General Theory:*

(1) Never in history was there a method devised of such efficacy for setting each country's advantage at variance with its neighbours' as the international gold . . . standard. For it made domestic prosperity directly dependent on a competitive pursuit of markets and a competitive appetite for the precious metals . . .[27]

(2) But if nations can learn to provide themselves with full employment by their domestic policy . . . there need be no important economic forces calculated to set the interest of one country against that of its neighbours . . . there would no longer be a pressing motive why one country need force its wares on another or repulse the offerings of its neighbour, not because this was necessary to enable it to pay for what it wished to purchase, but with the express object of upsetting the equilibrium of payments so as to develop a balance of trade in its own favour . . .[28]

(3) And it is the simultaneous pursuit of these policies by all countries together which is capable of restoring economic health and strength internationally, whether we measure it by the level of domestic employment or by the volume of international trade.[29]

In view of this, it would not be difficult to argue that Keynes, far from being a proponent of economic nationalism, is the true internationalist among modern economists. The change which his teaching has wrought in the general approach to international economics is fundamental. International trade is not a thing apart, but is merely that section of the total volume of goods produced and exchanged which happens to cross national frontiers; and anything that lowers or raises the total volume of

[26] The plainly derogatory term "beggar-my-neighbor policies" was introduced, in print at any rate, not by Keynes himself, but by one of his earliest disciples, Joan Robinson, in *Essays in the Theory of Employment* (New York, 1937), part III.
[27] *General Theory,* 349.
[28] *Ibid.,* 382.
[29] *Ibid.,* 389.

activity is bound to reflect itself also in the movement of foreign trade. The narrow "commercial policy" approach which has been usual in the past is quite inadequate to the task of expanding world trade.

The relationship between domestic employment and international trade is now generally recognized. Its significance has found expression in the very title of the commercial-policy proposals put forward by the United States in 1945: *Proposals for the Expansion of World Trade and Employment.* Under this scheme, the members of the proposed International Trade Organization "recognize that the attainment and maintenance of useful employment opportunities for those able, willing, and seeking to work are essential to the full realization of the purposes of the Organization. . . . Each Member shall take action designed to achieve and maintain full employment within its own jurisdiction through measures appropriate to its political and economic institutions. . . . In seeking to maintain or expand employment, no Member shall adopt measures which would have the effect of creating unemployment in other countries." [30] It is clear that Keynes' general ideas have had a considerable influence on postwar plans for international trade.

INTERNATIONAL MONETARY POLICY AND MULTILATERAL TRADE

The charge of economic nationalism which has been levelled against Keynes appears even less tenable when we consider his work for the construction of a new international monetary system, to which he devoted the last years of his life. There are two reasons for dealing with this work more briefly than with the influence of his general ideas. In the first place, the specific features of Keynesian economics, concerned as they are with the creation and regulation of effective demand, do not enter into, and indeed have no place in, the international monetary arrangements for the settlement of foreign balances. The maintenance of effective demand is, in the nature of the case, primarily a matter of domestic responsibility. The balance of payments merely trans-

[30] *Suggested Charter for an International Trade Organization of the United Nations* (United States Department of State, 1946), 2.

mits, it cannot create effective demand.[31] Some critics, seeing the name of Keynes prominently associated with the Bretton Woods scheme, seem to have feared that adherence to the scheme would mean compulsory deficit financing in every country. They must have been reassured on reading the text of the agreement: there is nothing in it to warrant such fears. The critics may have been right in one sense: the maintenance of high and stable levels of employment in the leading member nations is, ultimately, an essential prerequisite to the smooth functioning of the international monetary system. Keynes' main concern was the more modest one of ensuring that the new international currency arrangement would at least not discourage the appropriate domestic policies. He hoped, indeed, that it would encourage them by furnishing a favorable external setting. In defending the scheme he said: "It is as providing an international framework for the policy of full employment that these proposals are to be welcomed."[32] The Bretton Woods agreements proscribe measures "destructive of national or international prosperity." No country is to be forced into a state of deflation and unemployment as a means of adjusting its balance of payments. The agreements undoubtedly reflect a concern for economic stability and employment; yet they can scarcely be regarded as a direct offspring of Keynesian economics.

Nor can they be regarded as Keynes' personal offspring, even though his share in their formation, as well as in the formation of the Anglo-American trade and financial agreements in 1945, was very considerable. The grandiose Clearing Union proposal of 1943, which is generally attributed to him personally, foundered on the rock of creditor opposition. Even from the debtor countries' point of view, it was open to criticism since the resources which it would have made available, though ostensibly intended for international liquidity purposes, were liable to be drawn upon for postwar capital needs without, however, being distributed in anything like a fair proportion to the capital needs of different countries. John H. Williams and others suspected that the Clear-

---

[31] It cannot create effective demand except for one country at the expense of others, through the beggar-my-neighbor policies which we want to outlaw.
[32] Speech in the House of Lords, 23 May 1944 (above, n. 16), 377.

ing Union scheme, while cast in the form of a global plan, was essentially designed to meet Britain's balance-of-payments problem after the war. However that may be, it is interesting to note that the combined amount of the postwar loans which Keynes obtained for his country from the United States and Canada was very nearly equal to the 5.5 billion dollars which would have been the British quota in the Clearing Union. Moreover, both these loans took the form of a "line of credit," like the Clearing Union quota, to be drawn upon as and when required.

Keynes' opinions on the operation of the international monetary system under normal conditions, i.e., after the postwar transition period, may be summarized under five heads.

(1) *International liquidity:* Keynes was well aware that the additional liquidity provided by the International Monetary Fund, just like the liquidity provided by gold and exchange reserves, is useful to any single country pursuing a full-employment policy since it affords additional protection against temporary disturbances entering from outside. On this point he expressed himself as follows: "Do the critics think it preferable, if the winds of the trade cycle blow, to diminish our demand for imports by increasing unemployment at home, rather than meet the emergency out of this Fund which will be expressly provided for such temporary purposes? I emphasize that such is the purpose of the quotas." [33]

(2) *Exchange rates:* Exchange stability, if it is to be achieved, must be achieved in future no longer at the expense but as the result of domestic stability of income and employment. Keynes was skeptical about the possibility of coordinating the internal wage policies in different countries and consequently attached great importance to flexible ratios of exchange between the national currencies. By flexibility he did not mean continually fluctuating exchange rates, but rates subject to revision from time to time. Naturally he was in favor of the revision being performed by international agreement, under the auspices of the Fund, so as to prevent countries from taking undue advantage of exchange adjustment unilaterally. What he opposed above all, however, was any such rigidity as that imposed by the gold standard.

[33] Speech in the House of Lords, 23 May 1944 (above, n. 16), 372.

Speaking for his own country, he declared: "We are determined that in future the external value of sterling shall conform to its internal value as set by our own domestic policies, and not the other way round." [34] In this sense, as well as in the sense that international liquidity reserves are to be used as "insulators" rather than "transmitters" of international business fluctuations, the new monetary system was described by Keynes as "the exact opposite of the gold standard." [35] There is no doubt that Keynes secured a large measure of recognition for his point of view. We need only recall that the name of the Fund, which appeared as "Stabilization Fund" in the United States proposal in 1943, was changed to "International Monetary Fund" in 1944.

(3) *Control of capital movements:* Keynes had a clear idea of the distinction between equilibrating and disequilibrating short-term capital movements. He referred to the latter in his Clearing Union plan as "movements of funds out of debtor countries which lack the means to finance them." [36] The distinction between capital movements which promote external monetary equilibrium and those which, on the contrary, create or accentuate external disequilibrium is an important one in the conduct of international monetary policy. The transfer of private funds from a country with a high to one with a low interest rate, or from a country with a deficit to one with a surplus in the balance of payments, is just as contrary to the requirements of equilibrium as, for example, the export of wheat from England to Canada. There is now almost universal agreement that capital movements of the unbalancing kind — speculative transfers and capital flights — had better be subjected to control. The statutes of the International Monetary Fund not only permit, but, under certain conditions, may actually require member countries to exercise such control.

(4) *Rationing of scarce currencies:* Keynes welcomed the scarce-currency clause of the Fund agreement as a means of preventing the spread of depression from one country to others.[37]

[34] *Ibid.,* 374.
[35] *Ibid.*
[36] *Proposals for an International Clearing Union,* par. 35; see "Proposals for an International Clearing Union," *The New Economics,* 337.
[37] Speech in the House of Lords, 23 May 1944 (above, n. 16), 372.

If a depression were to occur in a major country such as the United States, that country's imports would decline and its currency would tend to become scarce in the Fund. Under certain conditions the Fund might then proceed to ration its supplies of the scarce currency, permitting member countries to impose similar controls in their transactions in that currency. The effect would be discrimination against the exports of the depressed country, tending to eliminate the export surplus which that country automatically acquires as a result of the fall in its national income and imports. Joan Robinson was the first to point out the attractions of this rationing device for an international system concerned with full employment.[38] The application of the scarce-currency clause would evidently mean a partial suspension of multilateralism. It is presumably intended as a temporary measure, to be introduced as a last resort in an emergency. The general underlying idea is to permit discriminatory devices only when they are urgently needed for the protection of external equilibrium and to subject them to international supervision and control, rather than leave each country free, as in the past, to apply them as and when it thinks fit.

(5) *Multilateralism versus bilateralism:* Normally, one of the supreme objectives of the new monetary and trading system is precisely to ensure full multilateralism in international settlements. On the general question of multilateral vs. bilateral methods of settlement, Keynes' attitude, as expressed in the speeches and writings of the last three or four years of his life, was quite unequivocal. Keynes is believed to have had a mild flirtation with bilateralistic ideas at some time in the late thirties or early forties; but, if this is true, there are no traces of it in his published writings. In the Clearing Union proposal, as well as in the speech he made in defense of that proposal,[39] he appeared as a determined champion of multilateralism, and this he remained until the end. In the text of the Clearing Union proposal, the very

[38] Joan Robinson, "The International Currency Proposals," *Economic Journal,* 1943. See, however, Sir William Beveridge, *Full Employment in a Free Society* (London, 1944), 222f, for a discussion of the practical difficulties in the way of carrying out this policy.

[39] Speech in the House of Lords, 18 May 1943; see "The International Clearing Union," *The New Economics,* 360.

first object of the plan was stated thus: "We need an instrument
of international currency having general acceptability between
nations, so that blocked balances and bilateral clearings are unnecessary." [40] In his speech of May, 1943, he said that the chief
object of the scheme was "to provide that money earned by
selling goods to one country can be spent on buying the products
of any other country; in jargon — a system of multilateral clearing." The multilateral theme was very prominent also in his later
speeches, in May, 1944, and December, 1945. No one could have
put the case for multilateralism more forcefully.

This may be surprising, since one of the two principal advantages claimed for the bilateral system is the supposed convenience
and security which such a system affords to a country pursuing
a full-employment policy at home. The proponents of bilateralism
stress the fact that, under the protection of bilateral clearing
agreements, a country can go ahead and expand its national income without worrying about its external accounts; for the induced increase in its imports will give rise simply to blocked
balances which foreigners can use solely for increasing *their* purchases from the expanding country. In brief, it is argued that
under this system a country in pursuit of full employment at
home does not have to worry about its balance of payments, and
is not deterred by external considerations from the pursuit of
internal equilibrium. But this should always be the case, even
under a multilateral system. As we have seen, there are a number
of possible devices, which have all been incorporated into the
international monetary and trading system which Keynes has
helped to create, which enable a single country to maintain
equilibrium in the over-all balance of payments while striving to
achieve or to preserve internal equilibrium. These devices may
be more difficult to handle than the crude and homely tool of
bilateral clearing. But surely there has been some advance in
economic insight among government officials in charge of international relations; and, under the guidance of new international
institutions such as the Fund and the proposed ITO, the new
devices should prove effective enough for the attainment and

[40] See "Proposals for an International Clearing Union," *The New Economics,*
325.

preservation of international equilibrium without resort to bilateralism.

The other main advantage which is claimed for the bilateral system is that it enables a country to improve its barter terms of trade by discriminatory treatment of its neighbors, by squeezing out the best possible export-import price relationships for itself, by bullying and bargaining with its weaker trading partners one by one. This policy of improving the *terms,* as distinct from the *balance,* of trade is of course a beggar-my-neighbor policy — not, indeed, as a means of creating employment through the export-multiplier mechanism, but simply as a means of extortion. Admittedly it may bring some gain, though probably only an ephemeral gain, to an individual country practicing such methods. But these methods are open to all, and they inevitably lead to commercial warfare pure and simple. In defending the international currency and trade proposals, Keynes had to face constant opposition from a small but vocal group of adherents to the bilateral school of thought in his own country. What he felt about the "neo-Schachtian" school is eloquently expressed in the final paragraph of his last great speech.[41] Can anyone read that paragraph and still maintain that Keynes was an economic nationalist?

What Keynes sought and, we may hope, achieved, was a multilateral solution to the postwar currency problem. His aim was a truly international monetary system. It is evident that the bilateral alternative offers, in essence, not a monetary system at all, but a system of international barter entirely analogous to interpersonal barter in a primitive society. Just as interpersonal barter, preferable though it is to complete self-sufficiency, inhibits that division of labor which money as a medium of exchange makes possible, so the policy of bilateralism cannot but cramp and cripple the international division of labor, especially the more refined and complicated division of labor which the spread of industrial techniques all over the world tends to develop. Keynes was modern enough to see that in the modern world nothing but a multilateral system would do. His distinctive contribution was

[41] See "The Anglo-American Financial Arrangements," *The New Economics,* 395.

to equip this system with the controls and safeguards required to make the pursuit of modern full-employment policies compatible with the equilibrium of international settlements. For the operation of these controls and safeguards, he left the necessary criteria — national income, employment, and the balance of payments — and, explicitly or implicitly, a set of general working principles which this essay has tried to indicate. These principles may still seem strange to some, and hard to understand; but they do possess the merit of consistency, seeking in every way to combine the advantages of international trade with the benefits of full employment.

4

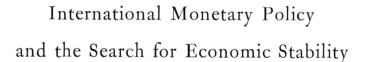

International Monetary Policy
and the Search for Economic Stability

(1947)

The object of this paper is to consider the international implications of national policies aimed at maintaining high and stable levels of employment. It is now widely realized that such policies are not only compatible with, but actually prerequisite to, a large and steady flow of world trade. Substantial progress has been made since the end of the war in setting up the framework for a new international system of monetary and trading relations. The two Bretton Woods institutions are ready to start operations; and a conference just concluded in London has produced a draft charter for an International Trade Organization. This is a good time to inquire how this new system can be operated so as to agree rather than conflict with the domestic objective of stability at full employment.

The search for domestic stability at full employment must nowadays be accepted as a datum. The international monetary system should be — and, I believe, is now — so devised that the

American Economic Review, May 1947, by permission of the publisher.

balance of international payments can never force a country into a state of deflation or inflation. Foreign trade fluctuations may continually necessitate *relative* shifts in the structure of prices and production, but should not compel any country to depart from the *general* norm of domestic stability. On occasion, domestic stability may of course break down; inflation or deflation may occur; but, if so, it will be for autonomous internal reasons, not as a means of bringing a country's external accounts into balance. Historically, resistance to deflation as a means of adjustment was not the only factor that led to the collapse of the gold standard. Resistance to inflation on the part of surplus countries — countries such as the United States, France, and Sweden at certain times in the interwar period — was perhaps just as important.

The problem that arises under these conditions may be stated as that of harmonizing the requirements of internal equilibrium with those of external equilibrium. It will suffice in this context to define "internal equilibrium," very roughly, as the maximum level of national income and employment that can be continuously sustained without an inflationary rise in wages and prices; while "external equilibrium" is simply a balance of payments that maintains itself in equilibrium without the persistent use of monetary stopgaps such as gold movements or short-term borrowing, and without a permanent increase in trade barriers.

Responsibility for internal equilibrium — for the maintenance of a high and stable level of employment — lies primarily in the sphere of domestic policy. There may be limits to what a country can do alone, but there is always something it can do to keep its own house in order. This need for self-reliance is the first point to stress, and it applies to the prevention of deflation as well as to that of inflation.

The next point is that, in principle, a country striving for internal equilibrium need never be deterred by difficulties in its balance of payments. There exist specific methods of influencing the external balance so as to keep it in equilibrium. (We shall discuss them presently under the two broad headings of commercial policy and exchange-rate adjustments.) For a single country, consequently, a unilateral expansion policy even at a time of general depression should be not only desirable but also to some extent practicable, in much the same way as a unilateral free trade policy was shown to be by the classical doctrine of foreign trade. The means available for preserving external equilibrium should afford each country some scope for the pursuit of internal equilibrium independently.

Naturally it would be better to find a way of coordinating the domestic stabilization policies of at least the major trading nations. But, in the first place, such policies must exist before they can be coordinated. Secondly, even if they existed everywhere, they would probably not be equally effective in the different countries. Thirdly, this coordination may require a degree of supernational control quite impracticable in the present state of the world. Coordination may come about ultimately as a result of the spontaneous adoption and attainment by like-minded nations of the same goal of internal equilibrium. We can hardly hope for more than the kind of spontaneous development that characterized the rise of the gold standard system, in which exchange stability was the primary common aim.

In the meantime, the international monetary system must be so designed as to provide "buffers" in order to prevent such departures from domestic stability as may occur in individual countries from upsetting the internal equilibrium of other members of the system. It must ensure that any single country pursuing the goal of internal equilibrium has instruments at its disposal for maintaining external equilibrium at the same time.

II

Among these instruments, consideration must be given not only to exchange-rate adjustments but also to trade restrictions, whether enforced by customs duties, exchange controls or otherwise. A country expanding unilaterally at a time of world depression is likely to incur a deficit in its balance of payments. When its liquid monetary reserves are inadequate to meet the deficit, there is generally some change in the exchange rate that will restore external equilibrium. Alternatively, there is the possibility of adopting import restrictions, not in order to reduce imports, but just enough to prevent them from increasing. This will prevent the expansion from "spilling over" abroad, but will not actually hurt the outside world.

A country enjoying internal equilibrium may suffer a deficit in its foreign accounts because of a depression occurring in its export markets. For the depressed countries abroad, this means a surplus, which will give them automatically some relief from their depression. But an export surplus is an unneighborly way of relieving a depression which could and should be remedied by domestic measures. Here again, therefore, a policy of exchange adjustment, or import restriction adopted by a country with a deficit in its balance of payments for the purpose of closing that deficit, cannot be regarded as inflicting any unfair injury to the internal equilibrium of other countries.

This leads us to a basic distinction which has to be made between the defensive and the aggressive use of measures such as import restrictions and exchange depreciation. The line between defense and aggression may be hazy in international politics, but it is fairly clear in international monetary policy. There is a simple criterion; namely, the balance of payments; more exactly, the balance of all current transactions and productive capital movements, excluding for obvious reasons gold movements, short-term funds, and hot money flights.[1] Exchange adjustments and import restrictions are defensive when they seek to prevent or to remove a deficit in the balance of payments; that is, when they are needed for external equilibrium. They are aggressive when they aim at creating a surplus in the balance of payments. The draft agreement of the ITO is in accord with this criterion. It permits the use of import restrictions, including even quotas, when they are required for the protection of a country's balance of payments. In the case of exchange adjustments, the regulations of the International Monetary Fund concerning "fundamental disequilibrium" are not so explicit. But it seems to me that the term fundamental disequilibrium must be defined primarily with reference to the balance of payments, especially

---

[1] I have discussed the balance of payments as a criterion of international monetary policy in *Conditions of International Monetary Equilibrium*, Essays in International Finance, No. 4 (Princeton, 1945), 4–8.

since any persistent disequilibrium in the balance of international payments is bound to impair the Fund's own position.

A single country at a time of world depression could conceivably attain a full recovery at home solely by an "aggressive" policy of exchange depreciation or import restriction, creating a surplus in its balance of payments, with the attendant favorable multiplier effects throughout the domestic economy. This it could do only, of course, at the cost of worsening the position in other countries. The balance-of-payments criterion would exclude any such beggar-my-neighbor policy. It would permit, however, exchange depreciation and import restrictions in their defensive uses, when they may be legitimate means of safeguarding a country's domestic stability as well as its external equilibrium.

III

As a method of influencing the balance of payments, trade barriers can be treated, and are here treated, as one form of international monetary policy. For the maintenance of external and internal equilibrium in the general sense indicated, exchange adjustments and import restrictions stand on the same footing. But their effects on the international division of labor are very different. Some advocates of full employment seem to welcome the restrictive effect of commercial policy on international trade, for the sake of domestic employment. This attitude is based on two distinct grounds. First, there is the argument in favor of minimizing the volume of foreign trade so as to minimize the possibility of foreign disturbances upsetting the domestic employment situation. This view must be rejected, for it should be realized that the effects of foreign business fluctuations can be offset or neutralized by other methods, without giving up the benefits of international trade. The second argument amounts to saying that the employment problem would be easier to solve if we made ourselves poorer all round by putting an end to international specialization. There is some substance in this argument. The international division of labor is a laborsaving device. Destroying it, just like destroying laborsaving machinery, may create jobs. But full employment achieved in this way can never be considered a true equilibrium position. It is senseless to cure unemployment by reducing the level of economic efficiency. There are other ways of solving the employment problem.

Trade restrictions operating through import quotas or exchange controls may be inevitable when there is a deficit in the balance of payments, when gold and other monetary reserves are inadequate, and when a change in exchange rates would be too slow a remedy. When exports fall off as a result of a depression abroad, or when imports increase as a result of domestic expansion toward the "internal equilibrium" level, protection of the balance of payments implies something more fundamental as well; namely, protection of the domestic employment situation. It is therefore right and proper that the new system of international trade and currency should have made provision for import restrictions through the quotas permitted under the ITO charter and through the exchange controls envisaged under the scarce-currency clause of the International Monetary Fund, when such restrictions are required for international monetary equilibrium. But commercial policy in this broad "monetary" function should always be subject to three general rules designed to minimize its restrictive effect on international trade.

In the first place, when import restrictions are imposed to close a deficit in the balance of payments (a deficit resulting, say, from a depression abroad), they should subsequently be removed as soon as the balance begins to show a surplus (as the depression abroad gives way to recovery). This rule is expressly stated in the ITO provisions adopted at the recent London conference. The surplus that might later appear could be removed by other methods, such as exchange appreciation or foreign investment; but the only proper way to remove it is by abolishing the import restrictions adopted previously. Our aim is not simply external equilibrium; it is external equilibrium with at least the preexisting degree of international division of labor. Now as a matter of practical politics, the international division of labor is usually not something that one can put in cold storage during a depression and take out again in better times. In practice, vested interests are liable to grow up and prevent the subsequent removal of the restrictions. Yet there is some hope that the rule laid down by the ITO could be made effective. The growth of vested interests might be discouraged by the very fact that the ITO charter requires the restrictions to be removed when they are no longer needed for the adjustment of the balance of payments.

The second rule should be this: import restrictions that seem to be needed more or less permanently for protecting the balance of payments should always, in principle, be removed simply by replacing them by an appropriate change in the exchange rate. There must normally be some rate of exchange at which a country's foreign receipts and payments will balance without the use of import barriers for this general purpose of external monetary equilibrium.

Thirdly, the International Trade Organization should see to it that commercial policy for the maintenance of external equilibrium should, as far as possible, take the form of reducing import barriers in surplus countries instead of increasing them in deficit countries. One country's balance-of-payments deficit is another country's surplus. And for the surplus country to reduce its own import barriers cannot be any worse than to have its exports subjected to higher barriers imposed by the deficit countries. Particular industries would be differently affected by the two alternative policies. But for the employment situation as a whole, one is as good or as bad as the other, while for international trade, one is much better than the other. Any unfavorable effect on employment in the surplus country, resulting equally from reduced import barriers at home or from increased barriers abroad, could be offset by domestic measures.

This point arises, for example, in the case of the scarce-currency clause of the Fund. Member countries would be permitted under this clause to impose discriminatory restrictions against the exports of a country whose foreign balance shows a surplus and whose currency therefore becomes scarce in the Fund. The surplus may be due to a slump in that country, and the restrictions would be justifiable as a means of safeguarding domestic stability in the deficit countries. But instead of allowing these countries to impose discriminatory trade restrictions, why not get the surplus country to lower its import barriers? Incidentally, while the former alternative represents a discriminatory trade policy, the latter does not imply any discrimination except in the sense that import barriers are reduced only by one country; namely, the surplus country.

IV

Thus there exist possible ways of mitigating the restrictive effects of the commercial-policy method of securing international equilibrium. Yet the method of exchange-rate adjustment is in general far preferable. The only trouble is that this method may not always be sufficiently effective in the short run. In the long run, a system of exchange rates should be established ideally in such a way that, when the domestic economies of the member countries are functioning at satisfactory levels of activity, each country's balance of payments maintains itself in equilibrium. There is in my view no good reason to doubt the general efficacy of exchange adjustments in righting a country's balance in the long run. It may conceivably happen that no degree of devaluation or appreciation will bring the external accounts into equilibrium. But this can be true only under rather exceptional conditions of demand and supply elasticity, which are unlikely to persist for a long time. It may be true in some countries today, but the present postwar conditions are exceptional and, we may hope, temporary. Our discussion here is mainly concerned with the working of monetary relations under the more normal conditions we hope to reach after the period of immediate postwar reconstruction.

The object of the International Monetary Fund is to keep exchange rates stable in the short run but to permit step-by-step adjustments of rates from time to time, as and when the trend of international payments requires it. The method of exchange adjustment can under the new system be used in a way entirely compatible with the objectives of internal as well as external equilibrium. The Fund, we may note, has now explicitly recognized the domestic employment situation as one of the criteria to be taken into account.[2] A true equilibrium rate of exchange is one that maintains the balance of payments, not simply in equi-

[2] The resolution adopted to this effect is reported in the *Federal Reserve Bulletin*, February 1947, 128.

librium, but in equilibrium at a satisfactory level of domestic employment.[3]

Some liberal-minded economists are so impressed with the restrictive dangers of commercial policy that they would rather leave the maintenance of external equilibrium entirely to the care of fluctuations in exchange rates. This view may be attractive theoretically, but it places too much reliance on exchange-rate variations. Owing to the speculative tendencies which they provoke in commodity as well as capital flows, such variations are likely to be disruptive of internal stability. Experience has shown that the distinction between exchange stability and domestic stability may become quite unreal when exchange rates are left free to fluctuate under the influence of speculative anticipations creating excessive and "nonfunctional" disturbances, not only in foreign trade, but also in domestic prices and production. This, at any rate, is apt to be the case when exchange variations are uncontrolled. When they are controlled by some form of official "pegging," then we have before us a quite different method — one which aims at offsetting, instead of correcting, discrepancies in the external accounts by means of gold or other liquid reserves.

V

The use of liquid external reserves as a buffer for temporary discrepancies in the balance of payments should be the normal method of operation of the international monetary system from day to day, or rather from year to year, exchange rates being thus held stable in the short run. That is the general function of what we may call "international liquidity," including in this term not only gold and exchange reserves but also the drawing facilities (quotas) provided by the Fund.

International liquidity is a buffer, not merely in regard to the balance of external payments, but also in regard to internal economic stability since it makes it possible for a given country

[3] This idea is clearly implied in the section on Exchange Rates in the *First Annual Report of the International Monetary Fund,* which speaks of "the maintenance of a balanced international payments position at a high level of domestic economic activity." (See *Federal Reserve Bulletin,* October 1946, 1130.)

to offset, within limits, the effects of foreign business fluctuations upon the domestic economy. Suppose a country is striving to keep up both external and internal equilibrium, but suddenly finds itself faced with a depression in its export markets abroad. Exports fall off, and the export industries will suffer a depression which, through the familiar multiplier mechanism, may spread to the whole domestic economy. To preserve the general stability of the domestic economy in these circumstances, it is necessary to offset the fall in foreign expenditure on the country's products by an increase in the volume of domestic expenditure. This offsetting policy has its limitations in practice;[4] but insofar as total employment depends on total outlay, the compensatory increase in domestic demand will tend to prevent a general depression in the given country. The principle of compensatory domestic spending can and should be applied in reverse when foreign demand is excessive and threatens to produce an inflationary expansion of domestic money income. In either case the procedure is the opposite of what the gold standard would have required. But the gold standard rules were never very strictly observed, and the offsetting policy just described is in fact a logical extension of the central banking practice by which gold movements were frequently "neutralized" even in the best days of the gold standard.

Since the offsetting policy in itself does nothing to correct discrepancies in the balance of payments, it depends essentially on the existence of liquid reserves for covering such discrepancies. Reserves should be adequate to take care of all temporary discrepancies, "cyclical" or fortuitous. But if reserves are small, then even a small and temporary drop in exports may exhaust them, so that the offsetting policy cannot be continued until the balance rights itself again. Thus the extent to which this policy can actually be employed for the preservation of domestic stability depends on the volume and distribution of international liquidity. What the situation will be in this respect after the postwar transition period we cannot predict, but there are two favorable factors to be mentioned. First, the Fund represents

[4] See *Economic Stability in the Post-War World* (League of Nations, 1945), 232, or *Conditions of International Monetary Equilibrium*, 11–14.

a sizable addition to the volume of international liquidity. Secondly, there is now general agreement that speculative short-term capital movements should be controlled. This means that reserves of international liquidity will no longer be wasted on transfers of hot money, but will all be available for the settlement of balances on account of trade and other normal transactions including foreign investment. There seems to be, consequently, a fair prospect for the successful functioning of the buffer system of international liquidity as the normal method of operation.

VI

When the liquid reserves of some particular country or countries are depleted, then — and only then — is the time to take measures to correct the balance of payments. Measures of deflation or inflation are excluded for this purpose, unless they happen to be required for domestic stability. We are then left with the two types of measures already discussed: commercial policy in the wide sense, on the one hand, and exchange-rate adjustments, on the other. It is the method of exchange-rate adjustment that should be relied upon to bring international monetary relations into long-run equilibrium. But coming in between this method and the normal buffer method of international liquidity, there may be need occasionally for commercial-policy measures as a temporary means of correcting the balance of payments.[5] This need may arise especially when demand and supply conditions are not immediately or sufficiently responsive to changes in exchange rates. The new currency and trading system does not prohibit commercial-policy measures; it lays down the conditions in which they are to be used; quite rightly, it looks upon such measures as exceptions rather than the norm. The presumption is that they are to be used only when the international liquidity system breaks down at some point, and when possibly a breathing space is needed for the restoration of long-run equi-

[5] It is because of the temporary nature and object of such restrictions that, following the ITO draft provisions, we have spoken of import quotas and not of tariff duties in this connection. Quotas can generally be imposed or removed by administrative action, while tariff changes usually require legislation.

librium through exchange-rate adjustment. And let me add once more that, in theory at any rate, the commercial-policy method of securing international monetary equilibrium can be handled, without prejudice to domestic employment, in such a way as to reduce rather than increase the barriers to trade.

The main conclusion of this paper is that the new system of international currency and trade is quite capable of being operated so as to allow scope for national policies aimed at high and stable levels of employment and at the same time to promote the flow of international trade. This system, which is developing largely at the initiative of the United States, presents an effective alternative to the bilateral solution. Bilateralism holds out two main attractions. First, bilateral clearing arrangements are supposed to have the advantage that a country can go ahead with any domestic expansion program without having to worry about its external accounts, since any increase in its imports will give rise to blocked balances available only for purchases in that country. But under a multilateral system providing for international liquidity, "defensive" commercial policies, and exchange adjustments, a single country should be able to enjoy substantially the same freedom from anxiety about its over-all balance of payments.

The second advantage of bilateralism is that it may enable a large trading nation to improve its barter terms of trade by bullying its weaker trading partners one by one. This policy of improving the terms, as distinct from the balance, of trade is of course a beggar-my-neighbor policy, not in the technical sense of "exporting unemployment," but simply in the sense of extortion. It leads to retaliation and so to commercial warfare all round.

The attractions of bilateralism are illusory. At the same time, we must realize that in the operation of the multilateral currency and trading system now in process of construction, we can no longer rely on traditional gold standard theory. The basic principles of the new system must be derived from the theory of employment as well as from that of international trade. It is useless to pretend that there is general agreement on these matters. The sooner such agreement is reached, the better will the system be able to function. The principles as I see them myself, and as I have tried to describe them, seem to have at least the merit of consistency, seeking in every way to combine the advantages of international trade with the benefits of full employment.

VII

We have discussed the principles in general terms without referring to any country by name. Such general discussion may be useful in clearing up our basic ideas, but sooner or later we must descend into the real world with its great diversity of national problems and national economic structures. In particular we must give some attention to the position of the United States in the new international system.

The position of the United States is important, first, because of the great preponderance of the American economy in the world today and, second, because of the wide fluctuations to which the American economy is subject or at least has been in the recent past. There is a widespread notion that all would be well in the international economy if only the United States could maintain high and stable employment at home. Some people even go so far as to say that, by way of international arrangements, nothing can be of any use unless there is high and stable employment in the United States.

This line of argument seems to me exaggerated and misleading. The general purpose of the new monetary and trading system is to interpose between the member countries a set of "buffers" (avoiding the use of "barriers" as far as possible), giving each country some leeway for domestic employment policy and some protection for its domestic stability. The position of the United States simply calls for a particularly strong and reliable set of buffers — not barriers — so as to provide means of cushioning or neutralizing the external effects of American business cycles.

One way in which business fluctuations here affect the outside world is the highly variable demand for imports in this country. In technical terms, this country has a high income elasticity of demand for imports. There are several reasons for this. First, our imports consist mainly of raw materials and hence are closely geared to the rate of industrial activity here. By contrast, British imports, for instance, consist more largely of foodstuffs, for which the demand is much steadier. Second, some of our imports are of a marginal character. Domestic materials are sufficient for a low or average level of industrial production, but when activity rises above the average, imports are suddenly required to supplement the domestic sources. Third, our imports are sometimes greatly affected, in quantity and even more in value, by speculative inventory fluctuations. In boom periods there is much forward buying of imported materials, while in depression years buying is postponed.

A possible remedy for this state of affairs would be for this country either alone or under international auspices to set up buffer stocks of the primary products chiefly affected. This is not the place to discuss the details of the buffer-stock proposal. Here we can only draw attention to the general point that a buffer-stock scheme might be an effective means of ironing out the fluctuations in American imports.

Another way to offset the effects of domestic fluctuations on the outside world would be a countercyclical timing of American foreign investment. This, too, would tend to stabilize the supply of dollars to the rest of the world and would make that supply less closely dependent on the oscillations of business activity in this country. The idea of countercyclical foreign investment, just like the buffer-stock idea, may not be easy to put into practice. But if it could be carried out, through the World Bank or otherwise, it would be a useful means, in addition to the other means we have discussed, of cushioning the external effects of American business cycles.

All this does not imply that the stability of the domestic economy in the United States is of no importance. It is important to the American people in the first place. Yet we might as well recognize that in a progressive and dynamic economy some ups and downs are inevitable, and at the high standard of living prevailing in this country such ups and downs are easier to bear than at a low level of existence. Let us have in readiness, therefore, a system of buffer devices to soften the external impact of such fluctuations as may occur.

As far as international economic relations are concerned, it would seem that such a buffer policy could, at least to some extent, take the place of internal economic stabilization in the United States (or, indeed, in any country). In particular, if we stabilize the American demand for imports through buffer stocks, or if we stabilize the supply of dollars to foreigners through countercyclical foreign lending as well as buffer stocks, is that not — for the outside world — an acceptable substitute for stabilizing the internal American economy? To be sure, there is the *volume* of trade to be considered, as well as the question of *stability*. At a high level of national income and employment in the United States, the volume of imports will be larger than at a low level. The buffer mechanism as such cannot produce a large volume of trade. It is only the stability problem that it is designed to solve, and the solution in terms of the various devices we have discussed should, on the whole, prove satisfactory to the outside members of the system.

The new system *can* be worked in such a way as to safeguard domestic employment in the member countries without prejudice to the international division of labor. We in this country should seek to ensure that it *will* be worked in that way. The search for stability at high levels of employment represents the dominant attitude of most countries abroad. The problem does not greatly concern a country like Soviet Russia, which, by the way, is not a member of the system. It does concern countries that rely largely on price incentives and private enterprise. The survival of economic freedom in some parts of the world may depend, in the years to come, on the extent to which international currency and trading arrangements, in their actual operation, conform to the requirements of economic stability.

5

~~~~~~

A New Look at the Dollar
Problem and the United States
Balance of Payments

(1953)

The most essential condition for achieving a fuller convertibility of currencies is a removal of the persistent disequilibrium
in trade and payments between the dollar area and the rest of
the world. Inconvertibility has not been the disease itself so
much as a symptom of the stubborn maladjustment commonly
called the dollar gap. In these circumstances discrimination in
trade and exchange control has appeared to the dollar–deficit
countries as a way of preventing their mutual trade from being
strangled by restrictions imposed on payments grounds on imports from the dollar area.

Absence of such maladjustment as a prerequisite to convertibility is particularly important for a currency like sterling, in
which some 40 or 50 per cent of the world's trade is conducted.

The pound sterling, being a world currency, would, if it were made more fully convertible, inevitably feel some of the strain of the world's dollar disequilibrium, even if the dollar position of Britain herself or the sterling area as a whole had been brought into balance.[1]

But now, as we take a new look at the dollar gap, we find that it seems to have closed. Since the middle of 1952 the current account of the United States balance of payments has been practically in equilibrium: United States exports and imports of goods and services have almost exactly balanced. For a statistical account of this remarkable change I refer to the *Federal Reserve Bulletin* of October 1953. On top of a balanced current account there has been a small trickle of private capital exports from the United States and a reduced though still substantial flow of United States government foreign aid. The net result has been an increase of over two billion dollars in the gold and dollar reserves of the outside world.

This being so, is there any dollar problem left? If balance-of-payments statistics are to be the sole criterion, then I think we must admit that the problem, for the time being at least, has vanished. It can be argued that this marks the end of the post-war transition period (which thus turns out to have lasted seven years instead of the expected five) and that the basic prerequisite to making currencies such as the pound more freely convertible into dollars has been established.

There is no denying that prospects for success on the road to convertibility have improved. Yet it does not follow that there is nothing more to be said on the dollar problem. I think there is something to be said, on its short-term as well as its long-range aspects.

II

To take the short run first, it is possible that if we look a little more carefully behind the balance-of-payments statistics, we may find that a dollar problem, even now, can still be said to exist, for a number of reasons.

[1] I have developed this point in "The Problem of Currency Convertibility Today," *International Economic Outlook,* Proceedings of the Academy of Political Science, 29 April 1953.

First, reserves of gold and dollars are, on the whole, still relatively low in the world outside the United States. The gain that occurred in 1952–53 is a modest gain that still leaves the degree of international liquidity far below what was regarded before the war as normal and desirable in relation to the dollar volume of trade. Governments are understandably reluctant to give up their trade and exchange restrictions, including restrictions on convertibility, as long as their buffer stocks of gold and dollars are so inadequate. The question of reserves is fundamentally inseparable from that of balance or imbalance in the flow of international payments, but I cannot enter into it at greater length.

A second reason for caution in interpreting the United States balance of payments for 1952–53 is that the position in that period was perhaps a little unusual. The twelve months from mid-1952 were marked by boom conditions in the United States combined with a certain amount of slack in the economy of Great Britain and Western Europe generally. We have yet to see what sort of balance can be maintained in a period of slackening in the United States and full activity in Europe.

Thirdly, about a quarter of the improvement in the world's current balance of payments with the United States in the last four or five years has been due to a very special factor: United States government purchases of goods and services, mainly for military uses abroad. This item, which includes an increasing amount of offshore purchases, is dependent, by and large, on the state of international political tension rather than on normal economic forces. It is dependent presumably also on the willingness of Congress to allow military purchases from foreign instead of domestic American sources, and this, apart from political factors, may vary with business conditions in the United States.

Lastly, we must remember that the world's demand for dollar goods is forcibly kept down by trade and exchange controls imposed on balance-of-payments grounds. To this extent the problem of disequilibrium is suppressed rather than solved. A "potential" dollar gap may still exist even if the accounts as actually realized are in balance. Much of the improvement in 1952 must have been due to stricter controls and discriminations, including the drastic import cuts of the sterling area last year. What we want is not simply an accounting balance, but a balance that can be maintained — with, of course, possible swings in either direction — without the need for the obnoxious discriminatory restrictions. We have to keep in mind here not only the restrictive controls affecting especially dollar imports, but also the government subsidies and other special measures of assistance designed to expand the production of commodities now largely imported from dollar sources. Such direct assistance amounts to protection quite equivalent to, though perhaps more effective than, discriminatory import restrictions. Another form of discrimination that may have kept down purchases from the dollar area is the European Payments Union and the trade–liberalization program which applies to each member country's imports from the rest of that group but not imports from outside. It is impossible to know what the United States balance of payments would have been in the absence of these various forms of discrimination, but it seems quite likely that instead of the approximately even balance actually realized by the outside world in 1952–53, there would still have been a sizable deficit.

For these reasons I feel that it would be rash to hail the latest developments in the dollar balance of payments as a return to "fundamental equilibrium." The improvement is encouraging: it should convince even the sceptics that the position is not as hopeless as some have believed it to be. Yet the present balance is precarious. It is a position of equilibrium on the surface only: superficial rather than fundamental equilibrium. When we take into account the need for more reserves, the role of American military purchases and the existence of dollar import restrictions in the soft-currency countries, we must, I think, admit that despite the favorable statistical showing a dollar problem still exists in the world even now.

III

So much for the short-term aspect of the matter. Casting our eyes beyond the present position it is relevant for us to consider also the possibility of a long-range dollar problem. As recently as

August last, a distinguished American authority, Mr. Lewis Douglas, in his report to the President, spoke of the "persistent tendency for the United States payment position to be in surplus with the rest of the world." Is this likely to be a chronic tendency and, if so, why? Now I am not one of those who would deny the possibility of balanced two-way trade between America and the rest of the world. The principle of comparative advantage still works or rather can be made to work so as to keep trade balanced, given proper exchange rates and proper domestic monetary policies. It can be done; but it takes deliberate effort. Automatic forces can no longer be relied upon to maintain balance. On the contrary, there now exist strong automatic forces making for imbalance. They stem directly or indirectly from the great predominance of the United States in the present world economy.

I am not convinced that the trouble comes only or mainly from a faster rate of advance in American productivity, as Professor Williams and Professor Hicks have suggested.[2] If that were so, even the poorest country could create difficulties for the rest of the world if it advanced more quickly than its wealthier neighbors. I would rather stress the general *level* of American productivity which is reflected in a level of real income, and hence a standard of living, far higher than in the rest of the world. The gap between real income per head in the predominant economy and in the world outside is now enormous. And this gap has been getting wider rather than narrower. At the same time the world has in an obvious sense shrunk in size. Modern communications have created a growing awareness of the international discrepancies in levels of living. The situation is quite without historical precedent.

Advanced living standards exercise a strong attraction on the poorer countries. This has been called the "demonstration

[2] J. H. Williams, in the Stamp Memorial Lecture, University of London, 1952, and J. R. Hicks, "An Inaugural Lecture," *Oxford Economic Papers,* n.s., June 1953. In Hicks's model the trouble (a worsening in Europe's terms of trade) arises from American advances that are "import-biased" rather than "uniform" or "export-biased." The model is faultless; but does it fit the facts? Productivity in U.S. export industries (even farming) seems to have advanced at least as much as in domestic industries since the 1930's. And the U.S. terms of trade have certainly worsened.

effect." In a recent book[3] I related it particularly to the world's backward areas. But the point is of general significance. The demonstration effect tends constantly to create new wants and so to stir up the propensity to consume in the poorer countries; it makes for inflationary pressures there and ultimately for balance-of-payments difficulties. The orthodox prescription is that a country should always endeavor to live within its means. In the contemporary world, however, the trouble is precisely that it becomes peculiarly hard for the poorer countries to keep their money incomes in line with their productive capacity or, in other words, to live within their means. In these circumstances the stage is set for a persistent or recurrent tendency to disequilibrium in international trade and payments.

Although this theory relates partly to the action of monetary authorities as well as to "man's actions in the ordinary business of life" (which Marshall defined as the object of economic study), the former can never be entirely independent of the prevalent behavior and preference patterns of individuals in society. As I have remarked in a slightly different context, "through its central bankers, finance ministers and other authorities, acting under the pressure of public opinion, political institutions, business interests, demand for credit and demand for foreign goods, a nation will generally contrive — however imperfectly — to give effect to its scale of comparative necessity." [4]

Any gap in a country's external accounts is ultimately a question of real income. There must be some change in the terms of trade that will eliminate an external deficit. But, on top of the burden of closing the gap at the pre-existing terms of trade, an adverse shift in the terms of trade further affects real income. For the poorer countries to endure such shifts may now be harder because the attraction of advanced living standards is stronger than ever before.

There may be other arguments for the likelihood of a long-

---

[3] *Problems of Capital Formation in Underdeveloped Countries* (Oxford and New York, 1953), ch. 3, where much more is said on this than is here possible.

[4] "Conditions of International Monetary Equilibrium," reprinted in *Readings in the Theory of International Trade* (Philadelphia, 1949), 23.

range dollar problem. But the simple hypothesis put forward above is one that strikes me as plausible. It supplements rather than conflicts with the classical theory of foreign trade on which we have been brought up.

I do not wish to appear dogmatic. We cannot be certain that the dollar problem will remain with us in future years or decades. It would be unwise and dangerous to adopt a rigid policy attitude based on a preconceived notion. It is perhaps best for the non-dollar countries to keep their defenses flexible if and when the need for them arises. If it should happen that the dollar problem proved to be persistent or recurrent, it would not take us by surprise. Meanwhile all efforts should be made to attack the trouble at its roots.

In international trade and payments, one country's deficit is another's surplus. When there is a lack of balance or threat of imbalance, action on both sides is likely to be needed. On the side of deficit countries (or potential deficit countries) the emphasis should be on realistic exchange rates and the control of inflationary pressures. We do not want and cannot in the long run afford the economic waste that goes with discriminatory restrictions on trade and foreign exchange; and from a political angle we do not want a permanent dollar barrier splitting the free world in two.

The goal cannot, however, be reached without proper action also by the surplus country. Why was there no persistent imbalance in the nineteenth century? Some say because wages and prices were flexible. But nowadays we have flexible exchange rates; perhaps not flexible enough, but at least for major adjustments from time to time exchange rates are now universally recognized as a legitimate instrument. No doubt in the nineteenth century what I have described as the "demonstration effect" was not nearly as strong as now: the gaps in income levels were smaller, and things like the radio, the films, aviation, and television did not exist. But what needs to be remembered also is the action of the leader at that time in unilaterally scrapping all tariff protection while exporting capital on a relatively large scale. If in other respects conditions were more conducive to equilibrium in the nineteenth century than now, such action by the leader is of even more crucial importance today than it was a hundred years ago.

IV

As regards tariff policy it is sometimes objected that this comparison is not relevant to the present situation because Great Britain was highly dependent on essential imports of food. But surely, by abolishing protection, she *made* herself dependent, in the interest of her own national prosperity as well as of world trade and development. Had Britain remained protectionist a hundred years ago, she would have remained less industrialized, more self-sufficient, less prosperous.

Reciprocity has been a central feature of the American trade agreements program since 1934. Now the rule of reciprocity in tariff negotiations is in some respects a sensible rule, but it does not help to correct the particular problem of disequilibrium in the international balance of payments. The United States has made sizable reductions in its tariff duties, but only after long and hard bargaining in return for no less sizable tariff cuts by other countries. Since the other countries, however, have generally been in deficit on their dollar accounts, they have had to restrict their dollar imports, and the United States has had to agree to their use of quantitative trade and currency controls for this purpose. So the reciprocity rule in tariff matters has had a paradoxical and undesired result: tariff duties in dollar-deficit countries have come to be replaced by direct import controls and inconvertible currencies. Had the American tariff cuts been unilateral, the deficit countries would not have had to reduce their tariffs and would have had less need for the objectionable direct controls and discriminations.

The principle of reciprocity is based on the general idea of equality in international relations. But at least in economic affairs it is useless to pretend that countries are all equal. The world's most prosperous and powerful nation — Great Britain a hundred years ago, the United States today — can do things that weaker countries cannot so easily do.

Sir Dennis Robertson a few months ago spoke of a "quasi-

revolution in United States commercial policy" as one of the
conditions for a successful restoration of convertibility.[5] It is
clear that such a revolution would have to go a good deal beyond
the Reciprocal Trade Agreements Program, which even in its
original form cannot cope with the problem of imbalance, and
which more recently has had its usefulness further curtailed by
the escape and peril point clauses. The program remains important today mainly for its "defensive" value. For the tariff
cuts made by the United States since 1934 have not been nailed
down in any permanent legislation. The only tariff act that is on
the statute books is still the 1930 Smoot-Hawley tariff, to which
we should automatically return if the Trade Agreements Act were
allowed to lapse without anything else being put in its place.[6]

There are some who say that even a complete and unilateral
removal of the United States tariff might not be enough to banish
the dollar problem. I agree, it might not. We should not rely on
that alone. But I cannot see any reason for doubting that it would
contribute a substantial part of the solution. The Bell Committee
report,[7] which early this year came out with some moderately
drastic proposals for tariff reduction and simplification, estimated
the effect of these proposals at no more than one billion dollars
of additional imports. That would not be a negligible contribution,
though I should think that to put these proposals into effect
would probably not be much easier politically than to abolish the
tariff completely.

The advocates of tariff reduction in the United States often
voice what seems to me rather ill-founded optimism as regards
the competitive effects on American industry. Certainly some industries would have to be hurt or squeezed out of business altogether. The *Economic Survey of Europe since the War* (ECE,
Geneva, 1953) has some illuminating passages contrasting the
economic structure of Great Britain and Germany as it took
shape under different tariff policies in the past. Similarly, if tariff

---

[5] "Internal and External Conditions of Convertibility," a speech at the
Vienna Congress of the International Chamber of Commerce, May 20, 1953.

[6] See C. Wilcox, "Trade Policy for the Fifties," *American Economic Review*,
Papers and Proceedings, May 1953.

[7] Public Advisory Board for Mutual Security, *A Trade and Tariff Policy in
the National Interest* (Washington, D.C., February 1953).

reduction in the United States were to mean anything, there would have to be some change in the economic structure of the country, making it more dependent on imports for things like clothing, pottery, children's toys and other items (mainly, I presume, in the category of manufactured consumers' goods). What is needed is a partial reversal of the abnormal self-sufficiency forced upon the American economy by war as well as tariff policy in the past. It would not be a painless process. And it would take some time; which in technical parlance means that the elasticity of United States demand for imports is greater in the long than in the short run.

These structural changes would be very minor compared with those that the British economy went through under free trade, yet they would not be negligible. Some thought has been given in America (for instance, in the Bell Report) to the ways in which the impact of tariff cuts might be softened by measures to facilitate readaptation of labor and plant, through compensation, retraining and other schemes that might require government support. Such devices to promote structural change would no doubt be desirable. But it is important — and perhaps not always easy — to distinguish these devices from all measures that would simply replace tariff protection by other forms of open or concealed protection. For example, subsidies to industries exposed to foreign competition might easily be even more effective than tariff duties in keeping imports out.

It is not my task here to consider what the political chances are for a quasi-revolution in United States commercial policy. There is no Cobden today, and as one American writer has put it, "the American capacity for indifference to foreign trade is enormous." [8] It is partly perhaps because foreign trade plays so small a part in our economic life, though this, on the face of it, should make it easier to adopt the changes required by the nation's new position in the world. Congress might be swayed by some international emergency, but unfortunately a tariff cut is not and cannot be an emergency measure, depending as it does for its effectiveness on a gradual change in the make-up of Amer-

---

[8] Herbert Stein, "Next Steps in U.S. Trade Policy," *Lloyds Bank Review*, October 1953.

ican industry. A domestic emergency like the one that led to the repeal of the Corn Laws in Great Britain is hardly conceivable. But we need not despair. The Reciprocal Trade Program was an enormous step forward in American trade policy, and further progress is not out of the question. The dramatic repeal of the Corn Laws should not make us forget that the British revolution in commercial policy lasted at least from the Huskisson reforms of 1825 to the Cobden-Chevalier treaty of 1860, a period of thirty-five years. In the United States, less than twenty years have passed since 1934.

Those who cannot bear to face the need for increasing American imports are often inclined to favor another way of bringing trade into permanent balance. They invite Europe, including Great Britain, to go out and compete more effectively with the United States in third markets and to displace American exports to these areas. Especially in the rest of the Western Hemisphere, from which American imports have greatly expanded, dollars can be earned by this indirect route, as Europe is well aware. In the United States it might indeed be politically easier to let American exports decline — for that is what it would mean — than to allow imports to rise. But in general this would hurt our most efficient industries while increasing imports would tend to hurt the least efficient ones. An expansion of American imports would obviously make for a better division of labor and a higher potential level of real income even in the United States.

Besides, the displacement of American exports in third areas is not easy, partly just because these are generally products where America has the greatest comparative advantage, and partly because in markets outside the United States European goods are already relatively well established. It is above all in the United States itself that they need to enlarge their small and precarious foothold. This is illustrated by the astonishing fact that the rest of the dollar area (that is, mainly Canada, Cuba, Mexico, Venezuela and Colombia), whose combined purchasing power is only a small fraction of that of the United States, buys more goods from Europe than the United States does. The last *Economic Survey of Europe,* where this is pointed out (see page 108), shows also that the real volume of United States imports from

Western Europe in 1951, though it had increased, was still less than in the late 1920's, even though the 1951 imports contained many defense items, as well as wine, spirits, and liquor, which did not come in at all in the prohibition era of the twenties.

Yet the fact remains that American imports in recent years have increased. Let us not belittle what has been achieved. Comparing the position in the last twelve months with that in 1948 we find that more than half of the improvement in the world's current balance with the United States came about through increased commodity imports into the United States; exports declined little, if at all. That, as I have suggested, is the better way to balanced trade. The point is only that more along this way needs to be done to put international equilibrium on a sound and stable footing.

V

In contrast to American imports, private foreign investment throughout the period since the war has fluctuated at a low level and without any sign of an upward trend. This has been disappointing. We realize that one reason why the nineteenth century did not know of a chronic sterling shortage was the export of capital from the United Kingdom. There is in America a feeling of nostalgia for the nineteenth-century environment that made this flow of overseas investment possible. The question is asked: can we not recreate that environment?

Foreign investment might not be a substitute for, but at least it would be a good supplement to tariff reduction and increasing American imports. It could provide a valuable offset to any adverse effect which tariff reduction might have on the general level of employment. It could at least be used to "buy time" — time for the structural readaption of the American economy to take effect. Sooner or later, of course, private foreign investment leads to a return flow of dividends, interest and amortization, and the need for accepting more imports can then no longer be deferred. This return flow will be particularly quick to set in if the capital goes out in the form of direct business investments, and if these continue to earn anything like the high returns now obtained. But direct business investments are not enough. One of the most urgently needed developments is the restoration of public international investment as we used to know it (i.e., investment by public authorities financed by private foreign loans). The International Bank has hardly begun to fill the gap left by the disappearance of this type of investment, which was very important in the past. How important it was can be seen from the composition of Great Britain's overseas capital assets outstanding in 1914. Roughly three quarters of the total represented investments of the public or public-utility type: 30 per cent was in loans to governments, as much as 40 per cent in railway securities, and an additional 5 per cent in other public utility undertakings.

British foreign investment, as is well known, bore a high proportion to the British national income at that time. It is equally well known that if we were to apply similar proportions to the United States national income today, we should get almost absurdly large figures; which confirms, I think, the view that there was something unique about Great Britain's foreign investment. It was unique in that the greater part of it (about two thirds) went to the vast and empty fertile plans of North America, Australia, the Argentine and other newly settled regions in the temperate zone of the world. It was unique in that it went to these places hand in hand with a great migration of people, including many skilled and enterprising people, from the British Isles as well as Continental Europe. The conditions that made this flow of private capital possible do not exist today and probably cannot be recreated.

The migration of people and the flow of capital were *complementary* and supported one another. In the twentieth century the capital exports from the United States can be viewed rather as a *substitute* for the movement of people. Cheap labor, instead of being allowed to come to the United States, is supplied with American capital abroad. We want more capital to move out from the United States to work with the surplus labor in the world's backward areas. But we should notice that in this situation, in sharp contrast to the dominant nineteenth-century pattern, capital is being urged to go out to work with people that have not grown up in a capital-minded milieu, and may not be culturally prepared for the use of Western equipment and technology.

Keeping this situation in mind we can see the basic rationale for the American emphasis on direct American business investments as a means of financing economic development abroad. The advantages rightly attributed to this type of investment are, first, that it goes out with American enterprise, tied up with American know-how, and, secondly, that it is likely to be productively used, not swallowed up, directly or indirectly, by immediate consumption. But it has disadvantages also. It is apt to create not only a dual economy but also a dual society. Above all, it often tends to promote lopsided rather than balanced growth, concentrating on raw-material production for export and quite naturally tending to keep away from production for the home market, because the home market in poor countries is miserably small. In America we sometimes forget that this is precisely the so-called "colonial" form of foreign investment, in oil fields, mines, and plantations working for export to the advanced industrial countries. It played a relatively minor part in the nineteenth century. I doubt whether we can rely on it for more than a minor part today. Besides, even this "colonial" type of investment is not likely to happen on any significant scale unless there is an assured prospect of a steady and vigorous expansion in world demand for the raw materials which it aims to provide.

There is not much hope today for re-creating the nineteenth-century pattern of international investment, with its emphasis on the regions of recent settlement and the parallel migration of people. All the more imperative is it to devise a new pattern adapted to present needs and conditions. Much is heard nowadays of the unfavorable climate for private foreign investment. This includes political, social and cultural difficulties, but in many areas the physical environment too is unfavorable because of the lack of basic public facilities such as transport, power, waterworks. In the economic development of the United States a hundred years ago, public authorities played a leading role in the drive for "internal improvements" financed largely by capital imports. There is much room today for international financing of public improvements. Until the backward areas have acquired a skeleton framework of such overhead facilities, conditions there will not be particularly attractive for the more diversified smaller-scale business investments catering for domestic as well as export markets.

These public works may not be at all profitable to start with. Some of them may turn out to be "white elephants," especially if the smaller diversified enterprises fail to materialize. But any form of capital investments is, in the last analysis, an act of faith: faith in the future. We have to take a chance.

Such financing as may be possible on these lines should be based on the intrinsic merits and prospects of the schemes rather than on balance-of-payments grounds. Yet it could make an effective contribution to the balancing of the world's dollar accounts — which is the basic condition of convertibility. Stabilization loans directly for balance-of-payments purposes may be open to the objection that the aid which they provide for real investment or consumption is based on a one-sided criterion and may not go to the countries most in need of it. American loans or grants to, say, Southeast Asia can help even *Europe's* dollar balance if Europe is able, through increased exports, to compete for the additional dollars — provided the dollars are not tied to American goods.

Considering the needs of the backward areas, it is impossible not to conclude that an expansion of American capital exports for development purposes ought to be one of the principal ways of dealing with the dollar problem, not only by making dollars available for current purchases but also, in the longer run, by relieving the disparities in productivity and hence living levels, and so attacking the roots of the malady.

Mr. R. F. Harrod in his illuminating paper on "Imbalance of International Payments," [9] points out that the American export surplus in 1950–1952, financed by United States government aid, was relatively not much larger than in the 1930's or in the 1920's. In the thirties the surplus was covered by American gold purchases at the increased dollar price of gold; in the twenties it was covered by American foreign investment, though much of that was concentrated on Central Europe for other than normal

[9] *Staff Papers* (International Monetary Fund, April 1953), 9.

development needs and came to grief there for political reasons. Any policy conclusion that one may wish to draw depends entirely on which period one chooses as the standard of comparison. Mr. Harrod's choice is such as to support his case for an increase in the dollar price of gold. But it does not seem to me self-evident that the comparison should be with the 1930's rather than the 1920's. Surely the export of capital from the United States is more in line with the basic needs of world development than a "bonanza" to the world's gold producers.

VI

One sometimes encounters the simple notion that the restoration of convertibility abroad, coupled, if possible, with a relaxation of discriminatory trade controls, would open the way to an increase in American exports to the rest of the world. Some recent statements on foreign trade policy seem to me to have raised false expectations in this respect. As I see it, convertibility and nondiscrimination imply nothing more than a balance that can be maintained by other means than discriminatory restrictions on dollar payments. Such a state of balance would not necessarily enlarge the scope for American exports. Only if the United States were to increase the supply of dollars through still more imports and foreign investment, only then could this expectation of greater exports be realized.

In this paper I have set out my views as to what could be done on the American side towards creating conditions conducive to convertibility and nondiscrimination. These conditions, I would like to stress, are good for their own sake and should not be looked upon merely as technical prerequisites to greater freedom in trade and currency exchange. It is a good thing in itself for America to reduce its tariff barriers and to increase foreign investment for economic development.

Whether any action on such lines is likely in the near future is a question on which your guess is as good as mine. A substantial advance in United States foreign economic policy is by no means inconceivable. There is a danger, however, that the current improvement in the world's dollar balance, which may turn out to be short-lived, might reduce the political chances of getting some constructive action. As we all know, the foreign trade and investment policies of the United States are now in the melting pot. It would be a pity if the present favorable appearance of the world's dollar problem were to weaken the Randall report next March or compromise its fate in Congress.

All hopes for a better balance in foreign trade rest also, of course, on the assumption that no serious slump is allowed to develop in the United States. The promptness with which Washington seems to have reacted to the threat of a recession in recent months is encouraging. But it is wise to remember that nowadays a government or a party in power may feel that it cannot afford a slump, for obvious political reasons. Unfortunately, there are no similar political pressures working for an enlightened foreign economic policy. The best that can be hoped for is that an intelligent pursuit of the national interest will prevail.

6

Period Analysis
and Inventory Cycles

(1954)

A prominent feature of economic fluctuations in the United States is the part played by changes in inventory investment, i.e., in the net flow of goods into or out of commodity stocks held by the business system. These changes accounted on the average for 23 per cent of the changes in Gross National Product in the five upswings and for as much as 47 per cent in the five downswings that occurred during the twenty years between the wars.[1] In the period since the war the recessions of 1948–49 and 1953–54 have been strongly marked each time by a cutback in inventory investment. The quarterly data now available show that this accounted for practically the whole decrease in GNP from the fourth quarter of 1948 to the third quarter of 1949, and again from the second quarter of 1953 to the first quarter of 1954, according to the last figures reported.

Oxford Economic Papers, n.s., September 1954, by permission of the publisher.
[1] These percentages, computed from the Kuznets series of annual GNP at 1929 prices, are given in M. Abramovitz's *Inventories and Business Cycles* (National Bureau of Economic Research, New York, 1950).

The large share of inventory changes in the ups and downs of business activity cannot be explained without reference to the timing as well as the extent of the swings in inventory investment. If these swings occurred irregularly, their share in the fluctuations of aggregate output could easily turn out to be zero or even negative. In reality, net inventory investment fluctuates closely — more closely than we might perhaps expect — with the volume of activity (not with the rate of change in activity). As a rule, we find its maxima at or near the cyclical peaks in general business and its minima, usually in the form of disinvestment, at or near the troughs. After reaching its peak at the top of the boom, the rate of accumulation usually falls off, but continues positive for a while. Similarly, after the trough, decumulation tends to go on, though at a reduced rate, before investment becomes positive again in the later course of the upswing. This means that the total *stock* of goods lags substantially behind the peaks and troughs of the trade cycle. It is the *flow* of inventory investment that conforms to, and apparently in some sense dominates, the short-run ups and downs of productive activity.

These facts, clearly brought out by Abramovitz in his study of the interwar period, are characteristic of inventories and inventory investment as a whole. The pattern is very marked in the case of manufacturers' and traders' stocks, which constitute by far the greater part of the whole. Some minor segments, such as agricultural and mining stocks, diverge from the general movement. But even within the manufacturing field there is, needless to say, much diversity of behavior among different types of stocks and different industries. The chief aim of the Abramovitz study was to display and explain this diversity by means of data for some individual commodities.

The present paper takes the recurrent pattern of total inventory investment as its starting point and seeks very tentatively to confront it with a general hypothesis that might help in some degree to account for it, without, of course, contradicting the diversity found in particular commodity stocks. In this attempt some use is made of a simple form of period analysis which will be defended, more explicitly than before, by reference to certain technical conditions of production and trade, and which, finally, will be combined with a consideration of modern methods of "inventory control" increasingly used in American business. The reader will doubtless be aware of the limitations of macrodynamic analysis. The main concern of this paper is not simply to present a stylized model but to relate it to individual business motives and to the observed facts, though naturally nothing more than a sketch can here be given.[2]

II

Consider first the role of stocks of finished consumer goods held as a buffer to meet unexpected changes in sales. We abstract here from price changes, the possible alternative means of balancing supply and demand, and ignore for the moment the working stocks needed in the pipelines of production and trade. Our first approach is an adaptation of L. A. Metzler's well-known study,[3] which in turn was based in part on E. Lundberg's work.[4]

Let time be divided into unit periods the length of which is determined by the Output Lag, reflecting the time it takes to adjust the volume of output to a change in sales. Output decisions are assumed to be guided by the sales experience of the recent past. Hence production for sale (OC or output for consumption) in any unit period is equal to the amount sold (CE or consumer expenditure) in the preceding period: $OC_t = CE_{t-1}$. Businessmen take this to be their best guess, realizing, however, that it is only a guess and therefore holding stocks of finished goods. Any divergence of actual sales from this guess results in an un-

[2] What follows is in part a development of certain points I made incidentally in a review article dealing with Abramovitz's book, "The Cyclical Pattern of Inventory Investment," *Quarterly Journal of Economics,* August 1952, from which I retain in slightly modified form the three numerical examples shown below.

I have derived much benefit, however inadequately reflected here, from Professor J. R. Hicks's comments on a preliminary oral version of this paper given in Oxford in February 1954. At two or three points I have followed a suggestion by Professor W. J. Baumol. Throughout I owe a great deal to Mr. Alain Enthoven's expert assistance and lively interest in the subject. Professor J. S. Chipman has read the manuscript and offered some helpful observations.

[3] "The Nature and Stability of Inventory Cycles," *Review of Economic Statistics,* 1941.

[4] *Studies in the Theory of Economic Expansion* (London and New York, 1937).

planned inventory change, or passive inventory investment (VP), positive or negative. In any given period businessmen aim at reversing to some degree the unplanned inventory change of the preceding period, by stepping up output beyond, or letting it fall short of, the amount they expect to sell in the current period. The degree of reversal aimed at, α_1, which is our marginal inventory ratio or "accelerator," can be partial $(\alpha_1 < 1)$, full $(\alpha_1 = 1)$, or overfull $(\alpha_1 > 1)$, meaning in the last case that action is taken, not only to reverse all of the unplanned inventory change of the last period, but also to produce a further quantity, positive or negative, for stock so as to alter the volume of stocks in line with total output and sales. Output for inventory, OV (or active inventory investment, VA), in each period is therefore:

$$OV_t = \alpha_1(CE_{t-1} - OC_{t-1}),$$

the passive inventory change of the previous period having been

$$VP_{t-1} = OC_{t-1} - CE_{t-1}.$$

For the present we assume that there is no lag of consumer spending behind changes in income. Income earned, Y, is entirely disposed of within the same unit period for consumption or saving, any income change from one period to the next being divided between the two in accordance with the marginal spending ratio, β. The volume of consumer expenditure, or business sales, in any period is therefore $CE_t = \beta Y_t + k$, where k is a constant permitting the average spending ratio to differ from the marginal — an easy concession to realism — and dropping out whenever we deal with differences from period to period. Thus output for sale is

$$OC_t = CE_{t-1} = \beta Y_{t-1} + k. \tag{1}$$

The passive inventory change is $VP_{t-1} = \beta Y_{t-2} - \beta Y_{t-1}$, which gives rise to active inventory investment in the form of

$$OV_t = \alpha_1(\beta Y_{t-1} - \beta Y_{t-2}). \tag{2}$$

Total income created in each period will then originate from output for sale, output for stock, and "autonomous investment":

$$Y_t = \beta Y_{t-1} + \alpha_1(\beta Y_{t-1} - \beta Y_{t-2}) + I + k. \tag{3}$$

In an initial state of stability the second term, output for stock, is zero. The third, I, is taken to be a fixed magnitude subject to displacement for exogenous reasons. If now a once-over change occurs in I (which can represent government spending or foreign demand, as well as business plant and equipment outlays), this creates a change in income and hence an unexpected change in sales, met out of stocks. Although passive inventory investment does not enter into income produced in each period and does not figure explicitly in equation 3 above, it is nevertheless an element of causal significance and a source of change: so long as α_1 is greater than zero it determines from period to period the rate of active inventory investment. Production for stock as well as for increased sale is now undertaken; and so the system, in all likelihood, begins to oscillate.

With the "marginal" inventory accelerator in the sense indicated,[5] the stability conditions worked out by Samuelson and depicted in his familiar diagram (reproduced in *Readings in Business Cycle Theory*, p. 268) are directly applicable to this case, unlike Metzler's version (p. 126) based on the average inventory ratio, which perforce ignores the possible area of partial reversal and so contains nothing corresponding to Samuelson's Region A where combinations of small α's and large β's produce, not fluctuation, but a steady change in income asymptotically approaching the equilibrium level appropriate to the new rate of autonomous investment.

Net inventory investment realized (VR) in each period is the sum of active and passive inventory investment, viz.

$$VR_t = VA_t + VP_t = \alpha_1(\beta Y_{t-1} - \beta Y_{t-2}) + \beta Y_{t-1} - \beta Y_t. \quad (4)$$

Now from (3) and (4) it follows that

$$VR_t = Y_t - (\beta Y_t + k) - I = (1 - \beta)Y_t - I - k. \quad (5)$$

This formula implies that the peaks and troughs of realized inventory investment and of total income must of necessity coincide. If total income — that is, production — is our measure of the business cycle, as it surely must be, the cyclical conformity of inventory investment appears as quite inevitable. The formula is

[5] $\alpha_1 = \dfrac{OV_t}{CE_{t-1} - OC_{t-1}} = \dfrac{OV_t}{OC_t - OC_{t-1}}.$

indeed a tautology. It tells us that any difference between saving and autonomous investment is accounted for by inventory investment realized in each period. Saving must be at its peak when income is, and so must total investment be, but as autonomous investment is kept constant the gap has to be covered by inventory investment.

If we wish to look behind the scenes and see how this comes about, the accompanying numerical example may serve as an illustration. Active inventory investment conforms to the rate of change in output for sale, which tends to level off as income approaches its turning point. But the passive component of inventory investment (which is negative when sales are going up, positive when they are declining) is affected by the slackening of the rise or fall of demand in such a way as to drive the net amount of realized inventory investment to its maximum or minimum in the peak or trough period of the income series. Towards the end of the upswing, for example, the unexpected dispersal of goods due to rising sales is rapidly slowing down, so that on balance inventory investment is still going up even though planned accumulation is beginning to decline. In this way it is possible to interpret the observed cyclical pattern of inventory investment in terms that are familiar from common business experience: active and passive inventory changes (or whatever labels one chooses to use in place of these terms: e.g., planned and unplanned, desired and undesired). Moreover, the cycle of total inventory investment realized is seen to fall neatly into four phases: active accumulation in the boom, passive accumulation after the downturn, active decumulation later in the slump, and passive decumulation in the revival. These terms denote, however, only the predominant balance of forces in each phase and do not deny the presence of both components in varying degrees at all times during the cycle.

Despite the resemblances between the theoretical sketch and the observed pattern, we must keep in mind that the cyclical conformity of inventory investment in this model follows with absolute necessity from the assumptions made. The assumptions must be either relaxed or justified.

EFFECTS OF REVERSAL OF PASSIVE INVENTORY CHANGES

$(\alpha_1 = 1, \beta = 0.6, k = 300)$

Output of consumer goods		Autonomous investment I	Income produced Y $(OC + OV + I)$	Consumer spending CE $(\beta Y + k)$	Inventory investment		
For sale OC	For stock OV				Passive VP $(OC - CE)$	Active VA (OV)	Realized VR $(VP + VA)$
900	0	100	1,000	900	0	0	0
900	0	200	1,100	960	−60	0	−60
960	+60	200	1,220	1,032	−72	+60	−12
1,032	+72	200	1,304	1,082	−50	+72	+22
1,082	+50	200	1,332ª	1,099	−17	+50	+33ª
1,099	+17	200	1,316	1,089	+10	+17	+27
1,089	−10	200	1,279	1,067	+22	−10	+12
1,067	−22	200	1,245	1,047	+20	−22	−2
1,047	−20	200	1,227	1,036	+11	−20	−9
1,036	−11	200	1,225ᵇ	1,035	+1	−11	−10ᵇ
1,035	−1	200	1,234	1,040	−5	−1	−6
1,040	+5	200	1,245	1,047	−7	+5	−2
1,047	+7	200	1,254	1,052	−5	+7	+2
1,052	+5	200	1,257ª	1,054	−2	+5	+3ª
1,054	+2	200	1,256	1,053	+1	+2	+3
1,053	−1	200	1,252	1,051	+2	−1	+1
...	...	...	...	...	...	...	...

SOURCE: This is Metzler's Table 2 (p. 118), adapted in certain ways, especially so as to illustrate the movement of inventory *investment* and the interplay of active and passive changes that lies behind it.
ª Peak.   ᵇ Trough.

III

The first deficiency to repair is the neglect of pipeline inventories. It is true there is something to be said for starting, as we have done, with stocks of finished goods. They receive the first impact of unforeseen changes in demand; they are the object of the passive type of inventory change; they generally form, not an inert cushion, but a resilient buffer which, though it *absorbs* the impact temporarily, also *transmits* it through its influence on subsequent business action. But the more or less automatic changes in pipeline stocks that result from changes in the flow of finished output for sale *and* for stock cannot be left out of account. For they, too, contribute to changes in income and hence consumer expenditure, reacting on business stocks of finished goods. They must be counted as part of active inventory investment, in addition to output of finished goods for stock.

We now have a pipeline accelerator, α_2, riding, not alongside, but on the back of the previous buffer accelerator α_1 (both being interpreted in marginal terms, as the ratio of active inventory investment to the change in output for sale in the case of α_1 and in total finished output in the case of α_2). The two in combined operation are in general a more powerful source of oscillation than a single accelerator equal to their sum would be. The Samuelson stability conditions are not strictly applicable to this case. The income series is described, no longer by a second, but by a third-order difference equation, shown below. Analysis of its stability, a highly complicated matter, need not detain us as it is of little interest in this context. What concerns us is the interpretation of the cyclical oscillation of inventory investment, not the precise limits within which combinations of the coefficients will produce oscillation. These limits are wide enough to make oscillation appear as the normal case for practical purposes. Nor is the exact boundary between damped and ever-increasing oscillations of great importance, for it is obvious that the latter — and the former, too, for that matter — will in reality encounter constraints of one kind or another, such as monetary stringency or the full employment ceiling stressed by Hicks, and will not be left free to perform their antics in isolation.

The main point here is that even in the general case now considered, including goods in process in the broadest sense as well as stocks of finished goods, the cycle of inventory investment generated by the shift in exogenous investment will coincide with that of total income and production. This may at first seem surprising since the new element added — pipeline investment — varies of necessity with the rate of change in total output, turning down (or up) before the peak (or trough) of the income cycle, and might therefore be expected to produce a lead in the movement of total inventory investment. The absolute cyclical conformity obtained in this as in the previous case can be explained again by reference to the passive changes. If the active component is strengthened by the introduction of the pipeline factor, so is its income effect and hence the unforeseen demand reaction on stocks of final products. This rationalization may sound plausible enough, but the simple algebra of the model shows once more that the result — cyclical conformity of inventory investment — is an automatic outcome of our assumptions.

The added element, pipeline investment, is:

$$PL_t = \alpha_2[(OC_t + OV_t) - (OC_{t-1} + OV_{t-1})]$$
$$= \alpha_2[(1 + \alpha_1)\beta Y_{t-1} - (1 + 2\alpha_1)\beta Y_{t-2} + \alpha_1\beta Y_{t-3}], \quad (6)$$

using the definitions given earlier for OC and OV. This represents the input temporarily needed or released in the pipeline when the flow of finished output, for stock as well as for sale, expands or contracts. It cannot be properly represented by, or lumped together with, output of finished goods for stock, as Lundberg and Metzler have done. It must be included separately in the income equation:

$$Y_t = OC_t + OV_t + PL_t + I$$
$$= (1 + \alpha_1)(1 + \alpha_2)\beta Y_{t-1} - (\alpha_1 + \alpha_2 + 2\alpha_1\alpha_2)\beta Y_{t-2}$$
$$+ \alpha_1\alpha_2\beta Y_{t-3} + I + k. \quad (7)$$

This is obtained by inserting the expression (6) in the income equation used earlier (3). Here we have the troublesome third-order difference equation. It will, however, be swallowed up easily by our formula for total inventory investment realized, which is:

$$VR = VA + VP = OV + PL + VP;$$

$$VR_t = \alpha_1(\beta Y_{t-1} - \beta Y_{t-2}) + \alpha_2[(1 + \alpha_1)\beta Y_{t-1}$$
$$- (1 + 2\alpha_1)\beta Y_{t-2} + \alpha_1\beta Y_{t-3}] + \beta Y_{t-1} - \beta Y_t$$

$$= -\beta Y_t + (1 + \alpha_1)(1 + \alpha_2)\beta Y_{t-1}$$
$$- (\alpha_1 + \alpha_2 + 2\alpha_1\alpha_2)\beta Y_{t-2} + \alpha_1\alpha_2\beta Y_{t-3}. \quad (8)$$

As before, it follows from (7) and (8), when both sides of (7) are subtracted from (8), that

$$VR_t = Y_t - (\beta Y_t + k) - I = (1 - \beta)Y_t - I - k, \quad (5)$$

so here again the maxima and minima of income and accumulation must necessarily coincide.

The numerical illustration now brings in the pipeline factor

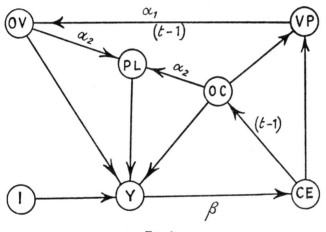

Fig. 1.

and is otherwise built up on the same lines as before. Here the value of the two accelerators, combined with the marginal spending ratio, happens to be large enough to produce, in response to the initial outside disturbance, fluctuations of increasing amplitude in total income and inventory investment. For our purposes, as explained, this feature of the illustration is of no particular concern or significance, but it is convenient in that it brings out the cyclical pattern more clearly than the previous example,

EFFECTS OF CHANGES IN PIPELINE STOCKS

$(\alpha_1 = 1, \alpha_2 = 0.5, \beta = 0.6, k = 300)$

Output of consumer goods			Pipeline stocks PL	Autonomous investment I	Income produced Y	Consumer spending CE	Inventory investment		
For sale OC	For stock OV	Total OT					Passive VP $(OC - CE)$	Active VA $(OV + PL)$	Realized VR $(VA + VP)$
900	0	900	0	100	1,000	900	0	0	0
900	0	900	0	200	1,100	960	-60	0	-60
960	+60	1,020	+60	200	1,280	1,068	-108	+120	+12
1,068	+108	1,176	+78	200	1,454	1,172	-104	+186	+82
1,172	+104	1,276	+50	200	1,526ᵃ	1,215	-43	+154	+111ᵃ
1,215	+43	1,258	-9	200	1,449	1,169	+46	+34	+80
1,169	-46	1,123	-67	200	1,256	1,053	+116	-113	+3
1,053	-116	937	-93	200	1,004	926	+127	-209	-82
926	-127	799	-69	200	930ᵇ	858	+68	-196	-128ᵇ
858	-68	790	-5	200	985	891	-33	-73	-106
891	+33	924	+67	200	1,191	1,015	-124	+100	-24
1,015	+124	1,139	+107	200	1,446	1,168	-153	+231	+78
1,168	+153	1,321	+91	200	1,612ᵃ	1,268	-100	+244	+144ᵃ
1,268	+100	1,368	+24	200	1,592	1,256	+12	+124	+136
1,256	-12	1,244	-62	200	1,382	1,130	+126	-74	+52
...	...	...	...	...	...	...	...	...	...

ᵃ Peak.   ᵇ Trough.

where the oscillation was strongly damped. In either case, the behavior of inventory investment and of its two components appears as a characteristic mode in which the business system reacts to major autonomous displacements.

Some readers might wish to refer also to the accompanying schematic representation of the relations discussed, which gives as it were a bird's-eye view of the system we have considered. It supplements both the algebraic formulation and the numerical example, using the same notation and marking the places where relations are lagged $(t - 1)$ or governed by the familiar coefficients.

IV

Before attempting to defend the output-lag construction which forms the basis of this model, and which will therefore be our major point of interest, we must briefly indicate how some of the other simplifications of this approach might possibly be justified.

1. By considering changes in the pipeline separately from changes in stocks of finished goods, we have reverted, in a way, to the distinction between "working capital" and "liquid stocks" which Keynes made in the *Treatise* and which ever since has led an uneasy but enduring existence, appearing recently in Hicks's *Contribution*. It cannot give full satisfaction without a framework of inventory analysis in which uncertainty, obstacles to output adjustment, and the other conditions making for passive as well as active movements find their place. While it is hard to define, to do without some such distinction seems harder still.[6] One difficulty arises from the fact that production is in reality divided into stages of manufacture and distribution, and is not, as the models imply, an integrated process. However, businessmen at each stage are not blind mice reacting to nothing but the orders coming in from the stage immediately in front. They see

---

[6] Observe Lundberg's effort to do without it in setting up (*Studies,* 200) a formula for inventory investment in which the replacement of finished stocks and the pipeline change are added together in a way that obscures the pipeline needs of output for stock as distinct from output for sale. Besides, his numerical example fails at one point to follow even his own formula and to recognize the possibility of disinvestment in the downward swing.

or try to see what goes on in the market at large and adjust their decisions accordingly. Thus the whole process is influenced by "judgements and situations that are likely . . . to synchronize for all sequential operations performed on a single major raw material." [7] As a result, the system is capable of behaving rather like an integrated process. Nevertheless, passive inventory changes and attempts at their reversal occur, of course, at other stages than final sale to consumers. The "suction" of growing demand in the upswing and the "backing up" of the output flow in the downswing can transmit themselves to intermediate products all along the line. But can these movements not be subsumed under the head of finished-goods inventories? The pipeline category will catch all "automatic" changes in working stocks due not simply to physical quantity but also to value added in the process. Within the business system a mere shift in stocks from stage to stage, though it may mean unplanned decumulation in one stage and planned accumulation in the other, cannot affect total net inventory investment realized, the magnitude that is to be explained. Only changes in final sales can alter the passive component of inventory investment without a simultaneous opposite change in the active component. That is why a precise separation of "liquid" and "working" stocks does not seem absolutely indispensable for present purposes.

2. Our treatment of autonomous investment is debatable. There is no denying that an increase in fixed installations can be met from unintended drafts on stocks, at least of intermediate products such as bricks, cement, and steel if, as is usual, the plant and equipment are built to order. The direct income effect of the increased fixed investment may thus partly get lost at first and later take a cyclical form itself because of inventory movements in the fixed investment sphere. This complication must here be ignored but does not seem fatal, especially when we remember the preponderant share of consumable output in the American economy, as well as the fact that our initial disturbance can come from other things than fixed investment (government spending or

---

[7] Ruth P. Mack, "The Process of Capital Formation in Inventories and the Vertical Propagation of Business Cycles," *Review of Economics and Statistics,* August 1953, 196, where this statement is supported by evidence from the leather and shoe industry.

exports, not to mention possible autonomous changes in consumer expenditure or even in inventory investment, as in the postwar restocking boom of 1946).

3. The assumption that adjustment through price changes does not occur is a sweeping simplification. Yet prices, especially of finished consumer goods, do tend to be sticky for various well-known reasons. Sooner or later they respond, of course, to any substantial and lasting change in market conditions. Under the pressure of inflationary or deflationary forces the whole price structure will give way; but in the short run it is not perfectly fluid, and that is all that matters for our purpose. Price adjustment may indeed prove ineffective in the short run, if it sets up expectations of further price change in the same direction. A price cut especially will "spoil the market" if expectations are elastic and buyers in consequence postpone rather than accelerate their purchases.

4. Uncertainty and imperfect foresight, an essential part of the story, will be readily accepted.[8] There would be no need for unintended inventory movements if producers could foresee all changes in demand far enough to be able to adjust their output in advance. The output lag would then be of no consequence. Actually such foresight does not and cannot exist. It is assumed that businessmen, for want of a better guide, decide on current output in the light of recent sales experience. But they recognize the fallibility of this or any other guide. At least in part, inventories of finished goods are, in J. M. Clark's phrase, a "child of uncertainty." They are held because it is felt impossible to forecast future sales accurately. This being so, unforeseen changes in demand give rise to inventory movements which, though tolerated, are in themselves unwanted, and are subject to subsequent reversal in some degree.

5. Any rise or fall in total productive activity affects income, and produces reactions on stocks of finished goods through changes — which individual businessmen cannot foresee — in consumer demand. This demand reaction is related to the mar-

---

[8] I have had the advantage of seeing a paper, as yet unpublished, by E. S. Mills on "Expectations, Uncertainty and Inventory Fluctuations," where this point, taken for granted here, is rigorously worked out. [*Review of Economic Studies,* XXII (1954–55), 15–22. Ed.]

ginal spending ratio (β). It is clear from the structure of the model as well as from the numerical examples that the total swing in net realized inventory investment from peak to trough or trough to peak (combined with the increase in autonomous investment in the initial upswing), when expressed as a fraction of the corresponding change in total income produced, inevitably reflects the marginal saving ratio $(1 - \beta)$. But the strength of the demand reaction need not be constant during the cycle, as we assumed. J. S. Duesenberry[9] and Franco Modigliani[10] have found the data to be consistent with the view that any fall in income creates a pressure on consumption habits, which is met to some extent by keeping up consumption at the expense of saving. The simplest, though admittedly not the best, way to take account of the cyclical irreversibility of the relation between income and consumption is to assume a lower marginal spending ratio in the downward than in the upward phases of the cycle: say, 0.5 in the former and 0.7 in the latter. As an automatic result, shifts in inventory investment (including the exogenous displacement in the opening phase) come to form a larger share in the downward (50 per cent) than in the upward (30 per cent) movements of total production — just the kind of asymmetry found in reality (see p. 105 above). Undoubtedly there are other explanations for the observed asymmetry. The lopsided demand reaction is an hypothesis that illustrates at any rate the working of our model, although it is probably not without some empirical significance. The Duesenberry–Modigliani "ratchet effect" is in itself a steadying influence in recessions, but we find that it tends to get lost through the leakage, which it facilitates, in the form of drastic cutbacks in business inventory investment.

V

We must now stop to give fuller consideration to the particular method here used of dividing time into discrete intervals. This is not entirely a formal and arbitrary device; it can be defended on

[9] *Income, Saving and the Theory of Consumer Behavior,* Harvard Economic Studies LXXXVII (Cambridge, Mass., 1950).

[10] "Fluctuations in the Saving Ratio: A Problem in Economic Forecasting," *Studies in Income and Wealth,* XI (National Bureau of Economic Research, New York, 1949).

substantive grounds. A constant output lag, uniform and coterminous in all firms and industries, is a violent simplification, but it stands as a representation of the relative stickiness that characterizes the adjustment of output to variations in demand. The assumption that there is some such lag, and that it is probably of substantial length when compared with the lag of consumer spending behind changes in income (which Robertson has used in a wider context of monetary analysis) is consistent with what we know about the cyclical pattern of inventory investment. But how strong is the assumption on its own legs? It is similar to that underlying the "cobweb theorem": reactions on the supply side are more or less delayed while those on the demand side are relatively quick, if not instantaneous.

The output lag may be said to arise from two sets of factors, psychological and technical. The psychological component, which may be called the "plan revision period," is the time that elapses between a change in the rate of sales and a change in producers' plans and decisions concerning the rate of output. Hicks (in *Value and Capital*) speaks of the time it takes for entrepreneurs "to wake up and change their plans." The necessary "wake-up time" enters into the plan revision period, but it is not all. Even a perfectly alert and informed seller will usually need "some time to assure himself that what has occurred was other than a random fluctuation in his sales volume. Presumably, the more erratic his . . . sales, the longer it takes him to sort out the genuine increase from a mere random fluctuation." [11] But this, too, cannot explain his behavior alone. We must explicitly bring out the assumption — often taken for granted — that changing the rate of output generally involves certain costs, subjective as well as objective. To this point we shall presently return.

The technical component of the lag, which we may call the "output-adjustment period" proper, is the time that must elapse until the decision is put into effect and the output change actually materializes. We need not and cannot list all the relevant factors. The time it takes for the "primary" products of the soil to be

---

[11] Gardner Ackley, "The Multiplier Time Period: Money, Inventories, and Flexibility," *American Economic Review,* June 1951, 357. Sec. II of this article contains a useful discussion of the output lag.

processed and distributed for final use — the "period of production" — is not necessarily one of them. The idea of working capital having to be built "from the bottom up," so that any adjustment of finished output to a rise in demand cannot be completed before a lapse of time equal to the "production period," loses its cogency as soon as it is recognized that reserve stocks of intermediate products are likely to exist at the various stages so that a production increase can set in simultaneously and uniformly in all stages. Such reserve stocks are desired and widely held by businessmen precisely as means to flexibility in output flow.[12] The output adjustment period therefore may be quite independent of the production period (though when reserve stocks are insufficient this factor may still become operative in upward — not downward — changes). It is in the main a matter of altering production schedules, including, for example, labor, transport, and distribution arrangements.

Both plan revision and output adjustment thus tend to cause some delay. But when this is conceded, it is still not clear why the output response should be discontinuous instead of, as it well might be, gradual and continuous. The assumption of discontinuity rests on the presence of costs of altering the volume of output: "setup costs," as we shall call them, using in a wider sense a term current in American business parlance. Here we encounter a general reason why firms are likely to be unwilling, even if they were able, to alter production except at discrete intervals, and why the most wide-awake management will not even try to adjust output continually to changes in sales.

The problem of setup costs may be tackled by means of a formula used in distribution, but basically applicable also to manufacturing.[13] A trader wishing to minimize his carrying and procurement costs combined will have to balance one against the

---

[12] *Ibid.*

[13] The formula has appeared in many versions in business journals ever since the 1920's. T. M. Whitin presents it very instructively in his paper "Inventory Control in Theory and Practice," *Quarterly Journal of Economics,* November 1952, and in slightly modified form in his book, *The Theory of Inventory Management* (Princeton, 1953), 32f. Whitin concentrates, however, on the square-root relationship of sales to inventories, which we will discuss later, and does not bring out the particular implications of the formula that concern us here.

other. Small but frequent purchases may save him carrying charges on inventory but will cause him greater procurement costs; by purchasing larger quantities less often he saves on procurement but increases his carrying costs. If carrying charges (R) are a constant percentage of inventory, and procurement costs (S) a fixed amount per purchase regardless of its size, the optimum purchase quantity (Q) is that which minimizes the sum of annual carrying charges ($\frac{1}{2}QR$, since $\frac{1}{2}Q$ is the average inventory held) and annual procurement costs ($(T/Q)S$, where T is the annual sales volume or "turnover" and T/Q the annual number of procurement transactions). Differentiating $\frac{1}{2}QR + (T/Q)S$ with respect to Q and setting the derivative equal to zero, we get:

$$Q = \sqrt{\left(\frac{2ST}{R}\right)}.$$

The purchase interval, measured, as a fraction of a year, by Q/T, is seen to be relatively sticky, varying, not in direct proportion, but with the square root of S. (Variations in annual sales volume, T, will affect the interval also, but much less, since they enter directly into the denominator of the fraction as well.) What happens, however, if procurement costs disappear, so that S is reduced to zero? The procurement interval, too, becomes zero. The practical meaning of this is that the trader goes in for continuous hand-to-mouth buying, synchronized as far as possible with his sales. Though the same simple version of the formula is not literally applicable to manufacturing, it is easy to see that for a manufacturer faced with a varying sales volume the practical outcome of zero setup costs is, similarly, hand-to-mouth output in response to all variations in sales.

The square-root relation between Q and T will concern us later, while the inverse one of Q and R is too familiar to require comment. It is just worth noting that the unit period implicit in this formula will tend to be shortened by a rise and lengthened by a fall in carrying charges.

This formula makes no allowance for "depletion costs," incurred (e.g., through loss of good will) when stocks run out and customers cannot be immediately supplied. Strictly interpreted, it implies certainty about future sales, so that depletion costs need not arise at all. In reality, the possibility of actual sales diverging from the expected is always recognized and leads firms to hold reserve stocks of finished stocks. Uncertainty is one reason for holding stocks, but evidently not the most fundamental. Even with perfect foresight, inventories of finished goods, quite apart from goods in process, will arise from the inevitable costs and diseconomies of output variation. In the absence of uncertainty, the *precautionary* motive for stockholding drops out, but there still remains what can be classed as a *transactions* motive, the consequence of setup costs. If such costs did not exist, it would be at least conceivable that output could be adjusted instantly to any change in demand, however unexpected. Uncertainty and setup costs in combination create both the passive inventory movements and the discrete output adjustments featured in the model, the former being tolerated within a range set largely by the latter.

The adjustment interval that arises from setup costs applies to total output, for stock as well as for current sale. When the producer decides to change his rate of output, he will naturally take account of what he wants to do about his inventory as well as how much he has been selling and is expecting to sell. (Besides, we should remember that in reality a firm in one stage may be selling to the next stage, for both resale and stock replacement there.) If the output-lag construction has any validity at all, it applies to the two decisions being taken together. In the presence of setup costs it would be unreasonable to suppose that output is adjusted at certain times in the light of changes in sales alone and at other times with an eye to the inventory position alone.[14]

What can be said about setup costs? In this paper, very little. The subject is a big one and almost unexplored. A few remarks must here suffice. The higher the cost of output variation, the

[14] It seems therefore a little too pessimistic to say that in the theoretical-sequence mechanism the reversal of unintended inventory changes "does not have any very determinate time-shape," to quote J. R. Hicks, *Contribution to the Theory of the Trade Cycle* (London, 1950), 49, and "cannot be definitely located as to time" (Lundberg, *Studies,* 108). Lundberg himself answers his initial doubt when he writes later (199) that "decisions concerning the replacement of and addition to stocks . . . are part of the plans of an entrepreneur when he determines the volume of production."

greater the length of the unit period. A constant S, independent of the extent of the output change, is doubtless unrealistic as a general assumption, though some components of S may well remain fixed. Perhaps the most acceptable simple formula would be:

$$S = b + c|OT_t - OT_{t-1}|,$$

where b represents those elements that do stay fixed while the second term, in which c is a constant and OT is total output (for stock as well as for current sale), covers those that vary in proportion to the size of the output change.[15] For the moment we take S to be independent of whether the change is up or down, but we shall find that this is likely to make a difference.

No doubt the importance of setup costs varies. For instance, in shoe manufacturing they seem to be relatively low, in newsprint production relatively high. But generally they are a fairly significant factor under modern conditions of large-scale organization and mass production. They must be sharply separated from the changes in average production cost that ensue from changes in the volume of output. They include all the well-known diseconomies of output variation. They account for the desire of business firms to stabilize their activity; without steady operation some of the advantages of large-scale production are lost. They may include subjective costs which managers endure when there is frequent need for major output decisions or when the mental comfort that comes from a smoothly running plant is disturbed. In more objective forms they commonly arise from the hiring and training of labor, from readapting machinery, tooling up, rearranging assembly lines, and possibly from loss of output when plant has to be shut down to permit these things to be done.

We live here in the Marshallian short period, with a given stock of equipment. We may or may not share the view that monopolistic competition creates widespread excess capacity. Reserve capacity, however, does generally exist. Plants are typically built for a fluctuating world and deliberately endowed with some flexi-

---

[15] W. J. Baumol suggests a similar formula for an analogous problem in "The Transactions Demand for Cash: An Inventory Theoretic Approach," *Quarterly Journal of Economics*, November 1952, 546.

bility, so that output from the given equipment is capable of fairly wide variation.[16]

The cost of output variation is likely to depend to some extent on the direction of the change. For fairly obvious reasons (e.g., recruitment and release of personnel) the cost may generally be less when the change is a decrease than when it is an expansion of output. The conjecture that the output lag tends therefore to be shorter in the downward than in the upward swings of business fluctuations is in accord with the fact, observable at least since 1929, that the phase of what we have called "passive accumulation" after the downturn is usually shorter and less prominent than that of "passive decumulation" in the revival.[17] This asymmetry is not unnatural when we think of setup costs and of the other possible determinants of the output lag. The technical component of the lag is likely to be unsymmetrical: to stop a plant takes less time than to set it going again. We should also remember that the "period of production" from the primary to the final stages operates, if at all, unsymmetrically: it can for a while hold back an increase in finished output; it cannot delay a decrease.

The psychological component, too, is apt to work unevenly. If a firm cannot meet an increase in demand, it misses a business opportunity and incurs depletion costs; whereas an involuntary accumulation of unsold goods entails a loss of liquidity — absorption of cash reserves or resort to bank credit — at the very time when liquidity is most desired. Once liquidity is impaired and

---

[16] The point could be illustrated by a diagram (such as that first shown by George Stigler in the *Journal of Political Economy*, 1939, 317, and recently used in W. J. Baumol's *Economic Dynamics*, New York, 1952, 91) comparing the average cost curves of two plants. One curve is steeply U-shaped, the other more like a shallow bowl. One plant is the cheaper producer within a certain range at and near the point of minimum average cost; the other is better for all output levels on either side of that range. The latter is in this sense more flexible: output can be varied widely without big changes in average cost. But here too it is possible and indeed probable that output cannot be varied without incurring set-up costs. Another attribute, therefore, of a flexible plant is cheapness of output variation. This is perhaps less easily combined with large-scale operation and, above all, is not necessarily related in any particular way to the shape of the average cost curve as conceived in the usual comparative statics terms.

[17] Cf. my remarks in *Quarterly Journal of Economics*, August 1952, 404–406.

this becomes evident to outsiders, the firm's survival itself may come to be threatened if creditors press for payment, suppliers insist on cash, and bankers become difficult. Hence the importance that attaches to the orthodox prescription of easy credit after the downturn. An elastic credit or a liquid business system is one of the more general assumptions of the preceding sequence analysis. In this respect a phase of involuntary accumulation presents some peculiar difficulties in practice.

Once the underlying rationale of our period construction has been considered, it is not surprising to see — as I think we can see — that the output lag is more conspicuous in reality than the lag of expenditure behind income changes. In either case it is the transmission of changes that matters. Just as the production period need not be the main factor in the lag between sales and output, so the income payment period does not necessarily determine the interval that elapses between a change in disposable income and the subsequent change in consumer spending. In both cases this is so because there exist reserve stocks — of goods in the one, of cash in the other.[18] Besides, even if the income period were an effective determinant, a significant lag could arise only from the interval between corporate profits and dividend payments. But changes in profits are usually mirrored in the movement of Stock Exchange values, which in turn can quickly affect consumer outlay.

While the average lag between business sales and changes in output may be of the order of between three and six months, the consumer expenditure lag is almost certainly less than three months: quarterly figures do not reveal it.[19] This seems perfectly natural in view of the technical factors. The costs, delays, and inconveniences involved in altering the rate of production play a significant part in the relation of business sales and output. There is nothing quite like it on the income–expenditure side.

[18] Ackley, 359.
[19] L. A. Metzler, "Factors Governing the Length of Inventory Cycles," *Review of Economic Statistics,* February 1947, 11–12, and "Three Lags in the Flow of Income," in *Income, Employment and Public Policy,* Essays in Honor of Alvin H. Hansen (New York, 1948), 25–28. The Duesenberry-Modigliani "ratchet effect" might be thought of as providing evidence of a marked consumption lag in recessions, but strictly interpreted it concerns the extent, and not the speed, of consumer reactions to income changes.

We cannot go into the empirical evidence, but it is worth noting that the observed pattern of inventory investment itself tends to confirm this view as to the comparative importance of the two lags. As we have seen, a model sequence based on the output lag, assuming the expenditure lag to be relatively short or nonexistent, produces cycles of inventory investment rather similar to those observed. A sequence based, however, on the expenditure lag, assuming the output lag to be short or zero, yields inventory investment cycles that differ systematically from the observed pattern. On the latter assumption we have:

$$OC_t = CE_t = \beta Y_{t-1} + k, \tag{9}$$

meaning that output adjusts itself within the same period to consumer spending, which now, unlike (1) above, reflects the income of the preceding period with β and k as before. Because of the immediate adaptation of output to changes in sales, inventory investment can here occur, not in finished goods, but only through changes in pipeline stocks:

$$VR_t = PL_t = \alpha_2(\beta Y_{t-1} - \beta Y_{t-2}). \tag{10}$$

Income is the sum of consumable output, pipeline change, and autonomous investment:

$$Y_t = \beta Y_{t-1} + \alpha_2(\beta Y_{t-1} - \beta Y_{t-2}) + I + k. \tag{11}$$

From (10) and (11) we see that

$$VR_t = Y_t - \beta Y_{t-1} - I - k, \tag{12}$$

and this will generally lead Y_t. The cyclical conformity is broken.

The income equation (11) is identical with (3) above, except that the accelerator is α_2 instead of α_1. Giving α_2 the same value as the α_1 in our first example (p. 107), we show below a numerical sequence to illustrate the expenditure lag. The income series in this illustration, like the income equation, is the same as before, which is not surprising since we have merely replaced one kind of lag by another. The mechanism that lies behind it is different — and so is the behavior of inventory investment, which now shows its peaks and troughs before the cyclical turning-points of total production. No such persistent lead is found in actual fact. Since inventory investment now does not follow the observed pattern, while earlier it did, this furnishes at least a pointer as to which lag is the more important in practice. The comparison does not provide independent proof that the output lag is a good assumption. It does tend to throw doubt on its chief competitor, the expenditure lag. The latter may still have its uses, however, in other departments of dynamic theory.

The period analysis based on the output lag is designed here for the study of inventory investment. It cannot possibly apply to induced investment in fixed capital. Any lag that may exist in fixed investment behind changes in output arises from quite separate causes and will therefore be essentially different. The same unit period, if it is to be more than a purely formal and arbitrary

EFFECTS OF EXPENDITURE LAG AND IMMEDIATE OUTPUT ADJUSTMENT
$(\alpha = 1, \beta = 0.6, k = 300)$

Consumable output OC	Pipeline change PL	Autonomous investment I	Income produced Y	Consumer spending CE
900	0	100	1,000	900
900	0	200	1,100	900
960	+60	200	1,220	960
1,032	+72	200	1,304	1,032
1,082	+50	200	1,332[a]	1,082
1,099	+17	200	1,316	1,099
1,089	−10	200	1,279	1,089
1,067	−22	200	1,245	1,067
1,047	−20	200	1,227	1,047
1,036	−11	200	1,225	1,036
1,035	−1	200	1,234	1,035
1,040	+5	200	1,245	1,040
1,047	+7	200	1,254	1,047
1,052	+5	200	1,257[a]	1,052
1,054	+2	200	1,256	1,054
1,053	−1	200	1,252	1,053
...	...	...	...	...

[a] Peak. [b] Trough.

time division, cannot serve both purposes. We have treated fixed investment as autonomous. In fact, aside from the possibility that

Economic Essays

it may itself be swayed by the inventory cycle, it will be subject
to fluctuations of its own. The inventory cycle might perhaps be
superimposed on the fixed investment cycle by some device like
the ingenious one which Hicks uses for combining induced investment in fixed capital with fluctuations in autonomous investment
(*Contribution to the Theory of the Trade Cycle*, pp. 197–199).
But this interesting track cannot be pursued within the limits of
the present sketch.

VI

There remains the accelerator. We have departed from the
usual approach by using a constant *marginal* inventory ratio, for
finished as well as working stocks. The assumption of a constant
average ratio between total inventories and sales or output is
clearly unrealistic. The overall ratio is in fact very far from
constant, varying inversely with the level of activity.[20] Is there
any reason to think of the marginal ratio as being more stable?

The statistical relation between business stocks and sales, when
plotted on a scatter diagram with stocks measured on the vertical
and sales on the horizontal axis, usually produces a gently upward sloping regression line pointing to a positive intercept on
the vertical axis.[21] This is just another expression of the systematic inverse variation of the over-all inventory ratio in the
course of business fluctuations. The fact that a straight line gives
a fairly good fit might at once be taken to justify our assumption
of constant marginal inventory ratios. But the statistical picture
does not truly represent the "inventory function" we are seeking.
In the latter the amount of stocks *desired* by businessmen is
related to varying output levels. In the former the passive type
of change also plays a part. Inventories are generally smaller in
the upswing and larger in the downswing than businessmen want
them to be. In effect, the least-squares regression line fitted to

[20] Abramovitz, ch. 6. See also *Survey of Current Business,* April 1949. The
statement is broadly true not only of manufacturing but of business inventories
as a whole, according to the Kuznets estimates for total inventories and Gross
Commodity Product valued at constant prices, for the period 1919–1938.

[21] Such graphs have appeared from time to time in the *Survey of Current
Business,* e.g., September 1942, October 1946, May 1948, May 1953 (though in
some cases allowance must be made for draftsmen's tricks of scale).

the observations is deflected from the true inventory function in a clockwise direction, in a way analogous to the deflection which Hicks assumes for the consumption function in the *Trade Cycle* (p. 34).

The flatness of the regression line is not, however, entirely due to unplanned inventory movements, but undoubtedly reflects in large measure what businessmen want. It seems practically certain that the inventory desired increases in general much less than in proportion to output and sales. There are statistical indications to confirm this. As T. M. Whitin points out in his paper (pp. 518–519), the inverse movement of the stock-sales ratio with variations in sales appears not only over time but also in simultaneous comparisons between firms of different size,[22] all (presumably) affected more or less equally by the passive type of inventory change.

Yet it must be admitted that for want of conclusive statistical proof our main evidence about the probable shape of the aggregate inventory function is the relation which we think firms *ought* to pursue. And this, it seems, is a square-root relationship. The stock of inventories needed for most purposes varies with the square root of sales. This appeared from the formula for the optimum purchase quantity, $Q = \sqrt{(2ST/R)}$, of which we discussed earlier some implications with regard to period analysis. The size of the trader's inventory depends directly on Q, which in turn depends on the square root of T, his turnover. Inventories in this case are held for a purely transactions motive; yet they are evidently subject to substantial economies of scale. The square-root relationship emerges in essentially the same way from the calculation of optimum "lot sizes" in manufacturing. Moreover, the size of reserve stocks — or, in American business usage, "safety allowances" — needed as buffers against unforeseen changes in demand, is also found, on probability grounds, to vary with the square root of expected demand.[23] In short, the square-root relationship applies to precautionary as well as transactions motives of holding stocks.

From all this it seems to follow that the true inventory func-

---

[22] *Survey of Current Business,* June 1948 and April 1949.
[23] See Whitin, ch. 3.

tion is in general something like the parabolic curve shown below. It is clear at a glance that this tends to justify the use of constant marginal accelerators in our model sequences. The marginal inventory–output ratio as measured by the slope of the tangent to the curve at any point can remain practically, though of course not absolutely, constant over wide stretches of the curve, while the average ratio, measured by the angle of the vector from the origin to any given point on the curve, must undergo considerable changes as the volume of output is varied. In these circumstances the constant marginal ratio, though not by any means ideal, is likely to be a far better approximation than constancy

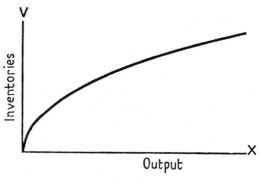

Fig. 2.

of the average proportion of total stocks to total sales or output. A constant average necessarily implies a constant marginal ratio as well, but the reverse is not true. A constant marginal ratio over the relevant range, quite compatible with an average ratio varying widely and inversely with output, is therefore a less restrictive as well as a more plausible assumption; and it is all we need for studying the flow of inventory investment as distinct from the stock of inventories.

We should bear in mind, however, that this parabolic curve represents a timeless, functional relationship between aggregates. If we wish to interpret it strictly for purposes of period analysis, we are faced with the need to distinguish between "liquid" and "working" stocks, remembering that in the former case, unlike the latter, the accelerator must cover production not only for additions to stock but also for replacement of passive changes. In terms of the timeless parabola it must be thought of, not simply as the ratio of a change in stocks to the corresponding change in output, but as that *plus* one:

$$\alpha_1 = 1 + \frac{\Delta V}{\Delta X}.$$

The accelerator, therefore, is not nearly as weak as the flatness of the inventory function in the higher output ranges might suggest.

American business managers have been finding that, for objective technical and "actuarial" reasons, a higher level of activity can be comfortably supported with a lower average inventory ratio. This has been partly a result of "inventory controls" introduced by scientific management experts and engineers in business, applying standard formulas with such modifications as special conditions may demand. One hears of big corporations retaining the services of individual business economists for designing inventory control systems suited to their needs, or purchasing such systems ready-made. Thus R. H. Wilson has attracted attention with the "Wilson Inventory Management Plan" which, as Whitin reports in his book (p. 208), has been purchased by the General Foods Corporation and the Westinghouse Electric Corporation, and is being operated by these companies to their satisfaction. There has been a spate of business literature on the subject ever since the 1920's but especially since the last war, ably summarized and discussed in Whitin's book. The question is essentially one of business engineering or, to use the German term, *Betriebswirtschaftslehre*. It is hard to find out what firms really want in regard to their stocks, which no doubt are sometimes affected by decisions that do not directly or consciously bear upon inventories at all.[24] But at least we know broadly what the scientific control methods recommend and what, therefore, business men "should" want to do about their inventories.

[24] Ruth P. Mack has stressed this point in an interesting way in her paper (above, n. 7).

VII

In one way the parabolic inventory function might be regarded as a steadying influence, compared with the pursuit of a constant over-all ratio. If, for example, the coefficients happen to be such that from a low initial output level the system begins to explode, this upsurge itself will tend to reduce the acceleration coefficient so that the system may after all settle down in a region of damped oscillation! Nevertheless, modern inventory management may be destabilizing in a more serious sense. It renders the economy highly sensitive to unplanned inventory changes. It makes for prompt reversal of such changes, *plus* generally something in addition to mere reversal. The action is becoming more and more automatic, responding quickly to built-in signals, instead of depending on the exercise of human judgment which even in the United States, and even with a constant over-all ratio as its main rule of thumb, is normally somewhat sluggish.

This type of inventory management is several stages removed from a stabilizing buffer-stock behavior. It implies $\alpha_1 > 1$; that is, more than simple replacement, which is the case when $\alpha_1 = 1$; much more than the neutral case $\alpha_1 = 0$, where firms may attempt, with a lag, to adjust output to changes in sales but pay no attention to their passive inventory movements. In this notation the deliberate buffer-stock principle would formally appear as $\alpha_1 = -1$: as sales, and hence output for sale, decline, output for stock is increased. But in this last case the previous framework of period analysis no longer has any real meaning.

In short, the spread of scientific methods of inventory control does not necessarily make for greater stability in United States economy; perhaps rather the reverse. And yet the inventory cycles we have considered arise only from technical needs of production and trade. They are, in Metzler's terms,[25] structural as opposed to speculative oscillations.

Speculation has not entered into our sketch at all. It is an exciting thing that easily attracts attention, but only occasionally

[25] *Conference on Business Cycles* (National Bureau of Economic Research, New York, 1951), 326.

does it take on a major role, accentuating movements set on foot by other forces. In his study covering the interwar period, Abramovitz, after some consideration, proceeds on the assumption that "price speculation is not a regular influence of great importance" and that "it may be neglected in seeking a first approximation to an explanation of inventory movements" (pp. 128–131). When it does come in, it tends to concentrate on primary products. A policy of "counterspeculation" through buffer stocks of basic materials is not to be despised. But it would not eliminate the structural inventory cycle. This can be sufficiently troublesome even without the added disturbance of speculation. The American inventory recessions of 1948–49 and 1953–54 can hardly be viewed as the aftermath of speculative excesses. Price speculation did loom large in the Korean crisis of 1950–51, but it soon petered out, partly under the influence of government controls.

The unruffled behavior of fixed investment in the United States has been remarkable both in 1948–49 and in 1953–54.[26] And yet the cycle of inventory investment goes on, giving us the jitters from time to time. No doubt something could and perhaps should be done to reduce its amplitude or to soften its effects, at home and abroad; for it does create instability. But this is no place to enter into policy considerations. Although we need not accept it as sacrosanct, there seems nothing pathological about this type of inventory cycle. In the light of the preceding conjectures it strikes one as something like the breathing of a giant in vigorous activity.

[26] Up to mid-1954, at any rate.

7

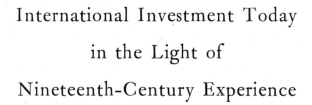

International Investment Today

in the Light of

Nineteenth-Century Experience

(1954)

To many Americans today the problem of international investment is doubtless a source of perplexity and even of some irrita-
tion. Ever since the last World War great expectations have been
placed on the export of private American capital as a means of
bridging the dollar gap as well as financing world economic
development. In reality, private foreign investment throughout
the period since 1945 has fluctuated at a low level and without
any sign at all of an upward trend.[1] This is most disappointing.
We suspect that the export of capital from Great Britain was one
reason why the international economy of the Victorian era did
not know of a chronic sterling shortage. We recognize, above

The Economic Journal, December 1954, by permission of the publisher.
[1] See *Federal Reserve Bulletin,* October 1953, 1039–1042.

all, that foreign investment was associated during that era with a tremendous spurt in world production and trade. There is in America a feeling of nostalgia for the nineteenth-century environment that made this flow of capital possible. The question is: why can we not re-create that environment?

The answer, I submit, must start from the fact that the circumstances in which overseas investment, and more especially British investment, went on in the nineteenth century (which I take to have ended in 1914) were in some ways quite exceptional. To realize this is of more than historical interest. So long as the peculiar features of that experience are not fully appreciated, memories of wonders worked by foreign investment in the past can only lead to false hopes and frustration.

Recent researches have made it possible to estimate approximately the percentage share of her national income that Britain used to lend abroad. Occasionally one finds the same proportions being applied to the present American national income as an indication of what the United States could or should do. Over the fifty years that preceded the outbreak of the First World War, it seems that Great Britain invested overseas an amount equal to about 4 per cent of her national income. In the later part of the period (1905–1913) the ratio was as high as 7 per cent. If the United States today were to devote similar percentage portions of her national income to the same purposes, she would be exporting funds to the tune of $12 billion or, if we apply the higher percentage, some $20 billion each year. These figures are almost absurdly large and tend to confirm the view that there was something unique about Britain's foreign investment.

It was unique in that the greater part of it — roughly two thirds — went to the so-called "regions of recent settlement": the spacious, fertile, and virtually empty plains of Canada, the United States, Argentina, Australia, and other "new" countries in the world's temperate latitudes. It was unique in that it went to these places together with a great migration of about sixty million people,[2] including many trained and enterprising persons, from the British Isles as well as Continental Europe. The conditions that made this flow of private capital possible do

[2] This is a gross figure; some of the migrants returned.

not exist to any great extent today, and probably cannot be re-created.

It was in the newly settled regions, which received two thirds of the capital exports and practically all the emigrants, that nineteenth-century international investment scored its greatest triumphs. The remaining third of British capital exported (or more accurately a quarter, since some went to Continental Europe) was employed in a different type of area, where its achievements were much more dubious: tropical or subtropical regions inhabited, often densely, by native populations endowed in some cases with ancient civilizations of their own. The areas that formed a minor field for overseas investment before 1914 are the major problem today: the truly backward economies, containing now about two thirds of the world's population. The empty and newly settled regions, from which international investment derived its brilliant general record and reputation, are today, in per capita income, among the most prosperous countries in the world.

Labor and capital are complementary factors of production, and exert a profound attraction on each other. The movement of labor to the new regions attracted capital to the same places at the same time. And the other way round: the flow of capital stimulated the migration of people to these places. To some extent, it is true, the parallel movements of capital and labor might plausibly be interpreted as two separate effects of a common cause; namely, of the opening up of the vast reserves of land and other natural resources. But the complementary nature of the labor and capital movements, based on the complementarity of the two factors, is equally plain. Any barrier to the transfer of one would have reduced the flow of the other. Labor and capital moved along side by side, supporting each other.[3]

In the twentieth century the situation is totally different. The capital exports from the United States can be viewed rather as a *substitute* for the movement of people. Capital and labor

[3] It is interesting to observe that the parallel nature of the two factor movements shows itself also, according to Professor A. K. Cairncross, in *Home and Foreign Investment, 1870–1913* (Cambridge, Eng., 1953), 209, in the close agreement with which capital exports and emigration from Britain varied from decade to decade between 1870 and 1910.

are still complementary, and still basically attract one another. But as things now are, restricting the movement of labor in one direction increases the need, if not the incentive, for capital to move in the opposite direction. Cheap labor, instead of being allowed to come to the United States to work with American capital there, is to some extent supplied with American capital abroad (supplied by the American government as in the years since 1945, if not by private profit-seeking investors, as in the 1920's). The underlying pressure — not necessarily the profit motive, but what we might call the global social pressure — is very strong for more capital to move out from the United States to work with the cheap labor in the world's backward economies. But notice that in this situation, in sharp contrast to the predominant nineteenth-century pattern, capital is being urged to go out to work with people that have not grown up in a capital-minded milieu, and may not be culturally prepared for the use of western equipment, methods, and techniques.

With this situation in mind, we can perceive what I think is the basic rationale of the present American emphasis on direct business investment as a means of financing economic development. The advantages rightly attributed to it are, first, that it goes out with American enterprise, tied up with American "know-how," and, secondly, that it is likely to be productively used, not swallowed up — directly or indirectly — by immediate consumption in the receiving country. Since, however, in the low-income areas the domestic market is small, this type of investment tends inevitably in such areas to concentrate on extractive industries — mines, plantations, oil wells — producing raw materials for export mainly to the advanced countries. This is, in effect, the so-called "colonial" pattern of foreign investment, of which American oil operations abroad are now an outstanding example. It has its drawbacks as well as its virtues. But, in any event, the stress laid — even in the original Point Four program — on direct investments in economically backward countries should not, in my opinion, be dismissed as merely a product of conservative business ideology; it reflects in part an essential difference in the present-day environment of international investment as compared with the nineteenth century.

In the aggregate flow of capital in the nineteenth century, the "colonial" type of venture played a minor role. Looking at Britain's foreign investment portfolio in 1913, we find that, of an estimated total of about £3,700 million outstanding at that time in nominal value, 30 per cent was in loans to governments, as much as 40 per cent in railway securities and some 5 per cent in other public utilities, so that no less than three quarters of the total was in public or public-utility investments. The rest includes banking, insurance and manufacturing companies, as well as investments directly in raw-material extraction. The total should be increased by making some allowance (say, £300 million) for private holdings and participations not represented by securities listed on the London Stock Exchange; but that would make little difference to the proportions indicated. It is therefore far from correct to assume, as is sometimes done, that the "colonial" form of enterprise in the extraction of mineral and plantation products for the creditor country was the typical pattern of foreign investment. To call it the "traditional" pattern might be justified in view of its history in earlier centuries. But in the nineteenth century its total amount was comparatively small; and what little there was of it appears to have been concentrated, as one would expect, in colonial and predominantly tropical areas.

To the new countries, by contrast, capital moved chiefly through the medium of securities carrying a fixed return (i.e., bonds and preference shares) issued by public authorities and public-utility undertakings. To these countries, it appears, capital could safely be sent in the form of relatively untied funds, with a good chance that it would remain capital there, because the people in these places, having come from Europe themselves, knew what to do with capital and how to handle it. Cultural adaptation was no problem.

These countries — the "regions of recent settlement" that absorbed the bulk of British overseas investment — were offshoots of European civilization.[4] For Britain, or at any rate for

---

[4] The precise composition of this group may give rise to some debate, though essentially the line is clear. It takes in Canada, the United States, Australia, New Zealand, and South Africa. In South America it certainly includes Argen-

Europe as a whole, investment in these areas was essentially a process of capital widening rather than deepening. Indeed, when Britain sent capital out to work with Swedes, Poles, Germans and Italians emigrating overseas, she may have done so at the expense of the deepening which her own economy is said to have needed in the period just before the First World War. But international investment in the nineteenth century was, of course, unplanned, and was determined by private rather than national advantages. French and German activities in Eastern Europe and the Near East were an exception in this respect. As Professor Viner has remarked, "the French loans to Russia . . . bore a close resemblance to the programme of military aid to Western Europe which we are now embarking on." [5]

Great Britain's national advantage, apart from the return flow of interest and dividends, seemed to be handsomely served through cheaper food and raw materials, though this benefit was shared by other importing countries that had made no corresponding investments and, besides, as we now realize, was derived in part from *Raubwirtschaft,* through soil depletion and erosion in some of the rich new plains (for example, in the virgin grasslands of the Mississippi valley).

Production of primary commodities for export to the industrial creditor countries is characteristic of the "colonial" pattern of direct investment in economically backward areas. In the regions of recent settlement foreign investment can also be said to have been induced essentially by the raw-material needs of the industrial centers — especially by Great Britain's demand for the wheat, wool, meat and dairy products, which she decided not to try to produce for herself, and which these temperate regions were particularly well suited to produce. The capital that came into these regions did not, however, enter into primary production

tina and Uruguay, rich farm and grazing lands in temperate latitudes settled predominantly by recent immigration from Europe. I would perhaps include also the southern tip of Brazil, to which the same description largely applies, and in which most of Brazil's productive capacity, including immigration as well as foreign capital, has been concentrated since the middle of the nineteenth century.

[5] "America's Aims and the Progress of Underdeveloped Countries," in *The Progress of Underdeveloped Areas,* ed. B. F. Hoselitz (Chicago, 1952), 184.

itself, but was employed above all in building up the costly framework of public services, including especially transport, which laid the basis for domestic industrial development, as well as for the production of raw commodities for export. These areas are now, and have been for some time, predominantly industrial,[6] a fact entirely compatible with the large or even preponderant share of primary products in their export trade.

Nineteenth-century foreign investment centered on the railway — that "great instrument of improvement," in Lord Dalhousie's phrase. If account is taken not only of railway securities but also of the use to which many government loans were put, it seems that well over half of Britain's external investment before 1914 went into railway construction. The great bulk of this was in the newly settled countries. The Indian railways, though an important individual item, accounted for less than one tenth of the total of overseas railway securities held by British investors in 1914. The United States and the Argentine alone accounted for more than half of that total. In the new countries the railway was important as a means of migration. The great pioneer lines — first in the United States, later in the Argentine and elsewhere — were deliberately planned and built *in advance* of current traffic needs; they themselves created the settlement and economic growth that eventually led to a full demand for their services.

Although individual promoters sometimes played the most conspicuous part, the railways in the new countries were built, as a rule, if not directly by governments, at any rate with extensive government assistance in the form of land grants, subsidies and guaranteed returns to the investors. In view of this fact, one can safely say that the bulk of international investment in the nineteenth century depended on government action in the borrowing countries. In French and German capital exports, some of which also went to the New World, the proportion of government loans and other public investments was even higher than in the British case.

It is true that the transport revolution, to which the cheapen-

---

[6] See F. Hilgerdt, *Industrialization and Foreign Trade* (League of Nations, 1945), 26, 39, and passim.

ing of British food imports (especially in the years 1880–1900) was largely due, was a matter of steamships as well as railways. While railway construction overseas was a major object of international financing, British shipbuilding counted almost entirely as part of British home investment. Since ship and railway building had much the same effects on international trade and the terms of trade, the distinction between home and foreign investment appears in this case somewhat arbitrary. In the internal economic expansion of the new countries, however, the railways had, of course, a very special part to play, rather different from that of the ships. And so we hear, for example, that "in the Argentine, the railway is like a magic talisman: for wherever it goes it entirely transforms the economic and productive conditions of the country."[7]

Overseas railway investment became predominant from about 1870 onwards. But this does not mean that the earlier part of the century can be ignored. While the total of foreign investment was much smaller then, so was everything else. We should note that by 1870 Britain's overseas assets had already grown to about the same order of magnitude as her annual national income. Capital imports were a prominent feature in the economic history of the United States for many years before the Civil War.

It is clear that the main flow of capital in the nineteenth century was not to the neediest countries with their "teeming millions," which were indeed neglected, but to sparsely peopled areas where conditions for rapid growth along familiar western lines were exceptionally favorable. If we were to look round for similar opportunities in the twentieth century, I do not know where we should find them if not in the further development of the same regions of recent settlement; or else perhaps in Siberia — a vast area reputedly rich in natural resources, which may be

[7] A. B. Martinez and M. Lewandowski, *The Argentine in the Twentieth Century* (London, 1911), 108. A statement such as this applies to a type of region with the particular physical and human characteristics already noted. It would not apply in the same way to a country like India, where, for reasons that cannot be entered into, the railway "did not give rise to a flood of satellite innovations" and "destroyed more employment opportunities [e.g., in traditional village industries] than it opened up." L. H. Jenks, "British Experience with Foreign Investments," *Journal of Economic History*, 1944, Supplement, 75.

longing for an injection of skilled labor from Europe and capital from the United States.

Once the main facts about the nineteenth-century capital flow are set out in something like their true proportions,[8] it is curious to see how little they fit in with some preconceived notions that have been widely current. Bernard Shaw, for example, in Act I of *The Apple Cart,* made one of his characters talk about England sending her "capital abroad to places where poverty and hardship still exist: in other words, where labour is cheap. We live in comfort on the imported profits of that capital." Consider, more seriously, the summary which Mrs. Joan Robinson gives (in *The Rate of Interest and Other Essays,* 1952, pp. 157–158) of the views of Rosa Luxemburg:

> The capitalist nations are surrounded by primitive economies, each insulated from the others like a nut within its shell, waiting to be cracked. The capitalists break open a primitive economy and enter into trade with it, whether by enticing its inhabitants with commodities they have never seen before, by political cunning or by brute force. Now exports to the primitives provide an outlet for the product of the last batch of capital goods created at home. After a little while another nut is broken, a use for more capital is thereby found, and so on, as long as the supply of untouched primitive economies lasts. . . . When the stock of unbroken nuts is exhausted, the capitalist system collapses for want of markets.

This is one variant of neo-Marxist doctrine and, like others, it neglects some crucial facts. No pre-existing markets were

---

[8] I have thought it superfluous to give detailed references to the well-known sources, such as the works of C. K. Hobson, L. H. Jenks, H. Feis, and the Royal Insitute of International Affairs. Among recent essays and articles that I have found useful, the following should be mentioned: N. S. Buchanan, "International Finance," *Survey of Contemporary Economics,* American Economic Association, ed. B. F. Haley, II (Homewood, Ill., 1952); P. Hartland, "Private Enterprise and International Capital," *Canadian Journal of Economics and Political Science,* February 1953; Sir Arthur Salter, *Foreign Investment,* Essays in International Finance, No. 12 (Princeton, 1951); Brinley Thomas, "Migration and the Rhythm of Economic Growth, 1830–1913," *The Manchester School,* September 1951; L. H. Jenks, "Railroads as an Economic Force in American Development," *Enterprise and Secular Change,* ed. F. C. Lane and J. C. Riemersma (Homewood, Ill., 1953); H. S. Ferns, "The Establishment of the British Investment in Argentina" and J. F. Rippy, "British Investments in Latin America, End of 1913," *Inter-American Economic Affairs,* Autumn, 1951; A. H. Imlah, "British Balance of Payments and Export of Capital, 1816–1913," *Economic History Review,* V, no. 2 (1952).

conquered in the new countries. Markets were *created* there by labor, enterprise and capital all drawn from Europe. In the industrially primitive countries markets were and have remained unattractive because of mass poverty. Why is it, for example, that in the 1920's Canada, Australia, and New Zealand, with already quite highly developed industries of their own and with a combined population of only 17.4 millions, imported twice as much manufactured goods as India with her 340 million people? [9]

The American public also, perhaps because it lives in one of the new countries itself, does not always appreciate the peculiar nature of the nineteenth-century investment experience. Some of us are too apt to forget — or to take for granted — all that went with it and to assume, from that experience, a "simple equivalence of the pace of capital transfer and the pace of development." [10] Keynes in 1922 made a remark that is worth recalling: "The practice of foreign investment, as we know it now, is a very modern contrivance, a very unstable one, and only suited to peculiar circumstances." [11] He cautioned against extending it by simple analogy to a different set of circumstances. Private foreign lending in the 1920's can be viewed in part as a backwash of the great momentum which it had gathered before 1914. Was it because in Central Europe foreign investment was applied to a situation to which it was unsuited that it came to grief there? It might perhaps have worked; Hitler did not give it a chance. Yet the fact is that it did not work.

Will it work, and if so, how will it work, in the "underdeveloped" areas of which we hear so much today? The preceding remarks have all been leading up to this question. My purpose here is to present the question, against the background of past experience, rather than try to answer it. In the time that remains I will only hazard a few brief comments on three general topics: direct business investment, public-utility investment and governmental grants.

The assumption I am making here — that it is the low-income

[9] Hilgerdt, 84.
[10] Honor Croome, "The Dilemma of Development," *New Commonwealth,* 9 November 1953, 487.
[11] *A Revision of the Treaty* (London, 1922), 161.

areas that constitute the main problem of international investment in the mid-twentieth century — may be challenged as
arbitrary and not entirely justified. The most profitable opportunities may still be in the "regions of recent settlement." But
having regard to their high income levels, these fortunate regions
can, in the present discussion, be left to provide, by and large,
for their own development needs.

For reasons mentioned earlier, direct investments by American
business firms — usually financed from corporate reserves rather
than security issues on the capital market — are thought to be
particularly well suited to the economically backward countries.
But they have their shortcomings also. In the life of an industrially primitive community they are apt to create not only a dual
economy[12] but also a dual society, in which conditions for the
diffusion of western technology may actually be the reverse of
favorable.. Foreign business investment is not always a happy
form of encounter between different civilizations. Besides, if
techniques are to be of wide and permanent use, they must be
adapted to local conditions. The methods of giant corporations,
whose foreign operations are sometimes only a side show, are
often too standardized to favor such adaptation. And so the
local economy may not get much help from the example they
give; the example is often inapplicable. Let us remember that the
Japanese acquired industrial techniques very effectively before
they began to receive any substantial foreign business investments. Also the technical assistance programs now in operation
remind us that there are other ways of spreading technical
knowledge.

As a rule, when foreign business enterprise is attracted to
economically backward areas, it is mainly for the production of
raw materials for export markets, for the simple reason that the
domestic market in such areas, even if protected by import
restrictions, is generally too poor to afford any strong inducement
to invest.[13] The natural result is a "colonial" investment pat-

[12] See H. W. Singer, "The Distribution of Gains between Investing and Borrowing Countries," *American Economic Review,* Papers and Proceedings, May
1950.

[13] From the latest comprehensive figures for American direct investments
(*Survey of Current Business,* December 1952), it can be seen that of the total

tern, open to the familiar criticisms that it tends to promote lopsided rather than "balanced" growth, and that it makes for instability due to high dependence on foreign demand for one or two staple products. If this type of direct investment is to take place in any considerable volume, it presupposes a long-run prospect of rapidly expanding demand in the industrial centers for the raw materials which it seeks to provide. Despite the forecasts of the Paley Report, there is no firm assurance of such an expansion except for certain minerals. Governmental purchase agreements alone cannot give this assurance in the absence of favorable basic demand conditions. A temporary stimulus might be got from the removal of United States tariff protection on primary products (such as sugar, copper, wool), but little can be hoped for in this direction.

In the last few years one of the chief economic obstacles to a greater flow of business funds to low-income countries has been the high level of business profits obtainable at home, from developing American natural resources and catering to the American mass market. Conditions may change. It is not inconceivable that business investment abroad might greatly increase in the future, and that it might bring substantial benefits to the poorer countries. Yet, on the whole, it seems unlikely that direct investment alone can become anything like an adequate source of international finance for economic development. It played, as we saw, a minor part in the nineteenth century. Can we rely on it to play a major part today? I doubt it.

What is most urgently needed today is a revival of the public

---

invested in Canada and Western Europe at the end of 1950, 23 per cent was in extractive industries, as much as 60 per cent in manufacturing and trade, 6 per cent in public utilities, and 11 per cent in miscellaneous activities, including cinemas and other entertainments. Of the investments outstanding on the same date in all other countries, which with a few exceptions are economically backward, 60 per cent was in extractive industries, mostly petroleum and mining, with 20 per cent, 17 per cent, and 3 per cent respectively in the other groups. This pattern is by no means new. We know that in 1929 only one fifth of total American direct investment was in manufacturing, and 84 per cent of this was in Western Europe, Canada, Australia, and New Zealand. "Only to a very small extent, therefore, did American direct investments enter into manufacturing for the domestic market in under-developed countries." United Nations, *International Capital Movements in the Inter-War Period*, 1949, 32.

or public-utility type of international investment that used to
dominate the scene. The International Bank for Reconstruction
and Development (the World Bank) has hardly begun to fill
the gap left by the disappearance of this type of private foreign lending. If the past cannot be reproduced, it is all the
more imperative to devise a new pattern suited to present needs
and conditions. Critics have wondered how much of nineteenth-
century foreign investment would have survived the tests and
rules laid down by the World Bank. The Bank, being dependent on the private capital market for most of its loanable
funds, inevitably reflects to some extent the attitudes of the
private investor. And the private American investor is still
waiting for a change in the weather, and remains unimpressed by
statistics showing that only 15 per cent of the dollar bonds (not
counting direct investments) floated in the 1920's by underdeveloped countries — that is, aside from Central Europe — have
proved a permanent loss.[14]

It is said that there are not enough productive projects in the
low-income countries to absorb much more money than is now
going out. It is pointed out that the Marshall Plan, which
accustomed the world to the sight of a large dollar outflow, was
not a plan of new development so much as one of reconstruction,
in an area where a solid industrial foundation and the "know-
how" of a skilled population already existed.[15]

No doubt this point has considerable force. But if there are
not enough projects, can we not ask for international technical
assistance to design them and to draw up the blueprints? Lack
of basic services, such as transport, power, and water supply, is a
particularly serious bottleneck in the poor countries. Because
of this the *physical* environment — quite apart from the obvious
difficulties arising from the political or social climate — is unfavorable to private investment. A large foreign firm producing
raw materials for export may find it profitable to set up incidental
facilities such as roads or waterworks, of which the local econ-

[14] See the Gray Report, 1950, 62.

[15] It will be remembered, however, that some of the Marshall Aid was in
effect passed on to "underdeveloped" countries (especially by way of the United
Kingdom, whose over-all balance was in equilibrium in 1948–49 and in surplus
in 1950).

omy, too, can make some use. But the general utility of such things often depends in haphazard fashion on the technical features of the firm's main activity. It may be fairly high in the case of a railway built by a mining company from the interior of Peru to the seacoast. It is virtually zero in the case of the pipeline in which Arabian oil is pumped to the Mediterranean.

In the United States a hundred years ago public authorities, as well as private promoters, played a leading role in the drive for "internal improvements," financed in part by foreign capital. There is no question that ample scope exists for international financing of public improvements in the poor countries today. Until these countries have acquired a skeleton framework of such facilities, conditions will not be particularly attractive for the more varied and smaller-scale business investments there. Even with such basic improvements, of course, the individual business investments, domestic as well as foreign, may fail to materialize, because of other obstacles. It is conceivable, therefore, that some of these public works would turn out to be white elephants. But the risk has to be taken; any form of capital investment is, in the last analysis, an act of faith. However hard it may be for the pioneering spirit that opened up the new countries to apply itself to the low-income areas today, not much can be achieved without that spirit, and no international organization concerned with development can remain untouched by it.

Apart from the distribution of the promoter-function, there still remains the question of finance. If the profitability of American business at home has kept down direct investments abroad, a simple comparison of bond yields does not explain why "portfolio" lending cannot get started again. However, while the private investor has been standing on the sidelines, we may have witnessed the beginnings of a system of international grants-in-aid and low-interest loans from government funds. The reference to the principle of Equal Sacrifice with which Roosevelt defended the Lend-Lease program may some day appear significant in retrospect. I need not point to other signs and landmarks. Let me just quote a few recent expressions of opinion. The man who gave his name to the Marshall Plan, in accepting the Nobel peace prize last December, said that it was "of basic importance to any

successful effort towards an enduring peace that the more fa-
voured nations should lend assistance in bettering the lot of the
poorer." [16]

Dr. Herbert Feis, the historian of nineteenth-century foreign
investment, has expressed himself as follows:

> A sense of obligation has won its way in the world to the effect that a
> wealthy country has a call of vague dimensions to provide means to assist
> poorer and suffering countries. To give free admission to [it] would
> bankrupt us and demoralise others; but to ignore the obligation wholly
> would be . . . out of accord with the effort in which we are engaged, to
> bring together the nations of the world in peaceful and co-operative under-
> standing. [17]

Even if we hesitate to accept the assumption that world peace
can be bought or that material progress makes for contentment,
the fact of growing pressures for international income transfers
must nevertheless be recognized. It may be precisely because the
problem of international investment is now, unlike what it was
in the Victorian era, concerned in the main with the backward
economies that the need for such transfers is felt to arise.

The difficulties which American trade policy encounters in
following the British nineteenth-century example might also be
taken to point to unilateral income transfers as more in accord
with the underlying situation. With commercial foreign investment an adjustment of the trade balance to the return flow of
interest and dividends cannot normally be long postponed, while
gifts permit an export surplus indefinitely. [18]

[16] *The Times,* 12 December 1953.

[17] "International Economic Outlook," *Proceedings of the Academy of Political Science,* May 1953, 59.

[18] However, I cannot fully share the view that, just because of the growing
return flow to which it normally gives rise, foreign investment of the orthodox
sort can be no more than a short-period remedy for international imbalance.
When in support of this view it is said that the increase in Great Britain's
foreign assets from 1880 to 1913 "was due wholly to the reinvestment of a
part of the income derived from earlier investments" (Salter, 9, 53), it seems
to me that a somewhat arbitrary causal attribution is made between two items
on opposite sides of the balance of payments, a procedure always of doubtful
validity, and particularly so when one of the items represents payments on
capital account, while the other belongs to the income account. That the
individual British investor, on the one hand, was under no obligation to re-
invest the interest he got from abroad is obvious. From the national viewpoint,

The idea of international grants-in-aid is essentially a consequence of the increased gaps in living standards and of the closeness of contact that is creating at the same time an increasingly acute awareness of these gaps — a situation without historical precedent. This awareness is perhaps the most fundamental obstacle to the resumption of private international lending. In contrast to the position of the backward economies today, income per head in the principal debtor countries of the nineteenth century — the newly settled regions — can never have been far below European levels. Interest payments from poor to rich are now, it seems, not only basically unwanted by the rich countries but indeed are felt to be somehow contrary to the spirit of the age. And although public grants (for "social overhead capital") and private foreign lending (for more specific investments) can ideally be looked upon as complementary rather than conflicting sources of finance, it is easy to see why in practice the two do not mix at all well. This applies not only to grants but also in some degree to international loans from government sources.

Persistent attempts in the United Nations organization to set up a system of international grants under UN auspices — from the UNEDA proposal of 1948 to the SUNFED report of 1953 — have foundered on the rocks of American opposition. Yet American practices and pronouncements alike have kept world expectations alive, and this has continued to some extent under the Republican administration. Two notable declarations by President Eisenhower last year attracted wide attention: one was the statement in April about "devoting a substantial percentage of the savings achieved by disarmament to a fund for world aid," the other being the so-called "Atom Bank" proposal for the international provision of atomic energy for peaceful purposes.

It must be recognized that international unilateral transfers

on the other hand, all one can say is that the British current account, including foreign interest earnings as well as earnings from merchandise exports and shipping, showed a surplus, which was balanced by the outflow of capital. Britain had an excess of merchandise imports over exports throughout the period 1880–1913. Yet it is conceivable that if British foreign lending had come to a complete stop in (say) 1890, a disequilibrium in the international balance of payments — a "sterling shortage" — might have been felt in the succeeding quarter of a century.

have no necessary connection with the subject of foreign *investment*. They may be for current consumption or for military use. Even if they are intended for, or tied to, particular capital projects, a net increase in the over-all rate of accumulation is not always assured. If they are to make an effective contribution to economic development, they call for domestic action in the receiving countries — fiscal, monetary and other policies designed to withhold resources from immediate consumption and to direct them into capital formation.

But once the receiving countries are capable of devising the necessary controls for the productive use of outside aid, they should be equally capable of using such policies for the mobilization of potential *domestic* sources of capital (e.g., skimming off resources now absorbed by luxury consumption, making use of labor set free from the land through better farm methods or recruiting any surplus labor already existing on the land). It is far from my intention to suggest that in these circumstances foreign aid becomes unnecessary. Yet this consideration does shift the emphasis upon the need for domestic policies to insure that in the over-all use of resources, domestic as well as external, investment is given top priority.[19] Here is the main criterion, and a body such as the World Bank has in this respect an even more vital role to play in the backward economies than that which the ECA and the OEEC performed under the Marshall Plan.

These remarks on international grants and their possible uses may all be idle speculation, for which, perhaps, I should apologize. The practices alluded to may turn out to have been temporary devices related to particular emergency conditions. What I have said on these controversial matters should have been put in the form of questions — and extremely tentative questions at that. But they are, I think, questions which a survey of the present state of international finance inevitably draws to our attention.

[19] This theme is developed in my *Problems of Capital Formation in Underdeveloped Countries* (Oxford and New York, 1953).

8

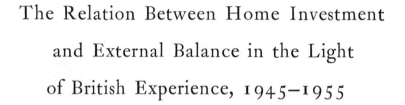

The Relation Between Home Investment

and External Balance in the Light

of British Experience, 1945–1955

(1956)

In the title of this paper readers will recognize a standard subject of theoretical discussion and practical concern. Yet the relationship in question is worth re-examining. Why exactly should two individual items — domestic investment and the balance of external payments — be picked out from the national income accounts and viewed as having some direct connection with each other? And why should this particular relationship be looked upon as one of rivalry? In the economy as a whole a given claim on resources competes with all other claims on resources, and any causal connection assumed between two particular groups of claimants must be *a priori* suspect. A peculiar link between home investment and external balance can nevertheless be said to exist on certain general grounds which will be considered later.

The connection is especially close in the British economy because of some structural features of British trade and industry. In fact, a recurrent conflict between the needs of internal capital development and external trade balance has figured prominently in British experience during the ten-year period since the war. In this paper we start, then, with a discussion of the United Kingdom's economic structure and experience (sections I, II, and III), attempting thereafter to look at the matter in more general terms (sections IV and V). In a final section we return to consider the special case of the United Kingdom, with some reference to current economic developments and policies.

I. STRUCTURAL FEATURES OF TRADE AND PRODUCTION

The first point to be stressed is the great change that has taken place in the composition of British exports. Just over half of total exports now consists of metal and engineering products. Machinery is by far the largest item in this group; next in order of importance are motor vehicles, electrical equipment, iron and steel (see Table 1). These products are typically capital instruments or producers' durable goods. Passenger cars are the leading exception, but even combined with bicycles, cutlery, and other consumer goods they account for less than one fifth of total exports of metal and engineering products — or "hardware," for short.

The preponderance of hardware is of recent date, though the shift in this direction has long been noticeable. The "hardware ratio" in British exports, which was 51 per cent in 1952–1954, was only 34 per cent in 1936–1938 and 25 per cent in 1913. A hundred years ago two thirds of British exports were textiles.[1] Although at that time most of the capital goods entering into international trade came from Great Britain they played a minor part in the country's export trade.

The share of hardware in total exports is now significantly higher in the United Kingdom than in the United States. Excluding military aid shipments, the United States ratio works out at about 40 per cent. This is not surprising since American food

[1] E. A. G. Robinson, "The Changing Structure of the British Economy," *Economic Journal,* LXIV (September 1954).

TABLE 1. COMMODITY COMPOSITION OF BRITISH EXPORTS, 1952–1954
(£ *million*)

	1952	1953	1954
Iron and steel	131	135	137
Nonferrous metals	52	60	56
Machinery other than electric	399	397	410
Electric machinery and equipment	180	172	170
Aircraft and engines	44	63	52
Motorcycles and bicycles	32	25	26
Passenger cars	104	96	109
Other road vehicles and parts	133	106	121
Railroad vehicles	37	42	44
Ships	36	40	50
Military equipment	23	44	47
Other engineering products	137	131	128
Total metals and engineering products	1,308	1,311	1,350
All other exports	1,276	1,271	1,323
Total exports	2,584	2,582	2,673

SOURCE: *Economic Survey for 1955* (Cmd. 9412), with additional detail from the *Trade and Navigation Accounts.*

and raw material exports are still considerable. The British ratio is, however, surpassed by that of West Germany, which has been just over 60 per cent in recent years.

Comparing British exports now (1952–1954) with the years just before the war (1936–1938), we find the hardware category alone contributing something like four fifths of the *increment* in volume. Prices in this category have risen less than in the rest of British exports. Calculations of the change in export quantum therefore yield somewhat varying results: the percentage increase turns out to be greater when prewar rather than postwar prices are used for valuing the quantities exported in the two periods.[2] Keeping in mind the index difficulty we may say that total British exports have increased by some 60 or 65 per cent in real volume from the late 1930's to the early 1950's. Over the same

[2] A. K. Cairncross, "Britain's Export Prospects," *London and Cambridge Economic Bulletin,* June 1954.

time-span exports of metal and engineering products alone have increased no less than two and a half times. The achievement is not so striking when the position before World War I is used as a benchmark. Indeed, the total volume of British exports appears now to be just about back at the 1913 level (which it never regained during the interwar period).[3] In the hardware field, however, the export quantum is now running at roughly double the 1913 level.

Underlying the shift in the composition of exports there has been a considerable expansion in the productive capacity of the United Kingdom's metal-producing and metal-working industries since the late 1930's. These industries came out of the war with good equipment and skilled personnel. They received nearly the whole increase in the country's industrial labor force in the ten years to 1946.[4] It is largely thanks to them that the early postwar export performance of the United Kingdom rose above expectations, the prewar volume being practically restored as early as 1946 with a hardware proportion already as high as 45 per cent. Further expansion of the engineering industries after the war was not always encouraged. According to the Government's *Economic Survey for 1947* (p. 29), it was to be deliberately checked because of a shortage of steel. Manpower and other bottlenecks, as well as steel shortages, have at times held back expansion, yet further expansion has occurred. The metal and engineering industries now employ nearly half of the total number of workers engaged in manufacturing (4.5 million out of 9.2 million workers at the end of 1954). They use a higher proportion of male labor than most other industries, and their total wage-bill is rather more than half of the wages paid in manufacturing as a whole.

These structural changes, though partly induced by war requirements, have conformed to the dominant trends in world markets. The growth in the share of capital goods in international trade, which has long been observed, has lately become even more pronounced.[5] These are goods in which the United

[3] See the long-period indexes published in the quarterly *London and Cambridge Economic Bulletin* since March 1955.
[4] C. A. R. Crosland, *Britain's Economic Problem* (London, 1953), 106.
[5] Figures illustrating the trend may be found in H. Tyszynski's study, "World

Kingdom may hope to have a comparative advantage, not only because external demand — present and prospective — favors them, but also because these goods embody productive factors such as capital and technical skills which, unlike land and labor, are relatively plentiful in Britain. These goods have a high conversion ratio — that is, their raw-material content is low. Their import content is lower still: only about 7 per cent, as compared with 30 per cent for textiles.

Britain has done better in the metal and engineering category than in world exports of manufactured goods in general, though since 1951 her share even in that category has once again tended to decline. Tyszynski's figures show Britain supplying 39.0 per cent of world exports of metal and engineering goods in 1899, 29.7 per cent in 1913, 20.4 per cent in 1929, and 19.6 per cent in 1937. Her share in 1950, however, shows a marked recovery to 26.9 per cent, according to the same source. Another series with somewhat different coverage is available for more recent years, comparing the share of the United Kingdom with that of the United States, West Germany, and other countries in world exports of machinery and vehicles. This is shown in Table 2.

It will be seen that the three great hardware exporters — the United States with a share of 35 per cent, the United Kingdom with about 25 per cent, and West Germany with about 15 per cent — together supply as much as three quarters of what is a fairly complete world total of machinery and vehicle exports. These figures put Britain's position perhaps in rather too favorable a light, since they do not include certain other metal manufactures, such as cutlery, which have declined. Nor do they cover steel exports, in which Britain's share remains lower than before the war. In contrast to Britain, where steel has repeatedly proved a bottleneck in the growth of engineering output, France has expanded her steel capacity under the Monnet Plan so much that her own metal-using industries have not been able to keep pace with it.[6] France is now ahead of Britain as a steel exporter.

Exports of Manufactured Goods, 1899–1950," *Manchester School,* XXI (September 1951); and for more recent years in the *Board of Trade Journal,* 22 January 1955.

[6] United Nations, *Economic Bulletin for Europe,* May 1955, 8.

TABLE 2. EXPORTS OF MACHINERY AND VEHICLES, 1951-1954

	1951	1952	1953	1954
Total, in million dollars:	9,518	10,651	10,833	11,674[a]
Exporting countries:	Percentage distribution			
United States[b]	39.1	35.6	35.8	35.0
United Kingdom	26.1	25.4	24.4	24.1
West Germany	10.0	13.7	15.5	16.1
Other countries[c]	24.8	25.3	24.3	24.8
Total	100.0	100.0	100.0	100.0

SOURCE: *Board of Trade Journal*, 22 January 1955.

[a] Annual rate based on first six months.

[b] Excluding military aid shipments.

[c] Belgium-Luxembourg, Canada, France, Italy, Japan, Netherlands, Sweden, Switzerland.

It is widely recognized that the consumer-goods component of British hardware exports offers little if any scope for expansion.[7] "More and more," Crosland says, "over the whole field of exports, we shall have to concentrate on heavy investment goods for the producer: textiles will cede to textile machinery, cars to commercial vehicles, radio sets to electronic equipment, bicycles to jet aircraft." It is in this direction that world markets are expanding and that further advances seem possible for British exports. The underdeveloped countries are a growing source of demand for capital goods. No doubt some of this demand is for the capital-widening type of extensive investment which these countries need merely to keep pace with their population growth. But this may suit the United Kingdom's export interest in the hardware field almost as well as investment for economic development in a more genuine sense. German competition may be troublesome at times, but there is likely to be room for all. Even in the depressed 1930's, when foreign lending had stopped, international trade in capital equipment — unlike other goods —

[7] E.g., *Economic Survey for 1952* (Cmd. 8509), 17; Crosland, 104; E. A. G. Robinson in *The Three Banks Review*, June 1955, 24.

managed to recover to previous boom levels.[8] The world wants these things and will pay for them, though salesmanship and the provision of some technical assistance with capital-goods shipments will no doubt remain important conditions of success.

In the commercial policy of underdeveloped countries today, nothing is so characteristic as the effort to cut down — or cut out — imports of consumption goods in order to make room for imports of capital equipment. This may be a shortsighted and in some ways ineffective policy (for reasons I have discussed elsewhere[9]), and it is fortunately not the only means employed for "economic development"; yet it is making a strong mark on the commodity structure of international trade. We should beware, however, of thinking of the development process merely in terms of substitutions within a constant total. An essential part of the process is the plowing back of output *increments* derived, for example, from fuller use of labor or from basic improvements in farming. The development process in itself does not preclude world trade expansion.

It is clear, then, that the United Kingdom's engineering industries have come to occupy a crucial position in the country's economy. Their task is to provide the extra exports the country needs for paying its way in the world. Compared with the prewar position, extra exports have been needed to make up for the loss of foreign investment income, to finance increased government expenditures abroad, and to compensate for the adverse shift in the terms of trade (which, measured by export over import price indexes, are about 15 per cent below prewar, though — according to the *London and Cambridge Economic Bulletin* — apparently still *above* the 1913 level). The quantum of imports, which seems to be approximately the same as in 1913, has been kept below prewar all along. This has been possible partly because of the decline of textile exports with their high raw-material import content, but mainly because of the expansion of domestic food production, in response to wartime needs and postwar subsidies. Further import saving along these lines would be a dif-

---

[8] *International Currency Experience* (League of Nations, 1944), 196–197.
[9] *Problems of Capital Formation in Underdeveloped Countries* (New York, 1953), ch. 5.

ficult, uneconomic, and unpromising policy. While the postwar export drive has been impressive in terms of the prewar base,[10] it has only just about restored the 1913 volume of exports. Additional exports are still required to strengthen the country's external solvency, to replenish the gold and dollar reserves, and to make possible the minimum flow of overseas investment appropriate to Great Britain's position as the center of the sterling area and the Commonwealth.

Here now is the problem: the metal and engineering industries form not only the major support of the country's external balance, but are also called upon to supply what is needed for the renewal and enlargement of the country's own capital equipment. Exports and home investment absorb in approximately equal parts the great bulk of what these industries produce. In the last national income report there is an input-output table relating to 1950, from which we can select the relevant figures (Table 3).

The table shows that exports absorbed 45 per cent and domestic fixed investment 36 per cent of total final output, so that the two divided between them as much as four fifths of the final output of the metal and engineering industries. Less complete figures, covering only the metal-using industries (that is, engineering and vehicle output, but not iron and steel and other metal production as such), are available on a somewhat different basis for more recent years (Table 4).

We notice a jump first in the share of defense (1950–1952), then in that of consumption (1952–1954). Yet exports and investment remain preponderant, absorbing even in 1954 over two-thirds of what corresponds roughly to the final output of metal-working industries.

The point stands out sharply: home investment and export needs are the two great competitors for the country's output of machinery, plant, and transport equipment. On structural grounds alone we have here clearly the makings of potential conflict between internal growth and external balance.

---

[10] The base period used here is 1936–1938. The use of 1938 alone is objectionable because of the slump in that year. From 1937 to 1938, import and export volumes fell off by 5 and 12 per cent respectively, while the terms of trade improved by 9 per cent.

TABLE 3. SALES BY METAL AND
ENGINEERING INDUSTRIES, 1950
(£ *million*)

Final buyers:	
Exports	1,070
Gross fixed investment	863
Personal consumption	265
Public authorities	205
Inventory investment	−40
Total final output	2,363
Intermediate output[a]	722
Total output[b]	3,085

SOURCE: *National Income and Expenditure, 1955* (Central Statistical Office, 1955), Table 17.

[a] Metal and engineering goods bought by other industries (building, farming, mining, food, furniture, etc.) for current uses such as repairs, components, and containers, not counted as fixed investment, and embodied in the output of these other industries.

[b] Excluding stock appreciation.

Internal growth means increasing productivity and real income per head. Capital investment is probably a necessary, though not a sufficient condition thereof. It was plainly a vital condition in Britain's postwar re-equipment phase. More recently, there has been talk about the "declining importance of capital" and about capital being in some way a consequence rather than a cause of progress.[11] Some indications will be given later concerning the adequacy of Britain's rate of capital formation. Our assumption in the meantime will be that investment is still a matter of considerable, though far from exclusive, importance for Britain's economic advance and that, despite possibilities of reciprocal causation, the conventional treatment in economic

[11] See Colin Clark's radio talk reprinted in *The Listener*, 10 March 1955.

TABLE 4. SUPPLIES AND USES OF METAL GOODS, 1950, 1952, 1954

	Value in £ million, 1953 prices[a]			Percentage distribution		
	1950	1952	1954	1950	1952	1954
Total supplies[b]	2,725	3,000	3,340	100	100	100
Used for:						
Exports	1,140	1,150	1,165	42	38	35
Investment	1,060	1,030	1,105	39	35	33
Consumption[c]	325	360	570	12	12	17
Defense	200	460	500	7	15	15

SOURCE: *Economic Survey for 1955* (Cmd. 9412), 51.

[a] This alone precludes comparison with the previous table. Prices of metal goods were about 25 per cent higher in 1953 than in 1950.

[b] Excluding "other industrial goods, repair work, etc." (i.e., intermediate output) and inventory investment in metal-using industries. Including imports, which represent only 2 per cent (in 1952, 3 per cent) of total supplies.

[c] Including passenger cars for the home market.

analysis of capital as a *factor* of production is not wildly unrealistic.

II. INVESTMENT POLICY IN PAYMENTS CRISES

The conflict between the needs of home investment and external solvency broke out sharply on three occasions during the postwar transition period. In the biennial series of sterling crises — 1947, 1949, and 1951 — the authorities reacted each time by taking vigorous measures to restrain or reduce the volume of capital outlay. These were not, of course, the only measures taken, but they played each time a very prominent part, and they recurred with greater regularity than other types of reaction (except for import restrictions, which showed the same regularity of recurrence, up to 1951–52). Whenever something went wrong with the balance of payments, domestic investment was hit on the head.

Whether the reappearance of a payments deficit in the latter part of 1954 and the tightening of credit policy early in 1955 can be said to conform to the same pattern we shall consider later. For one thing, these events are too recent to be reflected in the annual statistics used in this section.

A review of some of the earlier crisis measures will be instructive. In the White Paper on the "capital cuts" which Cripps announced in November 1947, it was explained that "as the credits granted by the United States and Canada are now almost exhausted, a great effort to balance overseas payments is necessary" and that more resources for the manufacture of exports "can only be obtained to any significant extent by postponement of certain investment projects. The size, scope and number of these projects must, therefore, be reduced . . . to save scarce labor and materials for diversion to even more urgent uses." [12] Full employment of labor and plant capacity made it impossible, then and on later occasions, to get more goods out for export quickly through further expansion of output; hence the need for "diversion." Another official report, issued early in 1948, stated the main reasons for the capital cuts as follows:

First, the exhaustion of the dollar credits at an earlier date than had been expected made it necessary to build up exports more rapidly, even at the expense of postponing re-equipment of the home industries. Second, the condition of achieving the necessary export targets was a release of certain materials, notably steel, which were in such short supply as to set an effective limit to production for export.[13]

In the next crisis, measures to restrain capital expenditure were taken in April 1949. But the main attack came in the autumn when, in a continuing state of strained capacity, the improvement in the foreign balance which devaluation was to bring about had to be matched by some form of domestic retrenchment: hence again a policy of investment cuts, announced in October 1949. In the words of another *Survey:*

Measures were adopted in the autumn of 1949 to reduce investment and Government expenditure in order to ease existing pressure and to ensure that the increase in exports which devaluation had made possible and necessary was not frustrated by too strong a pull from the home market. . . . In order to achieve the overall level of exports needed to balance our payments it is intended that . . . investment at home in engineering products

[12] *Capital Investment in 1948* (Cmd. 7268), 3–4.
[13] *Economic Survey for 1948* (Cmd. 7344), 38.

should be slightly less than in 1949, and that the products so released and the whole increment in output in 1950 should be exported.[14]

In 1951–52, when a sudden deterioration of the trade balance was aggravated by the rearmament emergency, both Hugh Gaitskell, the last Labour government's Chancellor of the Exchequer, and his successor, R. A. Butler, again relied heavily on a policy of cutting down fixed as well as inventory investment. The 1952 *Economic Survey*, the first issued by the Conservative government, had this to say on the new program of capital cuts:

In the long run our industries must have the equipment they need for expansion and efficiency. At the present time, however, some of these needs must be sacrificed because of the overriding importance of increasing exports of precisely those goods for which investment demand is heaviest. The Government has therefore taken steps to divert resources on a large scale from supplying engineering goods to the home market to production for export. . . . With regard to most capital goods made specially to order the Government has asked manufacturers to do everything they can to bring export orders forward for earlier delivery at the expense of home requirements.[15]

While the Conservative administration revived the instrument of monetary policy for curbing home investment, the new government, like the old, made use of tax measures and direct controls for this purpose. It imposed a higher tax on profits, the Excess Profits Levy, which remained in effect until the end of 1953. It suspended a system of "initial depreciation allowances" that was in force in earlier years, under which businessmen installing new equipment could claim certain benefits amounting to the postponement, though not cancellation, of tax liabilities. It maintained the licensing control of building and reintroduced a steel-allocation scheme which had been dropped in 1950.

The new monetary policy was reflected in two bank rate increases in November 1951 and March 1952 and in a general stiffening of credit terms and interest charges. In earlier years such conventional credit policies would probably have been ineffective because of the excess liquidity which the war had left behind and which Dr. Dalton had further increased in the course of his cheap money policy in 1946. "The holders [of excess

[14] *Economic Survey for 1950* (Cmd. 7915), 8, 28, 33.
[15] *Economic Survey for 1952* (Cmd. 8509), 18.

money] had no need to borrow, and consequently a restriction of credit had not the power to stop excess spending." [16] Excess liquidity was not removed by any of the special mopping-up operations in vogue on the Continent after the war; but it was gradually absorbed by the rise in prices and wage rates as well as by the expansion in the volume of production. The price rise caused by the Korean crisis was one big step that brought the ratio of money stocks to current money incomes, which in 1946 was far above prewar, closer to something like normal.[17] In these circumstances credit policy could hope to become once more an effective instrument. At any rate the authorities, disregarding prewar skepticism about the efficacy of interest policy, made it clear that they expected the higher cost and restricted availability of credit to curb not only the accumulation of stocks but also additions to fixed capital:

Both the defense demand and the orders from overseas customers are predominantly for the products of the capital goods industries, and for this reason a relatively heavy reduction has had to be made in resources devoted to investment at home, particularly in plant and machinery for civil use. This reduction will be brought about by tighter monetary policy and the suspension of the initial depreciation allowances, and by voluntary arrangements made by the manufacturers of capital goods with the Government about the proportion of production which should be devoted to export. The tighter monetary policy will increase the cost of carrying stocks and thereby may reduce the amount of investment in goods in process and in finished goods.[18]

Such were the policies — and tools of policy — affecting home investment in the balance-of-payments crises. In actual fact, the real volume of gross *fixed* investment, after a 36 per cent upsurge in the first two postwar years, showed a degree of steadiness surprising in view of the attacks that were made on it. This can be seen in Table 6. Though we shall find that the steadiness of total fixed investment is somewhat deceptive, it is nevertheless clear that *inventory* investment proved a far more flexible item in the short run. Throughout the period 1946–1953 it moved from year to year inversely with the foreign balance, as is shown in Table 5.

[16] R. G. Hawtrey, *Towards the Rescue of Sterling* (London, 1954), 92.
[17] See A. J. Brown, *The Great Inflation, 1939–1951* (London, 1955), 250.
[18] *Economic Survey for 1952* (Cmd. 8509), 45.

TABLE 5. BALANCE OF PAYMENTS AND INVENTORY INVESTMENT, 1946–1954

(£ million, at current prices)

	1946	1947	1948	1949	1950	1951	1952	1953	1954
Net balance on current account[a]	−298	−443	1	31	300	−407	131	78	136
Net inventory investment, total[b]	−54	309	175	65	−210	575	50	125	225
Of which:									
Private business	...	...	247	79	17	496	−77	106	402
Public corporations	...	...	−10	33	−15	4	51	−25	−59
Central government	...	...	−62	−47	−212	75	76	44	−118
of which:									
Trading stocks	...	...	−2	−15	−185	−29	34	9	−161
Strategic stocks	...	...	...	...	...	127	49	42	46
Surplus stores	...	...	−60	−32	−27	−23	−7	−7	−3

[a] Excluding U.S. Defense Aid. Source: *United Kingdom Balance of Payments, 1946–1955* (Cmd. 9585).
[b] "Value of physical increase in stocks and work in progress." Source: *National Income and Expenditure, 1955*, Table 52.

What made it move in this way? That is a difficult question, especially as we have no information on the import content of inventory investment. At times direct action by the government as a holder of stocks was important. Thus in 1950 the government allowed its own trading stocks, presumably of imported food and raw materials, to run down in order to cushion the effect of the devaluation. This accounted for almost the whole of the decumulation that occurred in 1950, and made it possible for the quantum of imports to remain unchanged in that year despite a continued rise in production and consumption. In 1951, on the other hand, government stockpiling of strategic commodities, again presumably imported, accounted for only one fifth of the total value of stock accumulation. The greater part of the 1950–51 upswing in inventory investment, and all of the 1951–52 downswing, occurred in the private sector. In fact private inventory investment alone, in the years 1948–1953, reflects faithfully the year-to-year countermovement in relation to the balance of payments. The behavior of government stocks alone cannot explain it.

It is often argued that import restrictions imposed on balance-of-payments grounds from time to time diverted expenditure on current imports to stocks of commodities imported earlier, causing in this way decumulation or reduced rates of accumulation in total stocks in the country. Moreover, by causing a deflection of expenditure away from imported goods, these restrictions may have had similar effects on stocks of home-produced goods, although business firms could react to such unintended disinvestment by rationing their customers, if they were not able to replenish their stocks through increased production or purchases, or by protecting stocks by raising their prices.

That import restrictions had some effect on inventory investment is probable, but from the data available it is not clear that this was the dominant influence. It should be noted that during the whole ten-year period 1952 was the only year in which the volume of imports was actually reduced below the previous year (see Chart 2, below). On the basis of annual figures, that is, import cuts failed to cut down total imports in any year except 1952. It is still possible that in other years *increases* in expenditure, being thwarted by import barriers, were directed instead to stocks of goods within the country. Except in 1952, however, the inverse movement apparent in Table 5 can hardly be explained by arguing that periodic import restrictions had the double effect of (a) redressing the external balance by cutting down imports and (b) forcing a reduction in inventories or at any rate in inventory investment. All we can say is that in 1948, for example, import controls may have tended to slow down the growth of both imports and inventories at the same time.

The import restrictions of 1947 and 1949 were dictated by the dollar problem (which is not our special concern in this paper) and were directed against imports from dollar sources. That they had no apparent effect on the indexes of total import volume (shown in Chart 2) does not mean that they failed to achieve their purpose. Besides, such restrictions when applied in the outer sterling area tended to help United Kingdom exports by shutting out competing supplies from the United States.

The element of inventory fluctuations has always played some part in the behavior of British imports.[19] Conversely, the import content of total inventory changes in Britain is probably considerable. In puzzling about the relation between external balance and domestic inventory investment some writers, however, have seemed to assume that the inventory changes have been entirely in imported goods. Thus Sir Henry Clay placed the stock changes side by side with the changes in Britain's external liabilities and gold and dollar reserves, stressing the importance of considering all these items together as an indication of the country's international financial position.[20] Tinbergen, too, has urged the need to take account of a country's stocks of internationally traded staple products as being virtually equivalent to international liquidity.[21] In the official Dutch report where he showed his balance-of-payments statistics and inventory-investment statistics in combination, he referred to a computation suggesting that in the Netherlands "the marginal import content in the stock changes is very

---

[19] R. C. O. Matthews, "The Trade Cycle in Britain, 1790–1850," *Oxford Economic Papers,* n.s. VI (February 1954), 22.

[20] "A Note on Stocks," *Journal of Industrial Economics,* April 1954, 86–88.

[21] J. Tinbergen, "The Relation between Internal Inflation and the Balance of Payments," Banca Nazionale del Lavoro, *Quarterly Review,* October–December 1952, 5.

high." [22] The point is doubtless important in Britain too, but probably much less so, if only because of the higher share of essential foodstuffs in British imports. Taking into consideration domestic raw materials, goods in process, and finished manufactures, it seems improbable that imported staple products alone should dominate the course of inventory investment in the United Kingdom, though lack of knowledge leaves the matter uncertain.

If import control has not been the only influence affecting inventory investment, it is conceivable that credit policy has played some part: not the level of money rates alone, of course, but also the varying stringency of the usual credit rationing, which at times was not unrelated to the state of the balance of payments. The value of total inventories at the end of 1952 is officially estimated at 7,200 million pounds (equivalent to 46 per cent of GNP at market prices in 1952), and though Hawtrey finds that "the proportion of stocks carried with borrowed money appears to be hardly one-sixth," [23] this still leaves a significant amount subject to some degree of banking control. But it must be conceded that especially before 1952 this influence was probably very weak in view of the liquidity of business.

Whatever the causal factors may have been it is clear, first, that the United Kingdom's balance of payments was quickly relieved through the reductions in inventory investment in 1947–48, 1949–50, and 1951–52; and secondly, that these reductions, though partly results of government action, seemed to be largely unintended and unforeseen. As is plain from the official pronouncements quoted above, the great object of policy in each crisis was to curtail the rate of *fixed* capital investment for the sake of expanding exports.

In these circumstances the unruffled behavior of the annual volume of fixed investment from 1948 to 1952 is perhaps surprising (see Table 6, line 3). However, the comparative stability of the total may be a little misleading. The total covers public as well as private investment. As the scope of these two categories was often changed by measures of nationalization and

[22] *Central Economic Plan 1954* (Central Planning Bureau, The Hague, March 1954), 8.
[23] *Towards the Rescue of Sterling,* 91.

TABLE 6. GROSS NATIONAL PRODUCT AT CONSTANT PRICES, 1946–1954

(£ million, at 1948 market prices)

	1946	1947	1948	1949	1950	1951	1952	1953	1954
1. Consumer expenditure	8,251	8,534	8,505	8,693	8,892	8,827	8,738	9,070	9,467
2. Current government expenditure	2,589	1,773	1,761	1,915	1,895	2,047	2,269	2,331	2,300
3. Gross fixed investment, total	1,032	1,272	1,406	1,513	1,570	1,545	1,546	1,741	1,826
a. New housing	...	355	342	327	315	318	388	491	497
b. Other building and works[a]	...	252	325	386	427	405	403	417	453
c. Plant and machinery[b]	...	655	739	800	828	822	755	833	876
4. Inventory investment	−69	336	175	62	−185	453	37	95	170
5. Exports of goods and services	1,482	1,575	1,991	2,229	2,540	2,672	2,614	2,574	2,762
6. Imports of goods and services	−2,882	−3,026	−2,998	−3,175	−3,211	−3,597	−3,295	−3,459	−3,639
7. Gross national product	10,403	10,464	10,840	11,237	11,501	11,947	11,909	12,352	12,886

SOURCE: *National Income and Expenditure, 1955* (Central Statistical Office, 1955).
[a] Including legal fees and stamp duties.
[b] Including vehicles, ships, and aircraft.

denationalization it is impossible to group the two in separate totals that remain comparable throughout the period. Yet there are indications that investment policy in balance-of-payments crises affected the two sectors unequally. We know that public investment on the whole was effectively protected against the impact of rising interest rates in the years 1950–1952. Government subsidies on new housing and public works offset the higher interest charges resulting from Mr. Butler's new monetary policy in 1951–52. Excluding new housing, the real volume of private investment appears to have declined from 1950 to 1952 by about one tenth in the private sector, while in the public it remained unchanged.[24] In 1947 as in 1952 the official policy of capital cuts seems to have affected private more than public investment.

It is possible that the government tended to attach a higher priority to its own investment projects. But a difference in the treatment of private and public investment can be explained simply by the needs of the balance of payments. Even if new housing is left out of account, the proportion of "building and works" to total fixed capital outlay is, as one would expect, much higher in the public sector than in the private. In 1953, for example, it was 44 per cent in the former sector, 21 per cent in the latter. Investment curbs for the purpose of helping the trade balance were likely to fall predominantly on private business because that is where most of the plant and machinery on the home market was absorbed. The building industry produces nothing for export as such, and the import content of its output is only about 3 per cent. The release of engineering products from the claims of home investment was capable of swelling the flow of exports directly, with no need for the inter-industrial factor transfers without which a cut in building activity could have done very little for the trade balance.[25]

Even outlay on equipment as distinct from construction could

---

[24] Rough estimates at constant prices, for public and private investment separately, can be derived from *National Income and Expenditure, 1946–52*, Tables 39 and 42. The only important change in the scope of the two sectors in 1950–1952 was the nationalization of steel in February 1951, but the figures for steel can be and have been excluded from this comparison.

[25] See F. A. Burchardt, "Cuts in Capital Expenditure," *Bulletin of the Oxford University Institute of Statistics,* X (January 1948), 5.

not always be turned on and off quickly if investment projects already initiated were not to be left unfinished. The government repeatedly declared that investment cuts were not to force interruptions of work already in hand.[26] Since individual projects take some time to complete, curbs on fixed capital formation could not become fully effective at once.

The changes that occurred in government policy with respect to investment — chiefly in response to the balance of payments —are strikingly illustrated in the varying number of approvals granted for industrial construction during the ten years, 1945– 1954. The annual totals are plotted in Chart 1, together with the

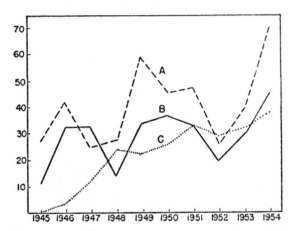

CHART 1. INDUSTRIAL CONSTRUCTION: APPROVED (A),
STARTED (B), COMPLETED (C)
(*Million square feet*)

data for starts and completions in each year. The yearly figures for construction approved vary a great deal. A detailed supplementary description given by the Board of Trade reveals even sharper changes at closer intervals: for instance, a drastic cut in approvals from the autumn of 1947 to mid-1948, then a peak

[26] With reference to the 1949 measures, for instance, it was stated: "The stoppage of building or the construction of plant and machinery on which work has begun is wasteful and disruptive. Work in hand will therefore be allowed to proceed, and for this reason the diminished rate of investment will not be achieved until the end of 1950." Cmd. 7915, 33. See also Cmd. 7862, 30.

level in the first quarter of 1949, followed by a tightening after
the devaluation and a still more drastic restriction in mid-1951.[27]
Even the series for starts of factory building shows wide enough
changes, while the curve for completions is much smoother. But
it is the approvals series that directly reflects policy. Of course
the factory building restrictions served indirectly but effectively
to control the demand for equipment.

It is important to bear in mind that Britain's metal and engineering output was continually expanding during the period here
reviewed. From 1946 to 1950 it showed a 50 per cent increase,
followed by another 20 per cent increase from 1950 to 1954. In
this situation, curbs on investment could make more hardware
available for export without having to force an absolute decrease
in supplies for the home market. Checking the expansion of
home investment was all that was needed. This, by and large, was
the case in 1947 and 1949. In 1951–52 an absolute decrease in
total industrial investment did come about. The fact that even
then the total volume of fixed investment remained practically
unchanged was due to the housing program started by the Conservative government in fulfillment of an election pledge. In the
plant and equipment field the cuts of 1951–52, however, unlike
the earlier ones, did not lead to increased exports, but were absorbed by mounting defense requirements.

For the postwar period as a whole, merely holding back the
rate of fixed capital formation at a time when re-equipment needs
were urgent and omnipresent may be counted as an achievement
from the viewpoint of the foreign balance. The worsening of the
commodity terms of trade, the loss of invisible receipts, and the
increased government expenditures abroad after the war de-
manded a strenuous effort of external adjustment. Loans and
grants from the United States were a great help, but after 1947,
when the United Kingdom's own external accounts were brought
into over-all balance, foreign aid can be said to have provided no
further net resources to the United Kingdom itself, though it
remained for a while of crucial importance to the *dollar* balance
of the United Kingdom and the sterling area. (Throughout this

[27] "Ten Years of Industrial Building in Great Britain," *Board of Trade Journal,* 20 August 1955, 422.

paper we are of course concerned with the over-all external balance of the United Kingdom alone.)

A comparison of the British economy in 1950 with the prewar position shows that the effort of redressing the external balance absorbed over half of the total increase in national output in 1950 over the 1938 level, so that, in spite of the considerable rise in output, consumption per head in 1950 had barely recovered to prewar standards.[28] For the period 1946–1954 we have the official yearly estimates of expenditure at constant prices shown in Table 6, from which we can observe the use to which the *increments* in national product were put. Table 7 below shows the way in which the increments, taken over two-year intervals, were absorbed by changes in the major categories of expenditure.

The wide swings in inventory investment are a disturbing element in a table of this sort, but cannot be left out of account. They produced on balance a big expansion in the aggregate volume of stocks. Aside from inventories, each of the four subperiods of Table 7 has its own characteristics. In the first, the postwar demobilization released an amount of resources nearly twice as large as the increase in production. In the first two subperiods the effort of righting the external balance stands out very prominently. In the third, rearmament claims the major share of additional output. In the fourth, an upsurge of private consumption dominates the scene. This corresponds closely with what we saw about the distribution of metal goods alone in 1950–1952 and 1952–1954 respectively (Table 4).

Viewing the period 1945–1954 as a whole, it is essential to remember that the real effort of redressing the external balance took place entirely on the export side (see Chart 2). The volume of imports, though more or less controlled, increased moderately (except in 1952), but was kept throughout below prewar. All was not quiet on the import side, yet there was comparative stability. Exports were the active element of adjustment. The quantum of exports went up by leaps and bounds from 1945 to 1950, rising far above the prewar level. In these circumstances the release of exportable goods from directly competing domestic claims was a

[28] G. D. N. Worswick and P. H. Ady, eds., *The British Economy 1945–1950* (Oxford, 1952), 46.

TABLE 7. CHANGES IN GROSS NATIONAL PRODUCT AT CONSTANT PRICES

	£ million at 1948 prices				Percentage share in GNP increment			
	1946-48	1948-50	1950-52	1952-54	1946-48	1948-50	1950-52	1952-54
Consumer expenditure	+254	+387	−154	+729	58	59	−38	74
Current government expenditure	−828	+134	+374	+31	−190	20	92	3
New housing	+374	−27	+73	+109	} 86	−4	18	11
Other fixed investment		+191	−97	+171		29	−23	18
Inventory investment	+244	−360	+222	+133	56	−55	54	14
Exports less imports	+393	+336	−10	−196	90	50	−3	−20
Gross national product	+437	+661	+408	+977	100	100	100	100

vital means of helping the external balance. No doubt the control of domestic consumption was the fundamental condition for the success of the export drive. Since, however, engineering products were the most readily salable and formed an almost steadily rising proportion in total exports, it is no wonder that investment curbs were resorted to whenever the balance of payments came under acute strain. And since engineering output was rising — strongly in the first, moderately in the second, half of the period —all that was needed was checking the growth of home investment from time to time: sharply in 1947, not quite so sharply in 1949, and most severely in 1951–52, when not only the rate of

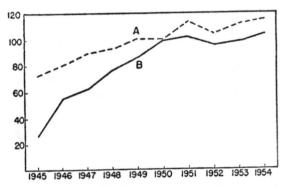

CHART 2. QUANTUM OF IMPORTS (A) AND EXPORTS (B)
(*1950 = 100*)

increase but the absolute volume of fixed investment other than housing was reduced.

Although the output capacity of metal and engineering industries was expanding over the period, it was at any given time limited and nearly always fully utilized. This is what caused the need for diversion of output from home investment to export requirements. Since resources everywhere were fully employed, any attempt to expand more rapidly the capacity of metal-working industries would have required transfers of labor from other industries. Such transfers, if carried out hurriedly under the pressure of external payments crises, might have involved some unemployment. Great Britain could probably not have kept her un-

employment ratio at 2 per cent and less if she had readily put up
with such transitional unemployment. And even if she had tolerated it, the required changes in her industrial structure might
still not have materialized quickly enough to alleviate the external strains. Mobility — occupational and geographic — was
limited. Through diverting the output of an identical group of
industries from domestic to external markets the frictional losses
and transfer difficulties of emergency shifts in the pattern of industry could be avoided. This meant merely changing the destina-
tion of the same or similar goods shipped from the same factories; it was much easier and could be done more quickly. In
this way the tussle between home investment and export needs
appears as a consequence of structural features of British trade
and industry operating in a state of even fuller employment than
anything that Beveridge had proposed in 1944 in his report on
Full Employment in a Free Society.

III. Investment Needs and Capacity

The tendency has been to treat home investment as a rival
claimant whose demands are curbed in order to release more machinery and equipment for export whenever any trouble arises in
the balance of payments. We have just noticed the substantial
advantages of this arrangement. What are its drawbacks? One
could object that it relegates domestic investment to the role of
a residual recipient having no priority in its own right. This might
not be a serious objection provided only that steps were taken
to promote a steady and adequate expansion in the output capacity of industries producing capital goods, not in response to
foreign-exchange crises but over the longer run. Given such expansion, the tug-of-war between home investment and export
needs might go on, but could then take place at a higher level of
both investment and exports. If, on the average, ample supplies
of equipment are assured for the domestic economy, there is less
objection to asking home investment from time to time to absorb
external shocks. The advantages of this arrangement, in minimizing the need for quick and costly readjustments and transitional unemployment, may be deemed to outweigh its remaining

disadvantage of causing some instability in supplies of capital goods for domestic use.

The spectacular growth of Britain's engineering output in the late 1940's was in part the result of turning to peacetime uses some of the capacity created during the war. This growth has not, since then, continued at the same rate and cannot be expected to do so without action designed to that end.

Suggestions have appeared recently in favor of creating *excess* capacity in Great Britain's export industries so that production for export could in case of need be quickly increased.[29] Now excess capacity must inevitably mean prolonged unemployment of some labor as well as plant; surely there is no need for that. The term "export industries" is misleading if it suggests that these industries produce exotic things fit only for export. Britain's export industries produce capital goods fit also for home use, and there is no point in leaving them at any time less than fully employed so long as domestic investment can make productive use of their output. Domestic demands would have to give way if the balance of payments called for a larger volume of exports, but this would be no cause for concern if capacity were large enough for an adequate level of home investment over the longer run.

Before turning to the problems involved in expanding Britain's capital goods capacity we should, however, pause to see what level of investment might be considered adequate. If the continuance of capital development at something like postwar rates should be found excessive and unnecessary, then the question of expanding the investment industries might not arise at all. Even the increase in hardware exports that will be required merely to offset the probable decline in textile and other exports could then perhaps be supplied from the same engineering capacity. The question of Britain's investment needs is a difficult and controversial subject. A few remarks, to provide a background for the rest of the discussion, will have to suffice.

Mr. Philip Redfern has produced estimates of net investment

[29] See the Symposium in the *Bulletin of the Oxford University Institute of Statistics*, XVII (February 1955), where G. D. N. Worswick (p. 68) and P. D. Henderson (pp. 82–84) defend the idea, while H. G. Johnson (p. 7) and R. L. Marris (pp. 26–27) criticize it.

at constant prices which suggest that the prewar stock of fixed
capital had been just about restored in 1950, and that by the end
of 1953 it had been exceeded by almost 10 per cent in real volume.[30] Now a net addition of 10 per cent, even when spread over
fifteen years, is not negligible. But if account is taken of the
growth of the labor force between 1938 and 1953 the rise in the
per capita quantity of fixed capital turns out less than 5 per cent.
As for earlier periods, we have the following conclusion from a
study by Phelps Brown:

Between 1870 and 1913 the physical quantity of capital other than buildings per occupied person almost doubled, . . . but from 1924 to 1938 it
did not on balance rise at all. . . . The outcome, in the virtual failure to
make any increase for fourteen years in industrial equipment per head of
the occupied population, was very serious, the more so because it occurred
even after the virtual abandonment of foreign investment. . . . It may
have escaped notice at the time, partly because of the extent of current
investment in building, as also in roads, which are not included in our
figures of capital, and these do indeed provide some offset; but also because this proved to be a time of technical harvesting, when the wider
application of new techniques raised productivity at home substantially
despite the scantiness of industrial investment in the aggregate, and when
the terms of trade moved in our favor.[31]

There is a gap in the estimates between 1913 and 1924, but it
seems reasonable to assume that the wartime disinvestment had
just been made good by 1924. If so, we have a forty-year period,
from 1913 on, during which the industrial capital stock per
worker seems to have increased very little. On the other hand,
output per man-hour increased a great deal. No rigid or close
relation can ever be expected between capital accumulation and
industrial productivity. Capital replacement alone, when it embodies improvements in technique, as it usually does, can make
for higher productivity. Such improvements in the quality of the
industrial capital stock are necessarily ignored in attempts to

[30] P. Redfern, "Net Investment in Fixed Assets in the United Kingdom, 1938–
1953," *Journal of the Royal Statistical Society,* vol. 118, part 2 (1955).
[31] E. H. Phelps Brown and B. Weber, "Accumulation, Productivity and Distribution in the British Economy, 1870–1938," *Economic Journal,* LXIII (June
1953), 281. See also Walther G. Hoffmann, *British Industry 1700–1950* (Oxford,
1955), 207–208, where an estimate of the growth of real capital is compared with
long-term changes in the rate of growth of British industrial output.

Economic Essays

measure changes in its quantity in terms of real factor cost.[32] How important these qualitative improvements are, and whether they can render superfluous any quantitative enlargement of the stock, are questions we must leave open, echoing only Sir Dennis

TABLE 8. GROSS AND NET INVESTMENT IN FIXED CAPITAL
AT CONSTANT PRICES[a]

(£ *million, at 1948 prices*)

	Manufac- turing and distribu- tion, etc.	Agri- culture	Public services, transpor- tation, fuel and power	Housing	Total
Gross investment:					
1936	472	12	419	522	1,425
1937	513	17	453	462	1,445
1938	474	12	471	474	1,431
1948	479	58	381	342	1,260
1949	532	50	452	327	1,361
1950	593	47	470	315	1,425
1951	595	46	454	318	1,413
1952	555	40	456	388	1,439
1953	570	37	513	500	1,620
Net investment:					
1938	191	3	149	333	676
1948	186	26	74	173	459
1949	225	16	134	155	530
1950	267	11	145	140	563
1951	249	8	122	140	519
1952	193	0	116	207	516
1953	191	−5	165	316	667

[a] These estimates are based on the official data, but the totals for gross investment are smaller than those in Table 6 above, because they exclude land, legal fees, stamp duties, and certain types of assets such as farm buildings, mine workings, and some assets of the central government, notably hospitals, offices, and research establishments. (See Redfern, paragraphs 30–32.)

[32] See Redfern's discussion of this problem in paragraphs 10 and 11 of his study.

Robertson's doubt "whether it would be wise . . . to rely wholly on these beneficent forces." [33]

Redfern's estimates of net investment, which attempt to fill a gap in the official statistics, throw new light on Britain's postwar investment effort. These estimates rest on highly tentative assumptions concerning current depreciation of the capital stock, but according to their author they "do indicate broad orders of magnitude." Estimates are given for net investment in 1938 and for gross investment in earlier years as well, and although these are much more uncertain than the data available since 1948, the figures summarized in Table 8, expressed at constant prices, afford a useful comparison of fixed capital formation before and after the war. The differences between the gross and net figures in this table represent the estimated amounts of capital consumption in each year.

According to the last column of Table 8, gross investment regained the prewar level in 1950–1952 and rose above it in 1953. However, the estimated amount of annual depreciation was larger than before, so that net investment remained below the 1938 level throughout the period 1948–1952, regaining that level only in 1953. The distribution by industry groups shown in the table reveals some significant variations. From the figures available for main types of assets it appears that residential and other construction in the period 1948–1952 was lower, while additions to plant, machinery, and vehicles, even when reckoned on a net basis, were higher than before the war. Nevertheless the Redfern estimates — which, though tentative, are the result of a thorough investigation based for the most part on periodic Census of Production data — leave us with a clear suggestion that, in the aggregate, real capital formation in postwar Britain has not been remarkably high in comparison with the years before the war. But of course this is not in the least surprising in view of the exceptional effort required after the war to right the external balance.

International comparisons of capital formation, as of other

---

[33] D. H. Robertson, *Utility and All That* (London, 1952), 130. See also page 127 on the difficulty of drawing a clear line between changes in quality and changes in quantity of fixed capital.

TABLE 9. NATIONAL PRODUCT AND FIXED INVESTMENT PER CAPITA IN 1950
(*U.S. dollars per head of population*)

	In United States prices				In average European prices			
	U.S.	U.K.	France	W. Germany	U.S.	U.K.	France	W. Germany
Gross national product	1,810	1,136	968	785	1,810	954	764	604
Investment:								
Producers' durables	149	65	58	49	191	86	72	62
Residential construction	91	47	27	67	44	25	10	32
Other construction	104	24	52	28	85	22	43	23
Total gross fixed investment	344	136	137	144	320	133	125	117
Per cent of GNP	*19*	*12*	*14*	*18*	*18*	*14*	*16*	*19*

elements of national product, are notoriously difficult, but the figures in Table 9, taken from a pioneering study by M. Gilbert and I. B. Kravis,[34] are probably significant. That the ratio of fixed investment to national product should be lower in the United Kingdom than the United States is understandable.[35] But in the three European countries, additions to fixed capital in 1950 seem to have been about equal in absolute amount. Contrary to the usual correlation, the country with the highest per capita product among the three shows the lowest percentage of product invested. This remains true, though less markedly so, if the ratio is computed for producers' durables alone. Again the strains of the external balance may provide a partial explanation. But the fact remains that United Kingdom investment does not come out high in this comparison.

No satisfactory data exist for comparing the capital stock per worker in different countries, but a rough and simple index for this comparison is the use of inanimate energy. The average industrial worker in the United States has about 8 horsepower of mechanical power to help him. The corresponding figure for Britain, though higher than the West European average, is said to be between 3 and 4 horsepower.[36]

If the capital-output ratio has shown a tendency to fall, as Colin Clark has pointed out, this may have been due not only to capital-saving innovations but perhaps even more to fuller employment of labor and fuller utilization of public overhead installations such as railways and power plants which bulk so large in the total stock. In these circumstances it seems rash to draw conclusions about the "declining importance of capital." The fall in the capital coefficient over the past few decades does not necessarily make capital less important for future progress. The contrary can be argued. The capital stock, now pretty fully utilized,

[34] *An International Comparison of National Products* (O.E.E.C., Paris, 1954), Table 12.
[35] These figures are at least comparable in scope. Comparisons more favorable to the United Kingdom have sometimes been made by ignoring governmental capital outlays in the United States while including them in the United Kingdom, and by expressing the British figures of investment at *market prices* as a percentage of the official British GNP estimates at *factor cost*.
[36] Graham Hutton, *We Too Can Prosper* (London, 1953), 61.

may well become a major bottleneck to further output expansion. Besides, the high rate of obsolescence that goes with technical progress calls for high rates of capital outlay even if it is true that the balance of technical advance is shifting in favor of capital-saving inventions (which in fact seems doubtful).

It is therefore not surprising that, since the general easing of the dollar crisis and the rearmament emergency, economic policy in the United Kingdom has become increasingly concerned with stepping up the rate of domestic capital formation. In 1953 the initial depreciation allowances were restored. In that and the following year, credit policy was relaxed and the physical controls over capital works and installations almost entirely removed. In his 1954 budget statement the Chancellor of the Exchequer, after expressing concern about "the inadequate level of investment by private industry," announced a new system of investment allowances, amounting to a form of tax exemption, not simply tax postponement. Later in 1954 his slogan "Invest in Success" received wide publicity. Early in 1955 the authorities in charge of transport, steel, fuel, and power put forward plans which all added up to "a massive investment program," in the words of the 1955 *Economic Survey* (p. 44).

What actually happened in 1955, when again the British balance of payments came under pressure, will be discussed in a later section. Here we are still concerned with the general problem in its two aspects: (a) the widely recognized need for increased capital formation at home for the sake of long-range economic advance; and (b) a realization that "no satisfactory solution can be found for the balance-of-payments problem without a further substantial increase in the exports of the metal-using industries." [37]

The case for an expansion of the industries producing capital equipment presents itself on both grounds. How is it to be accomplished? Through increasing investment in the capital goods industries, which in recent years seems to have been disproportionately low. In 1953 (the latest year for which detailed figures are available) these industries, while accounting for more than half of the total payrolls in manufacturing and apparently for over half

[37] *Economic Survey for 1952*, Cmd. 8509, 32.

of the net value of manufacturing output as well, absorbed only 34 per cent of the gross fixed investment in manufacturing, which in turn was little more than one fifth of total gross outlay on fixed capital (or just under one third of the total if home building is left out of account).

Given full employment of resources in these as in other industries, greater investment in capital goods industries must mean that a larger part of the finished output of equipment is turned back into these industries for the expansion of their own capacity. Now if exports of engineering products are not to be cut down, this implies that, for a time, consumer goods industries (as well as consumers themselves) may have to go without the durable goods they need for mere replacement, to say nothing of expansion. In short, in a fully employed economy the enlargement of engineering capacity needed for easing the clash between internal growth and external solvency must entail some restraint on consumption: reducing the consumer's share in any output increments resulting from current improvements in productivity or perhaps even cutting the absolute total of consumable supplies.[38]

Renewal and expansion of capital equipment in the wide range of miscellaneous industry catering directly to consumers' needs are, of course, the ultimate aim. But until the total capacity of capital goods industries has been substantially enlarged, investment in consumption industries cannot be fostered on any extensive scale without endangering the external balance.

The grand totals of national product estimates that lump together investment in different industries are inadequate in this context since they fail to take into account the internal structure of the investment process: the need for *reducing* investment in consumer industries in the course of *increasing* investment in investment industries. This prior enlargement of "investment capacity" is, in the light of preceding considerations, important enough to merit specific attention. How is it to be "financed"?

It might be thought that some of the resources required could come from reducing expenditure on the basic overhead services which seemed so large in the years immediately after the war.

---

[38] Apart from personal consumption, possible reductions in current government spending on goods and services must also be kept in mind in this context.

However, while investment in coal, gas, and electricity has been greater, roads and railways have throughout received far less than before the war. Consequently the estimates of Table 8 above, though they leave out certain government assets, do not show public services as securing larger amounts after the war than before. Only in 1953 does investment in this category rise above earlier levels. Recognizing the capital needs of basic services the government published in January and February 1955 a series of impressive development programs for railroads, roads, and nuclear power. If these plans are acted upon they will almost certainly lead to an increase rather than a reduction in capital formation of the public overhead type. Nothing will be left over in this field for use in the expansion of equipment industries.

It seems unlikely, therefore, that any considerable enlargement of investment capacity can be carried out under conditions of full employment without withholding, or perhaps even withdrawing, resources from the consumption sector. This means increased saving — personal, corporate, or public. The marked revival of personal saving in 1951–1953 was highly welcome, but it was offset by a drop in the investible funds accruing in the government sector.[39] A mere switch of this kind in the sources of aggregate saving cannot increase the margin of real resources available for investment.

It is true that, until 1954 at any rate, business firms in general had fairly ample financial means of their own available for investment. But this too, considered in terms of the whole economy, did not mean that total investment could have been stepped up significantly without a rise in the concurrent rate of aggregate saving. It has been said that "as shortage of finance does not at present appear to be curtailing investment, it is misguided to advocate higher savings as a means to higher investment."[40] This view seems to me to draw, from the state of individual business finance, an illegitimate conclusion in regard to the national resources budget. At full employment a shortage of saving does become a basic obstacle to increased investment.

[39] *National Income and Expenditure, 1955*, 44.
[40] *Bulletin of the Oxford University Institute of Statistics*, XVII (February 1955), 2.

But a policy of restraint on consumption, while releasing the means, might damp the will to invest. The fiscal method of forced saving emerged under the Cripps regime in 1948–1950 as a major source of investible funds. But its possible effect on private investment incentives cannot be disregarded. A remarkable feature of the present British economy is the fact that the public sector, which accounts for less than 20 per cent of GNP, performs well over half of the total gross fixed investment. In 1954 (after the completion of certain denationalization measures), the capital outlays of the central government, local authorities, and nationalized industries still amounted to £1,309 million, or 53 per cent of the national total of £2,452 million. Even with new housing excluded the share of public investment was as high as 49 per cent.

Could it be that private incentives have been depressed by the forced saving imposed by the state, so that the state has been led to take over the act of investment as well as that of saving? The hypothesis is perhaps not entirely unreal, although the main practical explanation of the disproportionate share of public investment is to be sought elsewhere: namely in the exceptionally high capital requirements per unit of output in the field of public services and public utilities, which in Britain are all nationalized.

If public investment is one possibility, there is, however, another way out of the dilemma. It is to provide special incentives to private investment, if and when consumer demand has to be restrained to make room for the increase in investment capacity. Such incentives can take many forms, ranging from credit policy to government guarantees or outright subsidies. Something could be done by the tax authorities through further liberalization of write-off rules, and there is no reason why this stimulus should not be made stronger in some industries than in others.[41]

As already indicated, the building of additional capacity in the investment industries may for a time leave less equipment for consumer goods industries. Investment in the latter, instead of being stimulated, might have to be discouraged during that time (if it is not sufficiently discouraged by the check to consumer

[41] Suggestions to this effect were made by N. H. Leyland and G. D. N. Worswick in the Oxford *Bulletin*, XVII (February 1955), 61-62, 68.

demand which increased saving would involve). Once the expansion of investment capacity has been accomplished the special incentives might be turned to the consumption industries, if their demand — *plus* export demand — for plant and machinery should fail to absorb the increased supplies then forthcoming.

Capital development in industries producing capital goods is always subject to peculiar uncertainties and requires greater faith in the future than does investment in the common run of industries producing directly consumable goods and services. Cautious managers may prefer to let their order books fill up and to lengthen delivery dates even at the cost of losing export orders, rather than take action that might increase the risk of surplus capacity in the future. Any measures devised for the encouragement of expansion in the investment industries would need to be strong enough not just to compensate, but to overcompensate for the probable deterrent effect of restraints on consumption. How great the deterrent effect would be cannot be predicted, but one thing is certain: any mechanical application of the acceleration principle would be misleading and inappropriate. The induced investment to which that principle relates is in the main of the "capital widening" type that goes with changes in the volume of employment. What Britain needs for increasing productivity is a deepening of capital: an increase in the stock of capital per worker, a structural change in methods of production, a shift to more capital-intensive techniques. Expanding the country's engineering capacity is the means to achieve this without prejudice to exports and external equilibrium.

IV. BALANCE-OF-PAYMENTS POLICY AT FULL EMPLOYMENT

At a given level of productivity, a fully employed economy has no possible way of closing a deficit in its foreign balance unless it can cut down its absorption of resources for domestic purposes — that is, for consumption, investment, and government use. A country's net foreign balance on account of goods and services (exports less imports, or $X - M$) necessarily reflects the difference between its aggregate income (Y), derived from its production of goods and services for all purposes, and its aggregate expenditure (E), the volume of goods and services which the country absorbs from all sources for its own uses. The formula $X - M = Y - E$ is an accounting identity and holds true at all times. It acquires pragmatic interest when we impose constraints on it: postulating that $X - M$ be reduced to zero and that Y be kept at the level corresponding to full employment. An improvement in the foreign balance not only implies in logic, but requires in policy terms, a reduction in domestic expenditure relatively to income.

In short, if a country is to live within its export earnings on foreign exchange account it must keep its total expenditure within its income. In an open economy income and expenditure are not necessarily equal. An excess of expenditure over income can persist and will express itself in an external deficit so long as reserves or other means of financing it exist. If action is taken focusing narrowly on closing the external gap alone, excess expenditure may go on but, when thus confined to the home economy, will force up money incomes and prices. A trade deficit constitutes a leakage of purchasing power. If the external escape valve is shut off, the increased pressure in the system cannot fail to affect the home economy in such a way as to reopen the external gap.

Balance-of-payments measures such as import restrictions or exchange-rate changes cannot be relied upon as automatic means of bringing about the required adjustment in aggregate expenditure or, in real terms, of keeping a country's absorption of goods and services within the limits of its total production. Consider import restrictions first. When expenditures on foreign goods are forcibly curtailed it is possible that (a) the money income which consumers spent on them is spent instead on domestic goods and services. In this case the result will be a tendency toward increased pressure of demand in the home market encroaching directly or indirectly on supplies available for export. Some temporary relief may come, it is true, to the extent that the increased demand in the home market is met out of stocks. If these are stocks of imported goods the diversion we have assumed can be postponed as long as they last. If they are homemade goods, action taken to arrest and reverse the unintended inventory drop will spread and possibly reinforce the inflationary pressure. Only in conjunction with some deliberate measure of restraint on total spending can the restriction of imports in this case bring any lasting relief to the balance of payments.

It is conceivable, however, that (b) consumers save that part of their income which they used to spend on imports. If so, the reduction in total spending that is necessary for correcting the trade balance comes about directly as a result of the import controls. Here the balance-of-payments measure produces "automatically" the right effect on the income-absorption relation as well. This is possible; but how likely is it? How much can we expect from it? The answer depends on a great many circumstances rarely considered in the popular discussion of balance-of-payments restrictions on imports. It is easy to see, for example, that if spending on home-produced goods and services is widely restricted by rationing and other physical controls, money previously spent on imports may, as a consequence of import restrictions, now remain unspent.[42] But when there is freedom from controls in the domestic economy, import controls are much less likely to have any effect on total spending. We may note that this was the case in Britain in 1954–55, when the authorities repeatedly expressed their determination to avoid resort to import restrictions to deal with the setback which then occurred in the payments balance.

In the popular argument, an increase in domestic production of import substitutes is almost invariably presented as a means of improving the foreign balance. Such a shift in production is indeed a common result of balance-of-payments restrictions on imports; but, at full employment, it can only happen by increasing the pressure of demand and weakening the capacity to export. And it is just the wrong result if what is needed is increased saving induced by import cuts. Why this is needed is clear: external balance cannot be attained without bringing aggregate outlay and income into line. The efficacy of import restrictions as a means to this end is limited and uncertain.

---

[42] It may also be confined to spending on various services where, despite full employment, it may not do much harm. But still the foreign balance can improve only insofar as the additional income so created is saved. As a practical matter British experience suggests that not much reliance can be placed on the supply elasticity of dog racing and other entertainments furnished from a given stock of factors engaged in such activities.

Next let us turn to exchange-rate adjustment. However favorable the price elasticities, a devaluation at full employment can be of no use unless in the field of domestic expenditure an act of retrenchment is enforced that serves to make room for an improvement in the foreign balance. (A possible secondary burden due to a worsening of the terms of trade would entail some additional retrenchment.) This does not mean deflation; it means counteracting the inflationary effects of devaluation. If this is done, total money income corresponding to the full-employment level will tend to remain unchanged (and if it does, income elasticities and propensities, when strictly defined in relation to income changes, will be irrelevant). If the inflationary effects of devaluation are not counteracted, any increase in exports or decrease in imports resulting from devaluation must cause inflation of money incomes and prices, leading to renewed weakness in the balance of payments.

This is the so-called "absorption approach" to balance-of-payments analysis. There is nothing new about it: the notion that a country's net foreign balance is necessarily equal to what the country produces *less* what it "absorbs" for its own uses forms a central theme in Isaac Gervaise's *System or Theory of the Trade of the World* (London, 1720).[43] Some writers have opposed the "absorption approach" to the "elasticity approach." The opposition seems to me unreal; both are needed. We find, however, one prominent advocate of the absorption approach devoting an excellent paper to a search for *automatic* effects of devaluation on domestic absorption; and these, admittedly, prove to be tenuous, if not actually perverse.[44] But why assume that some self-regulating mechanism of international adjustment *must* exist, if

[43] See J. M. Letiche, "Isaac Gervaise on the International Mechanism of Adjustment," *Journal of Political Economy,* LX (February 1952). A reprint of Gervaise's pamphlet is now available (Baltimore, 1954).

[44] These are the "cash balance effect," the income redistribution, money illusion, and other direct effects on absorption, which S. S. Alexander discusses in his paper, "Effects of a Devaluation on a Trade Balance," I.M.F. *Staff Papers,* April 1952. "Tenuous" is the adjective which Alexander himself applies to them (p. 268), and possibilities of perverse reaction are also recognized (p. 273). G. Stuvel's *The Exchange Stability Problem* (New York, 1951), is another work in which an exhaustive search for automatic effects on expenditure proves, on the whole, fruitless: the outcome depends on "the way home demand reacts to changes in incomes and prices" (p. 231).

only we could discover it? The conclusion is unavoidable that domestic expenditure must form an essential *policy variable* for the maintenance of external balance.

If contractual income payments such as wages can be kept unchanged, the rise in import and export prices following a devaluation will cut the real purchasing power of these incomes. (The "if" is a big one, though British wage restraint in 1950 is a notable case where the condition was met.) But even this does not guarantee the "disabsorption" necessary for an increase in the trade balance. The income-receivers affected may seek to maintain their consumption by reducing their saving or by dissaving, and moreover they are likely to do so. This possibility figured prominently in the Laursen-Metzler analysis of the terms-of-trade effects of devaluation,[45] but it is not necessarily dependent on any change in terms of trade: it may happen even when export prices rise as much as import prices.

On the other hand, the necessary disabsorption *may* come about even if wage rates are fully adjusted. A wage-price spiral incorporating a wage lag and a shift to profits may after a while grind out enough forced saving to satisfy the income-absorption relationship. But this is likely to spoil the international price adjustment which devaluation was intended to achieve and which remains a prerequisite for its success.

The income-absorption analysis, though its practical emphasis may be on the problem of "living within one's means," is readily applicable to surplus as well as deficit countries — countries that underspend their income as well as those that overspend it. The manner of its application will depend to some extent on the pattern of international balances — on whether, for example, there is a dominant surplus country facing a great number of deficit countries, or one large deficit confronted by many small surpluses. Similarly the analysis can take account of international investment, which in a borrowing country creates a margin for "overabsorption" and "overimporting" and which calls only for a modified definition of external equilibrium (not simply as

[45] "Flexible Exchange Rates and the Theory of Employment," *Review of Economics and Statistics*, XXXII (November 1950).

$X - M$ reduced to zero, but $X - M$ *plus* the foreign borrowing).

The initial assumption of a given level of productivity simplifies discussion but is easily dropped. The secular growth of output due to rising productivity can be substantial even in the short run, from year to year. In Britain it is something that Chancellors of the Exchequer count upon in their annual budget statements. It renders the conditions of external balance less stringent and makes it possible for the income-absorption equation to be satisfied by altering the proportions in which different claimants share in output increments. At a given wage and price level the aggregate money income corresponding to full employment is increased and the deficit country's problem may reduce itself to checking the concurrent growth of domestic expenditure.

H. G. Johnson's recent analysis of the effect of increasing productivity on a country's trade balance[46] has pessimistic implications that seem at variance with those suggested by J. R. Hicks.[47] Clearly, different results are possible, depending on varying circumstances and, more particularly, on the assumptions made as to whether productivity gains are taken out in rising money incomes or in falling prices. I have myself been inclined to think that, apart from the rate of its change, the *level* of productivity and hence of real income per head has also a bearing on the balance of payments.[48] Other things being the same, it should be easier for a country to live within its income if that income is high in relation to (a) past peaks experienced at home (the ratchet effect) and (b) current levels observed elsewhere (the demonstration effect). While other things cannot be relied upon to remain the same, these two factors nevertheless provide grounds for believing that greater productivity tends fundamentally to help rather than hinder a country in maintaining external balance. Yet some control over domestic absorption remains an essential condition.

Reliance on exchange-rate adjustment alone does not fulfill this condition. In particular, exclusive reliance on freely fluctuating exchanges as an automatic means of equilibration seems for this

[46] *Economic Journal*, LXIV (September 1954).
[47] *Oxford Economic Papers*, n.s., June 1953.
[48] *Economia Internazionale*, February 1954 (see chapter 5, above).

reason mistaken.[49] It does not meet the need for a domestic expenditure policy. But this need arises when there are no idle resources. In an economy in which, by contrast, ample slack exists there may be room for *increasing* domestic absorption and improving the foreign balance simultaneously. In such circumstances the income effects of exchange adjustment, though they generally reduce the power of devaluation to improve the trade balance, need not by any means destroy its efficacy. The frequent neglect of the absorption aspects in postwar discussions of exchange adjustment may be a hangover from prewar depression economics, but such neglect is not permissible in the economics of full employment, in which classical doctrine in more than one respect comes back into its own. In the same way the classical tendency to deny that import restrictions are capable of improving the trade balance is seen to have some validity in an economy at full activity.

It is sometimes argued that a high level of employment means low supply elasticities and therefore tends to make exchange-rate adjustments ineffective. There is no doubt that inelastic supply, though it may be good for the terms of trade of the depreciating country, limits the extent to which international price adjustment can take advantage of elastic demand conditions for the correction of international imbalance. In the analysis of exchange variation a number of writers have equated full employment with low elasticity of supply.[50] But this need not be the case when devaluation is accompanied by the necessary domestic policies acting on the volume of absorption. How are we to take these policies

---

[49] See L. Robbins, *The Economist in the Twentieth Century* (London, 1954), 97–101. A similar view expressed by C. F. Carter with reference to the dollar problem is worth quoting in this connection: "The dollar problem is linked to the desire of non-dollar countries to maintain a standard of living not justified by their productivity. As long as this remains the case, changes in exchange rates do not solve the underlying problem, but shift its stress to a different place." ("The International and Domestic Financial Policy of the United Kingdom," *Public Finance,* no. 3, 1953, 229.)

[50] A. J. Brown, "The Fundamental Elasticities in International Trade," in *Oxford Studies in the Price Mechanism,* ed. T. Wilson and P. W. S. Andrews (Oxford, 1951), 103–104; W. L. Smith, "Effects of Exchange Rate Adjustments on the Standard of Living," *American Economic Review,* XLIV (December 1954), 822; G. Stuvel, *The Exchange Stabilization Problem* (New York, 1951), 204–208.

into account? How, in fact, are the two approaches — elasticity
and absorption — to be combined on this point? It cannot be
right to suggest, as one writer does,[51] that in the depreciating
country these measures will serve to increase the elasticity of
export supply. Elasticity is a functional relationship that cannot
properly take account of policy measures designed to cut down
domestic spending. It is surely better to regard these measures
as tending to lower the country's supply *schedule* of goods avail-

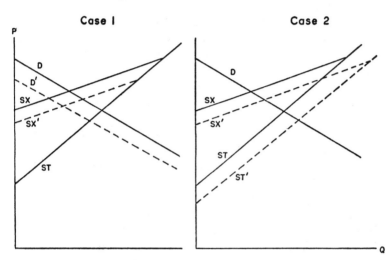

CHART 3. DOWNWARD SHIFTS IN EXPORT SUPPLY SCHEDULE RESULTING
FROM CUTS IN DOMESTIC EXPENDITURE ON (1) EXPORTABLE GOODS AND
(2) OTHER GOODS

able for export. There are two ways in which this downward
shift of export supply curves can come about (see Chart 3).

1. If the policy cut in domestic expenditure affects directly an
exportable commodity, this means a downward shift in the domestic demand schedule for this commodity (from *D* to *D'*). The
supply schedule for exports (*SX*) is the total supply of that commodity forthcoming at any given price (*ST*) *minus* the amount
sold at home at that price (*D*). The lowering of the domestic
demand curve implies necessarily a downward shift in the de-

[51] W. L. Smith, 822.

rived supply schedule of exports (from SX to SX'). At any given price more can now be sold abroad.

2. If the expenditure cut affects home-produced goods that do not enter into the export trade, factors will be released in the domestic industries and will seek re-employment in export industries, for whose products the home demand (D) has not decreased. This forces a downward shift in the total supply schedule of exportable goods (from ST to ST'), and hence also in the export supply schedule of these goods (from SX to SX').

Neither case 1 nor case 2 includes effects of devaluation proper, which will in addition bring upward shifts in foreign demand schedules expressed in domestic currency. For this reason alone it should not be assumed that case 2 must mean an intolerable volume of unemployment; there is a pull as well as a push of resources into export industries. Conceptually, apart from structural maladjustments, a proper combination of devaluation and "disabsorption" can preserve any given degree of employment that may be deemed desirable.

But in reality it is impossible to abstract from the problem of structural adjustment. The lowering of export supply schedules is incomparably easier in case 1 than in case 2. In the latter it depends on interindustrial mobility of resources and, if mobility is inadequate, will certainly involve some frictional unemployment. It is a considerable advantage for a country like Brittain to be able to rely largely on the method of case 1, even though this happens to affect, in the main, the domestic investment sector.

In short, exchange depreciation at full employment when combined with the appropriate absorption measures will cause a shift of demand and supply schedules, and in these circumstances there is no general reason to be afraid of supply difficulties. One arm of the combined operation makes room for the change in commodity flows, the other sets up incentives for the change to go ahead. Exchange depreciation under full-employment conditions *without* the complementary expenditure policies is likely to be disruptive of domestic stability and powerless to secure external equilibrium. Reliance on exchange fluctuation alone courts disappointment.

Reliance on domestic expenditure policy alone is liable to conflict with the maintenance of employment. If nothing else happens, the reduction of home expenditure is bound to lower national income below the full-employment mark. External equilibrium could be achieved in this way, but only by sacrificing internal balance. It is clear, therefore, that in general *two* policy handles are required for the simultaneous attainment of the two policy goals of internal and external balance. On the one hand there is need for instruments such as exchange-rate variation, import restrictions, export subsidies, or domestic price reduction. On the other, there must be an appropriate change in domestic outlay. What kind of outlay? This question concerns us in the next section.

Here we encounter a fruitful application of J. Tinbergen's theory of economic policy, centering on his distinction between target variables and instrument variables, and on his demonstration that "if more than one target is set, then a like number of instruments will be required." [52] Since in the present case we have two targets — a high level of employment and a net foreign balance of zero — we must make use of two policy instruments, one apparently designed to induce (or force) a change in external transactions, the other to keep domestic expenditure in line with the full-employment level of income. But although we may not be able to avoid using teleological terms and may be strongly tempted to link up each instrument with one particular target, all we can really say is that two policy variables are necessary for the simultaneous attainment of the two goals. As Tinbergen emphasizes, it is not strictly possible to hold the view that each instrument serves one of the goals.[53] In a system with an equal number of target variables and instrument variables a unique solution can be found, but there is complete interdependence be-

[52] J. Tinbergen, "The Relation between Internal Inflation and the Balance of Payments," Banca Nazionale del Lavoro (Rome), *Quarterly Review,* October–December 1952. For his general treatment of the subject see J. Tinbergen, *On the Theory of Economic Policy* (Amsterdam, 1952).

[53] As a matter of labelling and classification such measures as exchange adjustment and import restriction can of course be classed as "external," if only because in a closed economy they would be nonexistent and pointless. But in an open economy they do affect internal conditions and indeed have sometimes been used for this purpose.

tween all individual targets pursued and instruments employed.

J. E. Meade's monumental work[54] agrees in substance with this approach, but in its exposition is shot through with particular assignments of means to ends. To be sure, there are passages which expressly state that the problem is one of combined operation of two instruments acting on the internal and external position simultaneously; but the dominant method of presentation runs in terms of what particular instrument the authorities use for what particular purpose. Thus a sharp distinction is made (p. 157) between (1) the use of financial policy for the preservation of internal balance and price adjustment for the preservation of external balance and (2) the use of financial policy for the preservation of external balance and price adjustment for the preservation of internal balance. The pointlessness of such attributions is revealed in an elaborate analysis in the succeeding pages which brings out clearly that whichever principle is followed the results are in each case the same, which is not surprising. The only context in which Meade's teleology seems unquestionable is the case of the gold standard, which is characterized as "the automatic use . . . of monetary policy for the maintenance of external balance and of wage flexibility for the maintenance of internal balance" (p. 190), but here it becomes acceptable only because in effect the problem of internal balance vanishes with perfect wage and price flexibility.

Although many possible variations are recognized, Meade's general procedure is to assume that "whatever happens as a result of external developments" the authorities in each country pursue financial — i.e., monetary and fiscal — policies to maintain internal balance, defined as a high level of employment without inflation of prices and costs (pp. 233 and 345). The complementary retrenchment in domestic outlay accompanying a devaluation or import restriction in a deficit country is recognized as a necessity, but is almost invariably presented as being necessary "for the purpose of," "in the interests of," or "in order to preserve" *internal* balance (for example, pp. 166, 247, 318, 346ff). It is as clear as can be that the policy reduction of domestic expenditure is essential for the attainment of external as well as

[54] *The Theory of International Economic Policy,* vol. I, *The Balance of Payments* (London, 1951).

internal balance and that it forms indeed an absolutely basic means for a country seeking to pay its way in the world. When it is argued, for example, that "the authorities in B remove a deficit on B's balance of payments by restricting imports" and that "to preserve internal balance the authorities in B must adopt a deflationary financial policy" (p. 307), it is tacitly assumed that import restrictions *can* improve the foreign payments balance. But at full employment they generally cannot; and in the conceivable but unlikely case where they create their own "disabsorption," a policy cut in domestic expenditure will be required neither for internal nor for external balance.

Meade's characteristic method of presenting the change in domestic outlay as something required for domestic reasons (taking it for granted that, whatever the external disturbances, financial policy is always in some way adjusted to preserve internal balance), tends to conceal the external significance of domestic expenditure control. The income-absorption problem so vital for external equilibrium at full employment is wrapped up with the complex of policies said to be needed for internal balance, which, lying in the domestic sphere, are not further discussed. This makes for a sharp and neat separation between internal and external policies, convenient for purposes of exposition, but in reality untenable. It is, of course, a matter of presentation. No one can fail to profit from Meade's brilliant synthesis of price and income effects, nor to admire his enormous patience and skill. Yet one wonders whether the procedure described may not in some degree reflect, and in its turn support, the habit of keeping internal and external policy in closed compartments — a habit that has perhaps its roots in the slack of the 1930's, but has been out of place in the taut conditions of more recent times. Dr. Dalton's words in July 1947, when he was Chancellor of the Exchequer, are remembered as a classic (though inadvertent) expression of a then not uncommon attitude: "The contrast is most remarkable between the great difficulty of the overseas position and the relative ease of the purely domestic financial position, in which things are very much better and easier than we would have had any reason to expect two years ago." [55]

[55] Quoted in D. H. Robertson, *Utility and All That,* 56, 158.

V. INVESTMENT POLICY AND EXTERNAL BALANCE

The pursuit of external equilibrium and domestic stability at full employment requires, on the one hand, a policy variable such as exchange-rate adjustment or import restriction and, on the other, appropriate changes in domestic outlay. Now the question is: what kind of outlay?

We shall note three reasons why the brunt of adjustment is likely to fall on domestic investment.

The first is that, in a community's scale of necessity, investment may have a low order of priority. Food, shelter, luxuries, saving — this is the usual order in which major items enter into an individual's budget as his means increase.[56] In a nation's budget, too, investment can be treated as a luxury — and therefore as the first thing one lets go when in trouble. Investment is nearly always an early casualty in wartime. Provision for higher future consumption is in the nature of things an activity that can conveniently be reduced or postponed in case of need, without having to force a drastic change in a community's current habits of living and spending. This argument is necessarily somewhat vague, yet it strikes me as probably of basic empirical significance. In private enterprise economies, as in democratic welfare states, investment is consequently likely to be, in a sense, a residual recipient.

There is, however, nothing inevitable about this order of necessity. It may be the line of least resistance, but it is a matter of human choice, and in fact a concern for economic growth has caused many countries nowadays to attach a higher priority to capital outlay.

The second reason for concentrating on home investment is more specific and requires fuller consideration. Whenever a nation is running a deficit on its *external* accounts some kind of deficit spending must be going on somewhere in its *domestic* economy. According to the fundamental identity $X - M = Y - E$, in which E comprises consumption, investment, and gov-

[56] K. E. Boulding, among other writers, has discussed this "scale of necessity" in his writings on the consumption function and income elasticity. See his paper, "Equilibrium and Wealth," *Canadian Journal of Economics and Political Science,* 1939.

ernment outlays, a gap between exports (X) and imports (M) of goods and services reflects a gap between the aggregate income (Y) and expenditure (E) of all individuals, firms, and public organizations in the country. It is a homely truism (but true nevertheless) that a trade deficit could not exist if the households, companies, and other units composing a nation were not trying to spend beyond their income. Wieser's view of a country's balance of payments as the sum of the individual balances of its inhabitants[57] is applicable more generally to any group of people. In the international context, people are grouped according to the country in which they live; the deficits and surpluses they may have with each other inside the group cancel out; what remains is the net foreign balance. When their total income and their total expenditure are equal — that is, when the conditions of Say's Law are fulfilled (and of course they are not necessarily fulfilled) — only then will their external accounts be in balance.

Now deficit spending may, and in the popular view usually does, originate in the government sphere. It can also come from private households, as in Britain in the early postwar years (1946–1949), when people had abnormally large cash reserves available for consumption expenditure beyond current income, and when in fact dissaving occurred on a large enough scale to keep the net total of personal saving close to zero.

But the traditional and respectable form of deficit spending is capital outlay, which under modern conditions can normally be financed in part through the credit system. Accordingly it was capital outlay that tended to carry the burden of external adjustment under the gold standard rules of the game. In the nineteenth-century currency system, wages were flexible enough to permit continual price adjustments with tolerably full employment. Then what took care of the income-absorption relationship necessary for external balance? It was the interest mechanism of central banking policy acting on investment — perhaps most directly on inventory investment, but ultimately on fixed investment as well. Here was a gap in Wieser's theory that balance-of-payments equilibrium is brought about by individuals acting under the necessity of living within their incomes. For in-

[57] F. von Wieser, *Social Economics* (English translation, 1927), 451–454.

stitutional reasons this necessity did not apply to business investment expenditure, which at least for marginal amounts normally
depended on the credit system.

The gold standard can thus be looked upon as a system that
served to maintain external balance by keeping the member
countries in step as regards their investment activity and, to
this extent, their rates of economic growth. When capital outlay
in any country grew out of bounds so that the foreign balance
became unfavorable, brakes were applied to capital development
in that country through higher money rates and credit restrictions. The dominant preoccupation of central bank policy was
that of "relating the price of accommodation to the behavior of
the foreign exchanges." [58] The effects were not limited to traders'
stocks. We have a good description, for example, of the way in
which in 1837 a strain in Britain's foreign balance promptly
caused increasing stringency of credit and a reduction of new investment, chiefly in manufacturing.[59] We have the classic statement of the Cunliffe Committee's Report (1918) on the *modus
operandi* of the pre-1914 currency system: "The raising of the
Bank's discount rate and the steps taken to make it effective in
the market necessarily led to a general rise in interest rates and
a restriction of credit. New enterprises were therefore postponed
and the demand for constructional materials and other capital
goods was lessened."

Investment, being a form of private deficit spending linked to
the credit system, is that component of national outlay on which
the weight of external strains has in the past tended to fall. Harrod is right in saying that the relation between home investment
and the foreign balance has always been implicit in orthodox
doctrine about bank rate.[60] The substantive reasons are clear;
the relation is more than an accounting matter.

The term "monetary policy" may suggest something that is
"directly focused upon the supply of and the demand for money
in the sense of the aggregate of cash and credit," something
"whose influence is capable of covering the whole field of ex-

[58] R. C. O. Matthews, *A Study in Trade Cycle History, 1833–1842* (Oxford, 1954), 175.
[59] *Ibid.*, 209–210.
[60] R. F. Harrod, *And So It Goes On* (London, 1951), ix, 78.

penditure rather than special parts of it." [61] But let us not forget that, first and foremost, traditional monetary policy had to do with deficit finance for business investment, which indeed was the medium whereby money was injected into or withdrawn from a private enterprise economy. This, in the main, is still the specific province of monetary policy. "Essentially the aim of central banking is to operate upon private investment by manipulating the availability and cost of finance. This presupposes dependence of private investment on institutional channels of finance — including in this term both the banking system and the capital market." [62]

Monetary policy works by changing (a) the cost and (b) the availability of credit; in other words, by influencing (a) the desire and (b) the ability to invest. The effect under both heads is likely to be asymmetrical. "Interest policy . . . gets very high marks as a means of checking booms, but very low marks as a means of checking slumps." [63] Similarly, on the availability side alone, "You can lead a horse to water but you can't make him drink." To which we must add: but once he has started drinking, you can always turn off the tap. The availability concept refers to the element of rationing always present in reality — the "fringe of unsatisfied borrowers" in Keynes' *Treatise*. As the interest and rationing aspects of credit policy normally vary together it may be hard or even impossible to distinguish their separate effects in operation.[64]

It is conceivable that the interest mechanism of the gold standard may also come into operation as an automatic effect of exchange-rate adjustment or even of import restrictions. Pro-

---

[61] L. Robbins, *The Economist in the Twentieth Century*, 74.

[62] D. Rowan, "The Monetary Problems of a Dependent Economy: The Australian Experience 1948–1952," Banca Nazionale del Lavoro, *Quarterly Review* (December 1954).

[63] J. R. Hicks, *Value and Capital* (Oxford, 1939), 263. The famous Oxford survey in the late 1930's did not even consider the possibility of such an asymmetry (*Oxford Studies in the Price Mechanism*, ch. I). It was concerned only with the power of low interest rates to stimulate an increase in business investment, and even on this point its negative findings must have been greatly influenced by the then prevailing conditions of surplus capacity.

[64] See E. Lundberg's recent discussion of this, reviewed by S. Laursen in "Lundberg on Business Cycles and Public Policy," *Quarterly Journal of Economics* (May 1955), esp. 230.

vided only that the authorities hold the total quantity of money constant, the price rise of imports and import substitutes (and, in the case of devaluation, of exports as well) may cause an increased demand for cash for transactions purposes, which would force interest rates up and make credit tight. Private deficit spending would become more difficult to finance; once again investment would have to make room for the improvement in the foreign balance. But this automatic outcome depends on the proviso mention and is in any case likely to be quite unreliable in its impact on capital outlay, since the incentive to invest in at least the import-substitute industries would be increased at the same time.

But now a wider question demands attention. Is it not again a case of misplaced concreteness to strike out against particular deficit expenditures whenever a nation's aggregate accounts are in deficit? Is this not a rather narrow and arbitrary criterion based on institutional arrangements? From the viewpoint of over-all national budgeting, might it not be just as well to create a corresponding surplus in some other sector? Instead of forcing each individual sector or accounting unit into balance, could not deficits in one place be offset within the global accounts by surpluses elsewhere? Such queries may or may not throw doubt on gold-standard orthodoxy, but at least they suggest that the place and form of any internal retrenchment necessary for correcting the external balance are matters for the nation's choice. The burden does not have to fall on the accumulation of capital.

The third reason it tends to fall on capital formation is a structural point that applies in particular to the present British economy. If resources were fully mobile any disabsorption intended to offset the inflationary effect of devaluation or import restriction would establish a general framework leaving room for an improvement in the trade balance, and that would be all that was necessary. In fact mobility is imperfect; pockets of slack in some industries can coexist with bottlenecks in others for considerable periods. It is therefore natural that domestic expenditure policy should be designed to affect the kind of outlay that most directly impinges on the foreign balance, in order to minimize the transfer losses and the unemployment that occurs when workers have to change jobs.

But this is essentially an argument of short-term expediency. If on other grounds the community would choose a different place for disabsorption it can see to it that the adjustment is carried out slowly but surely in the desired direction. Factor mobility, though inadequate for meeting foreign-exchange crises, should be sufficient to permit a long-run shift, such as the expansion of Britain's capital-goods industries, which would make possible an adequate average level of home investment even though investment still had to give way to export needs at times of external strain.

When Harrod in a couple of forceful pamphlets[65] urged Britain to cure her balance-of-payments troubles by pruning what he considered an excessive investment program, he must have had the structural point in mind, though he did not stress it. It was uppermost in the minds of policymakers, as their statements showed. Investment policy in fact followed the line urged by Harrod, though for him it did not go far enough. Harrod at the same time was greatly concerned to expose the futility of trying, in an economy without slack, to redress the balance of trade by import restrictions alone. It may be that in 1947, when domestic expenditure too was hemmed in by direct controls, import restrictions did have some disabsorption effect (as described in the last section). Yet Harrod's view of the external deficit as being the "mirror image" of excess spending at home was in principle incontrovertible, based on the simple arithmetic of national income accounting so often ignored by adherents of the specific commodity approach, who, with their concrete view of things, would restore a balance of payments by cutting imports and fostering home production of this or that commodity.

Harrod's view was right, but to this writer still rather narrow in that he saw the excess expenditure not as an excess of domestic expenditure over national income as a whole, but as an excess of capital outlay over current saving. Investment was deficit spending and therefore to be cut. As a matter of fact many

[65] R. F. Harrod, *Are These Hardships Necessary?* (London, 1947); *And So It Goes On* (London, 1951).

British households in 1947 also indulged in deficit spending
(dissaving). But Harrod seems to have been influenced by gold-
standard doctrine. A reduction in home investment was what, in
the circumstances, would have happened in the past; it should
have happened in 1947 as well (though Harrod would have relied
on direct controls for this purpose, not on monetary policy).
Although his pamphlets were addressed to a popular audience his
references to the working of the gold standard, including particularly the traditional relationship between home investment
and the trade balance, were perceptive and enlightening (pp. 59,
62, 147 in *Are These Hardships Necessary?*; pp. ix, 78, 117 in
And So It Goes On). It was their relevance to the postwar condition of England that remained open to question.

Naturally some of Harrod's critics at the time found it hard to
see why in this condition investment should bear the burden of
retrenchment.[66] Though the subject of capital needs may be debatable, there must be a line below which even those who attach
little importance to them would not want gross investment to be
reduced for the sake of external balance. Investment in public
services, to which Harrod particularly objected, appears in the
light of Redfern's figures to have been considerably less in 1948
than it was ten years before (see Table 8, above).[67] It may be
that Harrod intended to protest not so much against a high level
of investment already going on as against overambitious plans,
some of which were later dropped or trimmed. The point remains
that reconstruction and development needs did not receive a high
priority in his discussion.

Moreover, his thesis was open to the charge that it neglected
the claims of internal balance as well as those of capital growth.
Investment cuts were for him not one arm of a two-pronged

[66] Among the critics were two — Haberler and Schumpeter — who were no
less steeped in gold-standard doctrine than Harrod himself. See *Review of
Economics and Statistics*, XXX (May 1948), and *Journal of Political Economy*,
LVII (October 1949). And the greatest of gold-standard authorities — Jacob
Viner — found Britain's postwar investment target set "incredibly low" and
thought this "the most discouraging aspect of the entire picture." "An American
View of the British Economic Crisis," *Lloyds Bank Review* (October 1947).

[67] There may have been a cut in this type of investment from 1947 to 1948,
but in view of the global figures of Table 6 this is not likely.

attack, the other being an external measure, such as devaluation. For closing the external gap he would have relied on investment cuts exclusively, believing that with big enough cuts of this kind devaluation would not have been necessary (*And So It Goes On,* p. 155). Quite possible; but this might have led to considerable unemployment. If there existed a pent-up foreign demand that would have absorbed at current terms all the equipment released from domestic demands, then total activity in the engineering industries could conceivably have remained unchanged so long as the backlog of export orders was being worked off. This might have been the case in 1947, but the backlog cannot have been so important in 1949, and in any event this factor played no prominent part in Harrod's presentation. He seemed unmindful of the employment problem, relying solely on domestic expenditure policy under conditions very different from nineteenth-century wage flexibility.

The upshot of this section may be stated in terms of Tinbergen's system of target and instrument variables, to which reference was made above. The simultaneous pursuit of the two targets, internal and external balance, calls for an equal number of instrument variables: what Meade terms "financial policy" on the one hand and foreign exchange or trade policy on the other. If in addition a third target is set, namely a high rate of capital formation for economic growth, a third instrument variable will be needed, and this may be labelled (briefly but perhaps recognizably enough) as varying the "fiscal" and "monetary" *ingredients* of financial policy in such a way as to provide the resources *and* the incentives for that rate of investment.[68]

[68] A question that branches off from here cannot be followed up in this paper. What if the target rate of capital growth persistently exceeds the amount which individuals choose to save at the full-employment level of national income? As Sir Dennis Robertson has put it (*Utility and All That,* 131), can it be taken for granted that collective saving decisions will in fact be honored and not evaded by individuals in their daily business of earning and spending money? Individual time-preferences cannot be ignored, but, for one thing, the large amount of company saving that is only remotely related to the wishes of individual shareholders suggest that there is some play in the system. Besides, insofar as the desire to save is directly related to the interest rate some method of interest subsidy on the investment side might more than repay its cost. But these and other related matters must here be left aside.

VI. Renewed Strains and Investment Curbs

We will conclude this discussion by focusing it briefly on the events of 1955 when the British economy, working at record levels of activity, developed strains that threatened to disturb all three of the policy goals just mentioned: internal balance, external equilibrium, economic growth.

It was observed from Table 7 that of the total increment in Gross National Product from 1952 to 1954, reckoned at constant prices, as much as 74 per cent went into increased personal consumption. An additional 11 per cent was absorbed by the growth in residential construction. These changes were at least partly related to government policies. The housing drive initiated at the end of 1951 has been referred to. The expansion of consumer spending had doubtless something to do with the sweeping tax reductions made in April 1953. There were minor cuts in purchase tax in January 1954, and consumer credit restrictions were removed in July 1954. The current surplus on the balance of payments (see Table 5) remained a good deal below the target of a £300 million annual surplus which the government was aiming at for the replenishment of gold reserves and the financing of Commonwealth development. Still, things seemed to be going well in 1954 when the Chancellor of the Exchequer spoke of a possible doubling of the British standard of living in twenty-five years, a goal which in view of the average 3 per cent annual rise of industrial output per worker in the years 1948–54 seemed quite attainable. The one dark spot was the lag in industrial investment. The concern felt on this score and the remedial measures taken by the authorities have already been indicated.

After some coaxing and exhortation, private investment picked up in 1954. The physical controls were gone, though building licensing was not formally scrapped until the fall of 1954; approval of new factory building was required only with respect to location. In the latter part of the year there developed indeed a vigorous investment boom — on top of the consumption boom that had developed since 1952. Some indications of increasing investment are given in Table 10. When the next balance of payments statement appeared early in 1955, it showed that in

Table 10. Quarterly Indicators of Investment Activity

	1953		1954				1955			
	III	IV	I	II	III	IV	I	II	III	IV
Industrial construction (million square feet)										
Approved	9.6	11.5	14.4	15.5	21.2	19.8	24.0	29.7	20.8	17.2
Started	8.0	6.6	9.4	12.6	10.4	13.4	16.0	17.9	15.9	n.a.
Machine tools (£ million)										
New orders:										
Domestic	8.8	10.5	10.9	12.4	14.2	20.3	18.5	20.2	17.7	n.a.
Export	2.9	4.1	4.2	5.3	6.0	5.5	5.5	5.5	4.8	n.a.
Deliveries:										
Domestic	9.7	12.1	11.6	11.6	11.4	12.7	13.2	13.7	13.8	n.a.
Export	5.1	5.0	4.6	4.6	4.4	4.5	4.8	5.0	4.4	n.a.

n.a. Not available.

the second half of 1954 the country had incurred a small deficit on current account amounting to £38 million (excluding United States defense aid), a figure subsequently revised to £5 million.

The trouble in the payments balance was largely on the export side. This was a time when most of Britain's customers were prosperous. The drastic import cuts which Australia imposed in April 1955 came after the deterioration of Britain's own balance and were quite overshadowed by the spontaneous effects of boom conditions elsewhere. British exports, on the whole, were keeping up, but they did not share fully in the expansion that was taking place in world trade.

The rise in British imports, on the other hand, was accentuated by large purchases of steel required to feed the domestic hardware boom, but was partly due also to the fact that imports in 1954 had been kept relatively low because of the liquidation of government trading stocks (see Table 5). Prices of both imports and exports remained fairly stable throughout 1953–55, increasing by about 2–3 per cent in the first ten months of 1955. The terms of trade changed very little.

The two dock strikes in the late fall of 1954 and the late spring of 1955 caused, however, some erratic movements in the trade returns, which must therefore be interpreted with caution. The bulges that appear in Table 11 in the first and third quarters of 1955 were largely due to shipments that had been delayed by the strikes. The adverse shift in the visible trade balance shows itself clearly in the quarterly movement of Table 11 but is perhaps best observed from the figures for the twelve months ending in September 1954 and September 1955 respectively, which (in £ million) are as follows:

	1953–54	*1954–55*	*Increase*
Imports	3,337	3,752	12%
Exports (incl. re-exports)	2,804	2,897	3%
Excess of Imports	533	855	61%

One of the most noteworthy features of British economic policy in 1955 was the government's refusal to try to correct the trade balance by means of import restrictions. As the domestic econ-

TABLE 11. QUARTERLY MERCHANDISE TRADE AND THE VISIBLE BALANCE

(£ million)

| | 1953 | | 1954 | | | | 1955 | | | |
	III	IV	I	II	III	IV	I	II	III	IV
Imports	825	826	821	852	838	868	1,005	898	981	1,002
Exports[a]	660	718	701	698	687	689	774	676	758	817
Excess of imports	165	108	120	155	151	179	231	222	222	186

[a] Including re-exports.

omy was characterized not only by full employment but now also by virtual freedom from direct controls, resort to import restrictions would probably have created additional inflationary pressure and so weakened further the export side of the external accounts, or would have given only ephemeral relief through the liquidation of stocks which would have had to be replenished later.

On the export side the 3 per cent rise in British export values from 1953–54 to 1954–55, as shown above, compares with an increase of 8 per cent in the imports of the free world outside the United Kingdom. At the same time Britain's chief competitors (Western Europe, the United States, and Japan) increased their exports by 13 per cent.

From the first to the second half of 1954 there was actually a slight decline in the value of British exports, which has been attributed to the first dock strike. But curiously enough this decline was more than accounted for by exports of machinery and electrical equipment alone. The $7\frac{1}{2}$ per cent drop in machinery exports was widely distributed among export markets. Import restrictions abroad were not being generally increased and, in fact, tended everywhere to favor capital goods. It may well be, therefore, that the export figures for the second half of 1954 reflected the spurt in domestic investment, which at all events interfered with the *expansion* of exports. Britain's engineering industries in 1954 were working overtime and expanding total output, but more of their output was drawn into domestic uses. The same was probably true in the first half of 1955, even though hardware exports then increased.

The insistent demands of the home market made themselves felt in many ways, but not, apparently, through any substantial price changes. Prices of British engineering products are notoriously sticky. They had not yet risen so much as to offset the advantage of the 1949 devaluation and were still, on the whole, competitive in world markets. But the pressure of home demand may have caused a comparative neglect of export orders. As Harrod put it: "Our engineering capacity is strained, to the detriment of prompt delivery to export markets. . . . Of the substantial growth of [export] delivery delays there is no doubt." [69] There exists no statistical measure that can fully reflect this difficulty. Comparison of new export orders and deliveries, shown for a single type of equipment in Table 10, affords some indication, but cannot take account of possible export orders lost because of failure to quote satisfactory delivery dates.

Evidently there was not enough room in the British economy for the expansion of private investment which had at last set in, and so the external gap re-appeared. The government's countermeasures in 1955 consisted largely in attempts to stem, or push back, the upsurge of private investment activity as well as to limit the capital outlays of the public sector. The aim was certainly to curb the increase in the aggregate volume of investment if not to cut it down. This time, however, there was another form of deficit spending of a postponable luxury character: consumer buying of durable goods on the installment system ("hire purchase"), which had rapidly increased since July 1954. Accordingly regulations governing minimum down payments and maximum credit periods were reimposed in February 1955, when they affected mainly household goods, and tightened up in July, when they were applied especially to motor cars.

Monetary policy was brought into action in January and February 1955, when the bank rate was increased in two steps from 3 per cent to $4\frac{1}{2}$ per cent. The liquidity of commercial banks was put under pressure. There was a general upward movement of interest rates, long as well as short. Between February and September the government increased, in four steps, the interest rates charged by the Public Works Loan Board on loans to local authorities from $2\frac{1}{2}$–$3\frac{3}{4}$ per cent to $4\frac{1}{2}$–5 per cent (the lower rates being applicable to loans up to five years, the higher to longer-term loans). Departing from previous practice the government refused to grant compensatory increases in subsidies to local authorities.

The business investment boom showed no signs of slackening in the first half of 1955. The psychological effect of the Bank rate increases was probably offset by the publication, in January and February, of the government's own investment plans (to which reference was made in section III), by the "optimistic and

[69] *Financial Times* (London), 23 April 1955.

expansive tone" of the budget speech in April,[70] and by other pronouncements preceding the general election in May 1955, when, for instance, the Chancellor declared once more that "we must, if we are to enjoy steadily rising standards of life . . . invest in and build up the productive power of our country and our Empire." [71] In this atmosphere the tightening of credit policy was of very limited efficacy. In fact bank loans continued to increase throughout the earlier half of the year. The banks sold government securities and allowed their liquidity ratios to run down. On June 16 the Chancellor observed that the amount of bank advances was not satisfactory, but that at least it was related to the continuance of investment, which was a major aim of the government. Later in the same month the banks put out a collective statement about the need to restrict their loans. Finally, in July 1955, the Chancellor issued, in the form of a letter to the Bank of England, a directive calling for a significant reduction in the amount of commercial-bank loans outstanding. This was interpreted as a 10 per cent reduction to be accomplished by the end of 1955. It heralded a fairly general quantitative limitation of credit, giving a somewhat unorthodox emphasis to the usual credit rationing side of monetary policy, while the bank rate was not further increased in 1955.

The statement in Parliament where these measures were announced on July 25 said in part:

Our primary aim must be to reduce home demand in order to leave room for the extra exports we need. All who can must try to spend less in order to save more. Business firms should endeavor to slow down investment not of the greatest national urgency. Since our principal object is to improve our balance of payments it would be undesirable to check investment leading to increased production for export. For the rest, even though a high level of productive investment is undoubtedly in our long-run national interest, all those embarking on investment projects should consider whether they could not postpone their initiation . . .

The appeal for *postponement* of investment projects used the same term as the 1947 White Paper on capital cuts (quoted in section II). The term occurs also in the Cunliffe Committee's

[70] *London and Cambridge Economic Bulletin,* September 1955, 1.
[71] *The Spectator* (London), 20 May 1955, 634.

description of the working of the gold standard (quoted in section V, above). New investment is inherently postponable expenditure; but postponement of individual projects is of course tantamount to reducing the aggregate rate of capital formation.

The statement just cited makes, however, a reservation in favor of export industries, which accordingly received preferential treatment in the commercial banks' credit restriction. The policy of confining new investment to expanding production for export is questionable on general grounds.[72] But its practical effect in the present case, from what was said in section I, may be to exempt especially the hardware industries from the cutback of capital outlay. From August to November 1955, when total bank loans to private borrowers declined by 5 per cent, loans to the metal and engineering industries alone showed a slight increase. It is important to note that these industries played a leading part in the upsurge of investment projects in late 1954 and early 1955. The share of the mechanical and electric engineering industries in the total approvals for new factory building in the first half of 1955 was 26 per cent, compared with 19 per cent in the period 1945–1954. The share of the other metal-using industries (motor vehicles, shipbuilding, and other metal goods) was an additional 25 per cent of the total space then approved, as compared with 18 per cent in the previous ten years.[73]

As may be seen from Table 10 above, the total volume of industrial construction approved was nearly 80 per cent higher in the first half of 1955 than in the first half of 1954. At the same time there was an increase by over 50 per cent in industrial building projects started. The upswing of investment activity was impressive.

Now if this upswing, as the projects approved suggest, was largely in the capital goods industries and if these industries, on the ground of their large and growing contribution to exports, were spared from the cutback imposed in mid-1955, the outcome might well be a substantial increment in the type of capacity required for both internal re-equipment and export expansion in

[72] See my note in the *Bulletin of the Oxford Institute of Statistics*, XVII (February 1955), 48.

[73] *Board of Trade Journal*, 20 August 1955, 426.

the future. The way in which the internal expansion of 1954–55 impinged upon the metal-using industries and, through them, on the external position demonstrated again the need for enlarging capacity in that particular sector. But, in these circumstances, what becomes of the cutback? In the United Kingdom a number of industries other than engineering can claim to be essential for the export trade. Moreover, by mid-1955 many new investment projects had already been started. (See Table 10 for figures on factory building starts.) Increased industrial construction could make use of resources released by the cuts that were imposed on public housing programs. But pressure to fill the added factory space with equipment was bound to continue for a time. Monetary policy is a flexible tool in the double sense that it can be wielded at any time and that it acts, in the main, on a type of expenditure that is postponable. However, a restrictive monetary policy may affect only the making of new investment decisions; it cannot always be expected to force the abandonment of projects already in hand. "In general, existing programs will not be affected," said the Chancellor on July 25 with reference to public investment schemes, repeating a principle expressed in previous cases of capital cuts (see section II, above). The principle could not easily be denied to private business. The abandonment of half-finished investment projects, as in some nineteenth-century downturns, seems today intolerable. The credit squeeze, except for its possible but uncertain effects on inventory investment, could therefore not be relied upon to bring immediate relief.

Despite our limited theme in this paper — which is not an over-all account of British economic affairs — we cannot at this point ignore the general state of the British economy in mid-1955 and the central problem, then coming to a head, of stability at high levels of employment. The labor force was far more fully employed than Beveridge had proposed in his report ten years previously. Instead of his 3 per cent unemployment, the ratio now was 0.9 per cent. The number of workers unemployed was the lowest since the war; the number of vacant jobs was more than twice as high; overtime work was widespread. It was a state of overfull employment that could hardly continue without either a return to direct controls or a serious open price inflation. Industrial disputes, a railroad stoppage, and the dock strikes set up inducements for business firms to increase rather than cut down their commodity stocks. Wage demands were pressed in excess of current advances in productivity. Increases in wage rates were particularly marked in the very first quarter of the year.

In this state of affairs the budget of 19 April 1955, which again brought substantial tax concessions, cannot be said to have followed the principles of "functional finance." These principles, while sanctioning budget deficits in times of sluggish private demand, call for a surplus in government accounts when private deficit spending imperils stability. Specifically, when private investment steps ahead while personal and business saving lags, the increase in government saving in effect finances the increased capital outlay. To some extent this happened in Great Britain from 1953 to 1954.[74] With a given progressive tax structure it tends to happen automatically. But in no democratic community is this an easy course to steer. When government revenue is booming as production and incomes increase, and when growing surpluses appear at least in the ordinary budget, it may be practically impossible to avoid tax concessions. It is easier under such conditions to adopt a tighter credit policy aimed at the more readily postponable expenditures on durable consumer as well as producer goods. Britain is not the only country in which a tendency toward tight credit and soft budgets was to be observed during the worldwide upswing of 1954–55. Remembering, however, the unsymmetrical efficacy of monetary policy and the possibility of a change in cyclical conditions, it is not inconceivable that this way of combining monetary and fiscal measures for economic stabilization might tend to produce over the years a shift in favor of consumption at the expense of capital formation.

In the overstrained economy of mid-1955 a cut in domestic expenditure was indicated for both internal and external balance. The latter part of the year witnessed a break in the prices not only of government bonds but also industrial shares, which by

[74] *National Income and Expenditure, 1955*, Table 45.

TABLE 12. SUMMARY OF GOVERNMENT REVENUE AND EXPENDITURE (£ *million*)

Fiscal years beginning April 1	Closed accounts		Budget estimate[a]
	1953/54	1954/55	1955/56
"Above the line": [b]	4,368	4,738	4,710
Ordinary expenditure	4,274	4,305	4,562
Balance	94	433	148
"Below the line": [b]			
Receipts	182	191	192
Expenditure	573	692	776
Balance	−391	−501	−584
of which:			
Met from surplus	94	433	148
Borrowed	297	68	436

[a] As published in April 1955, taking account of the tax concessions then announced.

[b] By and large, "above the line" denotes current and "below the line" capital expenditures.

itself was likely to restrain luxury consumption as well as business investment expenditure. In addition to any cuts in private fixed and inventory investment, the government had some scope for reducing its own spending, on current as well as capital account. Economies were possible, for example in the rent subsidies (apart from the local government building cuts). A shortening of the military conscription period promised to yield economies in defense expenditure. It was clear, however, that any further savings on current government spending were not large and could not be made quickly enough.

Consequently a supplementary autumn budget was introduced on 26 October 1955. The income tax relief granted in April was not withdrawn, but increases in the purchase tax (by 20 per cent), in the distributed profits tax (from $22\frac{1}{2}$ per cent to $27\frac{1}{2}$ per cent), and in postal charges together nearly offset, in terms of the revenue involved (approximately £150 million), the concessions announced in April. Aside from its effect on revenue, the supplementary budget was evidently designed to discourage spending and to encourage saving by households as well as business firms.

The autumn budget served also as an occasion for introducing a stringent system of curbing the capital outlays on the housing and public works schemes of the local authorities. Since the higher interest charges of the Public Works Loan Board had not appreciably deterred them, the Board was now to ration funds for these purposes and to consider loan applications only if private means of financing could not be found. More generally, the inception of new public investment programs was to be postponed and the execution of existing projects slowed down. The curtailment of investment schemes in public services, while regrettable on long-term grounds (as in the field of road building, where practically nothing had been done for fifteen years), must nevertheless be recognized as a useful short-term stabilizer.

Thus the government not only possessed strong enough means to bring the economy into balance, but showed a readiness to use them. The gravity of the British position in 1955 must not be exaggerated. Although the word "crisis" was often heard, the current difficulties were not of the same order of magnitude as in 1947, 1949, or 1951. The estimated payments deficit, though disappointing in comparison with the £300 million surplus aimed at, was quite small not only in the second half of 1954, but even in the first half of 1955, when United States defense aid amounting to £33 million actually resulted in a surplus of £17 million. Internally, the continued advance of industrial production, which since 1946 had increased more in the United Kingdom than in the United States,[75] was encouraging, even though the advance began to slow down in the latter part of the year.

[75] From 1946 to the first half of 1955 the industrial production index rose by 56 per cent in the U.K. and by 51 per cent in the U.S. Both indexes include coal, while construction, gas, and electricity are included in the U.K. but not in the U.S. Over the same period the index for manufacturing alone was up 74 per cent in the U.K. and 52 per cent in the U.S. The great difference is, of course, that in 1946 production in the U.K. was barely back to prewar while in the U.S. it was double the prewar level. The advance since 1946 has been interrupted by two recessions in the U.S. and only one (1951–52) in the U.K.

There is no doubt that the strains of 1955 will be overcome. The question is whether something like internal balance can be restored without a prior swing into recession and a rise of un- employment to something like the Beveridge level. But there is another — graver — question. Can stable balance, external as well as domestic, be achieved without a retreat on the investment front? [76] A minor tactical withdrawal is understandable and readily accepted. Can lasting harm to the investment program be avoided? One's mind turns back to the horse and the water. Will he be eager to follow the lead next time when he remem- bers that last time the water was turned off almost at once?

VII. Conclusion

It is too early to place the events of the last year in their proper perspective and to assess the effects of the policies adopted. Circumstances were in some ways very different from the years immediately after the war. In an economy which some have regarded as excessively rigid we have witnessed a vigorous investment boom of a type almost reminiscent of the Victorian age.

Yet the conclusions suggested by the 1954–55 episode tend to confirm those that emerged from our review of the earlier succession of payments crises. To summarize: the world economic environment today puts a premium on capital goods exports. This will not go on forever; but it is useless to try to peer more than, say, a generation into the future. A successful organism adapts itself to its environment. From being predominantly a

[76] The data for the last quarter of 1955, inserted in proof in Tables 10 and 11, suggest some slackening in the upsurge of investment, and an improvement in the trade balance. Moreover, the dollar rate on sterling which, within the permissible margin, had been below parity for over a year, returned to $2.80 in November 1955. But no firm reliance can be placed on such last-minute indications. Some time will have to pass before the flow of economic events and of economic information can give any answer to the questions raised. (In February 1956, when it was found that the external payments deficit for 1955 amounted to over £100 million, the new Chancellor, Mr. Harold Macmillan, made a fresh attack on the investment boom by raising the bank rate to 5½ per cent, suspending the investment allowance, tightening controls on private capital issues, and cutting public investment programs. Whether these meas- ures will actually reduce the volume of investment or merely check its further expansion still remains to be seen. [Note added by author in proof.])

textile exporter a hundred years ago the United Kingdom has turned into a capital goods exporter. The adaptation already accomplished has been impressive, but it is partly the product of abnormal war and defense efforts. Undoubtedly the adaptation could be promoted, steadily and deliberately, by peacetime incentives and financial policies. Besides, the 1955 boom, which is likely to leave behind a sizable addition to the capacity of Britain's capital goods industries, shows that cyclical forward jumps in the required direction are possible.

In the new structure of the British economy, however, coordination instead of conflict between export needs and internal capital development becomes imperative. In conditions of full employment, as we have observed, lack of integration between foreign-exchange (or foreign-trade) policies on the one hand and domestic-expenditure policies on the other must generally lead to trouble. In the particular British case there is considerable advantage in the use of home investment as an absorber of shocks in the balance of payments. Domestic investment is curbed when export needs are urgent. In a community intent on maintaining high levels of employment and minimizing the losses that would come from interindustrial shifting of resources for reversible short-term reasons, this mode of adjustment is a very real convenience. But it is unsafe to rely on it habitually unless special care is taken to enlarge or at least maintain the capital goods industries on which internal progress as well as external equilibrium in great degree depends.[77]

If home investment is used as a shock-absorber merely because it is postponable — like a luxury type of consumer outlay — or merely because it happens in part to represent deficit spending financed by the credit system, then under present-day conditions the long-term needs of internal advance can easily be thwarted. It is true that investment used to bear the brunt of external adjustment as a more or less automatic outcome of the gold-standard rules of the game. But the "natural" forces making for

[77] If it is objected that a bigger buffer of international currency reserves is what Britain really needs, the answer is a question: How can Britain, through her own efforts, best acquire such reserves? Which leads back to where we started.

accumulation are perhaps not so buoyant today as they were in the gold-standard era.

Price has not been the main reason for the virtual standstill of British exports since 1951. Nor can fault be found with the demand side abroad. A major reason has been limited capacity in the hardware sector, leading to delays in filling export orders and hence to failure of orders to increase. In the early 1950's hardware capacity was under pressure largely from rearmament demands, in 1954–55 largely from domestic investment. Capacity can surely be expanded to supply the needs of both domestic re-equipment and external balance at high levels of trade. But this implies an increase in national saving, contrived, if necessary, through public finance. The investment campaign of 1954 ran into trouble because there was inadequate provision for the corresponding additional saving; it was financed in effect by the adverse shift in the foreign balance and by the fall in the gold reserve. In a fully employed economy such provision cannot be neglected without imperilling domestic stability as well as the balance of payments.

In its simplest terms Great Britain's problem is to serve an expanding world market and to supply equipment for development overseas without stinting the means and checking the rate of her own economic advance. Let it be said once more that capital formation and economic growth are not identical. There is not necessarily any *close* relationship between them. Investment has bulked large in this discussion because it absorbs a large and statistically ascertainable portion of national product, while exports of capital goods enter into the balance of payments. Within the limited scope thus set, British experience in the ten years reviewed provides a lesson in international growth economics — a lesson of some general interest to any country determined not merely to live but also to grow within its means.

9

Reflections on India's

Development Plan

(1957)

The main features of India's development policies are matters of common knowledge. The First Five Year Plan placed the emphasis on agriculture. The Second Plan, which came into effect in April 1956, seeks to promote an expansion of small-scale village industries for the production of consumer goods. At the same time it calls for a big increase in steel production and engineering capacity. Before considering these specific programs it is necessary to deal with a subject that dominates the background of economic policy in India.

The Problem of Unemployment

Concern with the problem of unemployment is paramount in current Indian thinking. Professor P. C. Mahalanobis, one of the chief planners, regards this as "the most pressing problem." [1] A

Copyright 1957 by the President and Fellows of Harvard College.
[1] "The Approach of Operational Research to Planning in India," *Sankhya: The Indian Journal of Statistics,* XVI (December 1955), 14.

panel of Indian economists speaks of it as "a problem of enormous dimensions."[2] The urgent need to create more employment opportunities is stressed in nearly all documents relating to the current Plan.

This emphasis may seem surprising, perhaps even incomprehensible, to some economists outside India. What are the facts? There is first a certain amount of open unemployment, mostly in urban centers, which is said to have increased in the years 1952–1955 and is estimated at somewhere between five and ten million persons. India has rightly been proud of her success in expanding production since 1951 without any price inflation, at any rate up to the end of 1955. In fact, the general level of prices showed a slightly downward tendency during that period, despite a considerable increase in the money supply. This was possible not only because of the increase in crop yields and production generally, but also because of the progressive extension of the monetary sector of the economy. In view of the increase in unemployment, however, was India perhaps *too* successful in avoiding inflation? Could it be that investment, though it was increased, should have been increased still more?

That is what Professors Vakil and Brahmanand, of the Bombay School of Economics, suggest in a remarkable book that constitutes in part a critique of official policy.[3] They argue forcefully that the opportunity created by unusually good harvests in the years 1953–1955 should have been used to step up the level of investment more than was actually done. Their general analysis of the effect of crop changes runs as follows:

In a frictionless and resilient economy a rise in the level of agricultural output, other conditions being given, should lead to a fall in the level of prices of food-grains. This should lead to a fall in the level of money wages. This in its turn should lead to a fall in the rate of interest, which would bring about a rise in the volume of investment activity.[4]

[2] "Basic Considerations Relating to the Plan-Frame," *ibid.,* 120.

[3] C. N. Vakil and P. R. Brahmanand, *Planning for an Expanding Economy: Accumulation, Employment and Technical Progress in Underdeveloped Countries* (Bombay, 1956), xxx, 404. The comments that follow represent largely a review of this book, although reference will be made to a number of other publications also.

[4] Vakil and Brahmanand, 6.

The realization of this chain of events encounters obstacles at every stage. Since India is not a "frictionless and resilient economy," deliberate action would have been necessary. The increase in unemployment could have been avoided "if only capital construction activities of various types had been stepped up to the required extent." [5] As things turned out, "the possible increase in capital formation was partly nullified by a rise in the level of consumption standards." [6] The Planning Commission itself admits that "the increase in investment in the First Plan was not on a scale sufficient to absorb the new entrants to the labor market" and that the average rate of investment during the period of the First Plan, which was only about 6 per cent of national income, "cannot be regarded as impressive." [7]

The increase in open unemployment, whatever its cause may have been, is only a minor part of the problem. A far greater and more intractable mass of unemployment exists in agriculture where more than two thirds of India's total population is trying to make a living. The recent Agricultural Labor Enquiry revealed some open unemployment among landless laborers, who represent about 20 per cent of the agricultural labor force. Apart from this, agricultural unemployment may be said to take three main forms: (1) seasonal idleness of peasant cultivators; (2) underemployment of cultivators due to the small size of farms; (3) unemployment disguised through fragmentation of the individual holding.

(1) Seasonal idleness is a feature of farm life even in advanced countries. It may well be that its extent is peculiarly large in overcrowded peasant communities like India. Yet, as Vakil and Brahmanand emphasize, the essence of the problem of surplus farm labor is not merely a seasonal matter.

(2) Largely as a result of the fall in mortality the population of India has more than doubled in the last hundred years. At the same time, because of the decay of village industries, the proportion of the population dependent on agriculture has in-

[5] Vakil and Brahmanand, 16.
[6] Vakil and Brahmanand, 17.
[7] Government of India, Planning Commission, *Second Five Year Plan* (New Delhi, 1956), 3, 5.

creased rather than diminished. Population pressure has led to a steady reduction in the average size of the farm. In consequence peasants and their family members simply do not have enough to do: they are underemployed. The subdivision of land into smaller and smaller holdings means that, given the prevailing state of techniques, the work to be done on the land is shared among growing numbers of people. It amounts to a system of work-spreading.[8]

(3) In addition, the small individual holding has come to be subdivided into tiny strips and plots. This, too, is to a large extent a recent phenomenon in India, directly related to population pressure.[9] Progressive fragmentation of holdings on the operational level (quite compatible, of course, with a high degree of concentration in land ownership) absorbs labor in many ways, including the mere necessity for people to walk from their homestead to the scattered plots and from one plot to another. Because of the paths and boundary strips needed, fragmentation is wasteful of land as well as labor. It constitutes a make-work device which conceals the agricultural labor surplus. The term

[8] The extent of such underemployment is indicated in the *Second Five Year Plan* in the following terms: "There appears to be an agreement on the broad conclusion that under existing conditions, with present techniques of agriculture being continued, if cultivating units were to approach what might be described as family holdings affording the possibility of fairly full-time work in agriculture for a family of average size, agricultural production could be maintained with about 65–75 per cent of the number of workers now engaged in it. In other words, on certain assumptions, one-fourth to one-third of the existing labor force in agriculture may be surplus to its requirements" (p. 35). According to the 1951 census the agricultural labor force (including persons classified as "self-supporting" together with "earning dependents") numbered just over 100 million people.

[9] Professor D. R. Gadgil has summed it up as follows: "The vital problems connected with agriculture are the smallness of the farm unit and the scattered character of its constituent parts. . . . It is wrong in this connection to blame the laws of inheritance. . . . A large and jointly held cultivating unit has been traditional in India. Its break-up in recent decades is obviously the result of a pressure of population and a lack of alternative employment." ("Problems of Rural Life," in *India Calling: The Annals of the American Academy of Political and Social Science* 1944, 86.) The connection between population pressure and progressive fragmentation of land is not peculiar to India but can be observed in other backward economies suffering from excess population, as may be seen, for example, from the United Nations report on *Land Reform: Defects in Agrarian Structure as Obstacles to Economic Development* (1951), 6–14, 72, 82–85.

"disguised unemployment" fits this category best, though it is commonly used to denote all types of rural unemployment.

In these — and countless other — forms the "work-spreading" principle and the "make-work" scheme have come to dominate the rural economy. As the Indian public is only too familiar with the concrete manifestations of excess population, Vakil and Brahmanand do not enter into details but usually content themselves with such general statements as that "population pressure is absorbed through inferior organization." An essential element of the system is the Indian practice of sharing food, shelter and other necessities among distant as well as close relatives living together in peasant households. The marginal members of the farm labor force, if their own contribution to output falls short of their intake as consumers, are subsidized by the rest of the community. In such circumstances the marginal productivity of labor may easily be zero. To the extent, however, that the surplus labor is absorbed through fragmentation it cannot be withdrawn without loss of output unless the fragmentation is reversed and the plots are consolidated. Appropriate reorganization of the other factors of production is clearly a necessary and a reasonable prerequisite for purposes of policy as well as analysis.

Resistance to consolidation, however, is likely to be enormous because of the desire to protect employment. Attempts at farm reorganization are therefore unlikely to succeed unless and until a tighter labor market is created through increased investment activity. The Panel of Economists explicitly recognizes that agricultural reorganization encounters "difficulties [that] are related to the extent of employment that is available in the economy." [10] Significantly, Mahalanobis says that *"when unemployment has been decreased appreciably*, attempts should be made for the consolidation of operational holdings." [11] In the words of the Second Plan, "there is general agreement that cooperative farming should be developed as rapidly as possible. The practical achievements in this field are, however, meagre." [12] Government action for land reform and consolidation is left to

[10] "Basic Considerations," 129.
[11] P. C. Mahalanobis, "Approach to Planning in India" (based on a radio address delivered on 11 September 1955), 7. My italics.
[12] *Second Five Year Plan*, 201.

the individual states. This is not a field in which legislation alone can accomplish much. It is hoped that A. V. Bhave's land-gift movement, which favors joint cultivation on a village basis, will make some headway, but the results so far have not been notable.[13]

The economists in their panel report sound an optimistic note: "The First Plan has laid a solid basis for the development of agriculture."[14] An improvement in crop yields has occurred, but some of it has been due to good weather. The Second Plan counts on further advances through irrigation, better seeds, fertilizers and improved techniques. It is hoped to enlarge the area covered by the National Extension program. All these are promising developments. Yet a British observer[15] may perhaps be forgiven for reminding us that "there were many similar attempts at rural reconstruction under British rule, inspired by men . . . whose enthusiasm, knowledge and energy cannot easily be bettered even under self-government. Many of them had temporary success, but this was sooner or later submerged by the inert weight of local prejudice and ancient tradition."

In any case there is some doubt whether an agricultural revolution such as occurred in England, Japan and Russia as a basis for industrialization has yet begun in India. In particular, the deep-seated concern with employment may be a serious obstacle to the necessary reorganization of farm holdings and to other improvements as well. Without such reorganization the labor surplus in agriculture remains largely potential. On the other hand, reorganization may well prove impracticable without an active policy of absorbing the surplus manpower.[16] The way to absorb

[13] That the *bhoodan* movement has some serious drawbacks as well as merits is pointed out by D. R. Gadgil, *Economic Policy and Development* (Gokhale Institute of Politics and Eeonomics, 1955), 237–240.

[14] "Basic Considerations," 118.

[15] T. A. F. Noble, "Economic Progress in Underdeveloped Areas," *Scottish Journal of Political Economy,* June 1956, 113.

[16] That considerations of employment can baffle even a Western observer is shown by a comment which J. L. Buck made on proposals for cooperative farming in China in 1949: "Where three men are required to do the work on individual farms, only two are needed for the same amount of land in a 'cooperative.' But those who propose extending this system over all China fail to say what will be done with the third man." ("Fact and Theory about China's Land," *Foreign Affairs,* October 1949.)

it is by putting it to work on capital construction — the familiar roundabout way of increasing productive efficiency. This is the main prescription which Vakil and Brahmanand put forward in their study. India's unemployment problem is not of the Keynesian type, except occasionally to a minor degree. Its cause is not deficiency of effective demand but pressure of population on the land. The remedy, however, is the same: more investment.

REVIVAL OF HOUSEHOLD INDUSTRIES

The promotion of household production of light consumer goods is one of the chief objects of the Second Plan. Handloom weaving of cotton cloth, for instance, is to be doubled during the five-year period, according to a preliminary estimate.[17] This emphasis may be rooted in the traditionalism symbolized by Gandhi's spinning wheel, but it is more specifically a policy of employment creation. One of the documents relating to the Plan states that "the greatest importance is attached to the expansion of the household and hand industries as this would be the principal method of liquidating unemployment." [18]

The traditional cottage industries were largely destroyed by the competition of imported manufactures in the absence of tariff protection before World War I. In recent decades these industries have suffered from the competition of India's own factory output. Contrary to the normal development, the proportion of people engaged in agriculture has increased in the last hundred years from less than 60 per cent to about 70 per cent. In addition to its share of the population increase, Indian agriculture has had to find work for handloom workers who lost their living during this period.

Now the policy is to absorb redundant farm labor through a revival of cottage production. This cannot be done without protecting the hand workers from the competition of Indian factories. Hand production is less efficient; and the hand workers are expected to earn more than what they consumed in subsistence

---

[17] P. C. Mahalanobis, "Recommendations for the Formulation of the Second Five Year Plan," *Sankhya: The Indian Journal of Statistics*, XVI (December 1956).

[18] Mahalanobis, "Recommendations," 82.

farming. Consequently the price of handloom cloth would be about double that of mill-made cloth.[19]

Protection takes the form of direct or indirect subsidies. Electric power, where available, is to be supplied "at prices which the workers can afford." [20] Quotas and prohibitions are imposed on some factory products. The licensing of industrial investments is another instrument of protection. It is stated, for example, that in the interests of village production "for some time past no expansion of large match factories has been permitted." [21] But the most general protective measure is a system of excise duties on the products of Indian manufacturing industries. We have before us the curious case of an internal tariff protecting the rural hand workers against low-cost factory goods produced in the same country.

Under these conditions foreign investment in industrial production for the Indian market is practically out of the question, except in industries that are technologically outside the range of hand production (e.g., petroleum refining, basic chemicals, pulp and paper, as well as steel and heavy engineering).

The implications of this policy are worth considering. If the hand workers drawn from disguised unemployment in agriculture are to enjoy tariff protection from the competition of Indian factory products they will, through higher prices, still be receiving a subsidy from the rest of the community, just as they were subsidized on the farms where their marginal productivity fell short of their consumption. This means that the locus of disguised unemployment is shifted: one make-work scheme replaces another.

Vakil and Brahmanand go even further. They argue that this use of redundant farm labor, in view of the accompanying rise in earnings, leads to a *greater* subsidy than that implicit in disguised unemployment on the farms, and that the result is therefore a reduction in the resources that might have been channelled into investment.[22] They support the scheme only if

[19] Vakil and Brahmanand, 72.
[20] *Second Five Year Plan*, 433.
[21] *Second Five Year Plan*, 448.
[22] Pages 150, 282.

confined to the use of seasonal unemployment without any protective duties.[23]

The official handicraft policy is bound to affect factory industry adversely. Not only is there to be no fresh investment that might compete with hand production, but factories may be prevented even from making full use of their existing capacity. We are told that "it may be better to allow machines to remain idle rather than to keep human beings unemployed." [24] But idle manufacturing capacity is a waste of the scarcest factor of production: capital. And, as the Bombay authors never tire of repeating, any labor displaced through technical advances, or through the competition of capitalistic production methods, can and should be absorbed in investment. The official policy represents in their view a deliberate reversion to, and preservation of, less efficient methods of production. Can this be the way to economic progress?

It is true that the subsidies granted to hand production, whether directly or indirectly, may represent a case of infant industry protection. This is implied in the following passage in which the *Second Five Year Plan* sets out the rationale of the policy under discussion:

There is a case for using labor for increasing the supplies of consumer goods in a manner which economises the use of capital. A society in which labor is plentiful must develop the art of using labor-intensive modes of production effectively. In using labor-intensive methods, it may well be that the cost of the product is somewhat higher. This entails a sacrifice which can be reduced through technical and organizational improvements. In any case a measure of sacrifice in the matter of consumption is inevitable while the economy is being strengthened at the base. The sacrifice diminishes as more power, more transport, and better tools, machinery and equipment become available.[25]

As an adaptation to existing circumstances the pursuit of labor-intensive production methods with a view to economizing capital is undoubtedly right; but development policy must concern itself with changing these circumstances, not accepting them as they are. No useful change is promoted if the new

[23] Pages 369–372.
[24] Mahalanobis, "Recommendations," 16.
[25] Page 25.

production is of consumable rather than capital goods and especially if it is merely a substitute for goods that could be made more cheaply in existing factories. Moreover, the power and transport facilities needed for more efficient village production will not simply "become available"; they can and should be built right away with the aid of surplus labor.

Although handicraft industries are at present intended mainly as a means of employment creation, it is not at all certain that they are to be abandoned if and when the unemployment problem has been solved. Influential voices favor their retention as a permanent feature of the Indian economy. The Second Plan speaks of them as "the basis for an essentially decentralized society." [26] The leading authority has expressed himself as follows: "Working at home or very near home in the villages would be less fatiguing than in factories because the workers would be able to take some rest as and when necessary. Household activities and family life would not be disrupted. . . . Through a policy of industrial dispersal it would be possible to combine the advantages of both economic and political democracy in an effective manner. This would be a solution entirely in keeping with Indian social and cultural traditions." [27]

The economist as such cannot object to a goal set on noneconomic grounds. Besides, technological advance may recently have given some advantage to deglomerative tendencies in industry. The Indian movement of industry "back to the village" is to be supplied ultimately with modern machinery and electric power. It is contrary to the experience of other countries, which have progressed through the division of labor and the saving of overhead capital made possible by urban concentration. Yet it is not inconceivable that India may develop an original pattern of industrialization along these lines.

What is more dubious is the use of this policy as a means of providing jobs in the countryside. Is it not another reflection of the dominant make-work attitude? Utilizing idle labor should be no problem where there is so much to be done: the problem

[26] Page 432.
[27] Mahalanobis, "Recommendations," 55.

is to use it for capital creation rather than for inefficient production of consumer goods.

EXPANSION OF STEEL AND ENGINEERING CAPACITY

It is true that investment targets in economic and social overheads have been stepped up in the Second Five Year Plan. But a more distinctive feature of the Plan is its emphasis on expanding the capacity of steel production and engineering industries. At any rate in steel, India may well have a high comparative advantage, in the long if not in the short run. Physical conditions, at least as far as iron ore is concerned, are not unfavorable, and unskilled mining labor is cheap. These industries, however, are highly capital-intensive, in construction as well as in operation. They create very little employment and in this respect are inconsistent with the goals of the handicraft policy. What then is the rationale of this part of the program?

As in other underdeveloped countries, policy makers in India are impressed with the fact that the great industrial powers all have their own steel industries. Professor Mahalanobis tells us that, of any single factor, "the production of steel probably has the highest correlation with national income in different countries," and he quotes a correlation coefficient of $+0.75$ based on per capita figures for nineteen countries in 1953.[28] The dubious validity of any such argument need not be dwelt upon, especially since the policy has been supported by more substantive arguments as well. It is perhaps worth noting that Mahalanobis attaches still greater weight to "the development of the heavy machine-building industry," which he says "is so important that, if necessary, targets of even steel, coal or transport should be reduced to give higher priority to heavy machines because this would facilitate a much quicker rate of industrialization after four or five years." [29]

According to Vakil and Brahmanand, the steel and engineering program has been influenced by Soviet Russia's example. This in itself is not objectionable to them. Their criticism is

[28] Mahalanobis, "Recommendations," 19.
[29] Mahalanobis, "Recommendations," 51.

that the Soviet example is being followed out of context. In India there is nothing like the Russian farm mechanization drive of the 1930's; Russia never went in for a promotion of handi- crafts on current Indian lines. To Vakil and Brahmanand the handicraft policy and the steel program represent a basic incon- sistency in the Indian plan. Heavy equipment industries are not wanted for their own sake. If no market is created for new machinery through a mechanization of consumer industry, are the machines to be used merely to make more machines for the internal expansion of the machine industry? Even if we grant that village industries will develop new demands for light equip- ment and tools, and that public utilities present an outlet for heavy equipment, it is not easy to lay aside the doubts aroused by the contradictory nature of the Plan's two principal features.

The steel expansion program may have been partly due to the fact that foreign capital became available for this particular purpose. American, British, German and Russian capital and technical assistance are engaged in the construction or expansion of four separate plants. The American contribution has been made through the World Bank. There is no doubt, however, that the program originates from Indian demands and preoccupations. As Professor Mahalanobis has put it, "India's present dependence on imports of capital goods is a fundamental structural weak- ness which must be corrected as quickly as possible." [30]

What lies at the root of this sentiment? Defense considerations seem to have had relatively little weight in the formulation of the Second Plan. The threat of foreign exchange difficulties may have played some part, despite the surpluses earned on current ac- count of the balance of payments in the four years before 1956. But the external balance is not outside a country's control; it is basically a reflection of the extent to which investment outlay is being met by domestic saving. India's current terms of trade are not particularly unfavorable, not nearly as depressed at any rate as those of Soviet Russia in the early 1930's. India had some trouble in getting prompt delivery of British equipment in the years after 1950, when Britain's rearmament program led

[30] Mahalanobis, "Recommendations," 51.

to long delays in shipments of capital goods. But India can import such goods from America, Germany, Russia and Japan, as well as from Britain. She is not dependent on any single supplier. In fact world trade in capital equipment has been growing steadily and now accounts for one half of total international trade in manufactured goods.

Perhaps the strongest argument is that in the event of another major war foreign supplies would dwindle (as they did even in the Korean crisis). Apart from this, it is not clear why dependence on capital goods imports must be terminated "as quickly as possible." The Indian economy has other structural weaknesses: for instance, in agriculture, transportation and technical education. Undoubtedly India would sooner or later in any case build up a steel and engineering industry of her own in the course of her development. It is the top priority which the Second Plan has given to this goal at the present stage of development that may perhaps be questioned on economic grounds — and is in fact seriously questioned in the Vakil and Brahmanand study.

The Need for Public Overhead Facilities

In current Indian writings, official and unofficial, heavy engineering industries and public overhead services are often lumped together in the same category as "basic industries." While both are generally capital-intensive in their operation, the construction of public works such as river dams, irrigation canals, roads and even railroads can typically make use of masses of unskilled labor with relatively little equipment.

But the most elementary distinction between the two classes of industries is often overlooked. Steel and machinery can be imported from abroad (and are being imported by most countries in ever-increasing volume). Electric power, irrigation and inland transport services cannot be imported. The facilities for producing these basic services must exist within the country, or the services cannot be had at all. Investment in such essential public facilities as power and transport is therefore absolutely unavoidable. By contrast, investment in steel and machine production is in principle at least postponable.

As Professor Lewis has emphasized in his *Theory of Economic Growth*,[31] the share of public works in a country's investment program is apt to be "particularly high in the first decades of development, and declines thereafter. This is because initial development calls for the establishment of a framework of utilities." Although the Second Five Year Plan has set higher targets for public overhead investments the increase is hardly spectacular. Of the total public development expenditure planned, allocations for transport, communications and electric power represent 38 per cent in the Second as compared with 35 per cent in the First Plan.

Three types of public investment may be singled out for brief comment. Transport and communications, in the words of Professor Mahalanobis himself, are "extremely inadequate," even though India unlike some other Asian countries has in this field a good base on which to build.[32] The shortage of railway capacity proved a serious bottleneck during the period of the First Plan. Now the Second Plan points out that not even the wartime backlog of replacement has yet been made good;[33] that there is no provision for any new lines to open up regions not served by railways at present;[34] and that existing facilities may fall short of requirements during the period of the Plan.[35] Whether the present highway system can handle any considerable overflow of traffic from the railroads is doubtful. Roads capable of carrying motor vehicles are few and far between. The growth in total mileage of "national highways" during the Second Plan is set at only 7 per cent.

In electric power, as in railway traffic, the increase in requirements was underestimated in the First Plan and power shortages have persisted, in industrial centers as well as in rural areas. The Second Plan proposes a doubling of generating capacity, but even this may not be overambitious. To provide electricity for the expected increase in power needs is not enough. At present

[31] W. A. Lewis, *Theory of Economic Growth* (London and Homewood, Ill., 1955), 211.
[32] Mahalanobis, "Recommendations," 13.
[33] *Second Five Year Plan*, 70.
[34] Page 70.
[35] Page 464.

the great bulk of the country's fuel and energy requirements are still met from cowdung, wood and straw. It is of great importance to reduce reliance on these sources in order to stop the exhaustion and erosion of the soil, which have long been a result of using dung and wood as fuel. In 1956 there was electricity in less than 10 per cent of the towns and villages with a population of under 5,000. Under the current Plan electricity will still leave most villages untouched.

The Constitution states that provision for free and compulsory education on the elementary level is to be made within ten years from 1950. According to the targets of the Second Plan, however, the school facilities at the end of the Plan period (1961) will suffice for only 62.7 per cent of six- to eleven-year-old children and for no more than 22.5 per cent of children in the eleven- to fourteen-year group. In 1956 school facilities existed for only half the number of children in the six- to eleven-year age group. The shortage of schools is, of course, far greater in the countryside than in the cities. Understaffing begins to be a problem only when the schools have been built. At present, it seems, schools are not being built in sufficient numbers. The emphasis which Japan placed on educational investments in the early years of her industrial development after 1867 is worth imitating in India. The building of schools and other basic facilities in the countryside requires practically nothing but labor and local materials, of which there is no shortage. Cannot more be done to employ idle labor in essential public works?

EMPLOYMENT CREATION THROUGH CAPITAL CONSTRUCTION

The principal criticism of Vakil and Brahmanand is that India's Second Five Year Plan fails to attack the problem of agricultural overpopulation by drawing redundant labor into investment activities. Against the dominant school of thought which attributes unemployment to lack of capital equipment (e.g., Mahalanobis: "unemployment is chronic because of lack of capital goods" [36]), their view is rather that unemployment exists because there is too little production of capital goods, too little capital building going on. Their chief recommendation is that employment should

[36] "Recommendations," 15.

be created at once by increased investment, aimed at raising the productivity of labor in the future.

Much is already being done in this direction. The Community Development program is a well-known example: villagers come together to carry out useful works or improvements; and they do this in their spare time. Spare time is indeed the basic source of accumulation. But here as elsewhere division of labor is the more effective principle, implying the segregation of surplus labor — the community's spare time — into a separate working force devoted entirely to capital work.

According to Vakil and Brahmanand, population pressure results in a "deterioration in methods of organization," or, in the more concrete terms which I prefer, in work-sharing and make-work arrangements. It is recognized that any improvement of organization will throw people out of work altogether and will on that account alone be strenuously resisted. Organizational reforms in agriculture must therefore go hand in hand with the creation of jobs in capital construction.

In the same way technical advances are viewed by these authors as increasing the country's investment potential by releasing labor for capital work. There is, however, in their view no automatic absorption of labor displaced through technical progress. New jobs in the investment field must be deliberately created if the deep-seated prejudice against technical advance on employment grounds is to be overcome.

The main difficulty in the use of redundant farm labor for investment purposes stems from the fact, which the authors regard as inevitable, that the food surplus which at least potentially arises in the subsistence farm sector — through the removal of surplus laborers and the accompanying reorganization of agriculture — is insufficient to sustain the workers when employed on investment projects. This is so because the workers transferred will have to receive a rate of remuneration higher than their previous level of subsistence. Thus arises what this book calls the "wage-goods gap." I have discussed it elsewhere as one of three possible leakages. The difference between the Bombay authors and myself on this point is purely verbal.

The assumption that laborers will need to consume more on

investment projects than they did on the farms is undoubtedly realistic, yet it might have been a little more fully discussed. Sometimes this assumption is based simply on physiological calorie requirements: men must eat more when fully and actively at work. This is true when the original state is one of *under-*employment. To the extent, however, that unemployment is disguised in make-work methods (such as farm fragmentation) there is not necessarily any reason to suppose that the physical effort involved is any less than in "normal" employment.

The wage-goods gap appears as the great obstacle to the "employment-in-investment" program which is the main feature of the book. The authors leave, however, a gap between their demonstration of the existence of a rural saving potential and their emphasis on the obstacle to its realization. There is, of course, room here for alternative ways of presenting the matter: an optimist may claim that if only some complementary saving were available an investible surplus could be mobilized in the subsistence farm sector; while a pessimist may describe the same thing by saying that the investment potential concealed in the farm sector cannot be realized for want of outside resources to bridge the wage-goods gap. Vakil and Brahmanand seem on the whole inclined to focus attention on their positive program of using surplus labor in increased investment. There is, however, surprisingly little discussion of possible methods of bridging the wage-goods gap, although it seems often to be taken for granted that the gap *can* somehow be bridged. The reader will find only a few isolated references to foreign aid and hardly any consideration of fiscal policies for raising the necessary supplementary resources at home.

It is regrettable also that the authors make no clear distinction between the "marketable surplus" and the "investible surplus" of agriculture. The farm sector's marketable surplus of farm products evidently determines the volume of nonfarm employment.[37] It has no direct bearing on the volume of employment in investment, though the authors habitually write as if it had. A large marketable surplus is surely compatible (i) with a zero rate of investment in the economy or (ii) with a substantial rate of in-

[37] Vakil and Brahmanand, 201.

vestment financed by (a) nonfarm saving or (b) saving originating in the farm sector. The last case may become relevant when surplus laborers are transferred and farms appropriately reorganized. An investible surplus of farm products can then arise in the farm sector for maintaining the workers engaged on capital projects. Indeed the term "investible surplus" or "surplus available for investment" is occasionaly used in this sense,[38] but elsewhere the term "marketable surplus" seems to come in two varying senses, meaning sometimes the farm sector's saving, sometimes the farm products exchanged for nonfarm products. Often the context shows which meaning is intended. It is not, however, a matter of terminology alone. When the authors speak about bridging the gap through a quick expansion in the output of consumption goods,[39] they seem to forget that an increase in output creates an increase in income which may lead to an increase in expenditure as well. It is only insofar as the additional income is saved that employment in investment can be stepped up. If the reader himself is prepared to supply the necessary qualifications, the argument will nevertheless be found to offer some useful insights into the problems of what the authors call "accumulation policy" in a backward and overcrowded economy.

The Bombay authors' central objection to the official Plan, that it leaves untouched the problem of disguised unemployment and does not seek to mobilize enough redundant labor for capital works, would have been more strongly based if their own treatment of these matters had not confined itself to generalities. They speak of disguised unemployment in terms of "inferior" as against "optimal" organization, without really coming to grips with the agricultural revolution that would be needed for releasing farm labor for capital work and industrial employment.[40] Similarly, they do not deal with the practical difficulties of their employment-in-investment program: e.g., the discontinuous nature of employment on public construction projects, the difficulty of adapting them to local labor supplies, the extent to which such

---

[38] Vakil and Brahmanand, 205–206.

[39] Vakil and Brahmanand, 190.

[40] An excellent short account of the problems of farm organization and farm population is given in ch. 17 of D. R. Gadgil's *Economic Policy and Development* (see n. 13).

employment would require imported equipment, and the extent to which it might thus displace investment in other sectors.[41]

Compared with the critical part of the work (Part I: The Critique), the positive part is far more abstract (Part II: The Alternative). The theoretical analysis is sometimes marred, however, by the use of undefined terms, by the failure to state assumptions explicitly, and by the intermingling of stock and flow concepts. These blemishes reach their climax in an Appendix,[42] which, being so labeled, can presumably be skipped, and which this writer would advise any reader to skip. Elsewhere in this book the authors repeatedly contend or imply[43] that developed countries must have started from a situation of disguised unemployment in the past: otherwise how could they have increased their capital stock faster than their population? Here the authors overlook the fact which they stress in other connections, that technical advance and thriftiness can set manpower free for capital construction. When they advocate the working out of Indian solutions to India's development problems and are skeptical about the applicability of imported formulas, whether of Western or of Soviet origin, an outsider may well be inclined to sympathize. Neither the economics of business enterprise nor the Keynesian theory of employment nor the Anglocentric views developed a hundred years ago by Marx were designed to take account of India's overcrowded peasant economy. But when the authors try to apply their own view of development to the economic history of now advanced countries, they can only cause a raising of eyebrows among at least some of their readers. Evidently even Indian economists find it hard to avoid practicing "imperialism" in the sense of extending their constructs to conditions to which they are unsuited. Fortunately such attempts at generalizing their theory of underdevelopment are rare in this book.

Although the constructive part of the work presents, on the

[41] Some useful information on the "employment potential of development projects" may be found in chs. 5 and 7 of V. M. Dandekar's *Use of Food Surpluses for Economic Development* (Gokhale Institute of Politics and Economics, Publication No. 33, 1956). An examination of a number of specific projects shows that the direct labor cost is usually not more than about 60 per cent of the total cost of the projects.

[42] Vakil and Brahmanand, 252–272.

[43] Vakil and Brahmanand, 225, 235, 380.

whole, a plausible and challenging outline for accumulation policy in a backward economy, it does leave much to be clarified, amended and worked out in detail. The book is more interesting as a critique of current policies. The *Second Five Year Plan* is an exceedingly able and impressive document: what is debatable is merely the emphasis placed upon different parts of the program. It would not, perhaps, be entirely unfair to say that the plan relies largely on the introduction of a few big steel mills and engineering plants into an otherwise primitive economy. In this way presumably the Plan hopes to make possible "the elimination [specifically on public construction projects] of arduous human labor, which current social values would refuse to accept." [44] Arduous human labor has not proved avoidable in the early stages of capital growth elsewhere; but must each country go through the same stages? Short cuts are not impossible. We must hope that India, whose climate makes heavy labor particularly arduous, will find a way of eliminating it.

The shadow that lies on the land is the population problem: not merely the current rate of population growth but, above all, the state of excess population which the population explosion of the past hundred years has produced. Excess population breeds social institutions and attitudes that are hard to change. In particular it produces those instinctive and pervasive work-making and work-spreading tendencies which are not conducive to development. Herein lies a good part of the case for drawing more people into useful capital works at once, even before each man can be equipped with a bulldozer or steam shovel to lighten his toil.

All this, to repeat, is a matter of emphasis. To secure a perfect balance in any comprehensive development program is impossible. What matters most is that India is progressing — and that she is progressing in an atmosphere which permits unhampered public debate among her experts.

[44] *Second Five Year Plan*, 113.

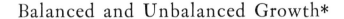

Balanced and Unbalanced Growth*

(1957)

THE CONFLICT BETWEEN "BALANCED GROWTH" AND INTERNATIONAL SPECIALIZATION

The idea of balanced growth is playing a prominent role in both the theory and policy of economic development. My purpose here is to consider whether this idea is compatible with the principle of international specialization or whether, on the contrary, it means throwing away the benefits which can be obtained through specialization. The dominant practical question in some of the less-developed countries is whether the available means, limited as they are, should be used to promote activities (a) specialized along lines of comparative advantage internationally or (b) diversified so as to provide markets for each other locally. In Western eyes the pursuit of balanced growth is causing only too often a pathetic misdirection of scarce resources. Some of the underdeveloped countries, on the other hand, feel that they can-

---

* These two lectures, delivered by Ragnar Nurkse in Istanbul and Ankara in 1957, were published that year by the Faculty of Economics, Istanbul and the Faculty of Political Sciences, Ankara, in *Lectures in Economic Development*, and are reproduced by permission of the publishers.

not rely on an external demand for their primary products, a demand which is usually inelastic with respect to price. Is there any guarantee, they ask, that the overspill of prosperity from the advanced countries, through changes in the volume and terms of trade and possibly, in response thereto, through private foreign investment in primary production for export, will induce a satisfactory rate of development — satisfactory in relation, for instance, to population change? The clash of prescriptions on the policy plane reflects what looks like a deadlock on the theoretical level also.

I

Before we attack the main problem it will be instructive to take a look at past experience and see how economic growth in certain areas was induced through international trade in the nineteenth century. The areas involved in this process of "growth through trade" were chiefly the regions of recent settlement in the temperate latitudes outside Europe. These areas (including especially the United States, Canada, Argentina and Australia) received a sizable flow of labor as well as capital from Europe, but the basic inducement that caused them to develop was the tremendous expansion of western Europe's, and especially Great Britain's, demand for the foodstuffs and raw materials which they were well suited to produce. Growth at the periphery was induced through trade by growth in the rising industrial center.

It was under the impression of this experience that Marshall in his *Principles* made the following significant pronouncement: "The causes which determine the economic progress of nations belong to the study of international trade." In the middle of the twentieth century this may seem to us a curious statement. It can be understood only in the light of certain historical conditions: it embodies the particular experience of Britain's economic relations with the new countries overseas. Economic growth in these areas was due not to international specialization alone but more particularly to the fact that the character of international trade was such that the rapid growth which was taking place in the center was transmitted to the outlying new countries. It was transmitted to them through a vigorous increase in the demand for primary products. Trade in the nineteenth century was not simply a device for the optimum allocation of a given stock of resources. It was above all an engine of growth. This profoundly important observation is one which we owe to Sir Dennis Robertson. It helps us to see things in perspective, but in doing so it serves also to put the classical trade theory in its proper place. The conventional tendency has been to credit international specialization as such with the spectacular growth of the new countries in the nineteenth century. In the light of Robertson's remark it can be argued that classical specialization theory, which in the nature of the case is a static analysis, has derived more credit and more prestige from nineteenth-century experience than it has deserved. The dynamic nature of trade as a transmitter of growth was overlooked during an era in which progress was taken for granted, like the air we breathe.

There is no doubt that international trade was peculiarly important in the conditions of the nineteenth century. In real volume it increased tenfold between 1850 and 1913, twice as fast as world production. Imperialism had very little to do with the expansion of trade. As was shown by J. A. Hobson himself, the tropical colonies took a minor share in the growth of British trade. The new countries, outside as well as within the British Empire, were more important. Their development was part of the growth of international trade itself. They were high-income countries from the start: effective markets as well as efficient producers.

It is true that, aside from the successful regions of recent settlement, economic growth induced through international trade in some cases carried with it certain features that were, and still are, regarded as undesirable. It sometimes led to a lopsided pattern of growth in which production of primary products for export was carried on with the aid of substantial investment of foreign capital while the domestic economy remained far less developed if not altogether primitive. This applies especially to tropical areas. It is the familiar picture of the dual economy resulting from trade and from foreign business investments induced by trade. An area of outpost investment producing for foreign markets showed often a lack of social as well as economic integration internally. In its export activities it was subject to the familiar hazards of cyclical instability.

In general, economic growth induced through trade, even when reinforced through foreign investment in extractive industries working for export, can hardly be expected to narrow the gap in income levels between the center and the periphery. Nevertheless, even "unbalanced" and unsteady growth through foreign trade is surely much better than no growth at all. Foreign capital working for export usually leads to an additional demand for local labor, increased wage incomes, expenditures on local materials, increased sources of taxation and, especially in the case of mineral concessions, lucrative profit sharing arrangements. All these benefits should help to promote progress in the domestic economy.

The traditional pattern of development through production for expanding export markets is not to be despised and ought not to be discouraged. Any opportunities that present themselves in this direction should be seized and fully exploited. The real trouble is that in the mid-twentieth century, with a few notable exceptions, conditions for this type of growth do not seem to be as promising as they were a hundred years ago.

Since 1913, as we all know, world trade has increased less than world production. To be sure, in the last five or six years we find the volume of trade in the non-Communist world increasing at just about the same pace as production. But when we look at it more closely we find that it is chiefly among the advanced industrial countries that international trade has been expanding in the recent past. These countries, including above all the United States, are themselves efficient primary producers, especially of food. Their demand for exotic raw materials like crude rubber, silk, nitrates, jute, and vegetable oils has been, and will almost certainly continue to be, affected by the growth of the chemical industry in the twentieth century. The latest technological casualty among American imports that I have heard of is chicle, which we used to import from Latin America for the manufacture of chewing gum. It appears that the American chemical industry has developed a substitute which is just as good or even better. In his comprehensive study of American imports Professor Humphrey takes the view that, in its effect on total United States imports, the displacement of imported raw materials by synthetic products has more than offset the 75% reduction in the American tariff which has taken place in the last twenty years partly through reductions in rates of duty and partly as a result of the price inflation which has diminished the burden of specific duties.[1]

The growth of synthetic materials is undoubtedly one explanation of the findings which Professor Kindleberger reaches in his recent book on *The Terms of Trade: A European Case Study*.[2] This study lends some support to the view that the poorer countries' terms of trade have shown a persistent tendency to deteriorate. Other recent studies have provided evidence that world demand for the poorer countries' export products has tended to rise much less than in proportion to the production and incomes of the advanced countries. For the postwar period this conclusion is very clearly presented in the last world economic survey of the United Nations (1956) and also in the remarkable report on international trade published by the General Agreement on Tariffs and Trade.

Only for minerals is the prospect favorable, although the demand for metals is being affected by the increasing efficiency of scrap collection and recovery of metals in the industrial countries. Besides, it should not be forgotten that the export of minerals, including petroleum as well as metal ores, involves in an obvious sense an element of living on capital. Professor A. K. Cairncross, in his careful statistical study of world exports of manufactured goods since 1900,[3] has shown that the manufactured goods which the industrial countries export to each other have constituted a steadily increasing proportion of their total exports.

It is therefore not surprising that, according to the GATT report already mentioned, we find the following distribution of international trade in the non-Communist world. The exports of twenty advanced industrial countries to each other (United States, Canada, Japan and Western Europe) constitute as much as 40% of total exports. Exports from these twenty countries to all less developed countries in the non-Communist world amount to 25% of the

---

[1] Don D. Humphrey, and others, *American Imports* (New York, 1955).
[2] C. P. Kindleberger (New York, 1956).
[3] *Economia Internazionale*, November 1955, 715–741.

total. Exports from the latter to the former group of countries represent another 25%. Only 10% of the total are exports of the less-developed countries to each other, even though the more than a hundred countries in this group contain two thirds of the total population. Why is it that so little of the coffee, tea, rubber and tin produced in the countries of this group goes to other countries in the same group? Obviously the main explanation is the low purchasing power of the inhabitants of these countries, which in turn is a reflection of their low productivity. The fact that the economically advanced countries are each others' best customers is now more than ever the central feature of world trade. It is chiefly within this small circle of countries that international trade is now expanding. With the exception of petroleum and a few other minerals, subject to the reservation noted, it can hardly be said that primary producing countries are enjoying a dynamic expansion in world demand for their exports. The unprecedented boom which the industrial countries have enjoyed in the last few years (1955–56) has had little or no perceptible effect in improving the terms of trade of primary producing countries.[4] In view of the tremendous growth of the American economy combined with the liberalization of American tariff policy in the last two decades, it is surely an extraordinary fact that, according to an official index, the real volume of American imports of agricultural products in 1956 was almost exactly the same as in the period 1924–1929. United States imports of all crude materials in 1955 were only about 25% higher in volume than in 1929, whereas the United States gross national product at constant prices has more than doubled since 1929. These trends are not confined to the United States. They affect the trade of other advanced areas as well.

If this is the situation of the mid-twentieth century, the mental habits which economists have inherited from the mid-nineteenth century may no longer be altogether adequate. It is no longer so certain that the less-developed countries can rely on economic growth being induced from the outside through an expansion of world demand for their exports of primary commodities. In these circumstances reliance on induced expansion through international

[4] See International Monetary Fund, *International Financial Statistics*, April 1957.

trade cannot provide a solution to the problem of economic development. It is not surprising therefore that countries should be looking for other solutions. It is important to keep these things in mind, because they form the background to the case for balanced growth which is now so much in vogue.

II

The circumstances indicated do not apply to all underdeveloped countries today: Kuwait and perhaps Iraq have nothing to worry about. But insofar as these circumstances do exist in reality it is clear that the poorer countries, even if they are only to keep pace with the richer, to say nothing about catching up with them, must expand production for their own domestic markets or for each other's markets. Now domestic markets are limited because of mass poverty due to low productivity. Private investment in any single industry considered by itself is discouraged by the smallness of the existing market.

The limits set by the small size of the local market for manufactured goods are so plainly visible to any individual businessman that we are fully justified in taking for granted conditions of imperfect competition, and not the pure atomistic competition which even in advanced economies does not exist to any significant degree, outside the economics textbooks.

The solution seems to be a balanced pattern of investment in a number of different industries, so that people working more productively, with more capital and improved techniques, become each other's customers. In the absence of vigorous upward shifts in world demand for exports of primary products, a low-income country through a process of diversified growth can seek to bring about upward shifts in domestic demand schedules by means of increased productivity and therefore by increased real purchasing power. In this way, a pattern of mutually supporting investments in different lines of production can enlarge the size of the market and help to fill the vacuum in the domestic economy of low-income areas. This, in brief, is the notion of balanced growth.

Isolated advance is not impossible. A solitary process of investment and increased productivity in one industry alone will certainly have favorable repercussions elsewhere in the economy. There is no denying that through the normal incentives of the price mechanism other industries will be induced to advance also. But this may be a snail's pace of progress. The price mechanism works but it may work too slowly. That is one reason for the frequently observed fact that foreign direct investments in extractive export industries have created high productivity islands in low-income areas and have had little impact on the level of productivity in the domestic economy.

Within the domestic economy itself, advance in one direction, say in industry A, tends to induce advance in B as well. But if it is only a passive reaction to the stimulus coming from A, the induced advance of B may be slow and uncertain. And B's slowness and passiveness will in turn slow down and discourage the initial advance in A. The application of capital to one industry alone may therefore be subject to sharply diminishing returns. As a way of escape from slowness if not from stagnation, the balanced-growth principle envisages autonomous advance along a number of lines more or less simultaneously.

Viewed in this way, balanced growth is a means to accelerated growth. Some economists treat the problem of achieving balanced growth as quite separate from the problem of speeding up the rate of advance in a backward economy. I admit that this may be a convenient distinction to draw on other grounds. But in my view, balanced growth is first and foremost a means of getting out of the rut, a means of stepping up the rate of growth when the external forces of advance through trade expansion and foreign capital are sluggish or inoperative.

In the existing state of affairs in low-income areas, the introduction of capital-using techniques of production in any single industry is inhibited by the small size of the market. Hence the weakness of private investment incentives in such areas. The balanced-growth principle points to a way out of the deadlock. New enterprises set up in different industries create increased markets for each other, so that in each of them the installation of capital equipment becomes worth while. As Marshall said, "The efficiency of specialized machinery . . . is but one condition of its economic use; the other is that sufficient work should

be found to keep it well employed." (*Principles,* 8th ed., p. 264).
The techniques that have been developed in production for mass
markets in advanced countries are not well adapted and sometimes
not adaptable at all to output on a more limited scale. It is easy
to see that the relationship between the size of the market and
the amount of investment required for efficient operation is of
considerable importance for the theory of balanced growth.

Frequently the objection is made: but why use machinery?
Why adopt capital-using methods in areas where labor is cheap
and plentiful? Why not accordingly employ techniques that are
labor-intensive instead of capital-intensive?

The answer is obvious. As an adaptation to existing circumstances, including the existing factor proportions, the pursuit of
labor-intensive production methods with a view to economizing
capital may be perfectly correct. But the study of economic development must concern itself with changing these circumstances,
not accepting them as they are. What is wanted is progress, not
simply adaptation to present conditions. And progress depends
largely on the use of capital, which in turn depends on adequate
and growing markets, which in the absence of a strongly rising
world demand for the country's exports means a diversified output expansion for domestic use.

Reference has been made to the importance of autonomous
advance in a number of mutually supporting lines of production.
How is this achieved? Autonomous advance in different branches
simultaneously may come about through the infectious influence
of business psychology, through the multiplier effects of investment anywhere which can create increased money demand elsewhere, or through deliberate control and planning by public authorities. According to some writers the balanced-growth argument implies that the market mechanism is eliminated and that
investments must be effected according to a coordinated plan.
This opinion, which is widely held, seems to me dubious. There
are many important reasons for government planning, but this is
not necessarily one of them. As a means of creating inducements
to invest, balanced growth can be said to be relevant primarily
to a private-enterprise system. State investment can and often
does go ahead without any market incentives. Planning author-

ities can apply capital, if they have any, wherever they may
choose, though if they depart too much from balance as dictated
by income elasticities of demand they will end by creating white
elephants and intolerable disproportionalities in the structure of
production. It is private investment that is attracted by markets
and needs the inducement of growing markets. It is here that the
element of mutual support is so useful and, for rapid growth, indispensable.

It is important to note that the doctrine under consideration is
not itself concerned with the question of where the capital is to
be found, for all the balanced investment which it envisages. I
have tried to make it clear in my discussion of it that the argument is primarily relevant to the problem of the demand for capital; it takes an increased supply of capital for granted. In my
presentation balanced growth is an exercise in economic development with unlimited supplies of capital, analogous to Professor
Lewis' celebrated exercise in development with unlimited labor
supplies.

In reality, of course, capital supplies are not unlimited. It may
be that the case for state investment stems chiefly from the fact
that capital is scarce and that government efforts are necessary to
mobilize all possible domestic sources of saving. Measures to
check the expansion of consumer demand may be necessary to
make resources available for investment but may at the same
time weaken the private inducement to invest. This is a famous
dilemma to which Malthus first called attention in his *Principles
of Political Economy*. A case for state investment may clearly
arise if and when the mobilization of capital supplies discourages
private investment activity and so destroys the demand for capital. But this case is entirely separate from the principle of balanced growth as such. It might only be added that the capital
supply problem alone creates a strong presumption against relying on the indiscriminate use of import restrictions which may
reduce a country's real income and therefore make it harder to
increase the flow of saving.

Elsewhere I have tried to explain how the balanced-growth
idea is related to the classical law of markets. Supply creates its
own demand, provided that supply is properly distributed among

different commodities in accordance with consumers' wants. An increase in consumable output must provide a balanced diet. Each industry must advance along an expansion path determined by the income elasticity of consumer demand for its product. This simple idea must be the starting point in any expansion of production for domestic markets in the less developed countries, insofar as external demand conditions do not favor the traditional pattern of "growth through trade." Yet, as often happens in economic discussion, critics have tended to dismiss this idea either as a dangerous fallacy or as an obvious platitude. It is hardly necessary to add that the pattern of consumable output cannot be expected to remain the same in successive stages of development. The content of a balanced diet of a man with a thousand dollars a year will differ from that of a man with a hundred dollars.

The relation between agriculture and manufacturing industry offers the clearest and simplest case of balance needed for economic growth. In a country where the peasantry is incapable of producing a surplus of food above its own subsistence needs there is little or no incentive for industry to establish itself: there is not a sufficient market for manufactured goods. Conversely, agricultural improvements may be inhibited by lack of a market for farm products if the nonfarm sector of the economy is backward or undeveloped. Each of the two sectors must try to move forward. If one remains passive the other is slowed down.

It is important in this connection to make a clear distinction between two concepts that are frequently confused: the marketable surplus and investable surplus of the farm sector. The farm sector's marketable surplus of farm products determines the volume of non-farm employment, including employment in manufacturing and other activities. It reflects simply the farm sector's demand for nonagricultural commodities. This is the concept that is relevant to the balanced-growth principle.

An investable surplus of farm products represents an act of saving in the farm sector. It can conceivably result from a transfer of surplus laborers from the farms to capital construction projects: a food surplus may then arise through forced or voluntary saving in the farm sector for maintaining the workers engaged on capital projects. This is the concept relevant to the problem of capital supply. It is obvious that even a large marketable surplus of food need not involve any saving by the farmers. It presents a very helpful inducement, but does not in itself create the means, for capital investment outside the agricultural sector. A fuller discussion of the interrelationship between marketable and investable surpluses would take us too far from our present subject. It seemed desirable to mention the distinction here merely for the sake of conceptual clarity. So much for the relation between agriculture and industry.

Within the manufacturing field alone the case for balanced investment implies a horizontal diversification of industrial activities all pushing ahead, though naturally at varying rates. The objection can be made that such diffusion of effort and resources over many different lines of activity must mean a loss of dynamic momentum in the economy. This is possible. The dispersal of investment over a variety of consumer-goods industries can undoubtedly be carried to excess. The balanced-growth principle can be and has been interpreted far too literally. Producing a little of everything is not the key to progress. The case for balanced growth is concerned with establishing a pattern of mutually supporting investments over a range of industries wide enough to overcome the frustration of isolated advance, in order precisely to create a forward momentum of growth. The particular factors that determine the optimum pattern of diversification have to do with technology, physical conditions and other circumstances that vary from country to country. There can be no standard prescription of universal applicability. We are concerned with a point of principle and cannot deal with the precise forms of its implementation in practice. Just as it is possible for manufacturing industry as a whole to languish if farmers produce too little and are too poor to buy anything from factories, so it is possible for a single line of manufacturing to fail for lack of support from other sectors in industry as well as agriculture; that is, for lack of markets.

The case for diversification which emerges from these considerations stands in sharp contrast, first of all, to the great concentrations of capital needed for public overhead facilities such as transport and electric power. This type of investment in public overheads will be reserved for a separate discussion in this lecture series.

Secondly, the diversification argument contrasts with the teaching of the doctrine of comparative advantage which tends to show that countries gain by concentration of effort on a limited range of activities rather than by trying to do everything at home. The first part of this lecture discussed certain reasons why possibilities of growth induced through international trade may have declined of late. Having considered the argument for balanced investment we are now ready to tackle the central point of our subject: the apparent conflict between domestic diversification and international specialization.

III

The classical theory of trade shows that at least up to a point a country can benefit by concentrating its effort and resources along lines of international comparative advantage. This is an important and familiar truth which no country that is seeking development can afford to ignore. But once a country has adopted an optimum pattern and optimum degree of specialization along these lines, how is it to achieve *continued* further growth if external demand conditions do not induce it? There is no doubt that the opening up of trade can bring very sizable gains to a primitive economy, but is there any guarantee that trade alone will thereafter cause a rate of growth that can be regarded as satisfactory in the light, for instance, of population increase at home or of the living levels prevailing abroad? There is no such guarantee, especially if the export products which the comparative-advantage principle tells a country to produce face an external demand which (a) is generally inelastic with respect to price and (b), what may be more important, shows only a sluggish rate of increase in total volume. Granted all the advantages of international specialization, there remains a possibility of deadlock and comparative stagnation.

In the nineteenth century growth was created through international trade not only because countries previously isolated and self-contained now decided to specialize. This was indeed an important factor in the opening up of Japan and more generally as a result of the great improvements in transport. But it was not all. Economic development was diffused through international trade because the pattern of advance in the rising industrial centers happened to be such as to cause a rapidly increasing demand for imported foodstuffs and raw materials. Insofar as this was the operating factor it should be kept distinct from the act of specialization. Much of the conventional theory of trade seems to me to be based on a very understandable, yet analytically illegitimate, generalization of nineteenth-century experience, an experience which in some ways was unique.

The theory of international specialization as such is a static analysis. It assumes a given pattern of comparative advantage, given levels of domestic productivity, and given amounts of productive resources. The theory can be and has been supplemented by considering the way in which factor supplies may react to the opening up of trade, but even in this form it remains an exercise in comparative statics.

The transmission of growth from a dynamically expanding center is a rather different story, in which a rapidly rising demand for imports of primary products is the decisive feature which in its turn generates outflows of productive factors to the peripheral areas to meet this demand. Now my point is that the case for specialization as such is just as strong as ever, but that the forces making for the transmission of growth from advanced to less developed countries may not be as powerful as they were a hundred years ago. In these circumstances, without giving up the benefits of international specialization, there may be a case for output expansion for the home market in a country where the supply of productive factors, including capital, is increasing. The idea popular in some quarters that a single country has to have all industries, including especially capital goods industries, derives no support from the economic concept of balanced growth in the limited sense in which I interpret it. This concept, based on the diversity and hence complementarity of consumers' wants, shows how a number of industries advancing simultaneously can create markets for each others' products. It is not an argument for indiscriminate industrialization. Let us remember that agriculture too is an "industry" in the framework of this concept. At low-income levels a large proportion of any addition to income is likely to be spent on food. Consequently, in low-income countries agricultural improvement is bound to be a crucial element in any process of balanced growth.

Nor is this an argument for autarky. There is plenty of room for home-market expansion without interfering with international trade. This becomes clear if we consider in particular the existence of transport costs, a factor often neglected in orthodox trade theory. If transport costs were zero, then a country's production pattern would not depend at all on the pattern of its own consumption and other expenditure. There would be no "localization of demand." Actually we find very considerable localization: countries usually spend most of their income on their own output. The presence of transport costs is at least one reason for this and certainly the most basic. It is for this reason that in poor countries, where income is spent mostly on food, the bulk of the labor force works in food production (and this is often true even of countries that are net importers of food).

Transport costs alone constitute an important barrier to complete international specialization. They create in each country a wide range of domestic goods and services within which the notion of balanced growth is applicable without prejudice to international trade. In fact, investment for home market production, so far from hurting international specialization, may lay the foundation for an increase in the volume of trade.

But transport costs are, after all, not a desirable thing but an unfortunate necessity. Is it not foolish to introduce in addition artificial barriers to promote balanced domestic development? The case for and against import restriction is a well-worn subject which I am reluctant to take up but cannot avoid altogether. In my own opinion the restriction of imports may sometimes help but should never be relied upon. Actually it is always apt to be overdone because it is a relatively easy thing to do.

The argument for balanced investment stresses the creation of investment incentives through the promotion of mutually supporting domestic activities. In the case of imported products evidently a market already exists in the country. The restriction or prohibition of imports may stimulate the domestic production of import substitutes.

Now in the first place this is an essentially unneighborly thing to do: it hurts your neighbor, and even though he may be comparatively rich and strong, it may weaken his demand for your export products. Moreover, if nothing else is done it is not at all certain that it will lead to a cumulative growth of the domestic market. The output of a certain commodity is increased until imports are replaced and at that point the expansion may stop if it is based on nothing broader than import restriction and import substitution.

There is a possibility that import substitution draws resources away from export production, which may force up prices of export products and so improve the country's terms of trade. But this is a risky policy: the world outside may learn to do without those export products. Besides, increased production for the home market need not, in my opinion, impinge on the export sector at all. The purpose of the balanced investment policy is not to draw labor away from export industries but to raise the productivity of people now working in subsistence agriculture and other activities for domestic consumption.

The main disadvantage of import restriction is that it may lead to costly and inefficient production of import substitutes. The market for an imported commodity, small as it may be to start with, becomes even smaller in real volume as the price to the domestic consumer increases. The initial effect on real income is bad and may well lead to a fall in domestic saving. If at the same time it increases investment incentives the result is likely to be inflationary. It is important to make the fullest use of opportunities for international specialization so as to maximize the real income level and hence the volume of saving available for investment. As we saw, the balanced-growth doctrine assumes increased capital supplies. Where are these to come from? A high level of foreign trade may be very useful as a source of saving (as it was, for instance, for Japan).

It is not to be denied that import restrictions can help in a policy of balanced domestic investment, but their unfavorable effect on real income and hence possibly on saving should always be remembered. They should therefore be used sparingly. Import restrictions enforced in spite of such unfavorable effects can be justified only on the grounds of greater future benefit; which is the infant industry argument for protection. On this point I am still inclined to maintain that infant creation is far more important than infant protection. If adequate development is not possible by means of international trade, at least we should take care that expansion of the domestic economy does not involve needless additional cost by destroying such gains as are being obtained from international specialization.

The upshot is that output expansion for domestic consumption can go ahead side by side with international specialization. It need not be a substitute for international specialization. It is a substitute rather for the growth transmission mechanism which for reasons indicated may not be as powerful today as it was in the nineteenth century.

The title of this paper has perhaps misled the reader. He may have expected to see a fight between domestic growth and international trade. The fight is not taking place. In fact, if we look at the two protagonists in my piece a little more closely we find that they are really friends, not enemies. Balanced growth is the best friend that international trade can have. Filling the vacuum in the domestic economy is the best foundation for foreign trade, since it means increasing the level of productivity and real purchasing power. After all, that is why the advanced nations are each others' best customers. That is the best hope for expanding world trade, although it is quite likely that trade will expand less than in proportion to national incomes. Trade as a *proportion* of world income may well decline as the domestic economies of the backward areas become more fully developed.

There is, however, a further problem that worries some economists. If production is pushed for domestic markets, will that not lead to balance-of-payments difficulties? The belief that it will is expressed in several places in Professor Lewis' book, *The Theory of Economic Growth*. Do we have a conflict here between balanced growth and external equilibrium? If external disequilibrium is inevitable, then this may lead to balance of payments restrictions on imports and so indirectly after all to a destruction of foreign trade.

Let me indicate very briefly how I would look at this problem. It is true that a new industry producing something new for the home market is likely to create an increased demand for imports because it may need some imported raw material and because part of the additional incomes earned in this industry may be spent on imported goods. But that is not the whole story; that is only one side of it. If this industry sells its products on the domestic market, the rest of the economy will have to divert its expenditure away from imported products: provided that expenditure is not increased by inflationary means — through a reduction in saving, through dishoarding or through credit expansion. If inflation can be avoided then the products sold by the new industry will necessarily act as import substitutes indirectly, even if they look totally different from anything imported previously. If there is a balance-of-payments deficit it is a result of inflation, not of output expansion for the home market. If there is no inflation then the rest of the economy will have to reduce its imports in order to buy the products of the new industry, and this will tend to offset the increase in imports caused by the new industry.

It may seem strange that an expansion of income in this model is not necessarily accompanied by any net increase in imports. It would seem that the marginal propensity to import is zero, which looks like a strange and unnatural result. But there is nothing strange about it if we remember that in this case there has been a structural change in the economy: the creation of a new industry. The usual concepts of income analysis in international trade assume a given economic structure. Economic development means changes in economic structure, and in this dynamic context the functional relationships between income and imports need not behave in the usual way.

There is no time to enlarge on this point. Perhaps I have said enough to suggest that it is not development for the domestic economy as such that creates balance-of-payments difficulties. It is the excess spending associated with inflation that creates balance-of-payments difficulties, and inflation is due in its turn to the difficulty which the poorer countries have in living within their means, when there is so much investment to be done and when there are so many temptations to spend on consumer goods as well. This is the great difficulty.

I may have seemed to take a rather optimistic — one may think perhaps an overoptimistic — note in regard to the particular subject of this paper. That does not mean that it is all very easy in practice. On this occasion I have neglected, for instance, the whole problem of capital mobilization. I would not for a moment deny that development on the home front is bound to be a painful and difficult process. But it is in some cases a necessary task and a promising one.

SOME REFLECTIONS ON THE INTERNATIONAL FINANCING OF PUBLIC OVERHEAD INVESTMENTS

Even though the circumstances affecting international investment today are in many ways totally unlike those of the nineteenth century, it is hoped that a comparative sketch of the same problem in two widely different settings may yet be of some interest. The problem is that of foreign lending for basic overhead facilities. This is the field in which the World Bank is now operating. Current practices will come up for discussion later. First let us take a brief look at past experience and try to size up the general nature of the problem.

I

International investment in the nineteenth century was mainly for the purpose of setting up public overhead facilities such as railroads. Of Great Britain's external investments outstanding in 1913, 30 per cent was in government bonds, as much as 40 per cent in railroad securities and 5 per cent in other public utilities, so that three fourths of the total represented public or public-utility investment.

Another prominent feature of British foreign investment was

that roughly two thirds of it was in the so-called regions of recent settlement, including the United States, Canada, Argentina and Australia. It is clear that the share of public or public-utility investment in British foreign lending was particularly high in the new countries. It is clear also that in these countries public overhead investment formed a high proportion of total capital formation in the nineteenth century. Despite a domestic railway boom this type of investment was not nearly so conspicuous in Britain's domestic economy where roads, bridges, canals, buildings and other improvements had been built up during previous centuries. In the United States the railway was introduced at a time when there was a veritable passion for "internal improvements." In contrast to England, railroads in the United States, at any rate west of the Alleghenies, were typically built in advance of traffic requirements. This has been called "the American railroad innovation of the nineteenth century." In the twentieth century we have the multipurpose river development projects of which the TVA in America is a well-known example.

In all such developmental projects we can distinguish between three periods: the period of actual construction, which is sometimes called the gestation period; then a period of infancy in which the project has not enough work to do to make it pay; and finally, the stage of maturity marked by sufficiently full utilization to make profitable operation possible. The biological analogy reflected in the three labels — gestation, infancy, maturity — is not strictly appropriate. The project itself does not change from the infancy period to the stage of maturity: it is the economy that grows up and so enables the project ultimately to become a paying proposition.

Public-utility projects often must be built, or anyway are actually built, before the economy can make full enough use of them, before they can be made to pay. They usually come in big units. They are built ahead of demand partly for this reason, that is because of technical necessity due to "indivisibilities," but possibly also as a result of deliberate policy of public authorities or of the speculative exuberance of private promoters. Whatever the reasons (and more will be said about them shortly) the consequence is a gap between the time of construction and the time of profitable operation. This infancy period is in some respects analogous to the case with which the infant industry protection argument is concerned. Tariff protection, however, is obviously useless here since basic services such as inland transport, electric power and water supply generally cannot be imported from abroad and do not enter into international trade. Tariff protection in the present case can help only if by attracting new industries it can accelerate the growth of demand for the transport of other basic services. Its effectiveness for this purpose is doubtful. For one thing, it is not likely to bring results quickly enough.

The infancy period of public overhead facilities presents a problem that has caused much trouble in the international investment experience of the past. Such facilities are as a rule highly capital-intensive in operation, which means that capital charges are likely to bulk very large in comparison with current maintenance and operating expenses. The gap in the infancy stage arises therefore chiefly from inability to earn enough to meet the fixed interest charges, though for a time there may be difficulty even in covering operating costs from current earnings. How is the gap to be bridged? There are three main possibilities. (1) new foreign borrowing; (2) government subsidies from domestic taxation; (3) elimination of capital charges through default or financial reorganization.

The first method is to raise new loans abroad with which to meet not only the existing interest charge but even perhaps to cover a part of current operating costs. This presupposes strong confidence in the ultimate growth of demand for the project's services. The loss incurred during the infancy period must be reckoned at compound interest. The cost of the gap is in the nature of a capital cost or investment. Filling the gap by additional borrowing creates an additional interest charge, and so increases the size of the gap. It is not a method that can be lightly recommended. Yet it may be a perfectly legitimate way of bridging the gap, just as proper as it is for a person to borrow in his youth and to pay off the loan when he reaches a mature working age. New borrowing to pay old interest obligations was abhorrent to orthodox principles, though the practices of international finance in the nineteenth century were such as to make it at least occasionally possible.

Government aid in the new countries often took the form of land grants made to railroad companies from the public domain. Although it may look like an outright subsidy, it is perhaps better regarded as a special method of raising capital to cover the infancy deficits. Once the railroad was built the company could sell such land to settlers from Europe or from the more developed regions of the same country. The settlers brought capital with them which thus, in effect, helped to meet the interest charges payable to foreign holders of railway bonds.

The subsidy method proper is quite different. The government of the country or region receiving the investment subsidizes it out of tax revenue so long as the investment cannot pay its own way. In effect, a tribute is imposed on the whole community for meeting the fixed interest charges and operating losses of the project. Such subsidies have sometimes resulted from government guarantees to foreign investors. Guarantee contracts relating to railway investments were worked out in two countries as far apart as Canada and India in the same year, 1849. At least in India the contract made it clear that the government was to pay not only the capital charges but also the ordinary operating deficits in any year when operating returns were insufficient. But the subsidy was to be repaid as soon as increased earnings made it possible to do so. In principle, therefore, the subsidy was a loan, though in practice, as was the case in Canada, it usually proved a permanent gift. This has been aptly characterized as a system of "private enterprise at public risk."

The government subsidy during the infancy period, when carried by taxation, constitutes a real burden on the community. It may discourage private business activity and slow down the growth of the economy, on which the profitable operation of the project depends. If this is the case then this method too tends to lengthen the deficit period of infancy. Finally, if the infancy period is indefinitely prolonged it is clear not only that there is a continuing burden on the country that taxes itself for this purpose, but also that the world as a whole suffers a loss in terms of opportunity cost: the capital could have been better used somewhere else.

This brings us to the third method of dealing with the problem: default, bankruptcy, repudiation — permanent or temporary, partial or complete. It could happen in the nineteenth century even in the most successful of the new countries; not necessarily because of bad faith or dishonesty, but rather because of the inherent difficulty arising from the quantitative importance and the essential lumpiness of public overhead investment financed by foreign loans.

Default occurred when any resources obtained through additional borrowing or government subsidies ran out, or the gap turned out to be longer than expected. The enterprise had not enough staying power to hold out until the maturity stage. Sometimes interest was paid in the form of funding bonds instead of cash, which meant that, even if all turned out well afterwards, a forced loan was imposed on the investors abroad.

Default is of course a serious matter not only for the original investors, on whom the burden falls, but from a world point of view. For one thing, default impedes the continuance of international financing. Moreover, a public utility financed by foreign capital should eventually pay. For a time it may be that charging what the traffic will bear cannot possibly bring in enough to service the investment. In the early development stage there simply is not enough traffic, or else what traffic there is will not bear charges high enough to make the project pay. Sooner or later, however, as the economy grows, it should be able to stand such charges. That is the test of the public utility of a project of this sort, at least if economic efficiency is the criterion. We all realize that welfare considerations may justify other policies. There are indeed certain types of social investment, in education and health for example, which may call for a continuous subsidy. But public overhead facilities such as transport, power and communications should be able to earn their way eventually. If they do not, then there has been a waste of resources; then default is due not to a temporary lag of earnings but to a basic malinvestment. In a few cases finished projects such as railroad lines have actually been scrapped or abandoned, at least for a time, but even serious malinvestment need not have any such physical consequences. The purpose of default or financial reorganization is to discard, not the physical plant, but the fixed interest charge. Once this is done the project may continue in operation, furnishing useful services, like a gift of nature. Yet waste will have occurred in the sense that the capital resources embodied in it could have been applied more usefully elsewhere. Our assumption must be that the infancy period represents only a gap, not a permanent drain.

Now let us recall that the gap is due to building ahead of demand. But why build ahead of demand? The reason first of all lies in the lumpiness of public overhead investment in conjunction with an expectation of growing demand. The element of lumpiness or indivisibility exists not only in relation to an individual project as a whole but also in regard to expansion costs. A canal company may start by digging a narrow and shallow ditch planning to deepen it later; or a railroad enterprise may lay down light and flimsy roadbed first with the idea of strengthening it as and when traffic increases. But this usually entails heavy costs of expansion. Traffic may have to be stopped altogether for a while, which alone makes it expensive in view especially of the continuous capital charges.

For reasons of this sort J. M. Clark in his *Economics of Overhead Costs* shows that there is a point at which, by building ahead of demand, total costs are minimized. If it is desired to keep the facilities closely geared to current traffic demand, any saving in interest charges might be more than offset by frequent expansion costs. On the other hand, if the project is built too far in advance, the fixed interest charges during the lean years will outweigh any saving in expansion costs. With a given interest rate the exact optimum point depends on future growth of demand and is therefore uncertain. Uncertainty is a distinctive mark of developmental overhead investments. The appraisal of profit prospects is liable to sudden change. Capital movements in the nineteenth century were associated with extreme waves of optimism and pessimism because of the peculiar difficulty of estimating the probable gains and losses on this type of investment.

As J. M. Clark presents it, the theory of building public utilities ahead of demand takes a certain-uncertain rate of growth for granted, as something given from the outside. But the growth of demand is itself determined to some extent by the overhead facilities available. A true pioneering investment is made not to meet an existing need but to create one. In the Great Plains of the Middle West there could be no great demand for transport until the land was settled, but settlement was slow and difficult until the railways provided access. This type of railway promotion became dominant in America in the 1850's. In Argentina about thirty years later railroads were built on the same principle: in advance of current traffic, to create the traffic needed to make them pay.

In this case the rate of growth in demand for transport or other basic services is not taken for granted. Investment is deliberately intended or at least expected to influence it: to induce an increase in miscellaneous economic activity and so an increase in demand for its services. Here too there is usually a long gap that has to be bridged, and the returns are not calculable with any close degree of certainty. Action is based on expectations that tend to be self-realizing, though whether they are realized fully and quickly enough can never be foreseen.

To the extent that an overhead investment project promotes the growth of the economy it creates its own demand. For this reason, even though physical lumpiness is usually an important part of the story, building ahead of demand seems often to have gone far in excess of anything made necessary by technical indivisibility. It has been an instrument of development policy used by public authorities. It has often resulted from the action of private entrepreneurs under the spur of competitive motives, in order to stake a claim or to shut out rivals. Competitive duplication has often been stressed in the literature and perhaps overstressed. Even if only one Pacific railroad had been built in America in the 1870's it might have failed, for want of traffic. Two competing railroad empires, the Northern Pacific and the

Union Pacific, entered into an agreement in 1870 to keep away from each others' preserves, and their preserves were vast. Yet bankruptcy overcame them both.

The first great project of the century in America was the Erie Canal built by the State of New York under Governor Clinton and completed in 1825. The drive for internal improvements reached a peak in the 1830's, when many American states sold bonds in England to finance canal, highway and railroad construction. To contemporaries these projects were gigantic undertakings. Many of them depended for financial success on future settlement and growth, and could not possibly earn their keep from the outset. There was also, however, an element of competition between states, each trying to attract settlers by building public facilities. Within some of the states there was in addition a tendency for public works to be scattered for political reasons so as to benefit all sections of the electorate. This caused too many projects to be started and some could not be completed before the crisis came. But more important was the fact that the new facilities, even when completed, could not be made to pay. In the early 1840's nine states defaulted on their bonds, which represented about 60 per cent of total state debt. Five of these states resumed debt payments after a few years, but the other four, accounting for about 10 per cent of the total, defaulted permanently. Another development crisis occurred during the 1870's, when a feverish railway building boom financed largely by capital imports came to an end. In 1876 railroads in receivership are said to have represented 17 per cent of total mileage in the United States. After the crisis of 1893 just over 20 per cent of the total mileage seems to have passed through foreclosure sales. These percentages are useful because the extent of bankruptcy and consequent loss to foreign investors has sometimes been exaggerated. Moreover, in the course of railroad reorganizations the bondholders, when their interest claim was cut down, often received preferred stock in exchange, so that later when earnings improved the investors' income was more or less restored. At the time, nevertheless, these crises caused serious convulsions in international finance.

The history of Argentina and Australia provides similar ex-

amples. It seems fairly clear that a typical nineteenth century
development crisis in the new countries was closely tied up with
the creation, through international investment, of temporary
excess capacity in the field of overhead facilities. This was so
not only in the experience of the countries already mentioned
but also in the Canadian case during the period 1900–1914. It is
said that the railways that Canada built in her great boom before
World War I turned out to be thirty years ahead of their time.
That may well be true, but the question is: would traffic requirements have increased as much as they actually did if as a matter
of public policy railways had not been laid down in advance?
Would the Canadian economy have grown at the same rate? Of
course we must not forget the extra tax load which Canada had
to carry in order to pay the "pure tribute" of external interest
before her railroads could earn their keep. This load may have
tended to slow down the growth of her economy, but it seems
doubtful whether this was a significant handicap. The existence
of ample overheads surely brought some benefits that could not
be appropriated in railway profit and loss accounts. It facilitated
a great deal of direct investment later. The net effect of anticipatory overhead investment was probably to accelerate Canada's
economic growth.

II

In an attempt to look at the problem in more general terms it
will be useful now to make an explicit distinction between two
types of capital formation: overhead investment and direct investment. Capital theory cannot make much headway so long as
it treats all man-made equipment as a homogeneous mass. The
structural content of the capital stock must be examined. Distinctions are necessary. But distinctions are always to some extent arbitrary and are made to suit their purpose. The labels
used for the present purpose are analogous to the overhead costs
and direct costs sometimes found in the theory of the firm.

The term "direct investment" refers to miscellaneous business
investment and is not restricted to foreign business investment in
the present context, though of course it includes foreign direct
investment. Within a given framework of public facilities, direct

investment occurs over the whole range of industry, trade and agriculture, is suited to individual enterprise, and typically results in quickly increased outputs of consumer or producer goods. It is within the sphere of "direct investment" that the balanced-growth principle, which was discussed in the preceding lecture, is applicable (in relation to the "horizontal" structure of consumer-goods production).

Overhead investment aims at providing the services — transport, power, water supply — which are basic for any productive activity, cannot be imported from abroad, require large and costly installations, and in the history of western economies outside England, have usually called for public assistance or public enterprise. Because of the monopoly element that attaches to them they are now everywhere subject at least to public regulation. Typically overhead investments take a considerable time to reach maturity in a growing economy. To be sure, all investment depends on expectations, but the time range of expectations is apt to be particularly long in overhead projects, because of their lumpiness combined with their high operational capital-intensity.

Capital goods are heterogeneous. The different types of capital in productive use, even within a single firm, are complementary to each other. This is true in particular of overhead investment and direct investment. There is an essential complementarity between them. Their mutual dependence can take two forms. An increase in direct investment induces an increase in overhead investment. Or it may be, as we have seen, the other way around. Overhead investment leads to a growth in direct investment. The former relationship may be part of what Marshall had in mind when he argued that the growth of an industry or of a whole region tends to create external economies. This notion includes not only improvements in organization but also apparently investment in overhead facilities such as transport. Marshall suggests more than once that external economies result from the use of modern facilities for communication, including steam transport and the telegraph. But railway and telegraph lines do not simply come into existence. They require investment. At least in part, therefore, we can perhaps identify overhead investment with the provision of external economies. This would leave out the organizational aspects but these are perhaps the most elusive part of the concept of external economies. In any case, on this view overhead investment seems to be induced by the growth of direct investment in miscellaneous productive activity.

This is a view that fits the condition of the late nineteenth-century British economy which was already well equipped with public facilities. It was an economy with a high density where the lumpiness of overhead investment was not of great consequence and where there was pretty full scope for the marginal analysis based on Marshall's motto: *natura non facit saltum.* Where additions to overhead facilities take place in response to prior increases in the demand for them the troublesome problems of infancy which we have discussed need not arise.

But these conditions were rather exceptional. Elsewhere in the nineteenth century, especially in the new countries, overhead investment in the provision of external economies appears as the active factor designed to induce growth in productive activity. Such investment led periodically to a state of maladjustment in the capital structure of the borrowing countries: too much capital in their overheads and too little in directly productive activities for export or domestic uses. Now this is not a simple horizontal maladjustment such as an excess of toothbrushes combined with a shortage of mouth organs. It is essentially a vertical maladjustment that tends to produce the kind of hiatus depicted by the Austrian capital and cycle theory. With the aid of foreign funds an extension of the roundaboutness of production takes place in the borrowing country and this leads to a crisis. Direct investment does not grow fast enough to justify the overhead investment financed by foreign lending. The structural distortion of the kind the Austrians stressed is here the essential trouble. Overinvestment in all lines proportionately would not be overinvestment at all but a case of balanced growth. The periodic overinvestment in the overheads of the new countries was the way these countries developed, and provides the main explanation of the crises associated with international investment in the past. Works of public utility were built in advance of the demand for them. This meant big forward jumps in boom times, alternating with the painful deficit periods during which the new projects were gradually absorbed through the growth of economic activity which they themselves helped to promote.

That is the picture derived from American experience and fairly generally from international investment experience in the century that ended in 1914. Is this picture of any relevance to the underdeveloped countries today?

III

Apart from political and cultural difficulties there is no doubt that in many of these countries the physical environment is unfavorable for direct investment, domestic as well as foreign, because of a lack of the public facilities which in advanced countries an individual businessman can take for granted. Electric power, water supply, transport, and communications are classed as basic services because they are essential for the use of producers although of course they can be a convenience for consumers also. They are often lumped together with the so-called "basic industries" such as heavy chemicals, steel, and engineering. Development plans usually give a high priority to both the heavy industries and the basic services, but in my view a sharp distinction between them is necessary. While both are generally capital-intensive in their operation, the construction of public works such as river dams, irrigation canals, roads, and even railroads is often labor-intensive and can make use of masses of unskilled labor with relatively little equipment.

But the most elementary distinction between the two is often overlooked. Steel and machinery can be imported from abroad and are being imported by most countries in ever-increasing volume. Electric power, irrigation, and inland transport services cannot be imported. If the necessary facilities do not exist within the country these basic services cannot be had at all. Investment in such facilities is therefore absolutely unavoidable from the very start of a development program. By contrast, the creation of steel and other heavy industries is in principle at least postponable.

The extent to which the lack of overhead facilities is a handicap varies in different areas, as can be seen in a study by J. F.

Gaston on *Obstacles to Direct Foreign Investment*.[1] In Southeast Asia this report placed the lack of such facilities very near the top of a long list of obstacles, immediately after commercial policy and exchange control, which in all areas came first in the list of obstacles. But that was some years ago when the dollar shortage was still acute. It is possible that the exchange-control obstacle has moved down in the list since then and that the public-utility shortage would now appear at the top of the list, at any rate in Asia.

One of the many reports on foreign aid that have appeared in Washington this spring (1957) rightly points out that while there are no limits to direct foreign subsidies for increased consumption in the poorer countries, what is wanted is an increase in their productive capacity. According to this report the capacity of poor countries to absorb foreign aid for increasing their productive power is very limited, so that the amount of external funds that can be productively used is not enormous. This argument has been heard before and is for various reasons probably true. What is interesting here is that among the reasons for the low absorptive capacity this report lists the lack of power and transport facilities, oblivious of the fact that such facilities can be and in the past have been the main object of international capital transfers. The main advantage of international investment in overheads is that it creates better conditions not only for foreign business firms but also for domestic enterprise and individual activity. If we believe that individual activity is the basis of development, here is something that can be done to promote the growth of such activity.

If individual enterprise is inhibited by the absence of essential public facilities, overhead investment is discouraged by the low level of directly productive activity in a backward economy. There is a deadlock. The public overheads have initially not enough work to do to justify their existence. That is why they require autonomous action, an act of faith. They will not be absorbed in the sense of being fully utilized for some time. On this side of the deadlock too, there is, in a sense, a limited absorptive capacity. The economy will have to grow into these structures,

---

[1] National Industrial Conference Board, Technical Paper No. II, 1951.

which can be deliberately put up to promote such growth, like the pioneer railways in America.

The situation of the backward economies today seems in one respect rather similar to that of the new countries in the nineteenth century: what is wanted in both cases is, or was, a rapid transfer of western techniques and production methods. In western Europe much of the basic framework had been built during previous centuries. But in the new countries this transfer required a special effort in the building up of public overheads, which absorbed the bulk of the international capital flow of the nineteenth century. The need for overhead capital may have been accentuated by geographic and demographic conditions in the regions of recent settlement, but it was basically due to the rapid-transfer feature of development in these areas. This feature is also present in the backward economies today, though otherwise the two cases are totally different. In both cases the importance of overhead investment tends to make for a high capital-output ratio during the period of initial growth.

The case for anticipatory overhead investment is widely accepted in the literature of development, but it is sometimes disguised under various phrases current in capital theory. For instance, Myrdal tells us that "what underdeveloped countries particularly need are investments that take a long time to mature." Joan Robinson says that "the basic investments take some time to yield any fruit." Professor Fellner similarly speaks of "the slow maturing of projects." These writers make it clear that they have overhead investments in mind. Why should such investments be slow to mature or to yield any fruit? Reference is sometimes made to the physical durability or long earning life of such investments, but this explains nothing and looks to me like misplaced concreteness. It seems to me that in all the phrases just quoted what is implied is the case for building ahead of demand in a dynamic setting of development.

Yet in the discussion of development policy the case is not universally accepted. There is both in America and in the underdeveloped countries a feeling that we cannot afford the waste that is believed to have occurred in the past. There is a fear of white elephants. The solution is comprehensive planning. Thus Professor Tinbergen's report to the World Bank starts off by saying that in the past "a good deal of misplaced energy and effort went into over-investments," but that now through development policy "it is hoped that some of the errors and wastes of the past can be avoided." Professor Mahalanobis, the Indian planner, in a remarkable econometric model, suggests that planning will eliminate excess capacity and will thus reduce the capital-output ratio to one half of what it would be in an unplanned capitalist economy.

The goal of planning is a closely coordinated advance of both overhead investment and miscellaneous direct investment. The latter is not left to individual enterprise but is directed increasingly under public auspices along with the former. In this way any disproportion between the two is reduced to the technically unavoidable minimum.

Under the force of circumstances, including the lack of funds, many countries are driven to adopt this approach to development planning. In the nature of the case it is a somewhat rigid approach and whether it can be universally effective seems doubtful. The planning of development in a backward economy is bound to meet difficulties into which we need not enter. Most of us in America feel that there is little hope of genuine progress unless there is a wide diffusion of individual effort and activity throughout the economy. In laying at least the physical groundwork for the growth of such individual activity the case for building the overheads in advance of demand still seems to me a strong and valid argument.

Besides, was there so much waste in the overhead investment financed by foreign lending in the past? Were the new countries densely populated by white elephants? It is probably true, as Cairncross and Rostow have maintained, that foreign lending was in the long run at the expense of domestic investment in Britain. But was there anything wrong about that? Great Britain, which had started the Industrial Revolution, was after all a tight little island, not exceptionally rich in natural resources, where opportunities for investment were limited in comparison with the new countries. The export of Britain's savings banished the Malthusian threat and produced cheap food for the British people even if individual investors suffered occasional disappointment. By contrast, the present American economy has ample opportunities for highly profitable investment at home and has on the whole little interest in developing cheap imports through investments abroad. This is a very important difference, but it is not clear that it destroys the relevance of past patterns of foreign lending for such financing as may now be forthcoming for economic development.

It must be admitted that public overhead capital represents an overhead capital charge, and can be neither an economic nor a financial success unless the economy grows up into it. The gap of the infancy period is not an argument for financing by free grants. There is no reason why public utilities should not be financed by hard loans, including if necessary loans to enable them to meet their capital charges during infancy. The rate of interest performs after all a useful disciplinary function. There is a rather different case for permanently subsidizing social investment such as education and health on the grounds that the existing expenditure pattern reflects the community's backwardness and should not be taken as it is but altered by public action. Even here the expenditure may be indirectly profitable by helping to increase government tax revenue. When people become educated they start paying taxes. But the effects of such expenditure cannot easily be traced and financing through intergovernmental grants is not altogether inappropriate. The new countries in the nineteenth century received a good deal of free investment in the social category through immigration from Europe.

IV

Now if we look at the total capital flow from the United States to the underdeveloped countries today we see a considerable volume of direct business investment going out. There is also a certain amount of intergovernmental grants. The big gap in international finance is in the category of hard loans for public overhead investments, the category in which most of the capital export of the nineteenth century took place. This is the World Bank's field of activity. Nearly half of its loans to underdeveloped countries has been for hydroelectric power projects. The rest of its loans is largely for transport facilities. The Bank has done very useful work, but the amount of its lending has been relatively small. Even if we include the loans made by the Export-Import Bank in this field (excluding postwar reconstruction loans to Europe) we find that in the last six or seven years the real volume of America's foreign lending for public and public utility investment has been much less than Britain's fifty years ago. In those fifty years total world production has grown threefold and United States production fourfold.

According to the World Bank the trouble is not a lack of financial resources but a lack of sound realistic projects. This raises some questions. If the shortage of projects were a matter of competent design, surely it could be remedied through international technical assistance. The Bank itself is providing a good deal of such assistance. One cannot help surmising that the lack of sound projects reflects the uncertainties of the infancy period which are characteristic of any pioneering investment in the field of public overheads. For a debtor country to borrow in order to meet interest charges on previous loans is not respectable, even though in the Victorian era it was possible for this to happen. That is how projects could be nursed along at least part of the way to maturity. A foreign loan to be serviced is a heavy burden during the initial lean years when returns are not coming in. Yet the burden may be worth carrying. It is perhaps not impossible to devise arrangements to help debtor countries to carry this burden.

The Export-Import Bank has financed a remarkable enterprise in Afghanistan, the Helmand Valley Project, which seems a good illustration of the trials and troubles that plague the early life of a big developmental investment. The scheme has received some unfavorable publicity in the United States. The difficulties it has encountered are typical of the infancy stage. Here is a white elephant if ever there was one. But with a project of this sort it is clear that ten or twenty years must pass before a judgment is possible about its true success or failure.

The World Bank's "specific project approach" has been criticized, but this stems naturally from the lumpiness of overhead

investment and is not in my opinion a matter for serious objection. Of course, it may be pointless to define the purpose of a
foreign loan if offsetting shifts in domestic capital are possible.
But the type of project with which the Bank is concerned is
usually so large and new to the local economy that such substitutions can hardly be of great importance.

Lastly, a word about the principle under which both the World
Bank and the Export-Import Bank generally finance only the
direct foreign exchange cost of a project, while expenditure on
local labor and materials must be met by the borrowing country
itself. This requirement seems to have its origin in the procedure
adopted by the Export-Import Bank in the 1930's as an anti-
depression policy of promoting American exports.

This "matching principle" calls for three comments. In the
first place, it is clear that lack of home finance may render in-
eligible projects that are otherwise sound and realistic. Secondly,
it should be noted that, in the case of projects accepted for
Bank financing, a limited supply of home finance may cause
the direct import content of the project to be higher than it
would be if foreign finance were available for meeting local costs
as well. Construction methods can be varied: the division between foreign exchange and local costs is not always rigidly determined by technical factors. Shortage of local funds may lead
to the adoption of capital-intensive methods of construction
using, for instance, imported bulldozers together with foreign
personnel, even though the use of cheap local labor might be
more economical. In the case of the Helmand River Project the
Export-Import Bank has invested $40 million, while local costs
are said to have been only $8 million, but even so they placed a
heavy strain on the Afghan budget.

There is a third difficulty that may arise from the division
between local finance and foreign exchange costs. The idea is to
get the borrowing country to mobilize its own resources. This is
a very good idea. Moreover, the local contribution to the financing of the project gives an extra cushion of safety to the foreign
creditor as regards both the collection and the transfer of foreign
debt service. Now let us remember that the projects so financed
are usually in the overhead category. Suppose the local contri-

bution is effectively mobilized. If this deprives the local economy of funds that would otherwise have gone into miscellaneous direct investment it does not really make the project more viable. For in that case it may be that the growth of local direct investment is slowed down, and so it may take longer for the overhead investment to become self-supporting in the sense of being able to earn enough for its interest and operating costs. This may well offset the safety margin provided by local participation.

The difficulty is diminished if the matching principle actually results in a net addition to the investable funds forthcoming within the borrowing country. Presumably that is its purpose, and this purpose could probably be achieved even in some of the poorest countries. British foreign investment went mostly to new countries which were short of labor as well as capital. Capital had to be imported not only in the form of equipment but also, in effect, to provide subsistence for the immigrant laborers engaged in construction work. Most of the backward economies today are old and settled countries, some of them densely settled, and endowed with some domestic saving potential as well. The rationale of the matching principle is to get them to provide additional domestic saving.

Could it be argued that in these circumstances the whole case for international investment is not as strong as it was a hundred years ago? Some of the underdeveloped countries do have potential domestic resources available for capital construction. But it may be very hard for them to mobilize these resources, and it may be impossible to mobilize them without resorting to coercive methods. Even the necessary labor is not always readily available for construction: as a rule, it can be released from the land only through changes — and possibly revolutionary changes — in agricultural organization. So there remains a strong case for international financing of public works in underdeveloped countries.

The theme of this paper can be attacked by questioning the strategic role assigned to overhead investments. Let me make clear that I do not regard public overhead capital as the only crucial element which, if supplied, would now make economic development race ahead. Progress depends on countless other things, many of them outside the economic field altogether. Nevertheless, one cannot help being impressed with the Roman roads and aqueducts, and with the fact that river developments comparable with some present-day projects made the beginnings of civilization possible in the ancient world. These examples prove nothing, yet to my mind they do illustrate the importance of overhead investment as a means to development and as an object of international as well as national financing.

APPENDIX: NOTES ON "UNBALANCED GROWTH" *
(1959)

[Ragnar Nurkse died, very suddenly and unexpectedly, on 6 May 1959. During the last days of his life he had been reading a proof of the article 'Unbalanced Growth' by Paul Streeten, which had been sent to him by the author, prior to its appearance in the June issue of *Oxford Economic Papers*. To this it is evident that he was meditating a reply, but no more than a few fragments of it were actually written. These have been put together by the care of Professor James Tobin, who, like Nurkse, was spending a sabbatical year at Geneva. Though they cannot convey very much of what he would have said if his life had been extended, they do perhaps give some idea of the direction in which his mind was moving, and are worth preserving as his last thoughts on an issue with which he had been so much concerned.

One or two explanations should be given. Streeten's criticisms had been mainly directed against the first of the lectures which Nurkse had given at Istanbul in 1957. . . . It was Nurkse's view that a good many of the criticisms which Streeten advanced against his first lecture had been answered (or anticipated) in the second. Thus in the second lecture Nurkse had insisted on the importance of anticipatory overhead investment as a condition of economic growth (pp. 261–266) like Streeten on p. 179. (He did not see the footnote which Streeten subsequently added on that page.) It is from this point that his words begin.]

No doubt Streeten thinks I contradict myself in these two pieces, two lectures printed side by side, of which one seems to favor balanced growth, the other unbalanced growth. But

---

* This paper, here printed as an appendix, was published, with notes by J. R. Hicks, in the October 1959 issue of the *Oxford Economic Papers*, n.s., and is reproduced by permission of the publisher.

each has its special context. My interpretation of the phrase "balanced growth" is more limited and less rigid than he makes it out to be. Streeten seems to have no use for special contexts and seems anxious to establish a general doctrine favoring unbalanced growth. In this spirit he puts all who ever used the phrase "balanced growth" in the same camp. He then bombards this enemy camp with heavy cannon. Incidentally, why start with List? An interesting shipload of "balanced growth" economists could be made up of such diverse figures as Alexander Hamilton, Tench Coxe, Sir J. Steuart, and A. Smith.

The balanced growth notion, as I now tend to use it, is confined to the sphere of directly productive investment, as distinguished from overhead investment.[1] Even in the sphere of direct investment, balanced growth is necessary only if export demand is not "sufficiently" expanding. With an expanding export demand, direct investment would not need to follow a balanced-growth pattern but would take the form of direct investment in export production, and the complementarities in the make-up of additional consumption can then be implemented through international trade. This is not possible when the backward countries suffer from an export lag.[2] This export lag is a basic assumption without which balanced growth is untenable or pointless. It is only when "growth through trade" is not possible that the correspondence, implied in balanced growth, between national output and national consumption pattern is needed. I am sorry that Streeten cites nineteenth-century Britain as a counterexample to balanced growth, for the whole burden of my song is that conditions for the nineteenth-century type of growth through trade are no longer so favorable.

I am now inclined to think that it might be well to distinguish between balanced growth as a method and balanced growth as an outcome or objective. Even zigzag growth must have balance as its ultimate aim, in the sense of output expansion in accordance with national-income elasticities of demand. Suppose that a country's exports refuse to expand, while its factor supplies increase and its appetite rises. Production must then expand not for ex-

---

[1] See above, pp. 267–268.
[2] See above, pp. 245–247. See also Ch. 11, pt. 1, sec. 3.

port but for home market demand. What determines the pattern of home market expansion? In the main, national income elasticities of demand. This outcome leaves plenty of room for zigzags in the mechanics of output growth. As regards the mechanics I am inclined to be "liberal," accepting as alternative possibilities: central planning; generally optimistic expectations leading to spontaneous advance on a wide front; or the "disequilibrium" method of zigzag growth in successive industries or sections, each tugging the other along by signals given by the price-mechanism. I still think, however, that horizontal maladjustment (to be distinguished from vertical imbalance due to anticipatory overhead investment) is not good for its own sake and slows down growth.

[To this there are two shorter passages from Nurkse's papers which may perhaps be added. The first, from a lecture given at the Institut de Science Économique Appliquée in Paris, on 2 December 1958, elucidates what is said above about income elasticities of demand.]

Shortages in specific factor supplies, among other possible causes, can and will naturally produce changes in relative prices, to which consumer demand will tend to adjust itself. To this extent the output expansion will deviate from the path of income elasticity, which assumes a constancy of relative prices. No one has denied that price-elasticities, too, help to determine a community's pattern of demand. But changes in relative prices have no close or determinate relation to economic growth as such, whereas changes in income are a direct reflection and measure of growth. Hence the prominence given to income elasticities in a macroeconomic approach to the problem of international growth economics.

[The other is from a letter to Streeten, of November 1958.]

What I had in mind there[3] was the "basic contradiction of capitalism" as Marx put it and as Malthus dimly saw it before him, namely, the fact that when the means to invest are there the will may be lacking, and vice versa. A certain level of invest-

[3] See above, p. 250.

ment depends upon a certain rate of increase in consumption. From the technical viewpoint of capital theory, the case for socialism is that it cuts the connection between investment activity and consumption change; all investment becomes autonomous.

[But this must be read in the light of what is said above (J. R. H.)]

I I

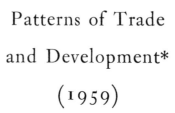

Patterns of Trade
and Development*
(1959)

CONTRASTING TRENDS IN NINETEENTH AND TWENTIETH CENTURY WORLD TRADE

In the Western world today some widely accepted doctrines of trade and development are still to a large extent influenced by the experience of the nineteenth century. It is inevitable that economic thought should lag behind the facts of economic history. Even economists are human; our mental activity is, and indeed should be, shaped in some measure by limits set by experience. When conditions change, however, conceptions and preconceptions derived from earlier experience can become a shell that inhibits the development of thought as well as action. Thus the nineteenth-century model of world trade is one which many of us still tend to carry in our minds as something like the normal or ideal. As it recedes in time, it appears more and more clearly to

---

* The Wicksell Lectures, delivered in Stockholm April 7 and 10, 1959, under the sponsorship of the Wicksell Lecture Society, reprinted by permission of the Society.

have been the product of very peculiar circumstances. We economists should always be ready to adapt the framework of our thinking if our work is to have relevance to the changing real world. It is in this spirit, and with these preoccupations as a motive force, that I venture to attempt a comparative sketch of long-term trends in international trade.

I. Trade Expansion and the Transmission of Economic Growth

The volume of world trade reached an all-time record level in 1957, but this is not surprising since nearly everything is bigger now than ever before. In relation to world production, international trade is smaller than it was some fifty or a hundred years ago. If we assume, as seems in fact to be the case, that roughly one tenth of the value of commodities produced in the world now enters into international trade, this proportion was probably something like one sixth in the years before the first World War.

But it is not just the *average* ratio of world trade to world production that adequately measures the relative weight of international trade in world economic affairs. More important was the *incremental* relationship between trade and production a hundred years ago. Trade played a crucial part in the economic growth not only of the "new" countries overseas but also of the "old" countries in Europe. In England at the time of Ricardo the margin of cultivation was creeping up the hillsides into poorer and poorer land and it is clear that without the burst of external trade which occurred soon afterwards, the struggle for food would have prevented industrialization from going as far as it did in Britain and elsewhere in western Europe.

Trade was an "engine of growth" in the nineteenth century. Sir Dennis Robertson, from whom this phrase is borrowed, observes in passing that it was not just a matter of optimum allocation of a given stock of resources.[1] It was certainly that, but it was something more as well. As I see it, it was also a means whereby a vigorous process of economic growth came to be trans-

[1] D. H. Robertson, "The Future of International Trade," in *Essays in Monetary Theory* (London, 1940), 214, reprinted in the American Economic Association's *Readings in the Theory of International Trade* (Philadelphia, 1949).

mitted from the center to the outlying areas of the world. This aspect of nineteenth-century experience was more or less neglected by the traditional trade theory, which focused its powerful spotlight on the beneficent specialization of productive activities that results when two economies previously isolated enter into contact with each other. The theory of international specialization, static though it is, is none the less fundamental; and it was in fact a highly relevant theory at a time when economies were opened up to one another by revolutionary improvements in transport, reductions in tariffs and by other means (as in the case, for example, of Japan). Yet it left something out. Trade was an engine of growth transmission as well as a means of improved allocation of existing resources. The classical trade theory derived a great deal of prestige from the brilliant record of nineteenth-century trade and development, even though it paid little or no attention to an essential aspect of that experience, namely, the dynamic spread of economic growth through trade. Why was this aspect neglected? Perhaps because economic growth was taken for granted, like the air we breathe. As it was going on at a pace satisfactory for both the new countries and the old, it seemed a matter of no particular interest compared with the fascinating theoretical problem of "entry into contact." Once economies had entered into contact through trade and reallocated their resources for increased specialization, what happened after that? Well, of course, they just grew and progressed, as everything did in the nineteenth century.

The focal center of economic expansion was initially Great Britain, whose population, despite heavy emigration, trebled in the nineteenth century while her real national income appears to have increased about tenfold and the volume of her imports more than twentyfold. (For our purposes the nineteenth century starts, in principle, in 1815 and ends in 1914.) The ratio of British imports to the national income was only about 12 per cent at the beginning, but in the latter part of the century had increased to about 30 per cent.[2] The change in commercial policy may be an

---

[2] See E. A. G. Robinson, "The Changing Structure of the British Economy," *Economic Journal,* September 1954. As everyone knows, the rate of Britain's growth slowed down after 1870, but it still remained of central importance in the international economy until the eve of World War I.

important proximate explanation, but basic conditions helped to force the change. The industrial revolution happened to originate on a small island with a limited range of natural resources, at a time when synthetic materials were yet unknown. In these circumstances economic expansion was transmitted to less-developed areas by a steep and steady increase in Britain's demand for primary commodities which those areas were well suited to produce. Local factors of production overseas, whose growth may in part have been induced by trade, were thus largely absorbed by the expansion of profitable primary production for export. On top of this, the center's increasing demand for raw materials and foodstuffs created incentives for capital and labor to move from the center to the outlying areas, accelerating the process of growth-transmission from the former to the latter.

II. The Role of the New Countries in World Trade and Investment

This pattern of "growth through trade" affected particularly the new countries or, as the late Folke Hilgerdt used to call them, the "regions of recent settlement" in the world's temperate latitudes: Canada, Argentina, Uruguay, South Africa, Australia, New Zealand. No doubt the United States, too, belongs substantially to this group, though Hilgerdt did not usually include it, since the United States is so big a trader and producer as to be in a class by itself for most purposes. These regions had certain essential characteristics in common, but in the present context what matters is their high, though varying, dependence on growth through primary commodity exports and on the private foreign investment which, directly or indirectly, was thereby induced.

Alfred Marshall referred to "the splendid markets which the old world has offered to the new."[3] He forgot to mention that these were *growing* markets, but this he seems to have assumed as a matter of course. The second-last chapter of his *Principles,* which deals with "General Influences of Economic Progress," begins as follows: "The field of employment which any place offers for labor and capital depends, firstly, on its natural resources; secondly on . . . knowledge and organization; and thirdly, on

[3] *Principles of Economics,* 8th ed. (New York, 1920), 668.

. . . markets in which it can sell those things of which it has a superfluity. The importance of this last condition is often underrated; but it stands out prominently when we look at the history of new countries." [4] It is perhaps significant that such remarks, though true almost to the point of platitude, were left unrelated to the traditional theory of international trade.

It was no doubt under the impression of contemporary experience that Marshall declared that "the causes which determine the economic progress of nations belong to the study of international trade." [5] In the second half of the twentieth century this may seem to us a curious statement. It can be understood only in the light of historical conditions. It embodies the particular experience of Britain's economic relations with the new countries overseas. Economic progress in these areas was due not to international specialization alone but also to the fact that the rapid growth which was taking place in the center was transmitted to the outlying new countries through a vigorous increase in demand for primary products. This was perhaps the most spectacular feature of nineteenth-century trade.

The new countries seem to have greatly increased their share in the rapidly growing total volume of world trade. At any rate their share in British imports rose from 8 per cent in the middle to 18 per cent at the end of the nineteenth century.[6] This does not include the United States, whose share in British imports during that period remained fairly constant at just under 20

[4] *Principles of Economics* (8th ed.), 668.
[5] *Principles of Economics* (8th ed.), 270.
[6] The percentage distribution of British imports by countries of origin may be summarized in the following figures, which I owe to the assistance of Dr. Robert M. Stern:

	1857–1859	1911–1913
United States	19	19
Other "new" countries[a]	8	18
Industrial Europe[b]	21	23
All other areas	52	40
Total	100	100

[a] Canada, Argentina, South Africa, Australia, New Zealand.
[b] Germany, France, Italy, Belgium, Netherlands.

per cent. The great increase in the United States share in British trade had taken place earlier.

While trade all over the world was expanding at a rapid pace, there is no doubt that the exports of the new countries enjoyed a particularly vigorous increase in demand. Correspondingly the outflow of British capital went mostly to these favored areas. The year 1870 is the earliest for which we can determine with any degree of confidence the geographical distribution of British capital invested overseas. The share of the "regions of recent settlement" in the British foreign-investment total outstanding rises from less than one third in that year to just about two thirds in 1913. Again the share of the United States in that total remains constant at about one fifth, while that of the other new countries shoots up from about 10 per cent in 1870 to 45 per cent in 1913.[7] But again we must remember that the rise in the United States share in British capital exports occurred in the earlier part of the century, for which the data are too poor to permit any confident statistical estimates.

The growth in British imports of primary products induced British capital exports to most if not all primary producing countries, but it is clear that the R.R.S. group was specially favored by the flow of capital as well as the rise in demand for its exports. Evidently there was a connection between the two phenomena. Private international investment in undeveloped areas was fundamentally, if not directly, induced by the growth in demand for essential foodstuffs and raw materials. The connection was not always a close one with regard to timing. Thus the 1880's were a period of active capital exports even though trade in agricultural products was relatively depressed. All the same, in that decade

---

[7] The total (gross) amount of British capital overseas increased from about £1,000 million in 1870 to about £4,000 million in 1913, and its percentage distribution by regions may be roughly indicated as follows:

	1870	1913
United States	20	20
Other "new" countries	10	45
Europe	50	5
All other areas	20	30
Total	100	100

Economic Essays

and on other occasions also, foreign investment was supported by a long-run prospect of expanding demand in the industrial centers for the raw materials whose supply it went out to augment.

These circumstances illustrate the essentially cumulative nature of economic growth. "To those who have shall be given": there is good reason for calling this "the first law of development." [8] It was Wicksell, whose great name we here commemorate, who originated the idea of "cumulative process" in the theory of short-term business fluctuations. This notion is based on the reciprocal stimulation of consumption demand and capital investment. When consumer buying increases, business investment appears more profitable, and vice versa; the two elements reinforce each other in the upward as in the downward direction. But cumulative causation need not confine itself to the short run. The notion can be fruitfully applied to long-run growth also, as Myrdal and Svennilson have suggested.[9]

In our particular case a cumulative process of development was produced by the relation between export demand and foreign investment. Areas that had natural resources whose products were in growing demand abroad received capital with which to exploit those resources and to increase the supply of those products. An increase in export demand alone is a favorable factor: it may improve the terms of trade, but even if it does not, it draws any increments in local capital and labor into lines in which the country enjoys a comparative advantage, so that increased supplies of imported goods in great variety can be got in exchange. If on top of this foreign capital comes in, this may lead not only to an enlargement of the export sector itself but also to the building of overhead facilities essential to the expansion of domestic activities as well. In fact, railways were the principal object of external investment in the areas of recent settlement. These areas include countries that are now among the most prosperous in the world. It is not suggested that the trade-and-investment relationship is the only explanation of their rapid growth in the past. There are other factors, but these lie outside our present subject.

[8] This remark has been made by Prof. A. K. Cairncross.
[9] See Gunnar Myrdal, *Rich Lands and Poor* (New York, 1957) and Ingvar Svennilson, "Den ekonomiska tillväxtens problem," *Ekonomisk Tidskrift,* Stockholm, 1954, 29.

Economists like Marshall and Robertson in contemplating the nineteenth-century scene spoke of the old countries (in Europe) and the new countries (overseas) as the world's workshops and granaries respectively. This was of course an incomplete view of the world. It ignored the exotic countries, the "outsiders." Such areas as China, India, tropical Africa and Central America were not unaffected by the forces of growth through trade, but compared with the newly settled countries they were relatively neglected by the expansion of export demand as well as the flow of capital. And in places where both trade and capital flows were exceptionally active, as in parts of Southeast Asia, the outcome was sometimes a "dual economy" in which a well-developed export sector coexisted with a primitive domestic economy. This lopsided pattern of development was surely better than no growth at all, yet it did show up the limitations of the external trade-and-investment engine when other conditions of progress were absent.

It is interesting to notice that J. A. Hobson in his influential study on *Imperialism* was perfectly aware that, with one exception (Malaya), the British colonies acquired in the second half of the nineteenth century — the products of the "New Imperialism" — took a relatively insignificant share in the expansion of Britain's trade. In the course of a dispassionate study of statistical evidence he found that continental Europe and the new countries overseas took the major share in this expansion. What then, he asked, was the economic motive of the New Imperialism? His answer was: foreign investment — the desire of a capitalist society to find an offset to its surplus savings, to gain exclusive control of colonial markets and to dump excess supplies in primitive economies. This is his economic explanation of imperialism.[10] But it contradicts in effect his earlier analysis of the pattern of trade expansion. Here the spirit of rational empiricism forsakes him; he cites no evidence. Had he tried to do what he did for

---

[10] To Hobson the underconsumptionist it looked as if a part of Great Britain's current saving had to be continually invested abroad — so as to maintain business profits and activity at home — because oversaving and underconsumption kept down investment incentives in Great Britain. In reality a part of British saving was invested abroad because the growth of British consumption expenditure, including expenditure on imported goods, created inducements to invest overseas as well as at home.

trade, that is, to show the geographical distribution of overseas investment, he would have found that British capital tended to bypass the primitive tropical economies and flowed mainly to the regions of recent settlement outside as well as inside the British Empire.

These fertile temperate regions, though now all more or less industrialized, became indeed, and still are, the world's principal granaries. They dispelled the Malthusian specter of world food shortage, at any rate for a century or two. This turns out to have been the main object and achievement of British capital exports.

III. The Current Lag in Exports of the Poorer Countries

In the twentieth century we observe first of all a marked slackening in the rate of world trade expansion. A period of about thirty years is generally sufficient to disclose long-term trends or changes in trend. In the period from 1928 to 1958 the quantum of world trade (outside the Soviet area) has increased by 57 per cent. A hundred years ago the pace of trade expansion seems to have been roughly five times faster.[11]

This slackening has occurred in spite of the fact that in the world as a whole economic growth is now taking place at probably a faster rate than ever before. It is true that in the last five or six years world trade and output have just about kept pace with each other, but this is too short a period on which to base a trend. In at least the latter half of the nineteenth century trade

---

[11] The following indications of percentage changes in the volume of world trade are available and may be quoted for comparison, though for the earlier periods they naturally rest on shaky statistical foundations:

	1850–1880	1880–1913	1928–1958
Changes in volume of world trade:	+270%	+170%	+57%

The percentages for 1850–1880 and 1880–1913 are based on an index that was used by Professor Bertil Ohlin in *International Economic Reconstruction* (Joint Committee, Carnegie Endowment and International Chamber of Commerce, 1936), 29. The figures are necessarily uncertain and can only serve as a rough indication, but they are not out of line with the volume indices for British trade now carefully revised in A. H. Imlah, *Economic Elements in the Pax Britannica: Studies in British Foreign Trade in the Nineteenth Century* (Cambridge, Mass., 1958), 96–98. The figure for 1928–1958 is based on GATT and UN indices excluding the Soviet area.

was growing faster than total production, though not quite so fast as manufacturing production.

The lag of international trade behind the growth of world output since 1928 is partly due to the fact that production has increased especially in countries such as the United States whose relative weight in world output is greater than in trade. Even if the United States had maintained its own, relatively low, ratio of imports to national product the rise in the United States share in world output would have reduced the average ratio of world trade to world production. In fact, America's own import ratio has declined, which has further contributed to the lag of world trade in relation to world output.

No doubt trends in commercial policy have also had something to do with the change in the overall ratio of trade to world production. But they cannot entirely account for certain shifts that have occurred in the internal proportions of world trade. In the years before 1914 exports of primary products were expanding more rapidly than exports of manufactured goods, in spite (or because?) of the rapid spread of manufacturing. In the mid-twentieth century we find, by contrast, a tendency for food and raw material exports to lag behind exports of manufactured goods. More specifically, we observe a lag in the exports of primary producing countries compared with those of industrial countries, although as may be seen from the following indices the lag is really significant only if we exclude petroleum, the twentieth-century boom commodity.

INDICES OF EXPORT VOLUME (1928 = 100)

	1955	1957
Exports from industrial countries[a]	139	162
Exports from nonindustrial countries[b]	138	151
of which:　1) Petroleum	479	...
2) All other primary products	118.5	...

SOURCE: *Trends in International Trade*, GATT, Geneva, 1958.

  [a] OEEC Europe, United States, Canada and Japan.
  [b] All other countries outside the Soviet area.

The exclusion, or at any rate separate treatment, of petroleum seems justifiable on the grounds that oil deposits are unevenly distributed gifts of nature, that they are exploited for export in only a limited group of countries, and that the great majority of underdeveloped countries have no means of benefiting from the present petroleum boom. This applies to other minerals too, but other minerals as a group have not enjoyed a trade expansion much above the average increase in world trade since 1928.

Although divergent price movements might be expected to change the picture, in fact the terms of trade between crude and manufactured products are now just about back to where they were in 1928. So we reach much the same conclusion if we look at the share of primary producing countries in the value of world trade.

PERCENTAGE SHARE OF NONINDUSTRIAL COUNTRIES
IN THE VALUE OF WORLD TRADE[a]

	Including oil-exporting countries		Excluding oil-exporting countries	
	1928	1957	1928	1957
Exports	33.8	31.3	32.2	24.4
Imports	28.0	35.0	26.9	30.4

SOURCE: *Trends in International Trade*. The figures for imports as well as exports are based on f.o.b. values.

[a] Excluding all Soviet-area imports and exports.

If the oil countries are included, the fall in the export share of the less developed countries is hardly significant. Here again an appreciable lag in exports is observed only if the petroleum countries are left out of account. On the import side we find in either case a rise in the share of primary producing countries. The gap which appears between the import and export figures for 1957, reflecting capital transfers and other invisible receipts, will concern us later. We shall find that the lag in the export trade of the less developed countries is quite troublesome enough, even though it seems to be counterbalanced by a "lead" on the import side.

But first we should notice that the figures just given cover the trade of primary producing countries with each other as well as their trade with the industrial countries. If we separate these two types of trade flows and if we apply the same distinction to the trade of industrial countries, we obtain an interesting *tableau économique* of world trade at the present time (1957).

Exports of:

Industrial countries to each other	(AA)	43%
Industrial to nonindustrial countries	(AB)	26%
Nonindustrial to industrial countries	(BA)	22%
Nonindustrial countries to each other	(BB)	9%

Total exports (excl. Soviet area):   100%

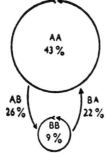

On the whole the industrial countries, which we may denote as group A, are high-income countries, while the nonindustrial countries — group B — are almost all in the low-income class. Countries such as Australia, New Zealand and even Argentina, which in the figures used here, computed from the latest GATT report, are classed with the B group, are exporters of primary commodities, yet internally are quite highly industrialized and definitely not low-income countries. But these few exceptions do not seriously affect the picture.

The picture is one that mirrors the basic lopsidedness of the world economy. The twenty countries in group A are each others' best customers. The more than a hundred countries in group B, containing two thirds of the total population of the A and B groups combined, have very little trade with each other — as a result, no doubt, of their low purchasing power and low productivity. Their exports to the A group are two and a half times as great as their exports to each other. By contrast, the A countries' exports to each other are far greater than their exports to the B group. It will be useful in what follows to keep in mind this unsymmetrical character of trade relations between advanced and backward economies.

There is no suggestion that the top-heavy structure of world trade is something new. On the contrary, trade in the nineteenth century seems to have been still more highly concentrated in the relatively advanced areas, as is clear from a useful though somewhat incomplete world trade matrix which Professor Lewis has tried to construct for the year 1887.[12]

The focal center of economic growth in the noncommunist world today lies predominantly in North America and Western Europe, or in what we may conveniently call the North Atlantic area. On closer inspection we should have to note that each of the two main parts of this center has its own dependent area of raw-material supply to the south, in the western and eastern hemisphere respectively. But here we have no time for such details.

The main point we must recognize is that this focal center, in terms of real income per head, is advancing vigorously, but is not transmitting its own rate of growth to the rest of the world through a proportional increase in its demand for primary products. The reasons for this are well known. 1) The composition of industrial production in the advanced economies is shifting away from "light" industries in favor of "heavy" industries (such as engineering and chemicals), that is, from industries where the raw material content of finished output is high to those where it is low. 2) As a special case, the rising share of services in the

[12] W. A. Lewis and P. J. O'Leary: "Secular Swings in Production and Trade, 1870–1913," *The Manchester School,* May 1955. The intratrade of Europe and the United States represented as much as 64 per cent of the (incomplete) total of world exports in 1887. Intratrade in Asia, Africa and South America is not known but was probably small and would not have made much difference to the percentage share of the advanced area's intratrade.

total output of advanced industrial countries tends to cause their raw-material demand to lag behind the rise in their national product. 3) The income elasticity of consumer demand for many agricultural commodities tends to be low. 4) Agricultural protectionism has adversely affected imports of primary products from the B to the A group, though this point should not be exaggerated. It affects especially Western Europe's imports from the R.R.S. rather than the North Atlantic's imports from the less developed tropics. Besides, there is plenty of protectionism hampering also the trade in manufactures. What we have to explain is a comparative lag in exports of primary producing countries.

5) Substantial economies have been achieved in industrial uses of natural materials (e.g., through electrolytic tin-plating and through systematic recovery and reprocessing of metals). 6) Last but not least, the leading industrial centers have tended more and more to displace natural raw materials by synthetic and other man-made substitutes produced from a few basic elements of mostly local origin. The demand for such staple commodities as crude rubber, silk, indigo, nitrates, jute, hemp, vegetable oils, hides and skins has certainly been held back and in some cases severely reduced by the growth of the chemical industry in the twentieth century. Among United States imports one of the latest technological casualties is said to be chicle, a vegetable product imported from Central America for the manufacture of chewing gum. It appears that the United States chemical industry has developed a synthetic substitute that is just as good or even better.

These are among the main explanations of the lag in the export trade of the less developed countries at the present time. It has been estimated that, since the late 1920's, exports from the primary producing countries to the United States and Western Europe have fallen from about $3\frac{1}{2}$ per cent to rather less than 3 per cent of the combined gross national product of this industrial area.[13] If again we exclude petroleum the fall would be from about $3\frac{1}{2}$ per cent to probably less than $2\frac{1}{2}$ per cent. This means that over the last three decades most primary producing coun-

---

[13] ECE, *Economic Survey of Europe in 1957,* ch. 4, p. 6.

tries have suffered a marked shrinkage in the importance of their exports in relation to the output and income of the industrial world.

If for a moment we consider the United States in particular, the fall in the ratio of United States imports to gross national product from about 6 per cent to 3 per cent over the last 50 years[14] contrasts sharply with the rise in the British import ratio in the nineteenth century. Professor T. W. Schultz of the University of Chicago has shown conclusively that the demand for raw materials as a whole, not only those imported, has lagged far behind the expansion of output in the American economy.[15] What we are considering therefore is merely the international aspect of a fairly general tendency. In a country so well supplied with capital and technical know-how it is a natural tendency for investment in "research and development" to displace crude materials with synthetic products. Some economists are more inclined to stress the future prospect of expansion in United States imports of primary commodities. They may prove right, but it is never safe to engage in long-term predictions. The facts for the past few decades are sufficient to reveal certain changes in trends. The report of the "Paley Commission" in 1952 gave a famous projection of United States demand for raw materials in the year 1975, but for this purpose it had to assume that "techniques of production do not change."[16] This has always seemed,

[14] According to Dr. W. Lederer, the economist responsible for United States balance-of-payments estimates, U.S. merchandise imports as a percentage of GNP have fallen from 5.70 per cent in the period 1896–1914 to 2.97 per cent in 1955. See *Review of Economics and Statistics,* May 1956, 184.

[15] In a paper on "Economic Prospects of Primary Products," presented under the auspices of the International Economic Association, Rio de Janeiro, August 1957, Professor Schultz has summed it up as follows: "We explain the slow increase in consumption of primary products in the United States in terms of the income elasticity of demand. Put in its simplest terms, the demand schedule has shifted to the right at a rate which has exceeded only a little the growth of population. A more than doubling of per capita real income has added only about one-sixth to the demand for primary products. . . . On the supply side, we infer that enough additional output has been forthcoming to satisfy the increases in demand at about the same . . . (relative) supply price, except in the case of forest products."

[16] U.S. President's Materials Policy Commission, *Resources for Freedom,* II, ch. 22.

to some of us, like a performance of Hamlet without the Prince of Denmark.

It is true in a sense that the United States is becoming more dependent on foreign mineral resources. Many people have been impressed by the fact, brought out by the Paley Report, that over nearly half a century the raw material consumption of the United States has increased by 98 per cent while its own production of raw materials rose only by 70 per cent. As a result, from a net exporter of raw materials at the beginning of the present century the United States has turned into a net importer. This change is sometimes referred to as the "scissors effect." [17] That the raw-material consumption of the United States has risen 40 per cent faster than its raw-material production is no doubt interesting and important. But even more impressive is the fact that the gross national product of the United States has, in its turn, increased about 150 per cent faster than its raw-material consumption. Most striking of all is the fact that United States manufacturing production has increased more than three times as fast as the American economy's intake of raw materials.[18]

Evidently the "scissors effect" has been overshadowed by the effect of raw-material economies, the growth of synthetics and the other factors mentioned. As for metals in particular, the tin,

---

[17] Sir Donald MacDougall, *The World Dollar Problem* (London, 1957), 186.

[18] These developments in the U.S. economy are summarized in the following table:

	1904–1913	1944–1950	
	(Billions of dollars at 1935–39 prices)		Percentage change:
1. Raw Material Production	4.8	8.2	+70%
2. Raw Material Consumption	4.4	8.7	+98%
3. Gross National Product	43.7	149	+242%
4. Manufacturing (1935–1939 = 100)	47	204	+335%

Items 1 and 2, which exclude agricultural foodstuffs and gold, are taken from the Paley Report. It should be noted that the production figures do not include secondary production of metals, derived from scrap, etc., the relative importance of which is increasing. Item 3: the GNP figures come from a paper by R. F. Daly (in *Studies in Income and Wealth*, XIV) and are cited by T. W. Schultz. Item 4: Federal Reserve Board index linked to the National Bureau of Economic Research index constructed by S. Fabricant which goes back to the beginning of the present century.

lead, and copper we import do not all get lost in the United States. To the extent that they are used over and over again, imports are needed only as additions to a revolving stock of metals, not to support a given volume of manufacturing output.

It is therefore in no way surprising that, as an over-all result, the increase of United States imports of primary commodities has failed to keep pace with the growth of the American economy. Similar tendencies are at work in Western Europe,[19] though in this area especially they have been masked to a large extent by the spectacular growth of petroleum imports in the last thirty years.

If the statistics of present-day world trade were considered in isolation, the lag in the primary commodity exports of the less developed countries might present something like a problem of "identification": has it been due to factors on the side of demand, external to these countries, or has it been due to limitations of supply in these countries themselves? Being aware of the major background factors, we have treated it as mainly a reflection of relative sluggishness in external demand emanating from the great industrial consumers. It cannot be denied that domestic policies causing limitations on the supply side in producing countries have also been effective in certain cases. But such policies can some-times be interpreted as reactions to relatively unfavorable demand conditions for primary export products. They may serve in effect to implement the terms of trade argument for protection by tight-ening up the supply of export products for which world demand is not only sluggish in expanding but also, at any given time, is apt to be price-inelastic in the lower ranges of the demand schedule.

It is possible that population pressure in certain countries such as India and Indonesia has hurt primary production for export by causing a reversion to subsistence production for local needs.[20] But this is not an inevitable result: an alternative is to maintain or increase the export crops as far as possible and to import the

---

[19] A. K. Cairncross and J. Faaland, "Long-term Trends in Europe's Trade," *Economic Journal,* March 1952, 26–27.

[20] This possibility is mentioned by H. Myint in his interesting article, "The 'Classical' Theory of International Trade and the Underdeveloped Countries," *Economic Journal,* June 1958, 325 and 331.

food needed for the growing population. And this is actually happening to some extent: the low-income countries are becoming an increasingly important outlet for the food poured out by the United States in competition with Canada, Argentina, and Australia.

The causal predominance of demand conditions suggested by the survey of particular factors fits in very naturally with the unsymmetrical pattern of world trade between countries at different levels of development, which our chart has served to illustrate. In a world in which (outside the Soviet area) over nine tenths of the manufacturing and over four fifths of the total productive activity are concentrated in the advanced industrial countries, the ideas of symmetry, reciprocity and mutual dependence which we associate with the traditional theory of international trade are of rather questionable relevance to trade relations between the center and the periphery. Despite the population masses and the vast physical areas of the underdeveloped countries, we must try to realize their pitiable smallness in aggregate economic terms, by comparison with the giant industrial economies. In such a world the distinction between dominant and dependent economies is a vital one in any dynamic view of international economic relations. It does not contradict the idea of mutual dependence that lies at the basis of *trade* theory pure and simple. It belongs to a different order of discourse: to the international economics of growth.

IV. Trade Trends and International Investment Incentives

For perfectly understandable reasons, then, the world's industrial centers on both sides of the North Atlantic in the mid-twentieth century are not "exporting" their own rate of growth to the primary producing countries through a corresponding expansion of demand for primary products. With the growing refinement of technology it is only natural that the raw products of the soil should tend in general to become relatively less essential in an advanced industrial economy. Equally natural is the fact that it is precisely in such crude and simple products of the soil that the poorer countries generally tend to have a comparative advantage, at least on a static view of the matter. This disparity is one of the basic factors that lie behind the increasing discrepancies in income levels.

In the nineteenth century conditions were different: they happened to be such that the growth of the dominant economy, Great Britain, did tend to transmit itself to the periphery through an even more than proportional expansion in demand for crude materials and foodstuffs. Again the main reasons, already mentioned, are obvious. Neither experience can provide the basis for anything like a universal law. As Professor Hicks has put it, a change has taken place in the economic atmosphere of international trade from the nineteenth to the twentieth century.[21]

The basic case for international specialization is not affected by this change. The point is merely that the forces making for the diffusion of economic growth from advanced to less developed countries are not as powerful in the trade field as they were a hundred years ago. The nineteenth-century pattern of development in outlying areas was geared to export markets for primary staples. This mechanism of growth transmission is now in comparatively low gear.

Nor is this all. Conditions in the trade field have some influence on international investment. The vigorous expansion of demand for primary commodities induced a massive flow of private capital to peripheral areas in the past. Conversely, the lag observed at the present time in the export trade of most of the less developed countries provides a simple explanation for the lack of incentive for private foreign investment.

Movements of private capital for productive investment in less developed countries have always depended to a large degree on the growth of external demand for the export staples of such countries. The home market does not generally offer any strong inducements in a thinly settled or backward economy.[22] There are other economic reasons for the now-limited volume of private capital flows to less developed countries. One of them is the highly progressive taxation in the advanced countries. There are

---

[21] J. R. Hicks, "An Inaugural Lecture," *Oxford Economic Papers,* n.s. V (June 1953), 130.

[22] By and large, it is only where the "take-off" has already occurred, as in some Latin-American countries, that the domestic market can offer substantial inducements for foreign direct investments to come in.

also political reasons. For most people the Cold War is the reason for the absence of large-scale private capital exports to underdeveloped countries. But there was a cold war for many decades in the nineteenth century too, between Great Britain and Russia. (A cheerful thought, but let us beware: historical analogies can mislead.) The cumulative interaction of raw-material demand and foreign investment so characteristic of nineteenth-century experience is naturally weaker today, for the reasons we have noted. For us economists this may be a sufficient explanation.

If anything is needed to confirm this hypothesis just look at the petroleum countries today. These are the exception that proves the rule. Here is a primary commodity that has enjoyed a tremendous expansion of world demand. The nonindustrial countries exporting this commodity have considerably increased their share in world trade.[23] And quite naturally these countries have managed to attract the lion's share of private foreign investment, at all events of United States direct investment since the last world war.

A curious parallel emerges in this way between the "new countries" of the nineteenth century and the "oil countries" of the twentieth. Both show a rising share in world trade. Both exert a strong attraction for private foreign capital. Both happen to be, on the whole, sparsely populated. The new countries banished the world food crisis that worried Malthus. The oil countries have banished the fuel crisis due to the exhaustion of coal supplies which in England worried J. S. Mill and Jevons. These are only some of the similarities. The dissimilarities are too obvious to enumerate. It may be that, of the two types of areas, the case of the new countries will long remain the more important and interesting illustration of the trade-and-development nexus. Yet the main point stands: the oil countries today like the new countries a hundred years ago demonstrate a cumulative relationship be-

---

[23] The exports and imports of the main oil-exporting countries as a percentage of total world trade (excluding all Soviet area trade) have gone up as follows:

	1928	1957
Exports	1.6%	6.9%
Imports	1.1%	4.6%

tween external demand for primary products and incentives for private international investment. It is the ancient rule again: Those who have (oil deposits) shall receive (foreign capital). If a wide range of primary commodities other than crude oil were enjoying an equally strong increase in world demand, is there much reason to doubt that a larger volume of private capital would be attracted to the underdeveloped countries, in spite of the political risks which, in varying forms and degrees, have always existed and will always continue to exist?

With things as they are in the trade field, governmental loans and grants are called upon to fill the gap left by the relatively modest level of private foreign investment. With the aid of such transfers as well as other noncommercial receipts (including American military expenditures overseas) the less developed countries have been able to increase their share in world imports and this, as we have seen, is true even if we leave aside the oil countries. The motive force of the mechanism is different; it has not come from market incentives to the same extent as in the past.

On this view of the matter there is a connection, then, between the lag in the export trade of most underdeveloped countries and the pressing need for official noncommercial transfers of funds from the richer to the poorer areas. It is this call for, and use of, noncommercial transfers that represents what is known as the Dollar Shortage, a phenomenon now limited, by and large, to the world's less developed areas. Perhaps a basic reason why we did not hear of a Sterling shortage in the nineteenth century was the rapid secular growth in Western Europe's and especially Great Britain's import demands for primary products and, on top of this, the stimulus so created for private capital exports to underdeveloped regions.

The governmental transfers on which we now have to rely are distributed not so much "to those who have," but rather, as François Perroux once remarked, "to each according to his need," though inevitably their distribution is influenced by political as well as economic considerations. As regards the magnitude of the total capital flow we find that, relatively to the value of merchandise imports of nonindustrial countries, it is now not much less than it was at the crest of the last big wave of foreign investment in what was still effectively the nineteenth century, namely in 1913. In that year the net outflow of capital from Western Europe and the United States combined was equal to approximately 20 per cent of the rest of the world's total imports from this industrial area.[24] All of this was private capital. In 1956–57 we find that the relative size of the total capital flow from advanced to less developed economies is just about the same — 17 per cent — except that now it consists mostly of official grants and governmental (or government-guaranteed) loans.[25] Most of this is coming from the United States.

In sum, though the mechanism is not the same, capital resources are moving from advanced to less developed areas much as before. The ratio of capital flows to import values may not be particularly significant. More interesting, though less certain, is the fact that the 5 billion dollars of private and official funds (including reinvested profits) which passed from the richer to the poorer countries in 1956 were probably equal to about one third of the total capital formation going on in that year in all the less developed countries outside the Soviet area. In any case there is no doubt that capital funds are moving in considerable volume in the right direction. But the conditions of world trade in which they move are for the most part very different.

These are among the essential facts of life in the world today. What are their implications for the doctrines as well as the pol-

[24] Again I am indebted to Dr. Robert M. Stern for collecting the data and computing this estimate.

[25] See the GATT report, 32–34. Departing slightly from the method apparently followed in that report, we compare the capital flows with the value of imports from the industrial into the nonindustrial countries outside the Soviet area. The percentages for 1956–57 come out as follows:

Private capital	7%
Official transfers	10%
of which: Grants	(8%)
Net loans	(2%)
Total	17%

This does not include the reinvested profits of United States subsidiaries. If these were included the total percentage would probably rise from 17 to about 20 per cent, of which private capital would account for 10 instead of 7 per cent.

304 *Economic Essays*

icies of international economics? Can the nineteenth-century prescription for growth through trade be as effective as it was in the past? Given the altered conditions of world trade, what are the major patterns and openings that present themselves for economic growth outside the industrial centers? Such are the questions we shall now attempt to consider.

THE INTERNATIONAL ECONOMY AND THE PROBLEM OF GROWTH

I. PAST AND PRESENT DEVELOPMENT PATTERNS

The nineteenth-century pattern of economic growth through international trade was one in which outlying areas of the world economy were favored by a rapidly expanding demand for their primary products. This tended in some cases to raise their real income directly by improving their barter terms of trade, which in a time of great reductions in transport costs was not incompatible with improving commodity terms of trade for the industrial centers as well. But changes in the terms of trade have perhaps received an exaggerated amount of attention in the trade-and-development literature. There were other ways in which the demand expansion for primary products helped economic growth in the outlying areas.

It gave, first of all, comparatively advantageous employment to any increases accruing in the domestic labor force or capital stock. Secondly, it may have tended to stir up dormant or idle resources and to draw them into economic activity for export production.[26] Thirdly, it could help by attracting to those areas a part of the increase in capital and labor that was going on in the dominant centers of growth. Buoyant conditions of external

[26] This point is stressed by H. Myint (above, n. 20). One way in which trade could lead to an "awakening" of domestic resources was through the creation of new wants that made people work harder and produce more cash crops for export. This particular point is perhaps to be looked upon as a once-for-all change rather than a truly dynamic factor of a continuing nature. Nevertheless it was also possible for trade expansion, by opening up additional opportunities for the advantageous use of productive resources, to create continuing inducements for additional domestic resources to come forward.

demand tended to encourage the application of capital and improved techniques to primary production for export. They helped in some countries — where other conditions also were suitable — to promote expansion in the domestic economy as well. All this constituted a pattern of "growth through trade" which was particularly characteristic of the nineteenth century.

It would be a serious mistake to think that all this belongs to the past. It has a part to play in today's world also. But if it is true that, for reasons indicated earlier, there is a relative lag in the industrial countries' demand for a wide range of primary commodities, this pattern is bound to be less prominent than in the past.

If there is such a lag — and the facts brought out by international economic organizations[27] suggest strongly that there has been one in recent years — then what are the less developed countries to do? Consider the problem that faces countries whose appetite for better living is rising, whose labor force and even capital stock is growing, but for whose exportable crude staples there is only a sluggish expansion of external demand. In the face of such conditions it might be useless, perhaps even worse than useless, to push the additional labor and capital into the traditional export sectors, in view of the inelastic demand which the traditional export staples are likely to meet.

In the last three decades the export volume of nonindustrial countries other than those exporting petroleum has increased by about 25 per cent.[28] Over the same period the economically active

[27] ECE, ECLA, FAO, GATT and the UN Secretariat, in their recent annual reports. Special mention should be made of the following: GATT, *International Trade 1955* (Geneva, 1956); UN, *World Economic Survey 1955* (New York, 1956), ch. 2; FAO, *The State of Food and Agriculture 1956* (Rome, 1956); ECE, *Economic Survey of Europe in 1957* (Geneva, 1958), chs. 4 and 5; GATT, *Trends in International Trade: A Report by a Panel of Experts* (G. Haberler, J. E. Meade, R. de Oliveira Campos, J. Tinbergen; Geneva, October 1958).

[28] This is based on the GATT index for 1956 (1928 = 100), which is the latest available, and which Dr. H. Staehle, Chief of GATT's Trade Intelligence Section, has kindly communicated to me. The index covers exports of nonindustrial countries to each other as well as their exports to the industrial countries. The value of the former, though still relatively small, has increased in importance compared with that of the latter. If this is taken into account, it appears that, leaving aside the petroleum countries, the volume of primary-commodity exports from nonindustrial to industrial countries has increased by just about 20 per cent from 1928 to 1956.

population in these countries has increased by about 50 per cent in numbers alone. From such indications as are available it seems possible that their capital stock has increased by even more.[29] Not only is there some domestic capital creation going on, but also capital imports are coming in from abroad in substantial volume, mostly in the form of governmental transfers unrelated to any investment incentives in primary production for export.

This emphasis on the continual increase that is going on in the productive — or potentially productive — resources in underdeveloped countries may seem surprising, but is in my opinion entirely realistic. No useful purpose is served by continuing to discuss matters of trade and development on the classical assumption of a constant stock of productive factors. The problem in some of the poorer countries may be that capital resources are not expanding as fast as the labor force; or that skills and education are not improving at the same rate as health, or as fast as numbers alone are increasing. These are serious problems relating to progress in income per head. But in reality all these factors of production are continually increasing in quantity and improving in quality in underdeveloped countries today, though naturally at varying rates.

If primary production for export, though of vital importance so far as it has gone, does not offer attractive opportunities for expansion, the question is what to do with the growing labor force and capital resources. In these circumstances it might seem best for the movable factors of production to emigrate from the less-developed countries to the centers of growth, the industrial economies. This is, we must admit, a rather academic solution. Nevertheless, where it is possible, some migration of working people and even of capital funds on private account does take place nowadays from the poorer to the richer areas. The migration of labor from Puerto Rico and Jamaica to the United States and the United Kingdom respectively is a well-known example. Transfers

[29] The problem of measuring capital is a notoriously hard nut to crack, conceptually as well as statistically. Nevertheless, we may note that the Economic Commission for Latin America has compiled estimates showing that the aggregate stock of real capital in that area, valued at constant prices, has increased by over 70 per cent in only twelve years (see *Economic Survey of Latin America 1956*, p. 7, and earlier issues).

of capital remain usually invisible but, until recently at any rate, private funds from such countries as Egypt and Thailand, for example, are believed to have leaked out fairly steadily to certain financial centers for safekeeping and investment. But on the whole such movements are severely restricted, either by the would-be receiving countries, as far as labor is concerned, or by the sending countries, in the case of capital.

The more realistic alternative is, of course, industrialization. Ten or twenty years ago development problems used to be discussed largely if not exclusively in terms of industrialization. This approach has gone out of fashion. Progress in agriculture is nowadays receiving equal emphasis. All the same, let us provisionally start with the old-fashioned concern with industrialization. I hope we can agree that it is in this general direction that the solution to the growth problem must be sought. It is largely in the building and operation of industrial production facilities that the increase in the labor force and in the other resources accruing in low-income countries will have to be employed.

Next it is essential, however, to distinguish between two types of industrialization: that which aims at producing manufactured goods for export to the industrial countries and that which caters mainly for domestic markets in underdeveloped countries. The significance of this distinction will become clearer later on. At this stage let me merely assert that the second type of industrialization generally requires, while the first does not require, a complementary advance in domestic agriculture. This is a basic, though not the only, reason for separating the two types. It is something that makes manufacturing for export much easier than manufacturing for home markets in the underdeveloped world. On the other hand manufacturing for export is vitally dependent on commercial policies in the older industrial countries, while industrialization for home markets is free from any such hazard and so in this respect easier.

Before dealing with the two development patterns in turn, let us note that they have one thing in common. Neither demands the abandonment or contraction of exports of the primary commodities which a country is naturally well suited to produce. To the extent that external demand for such commodities is growing there is even a *prima facie* case for expanding the traditional exports. It is to make use of growing resources which cannot with comparative advantage be absorbed by expansion in the traditional sectors that industrialization becomes really necessary. We therefore envisage industrial activities, whether for export or for home use, as being set up on top of the existing export sectors, so long as in these sectors a country still enjoys a high "established" comparative advantage even though, as a consequence of sluggish expansion of external demand, its "incremental" comparative advantage in these lines may be low.[30]

II. Industrialization for Export Markets

If demand conditions for a wide range of primary products are not conducive to growth in underdeveloped countries, is it not possible and desirable for at least some of these countries to start exporting manufactured goods in addition to their primary export staples? There is indeed an influential school of thought which sees the main road to progress in the poorer countries in the establishment of manufacturing activities working for export to the great mass markets of the advanced economies. Professor W. A. Lewis in particular has stressed this as a solution suitable especially for densely settled areas where labor is the most abundant factor of production in relation not only to capital but also to land. Similarly the recent report of four leading experts sponsored by GATT regards it as "a natural and economic development that relatively poor countries with high population densities like India and Hong Kong should export cheap labor-intensive manufactures in order to import food-stuffs like wheat from developed countries such as Australia, Canada and the United States which are rich in land and capital."[31] The theory of factor proportions in international trade, which is based on the pioneer-

[30] The distinction between "established" and "incremental" comparative advantage, which becomes necessary as soon as we apply the central concept of traditional trade theory to the problem of economic growth, is clearly set out in A. J. Brown's *Industrialization and Trade* (London 1943), 5–6, though the terms used are not the same.

[31] *Trends in International Trade: A Report by a Panel of Experts.*

ing work of Heckscher and Ohlin, seems strongly to suggest that the "incremental" comparative advantage of overpopulated countries poorly endowed with natural resources lies in increased exports of the simpler kinds of manufactured consumer goods such as textiles. This conclusion fits in well with the views of economic geographers who find that the most promising sources of increased food supplies in the world are still the temperate regions of recent settlement rather than the tropics.[32]

Industrialization for export would seem an attractive solution in that it avoids the need for carrying out any drastic and painful reform or "revolution" in domestic agriculture, under physical conditions that may be in any case unpropitious for agricultural improvement. The manufactured goods would be sold in foreign markets where there is no shortage of purchasing power, and would serve to pay for basic foodstuffs imported from regions better endowed to produce them. It seems for these reasons a relatively easy solution. Moreover, it does not necessarily depend on expansion of total demand abroad for the type of goods to be exported. It could displace high-cost suppliers in the older industrial countries, who would shift to more productive and more rewarding lines of activity such as skilled services, engineering and chemistry. This is indeed what could and should happen, but some obvious difficulties arise in this connection.

A word should be said first about possible difficulties on the supply side. Even in densely populated areas labor may not be really cheap for the purposes of industrialization, when it is illiterate, unskilled and undisciplined. The factor-proportions analysis was never meant to be applied without reference to quality. Just as land may not be really plentiful where it consists of marsh or desert, so even in an overpopulated country we should guard against the misplaced concreteness of concluding from the teeming numbers of people that labor is relatively cheap and plentiful. All we can say perhaps is that it is potentially cheap and abundant. It must be made cheap by raising it to a minimum level of economic efficiency. This is not easy. In fact, the history of the older industrial countries shows that the creation of an

[32] See especially Dudley Stamp, *Our Undeveloped World* (London, 1953).

industrial labor force is a task of formidable difficulty. It requires a lot of social overhead investment, especially in education and health, quite apart from investment in public utilities such as power and transport.

Today the showcase example of industrialization for export is Puerto Rico, an island which, fortunately for this purpose, lies within the United States customs area. Puerto Rico benefited from a great deal of social investment in the 1930's and the early 1940's (partly as a by-product of the war effort). It is only since then that Puerto Rican labor has tended to become cheap for industrial uses. Earlier, though numerically plentiful, it offered no strong attraction for industries to come from the mainland, and partly for the same reason, was handicapped in migrating to the mainland, though free to do so. The importance of social overhead investment is one of the chief lessons of Puerto Rico's recent development boom. But then, we should remember that investment in education, health and public utilities is necessary for *any* pattern of development. So the need for it should not be counted as an obstacle to manufacturing for export in particular. The difficulty is nonetheless real.

Industrialization for export markets may encounter other difficulties on the supply side. In the scale of comparative advantage there may be a wide gap, or at any rate a certain discontinuity, between the traditional primary products and the new manufactured goods which a country would seek to export. But let us now abstract from such impediments which, however serious, may perhaps be overcome with the help of export subsidies.

Equally serious are the obstacles which industrialization for export is liable to encounter on the side of external demand. This pattern of development depends for its success on a lenient commercial policy in the older industrial countries. From general considerations as well as from recent experience it would seem that such lenience can hardly be relied upon with certainty. The significance of the Puerto Rican success story is after all limited by the fact that Puerto Rico is a United States possession and, besides, is small enough to "get away with it." Moreover, Puerto Rico's industrialization is based in the main on American capital and enterprise, with a strong interest in the maintenance of free access to the American market.[33]

In the more general case of underdeveloped countries industrializing for export, the reaction of the advanced industrial centers does give cause for concern. The problem would not be so difficult if the manufactured goods which the poorer countries would start exporting were goods with a rapidly rising total demand (such as television sets or jet aircraft). Then these exports could find markets in the industrial states without hurting any existing producers there. It is true that existing producers may insist on a certain proportion of the growing market being reserved to them by protective measures of commercial policy. If so, the newcomers might not derive any great advantage from the fact that the demand for the goods they would wish to export is rising. But the main trouble is that in producing goods of this sort the advanced industrial centers themselves are likely to have an overwhelming comparative advantage.

The newcomers must therefore generally be content to export the cruder and simpler kinds of manufacture such as textiles. Now for these, as a rule, total demand is not rapidly expanding, so that existing producers in the advanced economies must of necessity be injured and displaced if such exports are to increase considerably in volume. The fact that export markets are found by displacement of existing high-cost suppliers in the older centers turns out to be, not an advantage, but a source of trouble, resistance, and frustration.

Just as textiles are usually the first manufactures to be started in the poorer countries, so also textiles are among the first to become sick industries in the more advanced countries, where workers as well as managers are quick to raise protests against "unfair" low-wage competition from backward areas. The "pauper-labor" argument, that great standby of protectionists, is brought forward again. Charges of "social dumping" are heard,

---

[33] This point should not be exaggerated. The predominance of American capital and enterprise in the Puerto Rican sugar industry has not prevented the restriction, by means of a quota, of access to the American market for Puerto Rican sugar.

even though the newcomers are only trying to make use of their one advantage: ample labor and cheap efficiency wages, an advantage which, as just observed, can be hard enough for them to make effective. When their low-wage competition is furthermore promoted by export subsidies conforming essentially to the accepted infant industry argument, the protests in the established centers of manufacture become even more indignant.

In any case there is a possibility of protective countermeasures being adopted in the older industrial countries. Such measures may force underdeveloped countries to export crude and simple manufactures to each others' markets instead of the mass markets in the advanced countries. In that case the solution turns out to be output expansion for *internal* consumption in the underdeveloped world, which we are proposing to treat as a different development pattern, to be considered in a moment.

Recent experience illustrates the risks and difficulties in the way of manufacturing for export to the advanced industrial countries. The United States early in 1957 secured an agreement by which Japanese exporters "voluntarily" restricted their exports of certain textile products to the American market. Britain did not take long to follow this convenient example, and managed to persuade the textile manufacturers of India, Pakistan and Hong-Kong similarly to curb their exports to the British market. In another predominantly industrial country, Canada, the government is pledged to give higher protection to domestic textiles. The Commonwealth Economic Conference held in Montreal in September 1958 stressed that "obstacles should not be placed in the way of the exports of manufactured goods from underdeveloped countries." The practical effect of this resolution will be watched with considerable interest.

It cannot be denied that industrial countries in these circumstances have some economic justification for protective measures, if labor mobility is low and if the alternative is wasteful unemployment in the industries injured by low-wage competition from less developed areas. Even Professor Haberler has admitted the validity of this argument for protection.[34] But it should be treated as an essentially short-term argument.

[34] *Survey of International Trade Theory* (Princeton, 1955), 16.

The industrialization-for-export pattern of development depends on a high degree of internal mobility and adaptability in the older industrial countries. These countries themselves would gain in real income by shifting out of industries where their comparative advantage is low or declining. Yet it is also natural that, for their own immediate comfort, they should wish to avoid or to cushion such adjustments at some cost in terms of their income growth. They feel they can afford to pay the cost.

Western Europe in particular is being urged to switch from consumer-goods production more and more to capital goods and chemicals.[35] This is in fact what is happening. In Great Britain the contraction of the Lancashire cotton industry has recently been described as "a catastrophic story." [36] In a sense it represents, on the contrary, a remarkable success story of drastic readjustment. Was it catastrophic for many individuals engaged in that industry? Surely in an otherwise active and expanding economy individuals, or their offspring, shift to other occupations and *improve* their lot in the process.

The United States tends to regard itself as a natural importer of primary commodities and to think of the less-developed countries as natural exporters of such commodities. Perhaps this reflects the continuing influence of the nineteenth-century trade model. What has happened within the United States has served to show that imports of manufactured products from poorer into richer areas are not necessarily against the laws of nature. On the whole the American economy, like the European, is moving in the direction of capital goods, chemicals, and other goods and services requiring much capital and skill. Is it prepared, however, to suffer a contraction in output of the simpler types of consumer goods? From this point of view it is particularly unfortunate that American trade policy has accepted the prevention of injury to domestic industries as one of its essential tasks. This concern with injury-prevention will not stop the United States industrial structure from changing in the right direction. Yet it does tend to slow down the change. The development needs of the backward

[35] ECE, *Economic Survey of Europe in 1956* (Geneva, 1957).
[36] A. J. Brown, *Introduction to the World Economy* (London and New York, 1959), 167.

economies may demand a faster rate of adaptation than is likely to be practicable in the advanced economies.

Critics of American trade policy have been pointing out for years that it makes no sense to restrict United States imports from countries which the United States is helping with free grants and other forms of foreign aid. From the business interests affected, however, one often hears the argument that the United States should help these countries precisely by means of governmental grants *instead of* by admitting imports which have bad effects on local employment conditions and possibly also on domestic income distribution. But this argument, which sounds curiously like a variant of the compensation principle in trade and welfare theory, leads to an awkward question. What are the receiving countries to do with the resources put at their disposal? If, first, their exportable primary products face a low rate of expansion in external demand and if, secondly, their exports of manufactured goods encounter obstacles, there remains only a third possible opening: output expansion for home consumption.

III. The Pattern of Home-Market Expansion

Industrialization for domestic needs in low-income areas runs from the very start into a difficulty well known to practical men and of great interest to economists. The trouble is this: there is not a sufficient market for manufactured goods in a country where peasants, farm laborers and their families, comprising typically two thirds to four fifths of the population, are too poor to buy any factory products, or anything in addition to the little they already buy. There is a lack of real purchasing power, reflecting the low productivity in agriculture. The other side of the same coin is that the local economy cannot supply the food needed to sustain the new industrial workers.

Therefore industrial development for domestic markets requires a complementary advance on the farm front, a rise in agricultural productivity. It is impossible to push domestic industrial development in isolation. This is now universally realized. It has become a platitude. Even the term "industrialization," still fashionable in the 1940's, is seldom found in the development literature today. This is not to say that the relation between agricultural and industrial advance is a new discovery. It is an ancient truth well known to economists in the 18th century.[37] But even the most ancient truths have to be rediscovered from time to time.

What modern economists have added to this notion is a simple application of the concept of income elasticity of consumer demand (a concept which, implicit in Engels' law, is itself over a hundred years old). Farming and manufacturing must move forward together, but not necessarily at the same rate. In a very poor country a given increase in manufacturing is likely to require a greater agricultural advance than in one that is not so poor. Conversely, a given increase in food output is likely to support a larger increase in manufacturing in an area where income per head is already fairly high than in one where it is still very low. The equilibrium relation between the two rates of advance may vary in the course of time as well as between countries. But this does not alter the basic principle of "linked progress" in the two broad sectors, farming and manufacturing.

As soon as agricultural improvement is recognized as an indispensable condition of it, industrialization for domestic markets appears as a much more formidable task. The difficulty stems largely from the fact that agriculture in most underdeveloped areas is a conservative, sometimes feudal, always tradition-bound, passive and noncapitalist sector of economic activity. Innovation in this sector cannot be relied upon to happen in response to market incentives alone. Even in the United States the agricultural extension service has long been a classic example of a nonmarket method of development policy in a progressive and predominantly market-oriented economy. In backward economies the necessary improvement and reorganization may demand a revolution in the countryside, affecting the lives of the great mass of the people. That is why industrialization for export markets

---

[37] Its essence may be found, for example, in Adam Smith's chapter on the Natural Progress of Opulence: "It is the surplus produce of the country only, or what is over and above the maintenance of the cultivators, that constitutes the subsistence of the town, which can therefore increase only with the increase of this surplus produce." Sir James Steuart is another eighteenth-century author who liked to harp on this theme.

would be so much more convenient, if only it were practicable to the requisite extent.

Another cause of difficulty may lie in the somewhat dubious physical potentialities of agricultural improvement in the tropics compared with the world's temperate zones. Nevertheless, there is surely ample scope for improvement through irrigation, new techniques of cultivation, and reform of the farm fragmentation that wastes so much land as well as labor in certain areas.

If the two-sector view of linked progress in agriculture and manufacturing is accepted, the question arises whether the same principle does not apply within the manufacturing sphere also. My own inclination is to think that it does, though this extension of the principle is not acceptable to some economists. Just as it is possible for manufacturing as a whole to fail if peasants can produce no marketable surplus and are too poor to buy anything from factories, so it is possible for a single branch of manufacturing to fail for lack of support from other sectors in industry as well as agriculture; that is, for lack of markets. To be sure, an expansion of one industry will have effects on income and expenditure tending to induce other industries also to expand. But if the others are only passive receivers of the external stimulus their expansion may be slow and uncertain. And their slowness and passiveness will in turn slow down and discourage the industry that first started expanding. In short, while it is true that the active sectors will tend to pull the passive ones forward (and this is what some advocates of "unbalanced growth" have in mind), it is equally true that the passive sectors will tend to hold the active ones back. Would it not be better if every sector were in some measure "active" in the sense of advancing spontaneously, imbued with some expansive élan of its own instead of waiting for signals from others? Price incentives and restraints would then be needed merely to keep each sector's rate of advance in line with the community's pattern of demand. The principle of balanced expansion can be looked upon as a means of accelerating the over-all rate of output growth.

The trouble of passive sectors holding the active ones back is suggested by the drag which a primitive agriculture can impose on the advance of manufacturing, but is probably not so serious within the manufacturing field where the various sub-sectors are likely to be more alert and progressive than the tradition-bound farm sector is apt to be. Within the manufacturing sector in particular it is of course not invariably true that output expansion in any single line depends on expansion elsewhere. A single industry might go ahead on its own if by reducing costs it can displace older and more primitive production methods in handicraft and village industries. In this case no increase in total demand for its product would seem to be needed. However, the existing volume of demand must be adequate to make the introduction of factory methods profitable; and in a low-income area this is not always the case. In the face of technical discontinuities such as the one represented by a transition from handicrafts to factories, output expansion elsewhere — implying demand expansion for the given product — may therefore be essential even for cost-reducing as distinct from output-increasing investments in the manufacturing field.[38]

These considerations need to be elaborated, and no doubt also qualified, on a number of points into which we cannot enter. They do seem to me a necessary ingredient of the international economics of growth. They boil down essentially to a simple point. If in an underdeveloped country the stock of productive factors is growing, but if development through increased exports to the advanced industrial centers is for one reason or another retarded or blocked, there arises a possible need for promoting increases in output that are *diversified in accordance with domestic income elasticities of demand* so as to provide markets for each other locally, in contrast to output expansion for export, which is *specialized in accordance with international comparative advantage.* That the increase in production for the home market in these circumstances must ultimately conform to the pattern of domestic demand expansion is indeed a platitude if not a tautology.

This view of the pattern of home-market expansion does not

[38] This distinction was used very effectively by Professor Viner in his address on "Stability and Progress: The Poorer Countries' Problem," at the Congress of the International Economic Association in Rome, 1956. See *Stability and Progress in the World Economy,* ed. D. C. Hague (London, 1958), 58.

in the least belittle the role of relative price changes in the efficient allocation of resource increments in the process of economic growth. Changes in relative prices are an essential means whereby in a market economy the pattern of output expansion is guided along an equilibrium path determined by consumer demand in conjunction with specific resource availabilities. Shortages of specific factors, among other possible causes, can produce changes in the scale of relative prices, to which consumer demand will tend to adjust itself. There is no denying that price elasticities will help to determine the community's pattern of demand. But changes in relative prices have no close or determinate connection with economic growth as such, whereas income changes are a direct reflection and measure of growth. That is why the emphasis in this context falls naturally on the notion of income elasticity of demand.

It is a mere matter of labels whether diversified output expansion in accordance with domestic income elasticities is called "balanced growth," to distinguish it from "growth through trade" which is specialized in accordance with international comparative advantage. This would be in some ways a convenient terminology, but "balanced growth" may mean different things to different people, and can have wider connotations not relevant to our special theme. The term is one we can easily dispense with.

Needless to say, there are limits to the diversification of output expansion. The minimum size of efficient plant is an important practical consideration which often limits the diversification of industry in any single country. This leads us at once to the crucial point that the case for diversified output growth for domestic consumption cannot be confined to national limits. Manufacturing for home markets in the less developed countries must include also production in these countries for export to *each others' markets*.[39] This is particularly important for the smaller countries, and it con-

---

[39] Following the table we used earlier, there is a tendency in a sketch such as the present to treat the advanced and backward economies respectively as all consolidated into two "countries," reducing the problem under discussion to the traditional two-country model of trade theory. This is a convenient simplification but cannot be long maintained without appropriate "frontier adjustments" between the two groups of countries and without a good deal of attention being paid to intratrade in each group.

stitutes a strong argument for liberalization of trade policies, leading up to customs unions if possible, among groups of countries in the underdeveloped class. The result of intratrade in manufactured consumer goods among such countries may be a reduction in their purchases of such goods from the older industrial countries, just as manufacturing for home consumption in a single country may lead to a fall in that country's imports of manufactured consumer goods. These results, however, are in my opinion not inevitable in the long run.

Industrial production for home consumption in underdeveloped countries is usually regarded as resulting in "import substitution." One objection to this description is that domestic output expansion can occur in the wide area of purely domestic goods which do not normally enter into foreign trade, as well as in the sphere of directly import-competing industries.

Moreover, "import substitution" can mean not only (a) the substitution of home-produced goods for imported goods, but also (b) the substitution of capital goods imports for consumer goods imports. In a more comprehensive sense, as well as commonly in fact, the two substitutions (a) and (b) can both occur in combination, at least to some extent. If a country cannot increase its export earnings sufficiently, it can still increase its imports of capital equipment by cutting down its imports of consumer goods.[40] In this way it can convert its own saving into imported capital goods even if it receives no capital funds from outside. But this involves the creation of additional productive capacity and hence also, sooner or later, an enlargement of the total size of the market in the country in question. With an increase in both domestic production and real purchasing power a displacement of imports by home-produced goods, though likely in the short run, appears in the end to be not at all inevitable.[41] Eventually imports of manufactured consumer goods, perhaps even of goods identical with those now made at home,

[40] We should not forget, of course, that import restrictions on consumer goods cannot lead to a net increase in capital formation without an increase in saving.

[41] One of the conclusions of Hilgerdt's celebrated study runs as follows: "To the extent that domestic industrial production is . . . accompanied by a corresponding increase in the total amount of manufactures that can be marketed in the country, it obviously does not encroach upon the market for imported man-

may well increase above the predevelopment level. Industrial expansion combined with agricultural improvement will have enlarged the size of the market.

On the export side similarly, the development pattern we are considering has some cheerful possibilities. When industrialization for the home market has taken root, it becomes easier to increase exports of manufactured goods to the more advanced economies. In discussing the policy of industrialization for export markets, we found that since the advanced centers themselves usually have a high comparative advantage in producing the articles for which their demand is rapidly expanding, the industrial newcomers are generally limited to exporting crude and simple manufactures for which demand is relatively stagnant, so that the result is injury to existing suppliers and strong resentment on their part. But once the less developed countries have established a certain minimum volume and variety of manufacturing for home consumption, they are likely to develop ways and means of producing more of the "progressive" products which can be exported to the mass markets of high-income countries without displacing any existing producers there. After all, the vigorous expansion that has been going on in trade among the advanced economies is also a result, not so much of any mutual displacement of manufacturing activities in these countries, but rather of expanding total demand for a wide and growing range of manufactures.

Japan, for example, has now reached a stage in which she has started exporting such items as optical goods and engineering products to the United States without meeting the same obstacles as in the case of her textile exports to the American market. Japan is often thought of as having developed her industry for export markets from the start. Recent research has made it clear, however, that the first stage of Japan's industrialization, in the latter part of the nineteenth century, was mainly based

---

ufactures." (*Industrialization and Foreign Trade,* League of Nations, 1945, 116). This is a truly dynamic view and, as Hilgerdt's study shows, an entirely realistic one, too. But it has never found a comfortable place in the traditional framework of trade theory.

on production for domestic consumption.[42] And the indispensable condition for the enlargement of the domestic market for manufactures was a remarkable advance in agricultural productivity during that period.[43] Japan profited greatly from an export boom in those early days, but that was in raw silk; and she made good use of it in financing imports of capital goods.

At any rate in the early stages of home-market industrialization there is usually a shift (relative if not absolute) away from imports of manufactured consumer goods in favor of capital-goods imports. An increase in food imports is possible, but is not an essential characteristic of this development pattern since, unlike industrialization for export markets, industrialization for home consumption necessarily involves an increase in domestic farm productivity and food output as well. The diversification of output expansion which we have discussed concerns the "horizontal" composition of final output in its consumable form. From the need for industrialization we cannot in any simple manner deduce a need for establishing capital-goods industries in underdeveloped countries, unless conditions for their establishment are favorable.[44] In general it is hard for any such country or group of countries to capture through domestic production the tremendous economies of scale that arise from the mass production of steel, machinery and transport equipment in the advanced industrial countries. Over 90 per cent of the total investment going on in the world (outside the Soviet area) now

[42] "The idea that the drive for foreign markets was *the* motor force of Japanese industrialization is nothing but a literary invention. It has little relationship to the facts. . . . The home demand for Japanese manufactures . . . absorbed continuously most of the output of industry . . ." W. W. Lockwood, *The Economic Development of Japan; Growth and Structural Change, 1868–1938* (Princeton, 1954), 309 and 369.

[43] B. F. Johnston, "Agricultural Productivity and Economic Development in Japan," *Journal of Political Economy,* December 1951.

[44] Public utilities deserve in general a higher priority than capital-goods industries for the simple reason that capital goods are importable, while basic services such as inland transport, water supply and electric power cannot physically be imported or, like electricity, cannot be brought from any great distance. If these services are to be had at all, the facilities for producing them must be installed on the spot. Their absence can be an absolute barrier to development while lack of home-produced equipment is not.

takes place in the industrial countries.[45] It is there that capital goods embodying the advances of modern technology can be produced on a large scale.

The less-developed countries, if they wish to benefit from the economies of large-scale production of modern equipment, must for the present import the greater part of their capital-goods requirements. It is not surprising that capital-goods have come to form a steadily increasing share, now nearly one half, of their total imports from the industrial world. This is one of the most conspicuous features of twentieth-century trade. Whereas in general the advanced countries export manufactured goods mostly to each other, in the capital-goods category their exports go mostly to the less-developed countries. Whereas a hundred years ago trade between the center and the outlying parts of the world economy consisted predominantly of an exchange of textile manufactures against foodstuffs and fibers, it now consists increasingly of capital equipment going out and of minerals coming in. The international division of labor, which used to be largely "horizontal," has become more and more "vertical."

IV. Summary and Conclusion

Let us quickly take a backward glance before closing. We have discussed three patterns of advance in less developed countries: (I) growth through exports of primary products; (II) growth through exports of manufactured consumer goods; and (III) expansion of output for domestic markets. This is in some ways an arbitrary division, but most divisions in economics have an element of arbitrariness, being made for convenience of communication and analysis. More important is the fact that in the real world we seldom find a single pattern in isolation, but usually a mixture of two or more. The three main patterns can easily be combined. Even an individual country may conceivably seek to follow all of them at once. The weight given to each of them will naturally vary in different parts of the world in accordance with a country's domestic resources and external demand conditions.

Besides, the relative weight of development patterns can

[45] ECE, *Economic Survey of Europe in 1957*, ch. 4, p. 2.

change over time. We have seen that Pattern I, which works through expanding demand for primary products, provided in the nineteenth century the principal opening for economic growth in outlying areas of the world economy. Advance is still possible along this line. But for reasons discussed earlier it now seems to offer relatively limited opportunities to the majority of countries in the lower income brackets. The petroleum countries are a rather special case.

Manufacturing for export to more advanced countries — our Pattern II — is being tried to some extent, in some places with success, and there are experts who predict great things for it in the near future. But it can hardly be described as a major factor at present. India, though she has less than 5 per cent of her labor force working in factories, has emerged as an exporter of textile manufactures, but even before she encountered obstacles in the United Kingdom these exports went mostly to other under-developed countries; and this is a different story.

More is happening along the lines of Pattern III, the pattern of home-market expansion. The local basis for it, in the form of food production in the less-developed countries (outside the Soviet area), has expanded by some 25 per cent in the last ten years, though on a per capita basis the increase is less than 10 per cent.[46] Industrialization for home markets is undoubtedly spreading.

The continuing and perhaps widening gap in income levels between the poorer and the richer countries should not blind us to the fact that economic growth in aggregate terms, if not per capita, is probably more widespread and, in the world as a whole, perhaps more rapid today, in the 1950's, than ever before.[47] But outside the lively intratrade of industrial centers, how much of it could be classed as "growth through trade"? If we found it to proceed largely along Pattern III, should we be surprised and disappointed? International specialization is an essential foundation of our material civilization. The case for it is firmly based on considerations of economic efficiency; and the world is not rich enough to despise efficiency. But why should

[46] FAO, *The State of Food and Agriculture 1958* (Rome, 1958), 12–13.
[47] See A. J. Brown, *Introduction to the World Economy*, 93.

we expect international trade to solve all problems of *development,* in any and all circumstances? Unfounded expectations may be due to the influence of a certain historical association

In the nineteenth century economic growth was so closely linked with international trade not only because countries previously isolated by high transport costs as well as other barriers, now came to specialize. This was a very important factor, but it was not all. On top of it, economic development was diffused to outlying areas through trade, because the pattern of advance in the rising industrial centers happened to be such as to cause a rapidly growing demand for crude products of the soil which those areas were well fitted to supply.

In the changed conditions of the present time, expansion of primary production for export — our Pattern I — still has a part to play. Even if we leave out petroleum, the volume of primary products imported from the less developed areas into the industrial centers, at roughly the same terms of trade, is now about 20 per cent greater than in 1928. There are countries, apart from those exporting petroleum, for which conditions of growth through staple exports have of late been quite adequate. And Japan in the late nineteenth century has demonstrated how effectively this type of growth can be used as a springboard for industrialization as well.

But in considering the picture as a whole it is hard to avoid the impression that for a great many countries under present conditions Pattern I, though excellent as far as it goes, does not go far enough. Let us keep in mind especially the rate at which productive factors in the underdeveloped countries are growing all the time, through the increase in population numbers, health, education and capital, homemade as well as imported. On the other side there is no doubt that world demand for a wide range of primary products is, for well-known reasons, relatively slow in expanding. In these circumstances any exclusive emphasis on the traditional pattern of growth through trade would be out of place, and could be interpreted as a hang-over from bygone days. We should try to understand the need for other patterns of development and the many new problems which they involve.

APPENDIX *

DYNAMIC ASPECTS OF TRADE THEORY

No attempt can here be made to deal with the theory of international trade in general terms. We concentrate on a particular situation: the lag in the export trade of less-developed countries. We should remember that this situation concerns a relatively minor portion of world trade. Far larger is the volume of trade conducted among the advanced industrial centers. It may be that the conventional trade theory, a product of advanced countries, is best applicable to the intratrade of countries already fairly well developed. In view of the quantitative weight of this trade such a bias would in fact be natural and legitimate. Nevertheless the situation on which we choose to concentrate is one that should not be neglected, and may have implications for trade theory generally.

I

The expansion of external demand for the primary commodity exports of the poorer countries appears in recent years, as we have seen, to have lagged behind the rate of increase in both the exports and national incomes of the industrial countries.

In the theory of comparative advantage, when a country experiences unfavorable demand conditions for its existing exports, certain forces operating through the monetary mechanism come into play that bring about two types of adjustment to these circumstances. At the export end of the scale of comparative costs, new commodities — the next in the scale — begin to be exported. At the import end of the scale, goods hitherto imported are displaced from the import list and begin to be produced at home. Two development patterns discussed earlier (patterns II and III respectively) correspond to these theoretical

* This appendix summarizes certain remarks presented for discussion in a seminar at the Stockholm School of Economics on April 13, 1959, insofar as they bear upon the subject of the preceding lectures.

alternatives, though the correspondence is not exact. If we are to keep in touch with the classical model we must modify it by making it dynamic and translating it into rates of change.

Static theory does not exclude change, but the type of change it deals with is of the once-for-all variety. The gains from trade which the classical theory of international specialization analyzes are of this character. Once trade has been opened up and factors appropriately reallocated, a higher level of real income is attained. The theory can accommodate without difficulty the "optimum-tariff" modification, supporting the terms-of-trade argument for trade restriction, which is similarly static in nature.

This type of trade theory is absolutely basic; it can be extremely useful. It is, however, limited in scope; and the more clearly we recognize its limitations the better for the realism and relevance of international economics.

Dynamics, by contrast, is concerned with effects of continuing changes and with rates of change.[48] The nineteenth-century type of growth transmission from an advancing economic center is an essentially dynamic story, in which a rising demand for crude products is a decisive feature which in turn may generate outflows of productive factors to the peripheral areas to supply this demand. The case for international specialization as such is as strong as ever. But the engine of growth transmission from advanced to less-developed countries is, in relative terms,[49] less powerful than it once was.

In a dynamic interpretation of the classical model as applied to the present situation, we must take into account two rates of change in particular: the rate of expansion of external demand for primary products and the rate of increase in productive resources in underdeveloped countries. On the one hand, we do not have a once-for-all downward shift in external demand for exports of primary products. What we have is typically a lag, in

[48] R. F. Harrod, *Towards a Dynamic Economics* (1949), 8.

[49] These are the terms that matter if we admit that the international "problem" of development has to do with income disparities and differential rates of advance. An excellent outline of this problem was given by Professor Erik Lundberg in his address on "International Stability and the National Economy" at the 1956 Congress of the International Economic Association (see *Stability and Progress in the World Economy*, especially 223–226).

relation to the exports and incomes of advanced countries, in the rate at which external demand is shifting upward.

Moreover, if we adhere to the usual distinction between shifts of the demand schedule and movements along a given schedule, we may say that external demand for primary commodities is generally price-inelastic as well as sluggish in shifting upward (to the right). This does not contradict the fact that, if price is increased, a demand schedule cannot remain inelastic for ever, and that any country trying to apply the optimum-tariff argument should actually, like a monopolistic firm, be operating on the elastic portion of the demand schedule with which it is confronted. It does mean that cost reductions and output increases in the face of such demand conditions may not do any good to primary producing countries. (If one of several countries exporting the same primary commodity were to cut its export costs and prices, its export earnings might well increase, but only at the expense of a fall in the other countries' earnings. The balance-of-payments adjustment mechanism alone, whether through exchange-rate variations or domestic price changes, would force the latter to cut their export prices too, and all would be worse off at the end than they were at the start.) Price-inelastic demand is not an obstacle to growth through primary commodity exports if the demand schedule itself is vigorously upward-shifting. Trouble begins only when such demand expansion does not occur.

So much for external demand. On the other hand, we must give up the constancy of factor supplies commonly assumed or implied in the classical trade model. In the typical case in reality, even a poor country's stock of productive factors is continually increasing, through growth of population and therefore its labor force, through improvements in health, education and skills, and through capital creation at home as well as capital imports from abroad. Indeed we can interpret the poorer countries' export lag in its most significant sense as *a lag in the rate of growth of external demand in relation to the rate of growth of domestic factor supplies.* This statement leaves, however, a good many loose ends, some of which we must try to examine.

II

An increase in numbers alone may constitute "growth" in aggregate productive capacity, but not necessarily "progress" in terms of per capita output and income. As a rule progress must involve an advance in the factors other than numerical size of the labor force. While this should be kept in mind, we must concern ourselves generally with growth in factor supplies whether or not it involves progress.

Factor supplies must be treated as a variable, but they can be a dependent, an independent, or a policy variable. (1) They can be incorporated as a dependent variable in a general equilibrium system of international trade, such as the one constructed by Professor Ohlin. This is a substantial advance, but not necessarily in the direction of dynamics. A given functional relationship between factor supplies and factor prices still need not take us outside the realm of static analysis. (2) It may be more realistic to treat certain factor supplies as an independent variable. This fits to some extent the growth of manpower, the spread of knowledge and perhaps even "official" capital imports, which may happen regardless of price incentives or domestic government policies. (3) Factor supplies may become a policy variable in development planning. The problem of "resource mobilization" is: how to get additional factors of production? It is here that special attention must be paid to increasing skills and material capital in relation to population numbers. The use of surplus farm labor for capital building is one example of resource mobilization. It may be that nothing can be done about the quantity of natural resources, which are said to be "the most permanent and powerful factor governing comparative costs." [50] But physical permanence need not be economically relevant. What matters is the amount of *useful* natural resources.[51] This depends on human knowledge. And knowledge is a variable.

On the other side we have the problem of "incremental resource allocation": what to do with additional factors of pro-

[50] A. J. Brown, *Industrialization and Trade,* 16.
[51] A point stressed by Viner (above, n. 38), 45.

duction? Allocation of resource increments is a central concern of dynamic trade theory.

But first, is it not somewhat arbitrary to keep resource mobilization and additional resource allocation in separate compartments (or separate paragraphs)? Admittedly in some cases the one may in fact be directly linked with the other. In business investment financed out of profits the link is particularly close. There are other possibilities of interrelation. In general terms the growth of factor supplies may depend to some extent on whether or not attractive or profitable openings exist for the employment of additional factors. When external demand expansion is relatively sluggish, and no attractive domestic opportunities come into being either, the growth of at least certain kinds of factors, including capital, may be slower than it would otherwise be. It may not be unrealistic then to think of external demand as an initiating force to which the stock of capital in an underdeveloped country will in some degree adapt itself. The most conspicuous instance of such resource adaptation is the international migration of private capital to countries enjoying a rapid rise in world demand for their export products (the new countries of the nineteenth and the oil countries of the twentieth century). All this amounts to saying that factor supplies may be a dependent variable in dynamic contexts as well as in static systems of analysis. Besides, it still remains true that factor changes may be, and perhaps increasingly are, an autonomous variable or one subject to policy action. And conceptually, in any case, it *is* a separate question to consider to what use additional productive resources should be put if and when they become available.

III

Is there a presumption that they should be channelled into the existing export sectors because these are the lines in which, for the time being, the country is comparatively most efficient? There is not. If external demand conditions are unfavorable the result could be a worsening of the terms of trade such as actually to reduce the country's total real income. This possibility has attracted some attention recently under the label of "immiserizing growth." It is a conceivable — and analytically very interesting — case, but, as will be seen, there is no need for it to happen.

Nor is there, on the other hand, anything to be gained by pulling resources out of the traditional export activities.[52] Since in the typical situation there is no absolute fall in demand for the traditional export staples, there is everything to be said in favor of at least maintaining production of these staples. And yet, to put *additional* resources into the existing export sectors might be of little or no use if export demand is inelastic as well as sluggish in expanding. Thus we see that while a country's established comparative advantage in the current export products may be high indeed, its incremental comparative advantage in these lines may be zero or actually negative. The only question, then, is whether the increment in the stock of productive factors should be utilized for developing new export activities, or whether it should be used to establish industries catering for home consumption and tending at least initially perhaps to displace existing imports.

Once more we face the two alternatives corresponding to the two possible adjustments to an adverse change in foreign demand under the classical trade model. In the classical model it is normally the shape of the comparative cost scale at both the export and the import ends of the scale that determines the proportions in which the adjustment occurs through increased exports and decreased imports respectively. If, for example, the scale of comparative costs has a kink at the import end but is smoothly ascending at the export end, the adjustment may come mostly through new exports rather than diminished imports; and vice versa.

Similar considerations may apply to our "dynamic" situation. It was argued earlier that even in densely populated countries labor is not necessarily cheap for purposes of industrial production for export markets.[53] In such a case indeed a country

---

[52] Unless previously unused opportunities exist for "optimizing" the country's barter terms through trade restriction. We may assume that such opportunities are being fully and continuously exploited.

[53] See Part 2 of "Patterns of Trade and Development," pp. 304ff.

may have no very marked incremental comparative advantage in any line on the export side. Yet the stock of resources may be growing. Is not this a situation in which the bulk of the factor increase would have to be employed for output expansion for domestic markets? In any event this is a solution that needs more consideration than it commonly receives. It may be obvious in general terms but it demands attention in the particular framework of international economics as well.

From the very fact that output expansion is for domestic markets it follows that it must to some extent be diversified in accordance with domestic income elasticities of demand.[54] The process of domestic output growth must of necessity observe a certain "balance" in its horizontal composition if the additional supply of goods and services is to create its own demand or, concretely, if the extra outputs are to find adequate markets. This is perhaps a mere tautology. The more substantive content of this view may be its "instrumental" (as distinct from its teleological) aspect which concerns itself with the mechanics of the process and looks upon concerted expansion of a range of sectors actively pushing ahead, as a means to accelerated growth.

Output expansion for home markets is of interest in the present setting as an escape from immiserizing growth.[55] This concept, as already mentioned, envisages growth in the factor stock as leading to impoverishment through bad effects on the terms of trade produced by output expansion for export in the face of unfavorable external demand conditions. As a theoretical scarecrow it undoubtedly has its uses, but it need not be accepted as an inevitable necessity in a spirit of economic determinism. It is not incompatible with the classical trade model; the immiserization is by comparison with the pregrowth and not, of

---

[54] Let it be recalled once more that the argument is not necessarily confined to national limits, which are arbitrary and accidental, but is applicable to a group of countries — or all countries — affected by the situation under consideration.

[55] For an ingenious formal presentation of the theory of immiserizing growth, see the two remarkable papers by J. Bhagwati, "Immiserizing Growth: A Geometrical Note," *Review of Economic Studies,* XXV, no. 3 (June 1958) and "International Trade and Economic Expansion," *American Economic Review* (December 1958).

course, the pretrade situation. But what is it that is supposed to produce the immiserizing growth? Obviously not the price system; if the terms of trade are falling, why should additional resources crowd into the export sectors? Immiserizing growth seems to rest on the novel concept of "output elasticity of supply," [56] which does not operate through relative price changes but assumes instead something like a fixed propensity of factor increments to go into certain predetermined lines of activity. If the output elasticity of supply of traditional export sectors is high, the fall in the terms of trade can more than offset the real income gains from output expansion in other sectors.

Output elasticity of supply is not an easy concept to accept. It is evidently constructed by analogy with the income elasticity of demand. Is the analogy a valid one? Although it has its difficulties too, the income elasticity of aggregate as well as individual demand is firmly based on the diversity of wants and the "limited capacity of the human stomach." Is there anything comparable on the production side? Is there any reason, independent of demand considerations, why factor increments should seek to distribute themselves along certain predetermined patterns? Institutional connections between factor creation and factor allocation do not provide a reason. Insofar as factor creation depends on attractive openings for factor allocation, one would not expect adverse demand conditions for exports to attract factor increments into export industries. It is no doubt a pedestrian question to ask, but what then is the empirical rationale of the concept?

Classical trade theory assumed domestic mobility of existing labor and capital. Actually there may be circumstances in which neither geographical nor occupational mobility of existing factors is necessary, as, for example, when the Indonesian peasant switches from rubber (for export) to rice (for home consumption) or vice versa. Flexibility in the structure of output is, after all, what matters.

[56] This notion appeared in Harry G. Johnson's powerful taxonomic investigation, "Economic Expansion and International Trade" (*Manchester School,* May 1955, now republished as ch. 3 in Johnson's *International Trade and Economic Growth,* 1958) and has been extensively used since then, notably in J. Bhagwati's papers just cited.

"Immiserizing growth" would seem to deny the mobility of factor increments, whereas general considerations suggest that increments in factor supplies are as a rule, and in the very nature of the case, "mobile" even if factors already existing and employed are not. Transformation of output structure is in any case essential to development, as Professor Svennilson's work has emphasized. It is perhaps only natural that a concept which implicitly denies capacity for transformation should point a way to impoverishment rather than development.

IV

If, by contrast, some mobility of resources and more especially of resource increments is accepted as generally plausible, a different approach suggests itself. It will be remembered that in Professor Hicks' celebrated analysis of trade and growth,[57] a balance-of-payments problem — the dollar shortage — resolves itself elegantly into a terms-of-trade problem. Aside perhaps from inevitable transitory difficulties in the foreign-exchange accounts, any country can normally restore its payments balance by accepting a worsening in its barter terms.[58] In this model external equilibrium is maintained by changes in the terms of trade.

Can we not go a step further? Although there are good reasons for the prominence which the terms of trade receive in the theory of international trade, there has been a tendency, in Britain and elsewhere, to exaggerate the actual extent and the economic significance of changes in the terms of trade in the study of long-term growth. One is too apt to think of these changes as if in each country resources were forever committed to the existing export industries or as if newly created resources were somehow predestined in certain proportions for these same industries.

---

[57] J. R. Hicks, "An Inaugural Lecture," *Oxford Economic Papers,* n.s. V (June 1953).

[58] This tends to happen as a by-product of price adjustment either through exchange rate variation or through the "gold standard" mechanism of internal price reduction. Import restriction in these circumstances might be preferred on terms-of-trade grounds, but this would seem to assume that unused opportunities in the optimum tariff direction exist; which may be contrary to fact and is in any case contrary to our assumption.

In the short and even the medium run, resources are indeed more or less fixed, and accordingly changes in the terms of trade are notoriously wide and disturbing in the business cycle. But in the longer run labor and capital within each country can and do move to other occupations. If the relationship of export prices to import prices undergoes a marked decline or increase, factors of production will tend to move from export industries to home-market industries (including directly or indirectly import-competing industries) or vice versa. In a growing economy this will involve changes in the allocation of increases in factor supplies rather than movements of existing factors. The effect on foreign trade will be a decrease or increase in the volume of both exports and imports, or quite possibly just a change in the rate of increase in trade.

In this way a change in the terms of trade tends to induce shifts in production and in the distribution of resources which will tend to reverse or counteract the change in the terms of trade.[59] In other words, changes in the terms of trade are apt to be "washed out" in the long run. What remains is growth or decline in the volume of productive activity, in the export and the home-market sector respectively, induced through international trade by external demand conditions. On this view changes in the terms as well as in the balance of trade are a transient element in the mechanism by which processes of economic growth (or decline) may be transmitted from one country to others. What may be a payments problem in the short run becomes a terms-of-trade problem in the medium run and a development problem in the long run.[60]

Because of the possibility of internal factor shifts in response

[59] If, for instance, a devaluation restores the payments balance but causes for the present a worsening in the terms of trade, in the longer run factors will respond to the change in price relations by moving from export to import-competing industries. This movement need not disturb the balance but will at least tend to repair the terms of trade.

[60] The present discussion is not concerned with the balance of payments, and there is no implication here that the troubles we are considering must start with a payments imbalance. Our starting point is not an absolute fall in export demand. Our purpose here is to view the terms of trade in long-term perspective. If we had to deal specifically with balance-of-payments problems in the present context, we would start from the "absorption approach" in which such problems appear as essentially monetary in nature, reflecting "excess" expendi-

everywhere as an American project" (p. 214). Accordingly, the Charter is, on the whole, "a product of the philosophy of economic liberalism" (p. 164). Well and good; but in our eagerness to restore the more liberal trading system of the past, let us not overlook the conditions that made it work, including the conditions which England provided for nearly a hundred years through unrestricted imports and large-scale foreign investment.

The Theory of International Economic Policy. Volume I: *The Balance of Payments.* By J. E. Meade. Issued under the auspices of the Royal Institute of International Affairs. London, New York, Toronto, Oxford University Press, 1951. xvi, 432 pp.

The Balance of Payments: Mathematical Supplement. By J. E. Meade. London, New York, Toronto, Oxford University Press, 1951. vi, 156 pp.

In this monumental treatise, Professor Meade of the London School of Economics has set himself two main tasks: (1) to combine the Keynesian income approach with the traditional price theory of the balance-of-payments mechanism; and (2) to analyze a wide range of policy issues centering on the problem of harmonizing the requirements of internal and external balance; that is, of full employment without inflation and of balance-of-payments equilibrium without undue trade restrictions.

The writers who in the past ten years have applied the theory of employment to the field of international economics have, for the sake of simplicity, almost entirely abstracted from price changes. A comprehensive synthesis of price and income analysis in this field is the outstanding achievement of Meade's work. The marriage is performed with the help of many simplifying assumptions, but even so the product is highly complex. The price theory used is of the Hicksian type, taking explicit account of both income and substitution effects of price changes. This does away with the dangerous models of partial-equilibrium analysis commonly employed in recent exchange-depreciation literature, in which export supplies and import demands depend solely on price and are treated as quite independent of each other.

Meade's synthesis encounters no difficulty in covering changes in productivity, shifts in demand, and capital movements, as well as deliberate policy changes. Meade himself attaches special importance to his analysis of capital movements, but some of his generalizations on this subject are admittedly rather uncertain. The theory of international investment cannot get very far without distinguishing between countries of different type and at different stages of economic development. On the level of abstraction on which Meade's analysis moves, such distinctions hardly appear at all.

On this level, Meade's model is undoubtedly a powerful and flexible tool of analysis. Some of the assumptions on which it rests are, however, open to question. It assumes throughout that domestic expenditure is not affected by changes in import prices; it assumes most of the time that the balance of payments is in equilibrium to start with and that, in effect, all goods enter into international trade (*Mathematical Supplement,* pp. 17, 46). In one case, the assumptions used are inconsistent (pp. 49 and 67 of the main book). While admiring the ingenuity and patience with which the model is composed, one cannot help feeling that here and there the structure creaks a little at the joints.

Changes in the terms of trade inevitably influence a country's real income in this analysis (e.g., p. 202). The corresponding effects of changes in the balance of trade are not so clearly brought out. In a state of full employment, an improvement in the trade balance has inflationary repercussions at home, and since these must be countered by cuts in domestic outlay to maintain internal balance, it thus affects real income (not consumption alone, as is recognized in a footnote on p. 318, but possibly also investment). On page 307, for example, a deficit country, B, restricts its imports, and "to preserve internal balance the authorities in B must adopt a deflationary financial policy. . . ." One misses an explanation of the basic rationale of the "deflationary financial policy" in this situation: namely, the need to enforce the unavoidable reduction in total demand as and when the import surplus is reduced. It is not just a question of internal monetary equilibrium; it is more fundamentally a matter of real resources available for national consumption, investment, and government use.

Even more characteristic than the marriage of price and income analysis is Meade's constant preoccupation with policy problems. This again distinguishes him from some earlier practitioners of the income approach to international trade. Chapter X on "Conflicts Between Internal and External Balance" is particularly interesting, and much of the rest of his work is directly concerned with the ways and means of reconciling the possible conflicts. Meade's treatment of the conceivable policy combinations, though formally unobjectionable, strikes me as somewhat mechanical, and does not permit a sharp distinction to emerge between the defensive and aggressive uses of such measures as exchange adjustment, changes in money wages and import restrictions (aggressive uses being those promoting internal balance at the expense of other countries). The distinction is fleetingly mentioned in a few places (pp. 154, 226, 306); it does **not** occupy the central position to which in my opinion it is entitled in any discussion of international economic policy.

Regardless of the formal range of possibilities, however, Meade comes out for exchange-rate variation as the main external equilibrator, relying on fiscal and credit policies to secure internal balance. With this general principle there is widespread agreement. But then there is a further choice to make: between the method of what Meade calls the "adjustable peg," which is the predominant one in the world today, and a system of continually fluctuating exchange rates. The author strongly favors the latter, subject to possible intervention by an international exchange equalization fund. His advocacy of this system may not convince those who are not already convinced, for they may find it a little one-sided. His hypothetical examples all refer to a situation in which a country gets into a "fundamental disequilibrium" that makes exchange depreciation sooner or later, in one way or another, inevitable. Little or no attention is paid to the case where a country, in external equilibrium to start with, experiences a highly favorable balance in one year followed by a big deficit in the next (or vice versa), ending up in equilibrium again in the third year. The comparative disadvantage of the adjustable peg system in the former case is matched by its comparative advantage in the latter. Since one can never predict whether an incipient disequilibrium will turn out to be of one type or the other, I cannot see that the score is all in favor of fluctuating exchanges. Nor can I find any recognition here of the peculiar difficulties that are apt to arise in the way of maintaining internal balance in the face of continually varying exchange rates. Meade implicitly endows the national authorities with an omnipotence and omniscience that make some of his solutions, complex though they may be, seem far too easy in comparison with the real world.

There is, moreover, a technical objection to fluctuating exchanges. If the price elasticities of demand in foreign trade are below a certain critical value, an appreciation instead of a depreciation of the exchange rate would be required to remove a deficit in the balance of payments. With a pegged exchange, the peg could simply be raised by an act of policy in these circumstances. With a free exchange rate, however, the deficit would lead to an automatic depreciation which in this case would worsen the deficit and lead to still greater depreciation. All this is clearly explained in the *Supplement* (p. 143), but in the main book I can find no mention of it. Since, as Meade frequently stresses, demand elasticities may be quite small in the short period even though they may be considerable in the longer run, this looks like a serious snag for a system of freely fluctuating exchanges.

The whole work is severely abstract. The only place where a real country (the United States) and a continent (Europe) are mentioned by way of example is a footnote on page 120. Anyone who might conclude, however, that the author is ill-acquainted with the real world would be greatly mistaken. When Meade comes to deal with international commercial policy in Part V of his book (pp. 263–332) he proves himself thoroughly conversant with all modern tricks of trade restriction and exchange control. The last eleven of the thirty-one chapters of the book constitute, in fact, a brilliantly perceptive, up-to-date and comprehensive theory of commercial policy in relation to the balance of payments, and are alone well worth the price of the book.

Part VI (pp. 333–425) gives up the assumption of a two-country world which underlies the earlier parts, and is notable especially for its balanced examination of the case for regional trade and payments arrangements involving discrimination against surplus countries outside. The point is that if deficit countries have to resort to import restrictions to balance their external accounts, it is senseless — and unnecessarily destructive of trade — to ask them to restrict imports from one another; what is needed in such a situation is a restriction of imports only from the surplus country or countries. This idea, set forth by Frisch in 1947, is here extensively developed, with due regard to the difficulties in the way of its application. The two main objections to the case for discrimination are found to be: (1) its failure to take into account "the relative essentiality of imports from different sources to different countries" (p. 415) — for example, imports from a surplus country may consist of irreducible necessities — and (2) the fact that deficit countries by restricting imports from one another as well as from the surplus country may make more goods available for export to the surplus country.

Meade's discussion of the theory of commercial policy, including that of discrimination, does not in the least obscure his strong preference for free trade and for allowing the fullest possible scope for the price mechanism — mainly through variable exchange rates — to promote international economic equilibrium.

The work appears under the auspices of the Royal Institute of International Affairs, the purpose of which is "to encourage and facilitate the scientific study of international questions." In sponsoring such a difficult theoretical investigation, the Institute has shown courage as well as discernment. This work may not be the last word on every aspect of the subject, but it is, without any doubt, a major contribution to the scientific study of international economic relations.

The Theory of International Economic Policy. Volume II: *Trade and Welfare.* By J. E. Meade. Issued under the auspices of the Royal Institute of International Affairs. London, New York, Toronto, Oxford University Press, 1955. xiv, 618 pp.

Trade and Welfare: Mathematical Supplement. By J. E. Meade. London, New York, Toronto, Oxford University Press, 1955. viii, 128 pp.

The second volume of Professor Meade's *magnum opus* takes full employment and balance-of-payments equilibrium for granted, and examines all other arguments for trade controls from the standpoint of world economic efficiency.[1] The volume is in four parts, the first dealing with general principles of economic policy, the second and third with controls on international trade and on movements of labor and capital, and the fourth with the question of multilateralism *vs.* discrimination.

The book is significant chiefly as a thorough and systematic exposition of the pure theory of international commercial policy. Its most original feature in this respect is the analysis of "second-best" arguments for trade control: arguments that recognize trade restrictions as bad in themselves, but as possibly useful for offsetting the effect of other bad things (such as internal taxes or monopolies). It cannot be said, however, that the discussion of "second-best" arguments, necessary though it may be for completeness, yields any very striking results. The author himself considers them "not very compelling." Even less compelling are the "distributional" arguments for trade controls, designed to shift the distribution of income in favor of one or another factor of production within a given country. Free trade maximizes economic efficiency; any desired change in income distribution can always be achieved by other means, such as fiscal policy.

The author is more impressed with the "structural" argument, which is essentially the infant-industry case for protection. To use his excellent metaphor, the ordinary "marginal" criteria of economic improvement can tell us whether we are going uphill, but not whether the mountain we are climbing is the highest of all possible peaks. Meade strongly believes in the importance of structural as distinct from marginal changes; what puzzles him is "how to tell whether a

[1] For a review of Volume I, see above, pp. 352ff.

Book Reviews

structural change will be economically efficient or not" (p. 568).
Thus we are given no easy rules as to the choice of the right mountain to climb. The choice must remain largely an act of faith or intui-
tion. While the reviewer is in sympathy with this approach, he has
nevertheless some misgivings about Meade's habit of discussing the
theory of external economies on the assumption that the size of the
market is constant or, at all events, is somehow given independently
of the changes discussed (pp. 259–270). The chapters on the structural problem are highly illuminating, but do not seem based on a
fully adequate view of economic growth as a whole. However, since
no one has yet developed such a view, this is no criticism of the
volume before us.

There is a further argument for trade control as a possible means
for a poor country to improve its terms of trade and thereby its real
income (a "distributional" argument on the international plane).
Meade accepts this, but stresses at the same time his preference for
the conceivable alternative policy of direct grants-in-aid from rich
to poor countries. In one place, however, he asserts that there is no
necessary connection between a country's per capita income level and
the strength or weakness of its balance of payments (p. 476). This
seems debatable and creates, moreover, an inconsistency in his treatment. When he comes to examine the case for discrimination, he
presents a group of countries in descending order of strength in their
balance-of-payments positions, the strongest having no import restrictions and the weakest employing discriminatory restrictions on imports from all sources (pp. 553f). Now if this descending order of
balance-of-payments strength is not also a descending order of real
income per head, there seems to be no justification for import restrictions by countries with weak payments balances. The only basic
justification is that, as Meade argues earlier, a poor country should
be allowed to improve its terms of trade with its richer trading partners, and that the richer countries should acquiesce in this — unless
they are prepared to offer outright grants instead.

But what is the use of improving the real income of poor countries
— whether through shifts in the terms of trade or through grants-in-
aid — if these countries suffer from population pressures of the
Malthusian kind? The result would be increased populations at physical subsistence levels and no increase in welfare. In such circumstances there is evidently a strong case for making any international
income transfers conditional on demographic restraints or, so long
as these are inadequate, for channeling any additional resources into

capital accumulation rather than consumable income. Meade himself presents on these grounds an interesting argument for controlling capital movements to countries of this type, entirely analogous to the case for curbing the emigration of labor from such countries. In a remarkable chapter on population problems he gives incidentally a very plausible theoretical account of the disguised unemployment in overpopulated peasant economies, showing that in such economies the marginal product of labor can easily be, not just zero, but actually negative (pp. 92–93).

Meade points out that differences in taxation and welfare-state arrangements in different parts of the world may create uneconomic incentives for international movements of capital, which it would be proper to check by means of direct controls. On the whole, however, he is a firm believer in freedom for factor movements as well as trade. Thus he finds no valid argument for restricting capital exports from a country that is losing in competitive power either because of chronic inflation or a persistent spontaneous shift in world demand away from its products. Some writers have feared that continuous exchange depreciation would lead to an excessive urge to transfer capital out of a country in such a predicament. Meade replies that if inflation alone is the trouble, money rates of interest may well be high enough to retain capital funds at home, while in the case of an adverse shift in demand the export of capital would actually be in accord with economic needs, and should not be prevented.

Much of the main volume is a translation into plain English of the models set out in a complex but well-devised notation in the *Mathematical Supplement*. Plain English is not always a good medium for essentially mathematical reasoning. Some parts of the main volume make rather cumbersome reading. Thanks to the author's expository skill and lucid style of writing, the book is not really difficult; yet it does place great demands on the reader's stamina and patience. Like its predecessor, the present volume is severely abstract. It is not, of course, entirely original. Some of it is based on work published by Fleming, Metzler, Samuelson and Viner in the years 1948–1951. Meade's characteristic achievement is to combine the ideas of others with many important insights of his own, to form a comprehensive treatise that is grand in design and coherent in texture. It is a truly impressive achievement.

International Economics — Studies. By Jacob Viner. Glencoe, Illinois, The Free Press, 1951. 381 pp.

This handsome volume is particularly welcome since many of the papers here reprinted appeared originally in somewhat inaccessible places. It is a collection of essays, addresses, and memoranda written by Professor Viner over a period of nearly thirty years, but mostly since 1943, and it forms an admirable complement to his *Studies in the Theory of International Trade* (New York, 1937) in that it covers the field of international economic policy rather than theory. Of the twenty-five papers included, nine deal with commercial, eight with financial policy, and six with more general topics such as peace, colonies, and the atomic bomb. Only two are strictly theoretical, appraising Taussig's synthesis of the classical doctrine. A trenchant introduction, written specially for this collection, takes issue with the Keynesian influences on international economics. It is critical in tone but, acknowledging as it does the usefulness of income elasticities and propensities, it amounts essentially to a plea for combining the theory of the income-mechanism with that of the traditional price-mechanism of adjustment in international trade and payments. This was probably written before Meade's work on the subject had appeared.

The bulk of the volume is nontechnical. It contains little of the history of doctrine that formed so marked a feature of the *Studies*. It does, however, reproduce two substantial pieces of historical research, one on the most-favored-nation clause, the other on international loans as a tool of balance-of-power diplomacy before 1914. These are the longest papers in the book and certainly among the most valuable. Other articles present Viner's views on policy problems such as the tariff, the gold standard, state trading, the Bretton Woods institutions, dollar diplomacy, and the foreign aid programs of the United States. Most of the papers are addressed to a wider circle than that of professional economists, and the author appears in them with his customary élan as an inveterate foe of national economic planning and an uncompromising free trader. On matters of trade policy he is generally a good deal more categorical here than in his *Studies*, where, after all, he left the theoretical case for free trade in no more than a "state of persuasiveness associated with incomplete demonstration" (p. 526).

American Economic Review, December 1952, by permission of the publisher.

In his discussion of the International Monetary Fund, Viner comes out in favor of stable, though not invariable, exchange rates (pp. 235, 287) and takes a remarkably lenient view of the scarce currency clause (p. 237). No less than five essays, dated 1945–1947, contain a proposal of his for a counter-cyclical international lending agency aimed at stabilizing employment (pp. 298, 322, 334, 340, 361). In a lecture delivered in 1930 he gives the best answer I have seen to Keynes' quip about our being all dead in the long run (p. 110). He shows some interest in the question of world government, on which his remarks are at first — in a wartime essay — sympathetic (p. 266) but later rather sardonic (pp. 304, 381). His strictures against intergovernmental grants as a permanent institution of international charity are profoundly significant and thought-provoking (pp. 371f). Even those who may not wholly share his nostalgia for the "middle years of the nineteenth century" (pp. 253, 374) will often find themselves agreeing with his judgment.

If I were to make a criticism, it would be of his failure to note the conditions which made the liberal nineteenth-century episode possible — among them the commercial policy of the leader at that time. That policy consisted not in selective and reciprocal tariff reductions, but in a sweeping and unilateral dismantling of the tariff. England made herself dependent on imports for her daily bread, whereas we — it seems — cannot even make ourselves dependent on imports for our Sunday cheese. I am sorry to see Viner writing in one place (p. 352) as if the principle of reciprocity in tariff cuts were somehow a part of the free trade doctrine. Viner would probably be the last person to deny the case for unilateral free trade. The American insistence on the reciprocity principle incidentally rules out tariff adjustment as a means of righting the international balance of payments and compels acquiescence in quantitative restrictions for this purpose. A relatively wealthy and powerful nation, as England was in the middle decades of the last century, can do things that weaker countries — with low reserves, with external deficits, with the terms of trade to worry about or infant industries to protect — cannot so easily do. Some of these essays reveal a disposition to accept "the traditional American pattern of economic isolationism" (p. 285) as something like a datum and to hail the American trade program as a great achievement in comparison with "American history and traditions" (p. 322). While Viner is aware of some of the shortcomings of our trade agreements procedure (pp. 290, 353), there is little or no hint that America's new role in the world may call for something more drastic and imaginative in the field of trade policy than the Hull program of limited, selective and reciprocal duty reductions tied to the "Mexican" escape clause. It seems to me a pity that the staunchest and ablest free trader in the United States has addressed himself not so much to this problem as, for example, to censuring the controls of the postwar British economy. I voice this feeling of regret even though the explanations are readily at hand: a book such as this does not aim at completeness or balance, and, besides, two of the papers were written during the author's stay in Britain in 1946, others being doubtless colored by that experience.

There is no short way of giving anything like an adequate idea of the rich and varied contents of this book. It is most of the time an easy book to read and all the time a very lively one. The style is forceful and scintillating, and the substance of the argument infused with a wisdom and humanism that become particularly moving in the essay on "Economic Foundations of International Organization," which brings the whole to a worthy and impressive conclusion. Quite apart from the classroom uses of this volume, economists as well as laymen with an interest in international relations will be grateful for an ample store of profitable and pleasurable reading.

BIBLIOGRAPHY

THE WRITINGS OF RAGNAR NURKSE

BOOKS AND PAMPHLETS

Internationale Kapitalbewegungen: Beiträge zur Konjunkturfor-schung (Vienna, 1935), x, 248 pp. Japanese translation, 1938.

International Currency Experience: Lessons of the Interwar Period (League of Nations Secretariat, 1944), 249 pp., mostly the work of Ragnar Nurkse, except for ch. VI. Japanese translation, 1953.

"Conditions of International Monetary Equilibrium," *Essays in International Monetary Equilibrium*, no. 4 (Princeton, 1945), 24 pp. Reprinted in *Readings in the Theory of International Trade* (Philadelphia, 1949), 3–34, and in *Foreign Trade and Finance*, ed. William R. and Clark Lee Allen (New York, 1959), 296–312.

The Course and Control of Inflation: A Review of Monetary Experience in Europe after World War I (League of Nations, 1946), 136 pp. Part I, pp. 3–84 by Ragnar Nurkse.

Problems of Capital Formation in Underdeveloped Countries (Oxford, New York, 1953), 163 pp. Spanish translation, 1955; Portuguese translation, 1957; Japanese translation, n.d.

Patterns of Trade and Development, The Wicksell Lectures (Stockholm, 1959), with an introduction by Eric Lundberg, 62 pp. (Chapter 11, above.)

PAPERS

"Ursachen und Wirkungen der Kapitalbewegungen," *Zeitschrift für Nationalökonomie*, V (1933), 78–96. (Chapter 1, above.)

"The Schematic Representation of the Structure of Production," *Review of Economic Studies*, II (June 1935), 232–244. (Chapter 2, above.)

"The Future International Bank Position of the United States, as Affected by the Fund and Bank," by Walter Gardner, Discussion by Ragnar Nurkse, *American Economic Review*, Papers and Proceedings, XXXV (May 1945), 291–294.

"Domestic and International Equilibrium," in *The New Economics*, ed. Seymour E. Harris (New York, 1947), 264–292. Partially reprinted in *Foreign Trade and Finance* (New York, 1959), 239–255. (Chapter 3, above.)

"International Monetary Policy and the Search for Economic Stability," *American Economic Review,* Papers and Proceedings, XXXVII (May 1947), 569–580. Japanese translation, 1953. (Chapter 4, above.)

"The Domestic Economy of Western Europe: Resources and Needs," and "Western Europe and the Shortage of Dollars," in Howard S. Ellis, *The Economics of Freedom* (Council on Foreign Relations, New York, 1950), 17–41 and 61–62.

"Capital Formation in Underdeveloped Countries," *Revista Brasileira de Economia,* December 1951, 11–190. Portuguese translation by João B. Pinheiro of six lectures delivered in English; short English and French summaries follow Portuguese text.) Incorporated in *Problems of Capital Formation in Underdeveloped Countries* (Oxford and New York, 1953).

"Some International Aspects of the Problem of Economic Development," *American Economic Review,* Papers and Proceedings, XLII (May 1952), 571–583. Incorporated in *Problems of Capital Formation in Underdeveloped Countries* (Oxford and New York, 1953). Reprinted in *The Economics of Underdevelopment,* ed. A. N. Agarwala and S. P. Singh (Bombay, 1958), 265–271.

"The Cyclical Pattern of Inventory Investment," *Quarterly Journal of Economics,* LXVI (August 1952), 385–408 (Review article of Moses Abramovitz, *Inventories and Business Cycles,* National Bureau of Economic Research, New York, 1950.)

"Some Aspects of Capital Accumulation in Underdeveloped Countries," *National Bank of Egypt, Fiftieth Anniversary Lectures* (Cairo, 1952). Incorporated in *Problems of Capital Formation in Underdeveloped Countries* (Oxford and New York, 1953).

"A Note on Investment Incentives in Underdeveloped Countries" ("Notas sobre o Trabalho do Sr. Furtado Relativo a 'Formaçao de Capitais e Desenvolvimento Economico' "), *Revista Brasileira de Economia,* VII, (March 1953), 67–78, English summaries, 78–87. Spanish translation, "Formación de Capital y Desarrollo Económico," *El Trimestre Económico,* XX (April–June 1953), 292–305.

"The Problem of Currency Convertibility Today," *International Economic Outlook,* Proceedings of the Academy of Political Science (New York, 29 April 1953), 61–78.

"A New Look at the Dollar Problem and the U.S. Balance of Payments," *Economia Internazionale,* VII (February 1954), 46–60. Résumé in several languages, 60–66. (Chapter 5, above.)

"Period Analysis and Inventory Cycles," *Oxford Economic Papers,* n.s., VI (September 1954), 203–225 (Chapter 6, above.)

"International Investment To-Day in the Light of Nineteenth Century Experience," *The Economic Journal,* LXIV (December 1954), 744–758. Reprinted in *Foreign Trade and Finance* (New York, 1959), 472–487. Spanish translation in *Revista de Economía Política* (Instituto de Estudios Políticos, Madrid, May 1953–December 1954), 155–173. (Chapter 7, above.)

"The Relation between Home Investment and External Balance in the Light of British Experience, 1945–1955," *Review of Economics and Statistics,* XXXVIII (May 1956), 121–154. Partially reprinted in *Foreign Trade and Finance* (New York, 1959), 363–371. (Chapter 8, above.)

"Internal Growth and External Solvency," *Bulletin of the Oxford Institute of Statistics,* XVII (1955), 38–50.

"Balanced Growth on Static Assumptions," *The Economic Journal,* LXVI (June 1956), 365–367. (Reply to Marcus Fleming's review of *Problems of Capital Formation* in *The Economic Journal,* LXV, June 1955.)

"Foreign Aid and the Theory of Economic Development, American Aid: A Reappraisal," *Proceedings of the Annual Fall Sessions of the National Academy of Economics and Political Science,* Special Publications Series No. 12 (Washington, D.C., 16–17 October 1956), 5–9.

"Fluctuations in Exports of Primary Products," *Contribuçoes a Analise do Desenvolvimento Economico,* written in honor of Eugenio Gudin (Rio de Janeiro, 1957), 251–265.

"Productive Investment and the Balance of Payments: The British Case," *Review of Economics and Statistics, XXXIX* (February 1957). Note by Thomas Balogh, 84–88, Reply by Ragnar Nurkse, 88–90.

"Reflections in India's Development Plan," *Quarterly Journal of Economics,* LXXI (May 1957), 188–204. (Chapter 9, above.)

"Excess Population and External Prospects," *The Scientific Monthly,* LXXXV (August 1957), 81–85.

"Excess Population and Capital Construction," *The Malayan Economic Review,* II (October 1957), 1–11.

"Excess Population and Capital Construction": Comments by Sir Sydney Caine, Reply by Ragnar Nurkse, *The Malayan Economic Review,* III (April 1958), 58–59.

"The Conflict between 'Balanced Growth' and International Specialization" and "Some Reflections on the International Financing of Public Overhead Investments," *Lectures on Economic Development* (Faculty of Economics, Istanbul University and Faculty of Political Sciences, Ankara University, 1957). (Chapter 10, above.)

"Trade Fluctuations and Buffer Policies of Low-Income Countries," and "Epilogue," *Kyklos*, IX (1958), fasc. 2, 141–154 and 244–265.

"Trends in World Trade," *Kyklos*, XII (1959), fasc. 1, 1–26. (Review of *Trends in International Trade*, A Report by a Panel of Experts, GATT, Geneva, 1958.)

"Notes on 'Unbalanced Growth,' " *Oxford Economic Papers*, n.s., XI (October 1959), 295–297, with notes signed by J. R. Hicks. (Appendix to Chapter 10, above.)

"Le Commerce des Pays Sous-Développés et les Conditions Internationales de Croissance," Cahiers de l'Institut de Science Economique Appliquée (Paris, October 1959). (French translation of "The Trade of the Poor Countries and the International Economics of Growth," lecture given at the ISEA in December 1958.)

"Comments on Professor Jacob Viner's paper, 'Stability and Progress: The Poorer Countries' Problem,' " in *Stability and Progress in the World Economy*, ed. Douglas Hague, First Congress of the International Economic Association, held in Rome in 1956 (London, 1958), 69–77.

"La Teoría del comercio internacional y la política de desarrollo," in *El Desarrollo Económico y América Latina*, trabajos y comentarios presentados en la Conferencia de la Asociación Económica Internacional celebrada en Rio de Janeiro en agosto de 1957, editados por Howard S. Ellis, con la colaboración de Henry C. Wallich (Fondo de Cultura Económica, Mexico and Buenos Aires, 1960), 278–312. (The English text will be published by Macmillan, London, probably in 1961.)

BOOK REVIEWS (* Contained in this volume)

Arnold, Arthur Z., *Banks, Credit and Money in Soviet Russia* (New York, 1937), in *Economic Journal*, XLVIII, no. 189, 81–83.*

Buchanan, Norman S., *International Investment and Domestic Welfare: Some Aspects of International Borrowing in the Post-War Period* (New York, 1945), in *Political Science Quarterly*, LXI, no. 2, 254–256.*

Halm, George N., *International Monetary Cooperation* (Chapel Hill,

1945), in *Journal of Political Economy*, LIV, no. 2, 179–180.*

Schwenter, Jürg J., *Kapitalexport und zwischenstaatliche Warenbewegungen, eine theoretische Betrachtung* (Bern, 1945), in *Journal of Political Economy*, LV, no. 5, 479.

Dehem, Roger, *Emploi et revenus en économie ouverte. Théorie et application à l'évolution belge et britannique de 1919 à 1939* (Louvain, 1946), in *Journal of Political Economy*, LV, no. 6, 616–618.

Mikesell, Raymond F. and Hollis B. Chenery, *Arabian Oil: America's Stake in the Middle East* (Chapel Hill, 1949), in *Journal of Political Economy*, LVIII, no. 4, 265–266.

Wilcox, Clair, *A Charter for World Trade* (New York, 1949), in *Political Science Quarterly*, LXIV, no. 4, 616–618.*

Hawtrey, R. G., *The Balance of Payments and the Standard of Living* (London and New York, 1950), in *American Economic Review*, XLI, no. 3, 483–484.

Chang, T. C., *Cyclical Movements in the Balance of Payments* (London and New York, 1951), in *Political Science Quarterly*, LXVIII, no. 1, 141–142.

Meade, J. E., *The Theory of International Economic Policy. Vol. I: The Balance of Payments* (London, New York, and Toronto, 1951) and *The Balance of Payments: Mathematical Supplement* (London, New York, and Toronto, 1951), in *Political Science Quarterly*, LXVII, no. 4, 604–608.*

Viner, Jacob, *International Economics* (Glencoe, Ill., 1951), in *American Economic Review*, LXVIII, no. 1, 978–979.*

Robbins, Lionel, *The Economist in the Twentieth Century, and Other Lectures in Political Economy* (London and New York, 1954), in *American Economic Review*, XLV, no. 3, 437–438.

Humphrey, Don D., *American Imports* (New York, 1955), in *Political Science Quarterly*, LXXI, no. 1, 138–139.

Meade, J. E., *The Theory of International Economic Policy. Vol. II: Trade and Welfare* (London, New York, and Toronto, 1955) and *Trade and Welfare: Mathematical Supplement* (London, New York, and Toronto, 1955), in *Political Science Quarterly*, LXXI, no. 3, 459–462.*

Index

and consumption, 206; and fixed investment, 185; growth of, 297; and imports, 296n
Growth: balanced, 100, 145, 244, 247ff, 278, 316, 318; and capital formation, 220; and consumption, 279; cumulative, 288; and disequilibrium, 280; diversified, 247, 254; *vs.* equilibrium, 257f; immiserizing, 331ff; and income, 159, 318; and industrialization, 307ff, 314, 342; internal, 159, 220, 253; and markets, 250f; patterns, 322ff; and population, 253, 327; and prices, 318; and public overhead investment, 265, 267ff, 274; and specialization, 242, 286; and terms of trade, 333f; total, 323; and trade, 242ff, 248, 253, 256, 279ff, 289f, 294, 299, 304f, 327, 335; transmission of, 294f, 300; in United States, 297

Haberler, G., 14n, 26n, 204n, 308, 312n
Halm, G., 346f
Harrod, R. F., 46n, 101f, 200n, 203ff, 210, 326n
Hartland, P., 142n
Hawtrey, R. G., 163n, 167
Hayek, F. A., 18n, 23, 24n, 26n, 31n, 34, 36n, 39, 42n
Heckscher, A., 309
Helmand Valley Project, 275f
Henderson, P. D., 176n
Hicks, J. R., 3n, 91, 106n, 115, 119, 122n, 128f, 191, 201n, 278, 300, 333
Hilgerdt, F., 140n, 143n, 285, 320n
Hill, M., 24n
Hobson, C. K., 142n
Hobson, J. A., 243, 289
Hoffman, W. G., 177n
Home market: expansion, 280, 317ff, 323, 331, 334f; industrialization for, 307, 314f, 321, 331; output for, 254, 257, 314, 317
Horizontal maladjustment, 280
Horsepower, per worker, 181
Humphrey, D. D., 244f
Hutton, G., 181n

Imlah, A. H., 142n, 290
Immiserizing growth, 331ff

Imperialism, 289f
Import demand: and income, 44f; and inventory fluctuations, 85, 166; United States, 62, 84, 102
Import prices, 353
Import restrictions, 55f, 74f, 77ff, 90, 93, 210, 256, 349, 355; and balance of payments, 52, 61, 78, 165, 187f, 203, 349f; and devaluation, 52f, 75
Import substitution, 319
Imports: British, 157, 166, 208, 286f, 302; and depression, 68; and Gross National Product, 296n; and imports, 43f; Indian, 232f; United States, 61, 97f, 246, 313, 350
Imputation, theory of, 33
Income: absorption and balance of payments, 188; and analysis of trade, 258; British, 284; and consumption, 118f, 125, 216; distribution, 357; elasticity of demand, 48, 48n, 84f, 250f, 280, 296, 315, 317, 331; and growth, 159, 318; and import demand, 44f; and imports, 43f; and inventories, 108f, 116; levels, gap in, 323; and savings, 44, 109
India: agriculture, 221, 225f; balance of payments, 232; capital growth, 223, 235f; development, 240; education, 235; foreign investment by, 222, 229, 231; foreign investment in, 228; imports, 232f; industrialization, 230f, 233f, 323; industries, 221, 227, 229f, 323; land reform, 225f; population, 223ff, 236, 240, 298; power needs, 234f; prices, 222; production, 220; steel production, 232f, 240; terms of trade, 232; unemployment, 221ff, 235, disguised, 225, 228, 237
Induced advance, 248
Industrialization: and agriculture, 236, 251, 255f, 315, 321; and development, 307, 313f; European, 226, 283; for export, 309, 313, 315f; and growth, 307ff, 314, 342; for home market expansion, 307, 314f, 321, 331; Indian, 230f, 233, 323; and raw materials, 299, 308
Industries: changes in, 313; Indian, 221, 227, 229f, 323; and markets, 252; and prices, 228

Infancy period of public facilities, 274f
Infant-industry protection, 357, 361
Inflation: control of, 93; and employment policies, 73; and investment,
222, 259; and payments deficit, 258;
Russian, 339
Interest: payment by borrowing, 261,
275; payments from abroad, 148f;
policy, effects of, 201
Interest rate: in Austrian School, 33,
199; changes, 15, 19f, 211; differential, 3, 16; function, 274; market
and natural, 15
International Bank for Reconstruction
and Development (World Bank), 85,
99, 146, 150, 232, 273ff, 346
International Monetary Fund (IMF),
346f, 361; and disequilibrium, 75ff;
and full employment, 79; and liquidity, 66; and stabilization, 67, 69f,
79, 81f
International trade: and employment,
64, 352; and full employment, 83;
and income approach, 41ff; theory,
242f
International Trade Organization
(ITO), 64, 69, 72, 75, 77ff, 348
Inventories: and balance of payments,
167, 200; and business cycles, 104f,
108, 116, 128; changes in, 104f,
109ff, 116, 122, 132f, 163ff; costs of,
121ff; and expectations, 117; and
income, 108f, 116; and liquidity,
124f; and output, 131; output for,
107f; pipeline, 111ff, 116, 126; and
sales, 128; and time periods, 106f,
120, 122
Inventory: cycles in United States,
132f; fluctuations and import demand, 85, 166; function, 128ff; investment of, 112, 116, 118, 126, 172;
management, 132
Investment: and balance of payments,
101, 151, 163ff, 169, 200, 202ff, 211,
219; balanced, 247f, 255ff; British,
158ff, 169ff, 174ff, 179, 183ff, 211ff,
216f, 259f; change in, 30; and consumption, 280f; as deficit spending,
200, 203f; demand, 39; vs. devaluation, 204f; diversified, 252; in downturn, 214; and exports, 219, 256; vs.

exports, 161f, 169, 174ff, 220; fixed,
and Gross National Product, 185; in
fixed capital, 127, 133, 167; and full
employment, 184, 198ff; incentives,
185, 248, 274; Indian, 222, 229, 231;
induced vs. autonomous, 118; and
inflation, 222, 259; international,
259f, 321ff; inventory, 112, 116, 118,
126, 172; and monetary policy, 201f;
and national product, 181, 220;
overhead vs. direct, 267ff, 271; in
overhead facilities, 267f, 273; by
state, 249f; United States foreign,
61, 85, 134, 137; wage rises through,
244. *See also* Colonial investment;
Direct investment; Foreign investment

Japan: development, 324; exports,
320; industrialization, 230f, 233f, 323
Jenks, L. H., 141n, 142n
Jevons, S., 301
Johnson, H. G., 176n, 191, 332n, 335n
Johnston, B. F., 321n
Joseph, P., 33n

Kähler, A., 32n
Keynes, J. M., 41, 46n, 49f, 52, 54n,
58ff, 65f, 69f, 115, 143, 201, 361
Kindleberger, C. F., 245
Knight, F. H., 29n, 36n
Kravis, J. B., 181

Labor: demand for, 244; division of,
53f, 76f, 86, 97; immobility, 137,
175; as production factor, 136, 306;
and public overhead investment, 233,
238f; supply, 250, 330; transfer of,
174, 307, 328; untrained, 137, 277,
309f
Labor-intensive production, 229, 249
Land: grants, 262; reform, Indian,
225f
Laursen, S., 190, 201n
Lederer, W., 296n
Letiche, J. M., 189n
Lewandowski, M., 141n
Lewis, W. A., 234, 250, 257, 294n, 308
Leyland, N. H., 185n
Liquid reserves: depletion, 82; and
offsetting policies, 81